9.95

C. D. HOWE

a biography

Robert Bothwell
William Kilbourn

C. D.
HOWE

a biography

McCLELLAND AND STEWART

Reprinted 1980

McClelland and Stewart Limited
The Canadian Publishers
25 Hollinger Road
Toronto, Ontario
M4B 3G2

CANADIAN CATALOGUING IN PUBLICATION DATA

Bothwell, Robert, 1944-
  C. D. Howe, a biography

Includes index.
ISBN 0-7710-4535-2 pa.

1. Howe, Clarence Decatur, 1886-1960. 2. Politicians—
Canada—Biography. 3. Canada—Politics and government—
1935-1957. 1. Kilbourn, William, 1926-

FC611.H69B69 1980   971.06'3'0924   C80-094572-7
F1034.3.H6B69 1980

Printed and bound in Canada
by John Deyell Company

Contents

To the memory of Frank Underhill

Preface

C. D. Howe is best remembered for something he did not say. Sometime after the end of the Second World War, Canadian political folklore tells us, Howe blurted out in Parliament, "What's a million?" in response to opposition questions about his estimates.

The image evoked by "What's a million?" has remained fixed in the morality play of Canadian politics. First exploited by the opposition, it was taken up by political commentators to illustrate the sin of pride that preceded the spectacular Liberal fall from power and grace in 1957. "Hubris," overweening arrogance which calls forth retribution, is said to be the lesson we should derive from the career of C. D. Howe.

C. D. Howe was not, originally, taken with the idea of a biography of himself. Reading other people's memoirs, he wrote in 1952, persuaded him never to attempt his own. Some five years later Howe revised his opinion. By then out of government, out of power, painfully aware that he was being pilloried as the Canadian version of a megalomaniac, and smarting under the doubtful conclusions of an unauthorized biography, Howe began to look around for a biographer of his own choice.

Howe knew few, if any, historians. It was a peculiar coincidence that brought one of the authors of this book to his notice in January 1958, at his favourite lunching spot, the Rideau Club. After a rambling indiscreet commentary on politics and personalities he knew, or had known, Howe told Kilbourn he had some "junk" over at the Archives: would he care to go over and take a look?[1] For various reasons Howe's suggestion came to nothing, and over the next couple of years he sounded out other possibilities. But before any firm arrangements could be made, Howe died and the matter of a biography was left in abeyance for several years.

The authors of this study were commissioned by the C. D. Howe Foundation (now the C. D. Howe Research Institute). Besides the Foundation, a great many people assisted us in the making of this book, and we are deeply indebted to them. We should like especially to thank the Howe family for their unstinting cooperation and the Howe Research Institute for funding our research. We would also like to express our gratitude to Yousuf Karsh for the use of his unique photograph of the Liberal cabinet.

This is not an authorized biography except in the sense that the Howe family's advisers in the matter, W. J. Bennett and J. W. Pickersgill, allowed us to use those few of his private papers not yet open to the public. For making this biography possible and for their many hours spent assisting us, we owe them our particular thanks. The selection of material and the viewpoints expressed are of course entirely our own.

There have been many others without whose assistance this book could not have been written. We should like to thank the staffs of the many libraries and archives who helped us; and for making available to us material in their possession: Ruth Smith, William Young, Burton T. Richardson, H. Carl Goldenberg, Mrs. C. S. Band, Col. G. R. Stevens, Floyd Chalmers, Kenneth Johnston, Mrs. K. R. Wilson, Norman DePoe, Margaret Mattson, David Wolfe, Ronald Hambleton, Mark Larratt-Smith, R. Whitaker, A. W. Rasporich, Professors Dale Thomson, C. E. S. Franks, and Donald Forster, Merrill Menzies, Clive Davidson, and the President, the Dean of Arts, and the Registrar of the Massachusetts Institute of Technology. The only exception to the rule of universal cooperation which we enjoyed was the Liberal Party of Canada. Our research assistants at various stages included Nancy Burpee, Ruth Pickersgill, Patricia Oxley, Tom Sherwood, Stanley Howe, David Lawrance and Hector Mackenzie. For reading and criticizing portions of the manuscript at various stages of completion, and for other helpful comments and suggestions, we are indebted to Charles Stacey, Craig Brown, Michael Bliss, John English, J. L. Granatstein, Mary Lou Dickinson, Pierre Berton, Joseph Carr, Norman Hillmer, Stephen Franklin, John Stewart, Michael Halloran, Norman Ward, Kenneth Kilbourn, Elizabeth Kilbourn, Heather Lawson, Elisabeth Howe Stedman, and James Dodge, and for their comments on the whole manuscript, J. W. Pickersgill and W. J. Bennett. The criticism and support of our editor, Diane Mew, were absolutely invaluable. We were assisted with the typing and other preparation of the manuscript by Gail Robinsky, Sue Colley, Elizabeth Kilbourn, Hilary Kilbourn, Anella Parker, and Doris Brillinger and her staff and in the assembling of photographs by Adriano Metelli, Stanley Howe and the immediate family of Rt. Hon. C. D. Howe.

On Borrowed Time

D awn, December 14, 1940. The North Atlantic, three hundred miles off Iceland. A torpedoed British ship, with a mighty heave of her stern skyward, tilted, plunged and vanished into the deep. A few yards from one of the sunken freighter's lifeboats a conning tower broke the surface. A lifeboat passenger at one of the oars observed beside him a man with craggy black eyebrows scowling at the German submarine; jaws set and fist clenched "as if he would grasp the black hull with his bare hands." The passenger was James Bone, London correspondent of the *Manchester Guardian*. It was his first glimpse of Clarence Decatur Howe at war.

The day he left for Britain, Howe wrote to his daughter Elisabeth, making light of the dangers of the ocean crossing, and describing the bulky woollen "costume" her mother had provided in case he had to take to the lifeboats: "Will try to send you a photo to show what the well dressed man should wear while being rescued." After seeing Howe off at Union Station, Ottawa, Prime Minister Mackenzie King wrote in his diary of his prayer that his colleague be spared, though he recorded no particular premonition of danger. But on the night of Friday, December 13, at midnight Canadian time (the exact hour, it turned out, of the torpedoing of Howe's ship the *Western Prince*), one of Howe's old friends from Port Arthur, who did not even know that Howe had left Canada, awoke and told his family that he feared Clarence was in grave danger. In a dream he had just had a vision of disaster at sea.

Howe himself looked forward cheerfully to the ocean voyage as a respite from his office routine. He boarded the *Western Prince* at its Hudson River pier on December 5, and was delighted to find that her master was his old friend Captain John Reed with whom he had sailed to Buenos Aires in peacetime.

Howe's party included three men he had coopted for war service: his executive assistant Billy Woodward, the Vancouver department store head, and his departmental advisers E. P. Taylor, the young Toronto business tycoon, and Gordon Scott, the Montreal financier and former Provincial Treasurer of Quebec. The four of them, with Captain Reed, went uptown to enjoy dinner, theatre and the bright lights of Broadway.

The ship sailed out of New York harbour the following day, with most of her passengers on deck to bask in the mild weather and watch the towers of Wall Street and the Statue of Liberty recede into the distance. As they headed on a far northern course close to Greenland, in hopes of avoiding German submarines, there was strict blackout at night and occasional lifeboat drill. Howe worked mornings with his group on preparations for their mission to Britain, and kept the rest of the day free for playing bridge, walking the deck, ship's entertainment, and the sociable company of the captain's table.

Bright, uneasy small talk was exchanged about the chances of a U-boat tracking them down. On Friday, December 13, as the *Western Prince* left behind her the last of the Greenland shore, Howe recorded in his diary a general feeling of edginess; people felt that "if we are going to be torpedoed this will be the day." Most passengers stayed up in the smoking room that evening and "at 12 midnight everyone breathed a sigh of relief and left to go to bed."

Howe was wakened by the sound of an explosion, which was followed by the ship's bells calling passengers to the lifeboats and the repeated short, sharp blasts of her whistle signalling disaster. He dressed quickly but before he could collect his things, the steward hustled him up on deck and into a lifeboat. Its passengers experienced some anxious moments as the boat was lowered away into the water. There was a high sea running and the lifeboat was nearly smashed into the side of the ship. A strong wind drove chilling drizzle onto the passengers, as they managed to row a few yards clear. In the grey light they could just make out Captain Reed and his second officer walking forward to inspect the damaged bow. He called out to them, "Stand by! I may need you shortly," and went back to his bridge. Moments later "there was a terrific explosion amidships. Captain Reed gave two toots on the whistle (somebody said 'The old man is saying goodbye!')" and the *Western Prince* dived precipitously and disappeared.

Most of Howe's thirty-five companions spent their time trying to keep the lifeboat bailed out and pointed into the wind, hoping for a rescue ship to appear. They were unsuccessfully looking for survivors or any of the other lifeboats, when the submarine rose ominously out of the sea just behind them. "For a moment I thought of being machine gunned or having a trip to Germany," Howe recalled, but it passed by and dived again.

As the seas kept running higher and the lifeboat perched on each crest and then plunged into the trough, practically everyone became seasick except Howe and two Newfoundland sailors aboard. But "as one of those rowing collapsed, someone else would take their place." Some Scotch whisky was broken out and distributed, which "helped considerably." Suddenly, as the afternoon grew dark and cold a tramp steamer appeared on the horizon. Red flares were fired off, and the steamer veered and headed toward them. Some singing broke out, and as the lifeboat came round to the lee side of the ship, her crew began the delicate task of lifting the passengers aboard their heaving ship via rope ladder or basket. With a tremendous effort Howe clambered up safely. The other lifeboats were found before dark. The rest of Howe's party were in them, but the ropes were too much for his friend Gordon Scott; as he clung to them against the side of the ship, his lifeboat was hurled against the hull; he was crushed, and dropped into the sea.

Howe's rescue was something of a miracle. Merchantmen were under strict orders not to go to the aid of torpedoed ships. But when the Scottish captain of this one heard the *Western Prince's* SOS he called his tiny crew together, and told them he had a sense that he must turn back. Knowing that this meant heading straight toward the submarine as well, they had agreed.

And so now, with two hundred extra souls aboard, the steamer sailed through the sub-infested ocean and the German minefields to Scotland. Her captain kept reassuring them, "I'll get you to Glasgow"; and when someone pointed out that there was lifeboat space for only thirty-two, "You'll not be needing lifeboats, I'll take you in."

On the fourth day, toward evening, they sighted land and by night they were sailing up the Clyde.

After arranging a collection for their rescuers and Christmas leave at home (the captain was later severely disciplined by the Admiralty for his disobedience), Howe let himself be outfitted with a suit to replace his rescue costume, and entertained by the Lord Provost for dinner. He was met next morning in London by the Canadian High Commissioner Vincent Massey, members of the British and Canadian governments and his son Bill, on special leave for the occasion. He held a press conference and made a short-wave broadcast to Canada, and spent the next night at Chequers with Winston Churchill. Then, after being received by the King at Buckingham Palace, he joined his colleagues and his British counterparts in their critical meetings to plan for the supply of Britain.

When told the news that Howe's ship had gone down, Mackenzie King wrote in his diary that he had spoken to Howe of the risks involved, but reluctantly agreed with him that the trip to Britain was absolutely essential:

> At this moment . . . I am far from despairing for his life though I believe if spared it will be as a result of a rescue at sea – a perfectly terrible experience. . . . Throughout the day I have been turning in my mind possible men to take his place but I can think of no one.

Howe's secretaries spent the day in his Ottawa office fending off newsmen and updating his obituary. That night when King got word that survivors of the *Western Prince* had been rescued, he immediately rang up Mrs. Howe. "It seemed as though she had been sitting right at the phone. She said she thought if he were saved it meant that he had some special work to do. I told her I was sure of that."

Howe himself was not given to brooding on the ways of Providence and the mysteries of life, but he did say after his rescue that he believed from now on he was living on borrowed time. He had always acted with a sense of urgency and a trust in the authority of his own instinctive judgment. Once he was home again these qualities seemed more than ever to centre at the core of his being and become absolute.

At the end of the war, when he was criticized in the House of

Commons for being too rigid and unbending, Howe replied:

> I am the only man in the world who took on the job of buying war supplies at the beginning of the war and [was] carrying it through at the end of the war. Perhaps if I had been more flexible I would not have lasted as long.

His austere upbringing on the rock of New England, his engineer's struggle with the intractable realities of nature, his twenty years hustling business on the Canadian Shield and prairie, his battle as a peacetime cabinet minister with the exigencies of the Great Depression – these had all tempered the will of a formidable man. But on that grey December in the North Atlantic, during the darkest days of the war, the iron entered his veins.

"But for him the war would have been lost": that was the way a close friend and colleague of Winston Churchill described Howe's part in the desperate struggle to save Britain from annihilation by Hitler's juggernaut. Though such judgments as this must remain a matter for speculation, there is no doubt whatsoever that Howe's twenty-two years in government changed the course of his own country's history, and radically affected the life of every Canadian in the second half of the twentieth century. His remarkable career and character are central to the story of modern Canada.

Yet scarcely two decades from the time when his name was a household word in the land, and he was the envy of his opposites in Washington and London as the only general manager of a free economy who could accomplish what he pleased, Clarence Decatur Howe is a blurring memory, all but forgotten.

In a sense, of course, he is already a figure from the remote past. He was born and bred in Horatio Alger's New England, a small-town America still innocent of the revolution in society to be wrought by the production line and the products of Henry Ford. He began his first three careers – as professor, civil servant and consulting engineer – in the Canada of Laurier and Borden. He founded his business before there was such a thing as the income tax, and even as an established entrepreneur he had no notion of the all-pervasive role soon to be played by government in everyday life.

The vast majority of his fellow Canadians in 1979 have never heard of him. For a few old men dozing out their days in the corporate board rooms and Mausoleum Clubs of Toronto and

Montreal, he is still the ultimate shining hero. But usually, if his name is invoked at all, it is as the arch-villain in the drama of Canadian nationalism, or as the terrible ancient of Parliament who once dubbed a Commons debate "the children's hour" and asked its members "What's a million?" and "Who would stop us?" Such images of the man all have more than a grain of truth to them. But the real story of Howe's life is still to be told, and its substance is more fascinating than any of the legends.

CHAPTER ONE

Yankee from the Rock of New England

Clarence Decatur Howe was born in Waltham, Massachusetts, on January 15, 1886, a ninth-generation New Englander.

His father was a quiet, genial carpenter-turned-housebuilder who served as president of the local board of aldermen. His mother was an intense, intelligent woman, who was determined that her only son should have the best education that family thrift and his talents could gain him. Both William Howe and Mary Hastings had grown up together on neighbouring farms in Bethel, Maine. William's father doubled as village carpenter and taught his son the trade. Mary attended the local academy which her grandfather, a blacksmith as well as a farmer, had helped to found. As a young man William left home to look for work in the rising factory towns of Massachusetts and then followed several of his brothers west to Colorado. But in his mid-thirties he determined to settle down, and in 1882 returned east to marry his childhood friend. Seven years his junior, Mary was by then a graduate of the Bethel Academy and a member of its teaching staff. They decided to move to the small industrial town of Waltham, outside Boston, and here William built their house, with his workshop at the back, and a driving shed and stable.*

* It was near Waltham that the Howe ancestors had arrived and settled in the 1630s during the founding of Massachusetts Bay, the strongest and sternest of the Puritan colonies in the new world. About the time the state of Maine was created in 1820, Clarence's great-grandfather moved north to take up land there. His mother's ancestors had also emigrated to Massachusetts, in the year

They lived on a large tree-shaded lot just south of the Charles River, in a district of skilled factory workers and craftsmen. Both lot and home were rather grander than those of their neighbours, and they had daily kitchen and cleaning help. They grew roses and fruit trees and kept a large vegetable garden. William eventually acquired the vacant land across the road and expanded his small business by taking on the agency for a roofing supplies company. He became both an Oddfellow and a Mason, and he and his wife attended the Baptist church regularly.

Mary Hastings Howe was from a Democratic family but became a staunch anti-Irish Republican like her husband (and most of the "better people" of Waltham) after a few years of seeing how "Honey Fitz" Fitzgerald and his kind ran things in Boston. William was elected alderman-at-large in Waltham and later represented the district in the State House for one term. He enjoyed being a legislator of the Commonwealth of Massachusetts well enough, but rather than seek re-election retired at the prospect of a distasteful battle with an Irish Catholic lawyer who had the Democratic nomination and strong political passions. Mary became president of the Waltham Women's club and trustee of a civic charity fund. After her children were grown, she was elected the only woman member of the Waltham school board.

Neither William nor Mary Howe was overtly ambitious for wealth or social status. But it was a principle so obvious as to be unspoken that poverty was a condition to be shunned like the plague or mental illness. Among the cardinal sins it ranked high – with lying and cheating, godlessness and poor household management. But to remain, as they did, in the same home all one's life and decidedly not to become rich was no sin either.

1638, and one of them, a Revolutionary War captain, had moved north to help found the town of Bethel, Maine, in 1796. Clarence's middle name derived from another military name connected with his mother's family, that of the American naval hero Stephen Decatur.

Most people named Howe who have lived in North America – including Gordie Howe, the hockey great, Elias Howe, inventor of the sewing machine, Julia Ward Howe, author of the *Battle Hymn of the Republic*, William Walsham How, the Episcopalian bishop, Mark de Wolfe Howe, the literary critic, and Joseph Howe, the tribune of Nova Scotia – are descended from, or related by marriage to, one of the Puritan Howes who came out from England in the 1630s.[1]

Clarence inherited his mother's keen intellect, her single-minded sense of purpose, and a lifelong dedication to the practical value of sound learning. Her husband was more easygoing and bequeathed to Clarence his geniality, his dry humour, his love of male company and a general air of contentment with his lot. William had a high forehead, beetling brow, large face and solid build – like all the Howes. The statue of his Canadian "cousin" Joseph Howe, the great leader of Nova Scotia, which stands outside the Province House in Halifax, was in Clarence's view the spitting image of his father. Clarence inherited from his mother his sharper features of nose and chin, the olive-dark complexion and piercing eyes.

There was only one other child in the family, a daughter, Agnes, three and a half years younger than Clarence. The depression of the 1890s meant that there would be only enough money in the family to provide one of the children with a college education. At an early age, Agnes acquired the distinct impression that it would not be her. She and Clarence got on well, when they played together at all, and she was allowed to participate, at least as an admirer, when her brother built an elaborate mechanical toy railway system in the attic. She went with him every week to Sunday School at the Baptist church. Their mother read them stories regularly and Clarence soon became an avid reader of adventure books on his own. He was particularly fond of the popular Horatio Alger books, whose heroes' pluck and virtue led inevitably to success and fortune.

Throughout his boyhood, his parents retained close ties with their home state of Maine and the family farm. Every summer from an early age Clarence stayed at the homestead of his grandfather Hastings in Bethel. The original farm cottage had been supplemented by a big white federal-style house, which commanded a magnificent view of the Androscoggin River Valley and the White Mountains of New Hampshire beyond. His uncle Fred Howe married his mother's sister, and their family lived on the farm next door, so that his second home was a place of cousins and aunts and uncles. From the day school was out in June to the day it began again in September, he could look forward to a summer of swimming and exploring, of mowing and helping with the machinery and the horses, of churning butter and doing the chores. Johnnycake and baked beans for Saturday night supper always remained Clarence's notion of a great feast. All his life he retained his love for the farm, and he visited Bethel whenever he could.[2]

The grand city of Boston, outstripped in size by New York and Philadelphia but still a prosperous and expanding metropolis of half a million people, was only twenty miles away from Waltham and reachable by regular train service. Trips there were a rare treat, but early on it was an unspoken assumption shared between Clarence and his mother that this was where he would complete his education and begin to make his mark on the great world. At twelve or fourteen, most of Clarence's schoolmates went to work as apprentice or office boy, seamstress or shopkeeper's assistant, hired girl or boy on the farm. But his parents had saved for the day when he would be ready to cross the river to the north side of town to Waltham High School and prepare himself for the Massachusetts Institute of Technology. A few young men from the richest families in town were sent away to board at one of the great New England academies – Phillips Andover or Groton or St. Paul's – but the students of Waltham High were still a privileged and small elite and their parents and teachers never let them forget it.

The three-storey red brick school building was new the year Clarence entered, but the old school's academic standards had long been high. Classes were small, and in Clarence's year only thirty-nine students received their diplomas.

He was not a brilliant student in any one subject, but every year ranked near the top of his class. The captain of the 1901 Waltham High rowing crew recalled Clarence at fifteen as the youngest of the oarsmen, "two years behind me, a very bright, hard-working boy, who stuck to things. I suppose people always say this afterwards, but he really seemed even then a boy who was going to get somewhere in life." He loved sports, and baseball in particular. For the rest of his life he followed the fortunes of the major league Boston teams, the Red Sox and the Braves, though when the latter moved to Milwaukee he switched his National League allegiance to the Brooklyn Dodgers – whose departure for Los Angeles he also regretted.[3]

In his relations with girls he preferred the company of those who shared his interests in sports and studies. He enjoyed the occasional sleighing or dancing party but there is no trace of a close relationship with any young woman nor any sexual excitement or romance throughout his school and college years. With the example of his female classmates before him every day, it was clear enough that in many things young ladies were the equals or superiors of young men. Certainly in his own family, it was his mother who had the education. She was the chief force for higher culture in the Howe household, the keeper of its conscience and the general manager of its daily economy.

The Young Men's Sunday School Class at Waltham Baptist Church reinforced the practical faith in which Clarence was brought up at home and school. There was not much in the way of strenuous learning or teaching – just a continual dwelling on the biblical passages that conveniently fitted prevalent New England notions of virtue, such as those about thrift, hard work, the good Samaritan, and the awesome importance of investing one's talents to the full without needing to be told how. The grander mystery and higher theology of the Scriptures do not appear to have had any influence whatsoever upon young Mr. Howe, nor were they, in so far as they were apparent at all to the congregation, intended to.

The High School graduating exercises of the class of 1903 took place late in June at the Masonic Temple. Besides the valedictory, five choral interludes, a ceremonial march, and the diploma-giving, the exercises featured an address by the eminent Professor Charles D. Adams (one of *the* Adams of Boston) on "Education for Life," and the singing of the class ode. Each verse concluded, alternately, with the Latin and English versions of the School motto *Facta non Verba* ("Deeds, not Words").*

The week after his graduation, Clarence took the train in to

---

* Most paths may seem strewn with flowers
And the future bright and fair,
Yet will surely come dark hours,
When we'll need to do and dare.
Each one for the right then standing,
We our battles must begin,
But with these, our words, commanding
"Deeds, not words," we'll surely win.

Now, as our farewells we're saying,
To our teachers, schoolmates, too,
We must on without delaying,
For there's much for us to do.
Ever onward, upward striving,
Toward our distant goals so bright,
We will find that in true living,
"Facta, non Verba" leads aright.[4]

"Boston Tech" (as the Massachusetts Institute of Technology was commonly called), and wrote his entrance exams. He was accepted, and in September began commuting each day from Waltham into Copley Square, where the modest Tech buildings were scattered among those of the Harvard Medical School, the old Boston Fine Arts and Natural History Museums and the magnificent new Boston Public Library.

It was an exciting time to be at MIT. The place was being transformed by an enterprising president and brilliant faculty into one of the world's great centres of science and engineering. It was also becoming a recruiting ground for business; "engineers were the first people in industry to attempt to apply systematically the intellectual methods of science to business management." It was no accident that one of MIT's recent graduating classes had contained four bright young men who would one day be chief executives of four of the world's largest corporations: General Motors, General Electric, Dupont and Goodyear. Engineers in the early 1900s were on the verge of becoming a new ruling elite in American industry. "It was a natural evolution," wrote William Wickenden, since "the engineer in his planning is dealing quite as often with money and men as with materials and machines." It was not that MIT deliberately set out to be a business school. But it did seek to instill a faith in its graduates: he who learned moral and intellectual integrity would be a better man and build a better world. The goal of the civil engineering course, as the 1907 calendar stated, was "to enable the student to apply intelligently to practical problems the principles he has studied; to give power, to avoid rule-of-thumb methods, and to train the student to have courage and self-reliance.[5]

The total student population at Tech was less than fifteen hundred; Howe's own graduating class numbered only 237. His professor of civil engineering, George F. Swain, was reputed to be the finest teacher of the subject in the country. For over forty years, interrupted only by a brief spell at Harvard, he trained MIT engineers who went on to build the railroads and bridges and waterworks and highways of an expansive America.

Something of a martinet, with his pointed handlebar moustache, black bow tie and rimless pince-nez, Swain inspired a mixture of awe and admiration in his young charges. An impatient and sarcastic man, he would compare a raw student's capabilities in engineering to those of "my black cat." He reserved his particular scorn for people who pretended to know what they did not. He insisted that a student think through a problem rigorously before committing himself to a solution, but once committed that he have the courage of his convictions.

With typical Yankee restraint, Tech students were categorized in three grades only: credit, pass or fail. Howe was a credit student throughout his four years, and as a result received a disproportionate share of Swain's attention. Swain afforded a role model for Howe. His interests and involvement were not confined to his students and the institution. He was a member of the Boston Transit Commission, and consulting engineer to the Massachusetts Railroad Commissioners as well as to a variety of projects needing his expertise on structural stress. Prominent in various engineering societies in Germany, Great Britain and Canada, he became the first academic elected as president of the American Society of Civil Engineers.[6]

After a thorough grounding in mathematics and physics, surveying and drawing, mechanics and hydraulics, Howe went on to advanced work in structures, bridge design, and railroad engineering, and a thesis on soils and stress in building foundations.

While he kept up faithfully with his demanding work schedule he did take part in the activities of his class. He managed the baseball team in his first two years, and helped organize the famous Tech Show; in his final year he was on the Class of 1907 executive. He was an excellent dancer – a talent he never lost – and there were always plenty of Radcliffe girls eager to go out with him. College football had been outlawed by the president as being distracting and dangerous, but Howe did not have time to train seriously in sports anyway. He was not an outstanding class leader or scholar or sportsman; the role of campus golden boy or student politician he was content to leave for others. But he was an efficient and affable field commander when his fellows wanted something done. Unsophisticated and unassuming, he could be counted on as good company and a reliable member of whatever group he committed himself to. A team player, but not fanatically or boisterously so, he kept a certain distance. His slight reserve made it all the more winning when a smile burst across the serious expression on his handsome broad face. He was of middling stature, sturdy build, with a high forehead and straight dark hair, altogether foursquare and commonplace in appearance, yet his steady gaze and dark eyes were piercing. At the very centre of the two hundred odd faces in his class photograph, his is the one, more than any other, that stands out and holds the beholder once it has been noticed.[7]

During his summers at Tech, Howe apprenticed as a draftsman. The experience was useful and the money essential. Academic fees, at $250, were among the highest in the country, and only partly covered by the bursaries he was awarded. Howe worked for one of the outstanding civil engineers of his day, Joseph Worcester. Worcester disapproved of Tech, as opposed to Harvard, for the narrowness of its educational and civilizing opportunities, but he welcomed its students to the hard and low-paid labour of his drafting rooms. These were located not in his office on Milk Street in downtown Boston, but at the rear of his capacious home property in Waltham. Inevitably, Clarence got to know one of the Worcester girls – a tom-boy who loved tennis and dancing and went to Radcliffe. In the end, however, it proved to be her demure and handsome sister Alice that he had his eye on; for one thing she was remarkably like his mother. But that is a story for a dozen years and many labours later.[8]

On a January morning just after his twenty-second birthday, Clarence Howe sat across the large double drafting desk from his closest friend at Tech talking about the future. Big business was the career for ambitious engineers these days, Jim Barker told him. Wasn't that what Andrew Carnegie and Pierpont Morgan needed now? Howe disagreed: "Business men are a dime a dozen" – an engineer should be more adventurous, find himself a new field, go out and build.

Neither of them in fact had a job lined up at all. A sharp recession in the winter of 1907-8 had made things tough for newly graduated engineers, and they were not as well connected as their more affluent classmates. Professor Swain had kept them on after their graduation to assist him with his teaching.

At that point Swain himself walked in and threw an envelope bearing a Canadian stamp on to their desk. It landed on Barker's side. He pulled out the letter and after a quick perusal passed it over to Howe. Dalhousie University in Halifax was looking for a professor of civil engineering and wanted Swain to nominate somebody.

There is a story which became a tradition in Howe's family that both men wanted the job, decided to toss a coin for it and Howe won. Years later, in his Chicago office, Sears Roebuck board chairman James Barker recalled the event. The decision, he said, was not left to chance. He himself was in no way interested in banishment to Canada, and determined to stick to his ambitions for a business career. But even if he *had* wanted the Canadian job he would never have tossed for it with his friend. "At Tech we recognized that Howe was lucky. No one who knew him would throw dice or play pitchpenny with him. He always won." And Howe's luck, Barker explained, somehow included both "keenness of perception" and a power to dominate. Howe told him yes, he just might be interested in that job.[9]

Until then, a teaching career was something he had never seriously considered. The $2,000 salary, though it was low by the standard of his classmates' expectations, was more money than his father made; and his mother did not need to tell him that having a professor in the family would please her. But the main facts were two: he had no other immediate prospects and this one would be an adventure. If he did as well as he believed he could, it was bound to lead to something even more interesting.

So it was decided. In the summer of 1908, at the age of twenty-two, Clarence Howe left for Canada on his first trip away from home.

CHAPTER TWO

Professor Howe in Halifax

Howe's luck could hardly have landed him in a better place from which to start out. Halifax in 1908 was foreign but at the same time familiar. It presented an exciting, even an exotic, new world of experience to such a green young man as Clarence Howe. The city was closer to Waltham in size and wealth, but in other respects more like Boston. It was an old and established provincial capital, the commercial metropolis for a farming, fishing and shipbuilding hinterland. Decisions were made there, in counting house and Province House. About Government House, the residence of the lieutenant-governor, revolved society and its aspirations to culture and sophistication. And Halifax was a strategic British coaling station, harbour of the world's mightiest navy and fortress of an empire on which the sun never set. Riding out into the North Atlantic, it seemed closer in character – or at least in its yearnings – to London than to the backwoods lumber village of Ottawa. Its citizens were closer, too, to their Yankee cousins in the "Boston States"; Haligonians until recently had more regular commerce with New England than with either the capital of the Dominion or of the Empire.

No matter that the place had seen better days (it seemed to one observer "less like a town than the debris of an old one for sale''), nor that it had always been petty and provincial. Clarence Howe was delighted with it. As a young university professor from Boston, he was taken immediately to the bosom of society, much as if he were a young British naval officer on tour of duty. By contrast, back home even his old mentor, Professor Swain, was not quite a "Proper Bostonian" nor a denizen of Beacon Hill. Nor was his former employer, the august Joseph Worcester, familiar though he might be with God, altogether spoken to by the Cabots and Lowells.

For Clarence there was the added surprise that the great man of his newly adopted home, the awesome presence whose memory older Haligonians still cherished, was none other than his own "cousin" Joseph, the great Nova Scotian reformer. Even Clarence's raw northeast accent was familiar enough in Halifax and in any case not markedly different from that of the natives. The young man from the provinces had clearly arrived in an appropriate capital.

During his first term, Clarence sent a postcard to his Aunt Agnes in Maine with a picture of "Government House, Halifax, N.S." on it. On the back he wrote:

I had a swell dinner here in this house last Monday (our Thanksgiving). Dinner was given by the Governor, and all the big officials of Nova Scotia were there. It was by far the best dinner I ever tasted. CDH.

On an earlier card mailed soon after his arrival, depicting "Regatta Day, Northwest Arm," Howe had written: "I attended one of these yesterday and saw some fine racing. Everybody is out for a good time, and I expect a great winter. The people here are very cordial." And on the back of a photograph of the solid three-storey Victorian pile that was Dalhousie University, Clarence proudly asked his cousin John, as his first term began, "What do you think of my college?"

When Clarence's mother came up in September for a two-week visit, she was pleased that her son had found his niche. She wrote that the city was "beautiful" and the people "more than cordial."[1]

Howe took a room downtown, southeast of Citadel Hill and not far from the harbour, near the corner of South and Hollis streets. It was on the second floor of a row of townhouses, a place which was still serving the same purpose nearly seventy years later, though it is rumoured to have been a place of decidedly ill repute for many years in between. Here Clarence was less than a mile's walk from work. He paid his landlady $5 a week, which scarcely touched his very comfortable professor's salary of $2,000 per year.

In August of 1908, before term began, Howe was sent to take charge of the fourth-year civil engineering summer camp. For their projects they were doing a topographical survey of Cole Harbour and the marshes about twelve miles east of Halifax, and planning a railroad spur from Cole Harbour over to the Musquedoboit line. They lived in tents, about twenty students in all, and except for supplies coming in by team and wagon, were pretty much isolated. The new Halifax streetcar system served only the city itself, and the automobile was still a rare curiosity and lacked paved roads to travel on.

Howe was only a year or two older than most of his students and less sophisticated than many of them. Denis Stairs, from the prominent Halifax financial family, and later head of a large Montreal engineering firm, recalled that Howe knew no more about the kind of survey assigned to the camp class than they did. "He did not pretend to. But he had the ability to reason out any problem that came up and find a common-sense answer." Howe settled in immediately and no one even attempted the pranks that new professors could expect from senior students. "We had a happy time at camp and by the time the college term began we had acquired a great respect for him."

Another student, C. J. Mackenzie, later dean of engineering at the University of Saskatchewan and eventually Howe's appointee to the presidency of the National Research Council, recalled that Howe was never a brilliant lecturer but that his presentation, punctuated with quick blackboard drawings when necessary, was always simple and crystal clear. The thing that meant most to him was Howe's response when he was stuck with a problem in his major thesis.

"It was about a bridge and I expected he would have the answer for me. But he told me instead, 'I don't know any more about it than you do. But look up such and such. And you might try so and so.' He really didn't know the solution, but he believed there must be one and that I was capable of finding it. This touched my confidence."[2]

Howe worked his students as hard as he worked himself. In reflecting on university education he later attacked the argument that the best preparation for life and a successful career could be found in student activities ("shifting about," as he called it) rather than in the classroom. "The worker at college continues to work, and becomes a successful engineer. The shirker continues to shirk and gets nowhere." To his students

Howe preached two supreme virtues. First, always have a target in life, even if it has to be adjusted from time to time; every successful man he knew had a goal. Second, respect the facts.

"The engineer deals with concrete problems, where facts are facts and all else is error. No engineer will long be tolerated who shows a tendency to temporize with the truth. . . . There is no devious route to the correct answer." That was why a thorough engineering course was naturally "designed for the training of character." Before you talk about the need for students learning how to think – "thinking is a highly dangerous performance for amateurs" – you must see that they have the necessary grounding "in hard facts and hard practice."[3]

Throughout his five years in Halifax Clarence enjoyed himself in other ways besides working. Most members of the faculty were old enough to be his father, and he was a more frequent guest in the homes of his students. On weekends he would take a ten or twenty-mile walk in the countryside with a friend; he played cards for small stakes several times a month, smoked continuously and usually drank root beer rather than spirits. Rum in Halifax was of little interest to Clarence and his friends, being a commodity kept on the family sideboard with the salt, pepper and vinegar and offered freely at every suitable occasion. Years later, Howe recalled with affection "pleasant afternoons in congenial company" spent at the Studley Quoit Club, "a famous institution of that day" where "many distinguished visitors including royalty were entertained." He also went dancing, and before long acquired the reputation of being one of the most eligible bachelors in Halifax. He was once seriously interested in Lois McKay, a sister of one of his students and daughter of the Nova Scotia supervisor of education, but it turned out that she had a mind to marry somebody else.

Dalhousie University, with a total student body of under four hundred, contained essentially within a single building, was small even by the standards of North American higher education at the turn of the century. Founded in 1818, ninety years before Howe's arrival, it had emerged from its even smaller eighteenth-century Nova Scotian parent, King's College, the Anglican institution which also had a role in the founding of Columbia University in New York City. Dalhousie maintained the high standards and something of the atmosphere of one of the better New England colleges. But it was also a true university, aspiring to a whole range of both liberal and professional higher education. The faculties of its small but renowned schools of law and medicine were supplemented by the most capable Nova Scotians in those professions, who considered it an honour and a duty to devote part of their time to teaching.[4]

Howe arrived during the declining years of an imposing, slightly eccentric grey-bearded Presbyterian minister, the Reverend John Forrest, who presided by means of benign neglect of academic subject matter, tempered by close personal attention to housekeeping details. "Lord John," as everyone called him, had become president at the behest of a relative from Pictou who had made money in printing and given much of it to Dalhousie. Lord John taught history and economics, and acted as bursar and registrar. One of Howe's students recalls going into the presidential office at the beginning of term, signing up for six courses, paying the portion of tuition fees he owed over and above his scholarship, and receiving change, fished out from the back pocket of Lord John's clerical suit. It was rumoured that he kept the university's ready cash in one pocket and his own in another. None of the students interviewed has a recollection of Lord John's economics courses, but given the thorough character of a Nova Scotia Presbyterian theological training, they probably made up in vigour and basics what they lacked in acquaintance with current academic fashions in subject. Adam Smith, after all, was a clergyman and had no graduate training as an economist. John Forrest was easy-going and approachable, if a bit distracted. He was a ritual target of student pranks. The engineers arranged to board a cow in his office one night, having made sure that she had a good meal first. The consequences the next morning were, in several senses of the word, terrible. Though the president did not much approve of engineering or of engineers at the university he did like Howe.[5]

Among other characters on the faculty, the most famous was Archibald MacMechan, professor of English and widely published belletrist and poetaster. Something of a dandy, he was a sight to behold in his plus fours on the golf course. By insisting that male students in his classes wear collar and tie, MacMechan set a standard for all classes in the university. Howe respected him for insisting that like everybody else engineers must speak and write clearly.

As with most of the other staff members, the scope and range of Howe's teaching obligations were formidable. He taught a dozen courses in all four years to classes ranging from about five to twenty students. After his first year, all upper-level engineering instruction was taken from the several universities of the province and placed in a purely technical institute, a separation which Howe thought misguided. He also missed his senior students. He later said that he liked Dalhousie and teaching well enough that had it not been for this loss he would have resisted the temptation to leave.[6]

The instrument of Howe's move from academic life to another career was a philosophy professor at Dalhousie named Robert Magill, an Ulsterman who had originally come over to teach at the Presbyterian Divinity College. When Walter Murray left Dalhousie to become first president of the University of Saskatchewan in 1905, Magill succeeded him as professor of philosophy. He was known as something of a free thinker: "not a very religious fellow" and given to "bad language" on occasion. He was blunt and unpredictable in his opinions. The students marked the contrast between Magill's erratic brilliance and Howe's stability and common sense. But the two of them got on well together.

Magill was spare and of middling stature, with keen sparkling eyes and hair worn uncommonly long and flowing. He had married a Stairs. The resulting social position in Halifax and ready acceptance among local Conservatives unquestionably helped his career; it did not matter that he was regarded as something of a leftist. He wrote a paper arguing that a man could do as much good work in an eight-hour as a ten-hour day, and he became locally renowned for arbitrating strikes to the satisfaction of both sides.[7]

If Magill could handle labour disputes, he could arbitrate other, even more ticklish, situations. In the early 1900s Saskatchewan was convulsed by a major political controversy. Saskatchewan grain growers were convinced that the large grain companies, through their ownership of country grain elevators, could manipulate the grain trade as they saw fit, and always to the disadvantage of the farmer. The Saskatchewan government was in a quandary: clearly something would have to be done, but it had no idea what. The provincial premier asked Walter Murray, the president of his university, for advice. Murray suggested a royal commission, with his successor at Dalhousie to head it up, and the premier agreed.

Magill knew nothing about the grain trade, but he willingly

undertook the novel task. As always, he performed superbly. His report became a classic analysis of western mistrust and discontent with the operations of the grain companies. He concluded that the farmers should enter the market themselves, and by putting pressure on private grain companies, secure a fair deal for their products. This they soon did. But in the meantime their political agitation also persuaded Prime Minister Sir Wilfrid Laurier to plan for a Board of Grain Commissioners to supervise the grain business. Laurier's government fell in 1911, before his Grain Act could be passed into law; but it was taken up the next year by the new Conservative government of Robert Borden.

Borden was the member of Parliament for Halifax, and when he turned to the task of finding a chairman for the new Board of Grain Commissioners, Robert Magill was a natural choice. In April 1912, as soon as classes were over, Magill headed west again, this time to stay. His headquarters were in the city of Fort William, the CPR's train-to-ship transfer point on Lake Superior for grain from the west bound for Montreal and Europe. After organizing his office and hiring a staff of inspectors, Magill decided that the board itself should participate in the grain business by building its own elevator terminals. He needed an engineer to advise on their siting and construction. Who better than his old friend Howe?

Howe was delighted. In the spring of 1913 he resigned his university position, packed his belongings and prepared to move west. Simultaneously he made another decision. He liked Canada, and he had a future here. He would identify himself with his adopted country. In 1913, at the age of twenty-seven, Clarence Howe applied to become a British subject.[8]

CHAPTER THREE

Twenty Years a Westerner

In the summer of 1913 the young professor from Halifax stepped off the CPR train in Fort William. His morning's ride had taken him among the engineering miracles of tunnel and trestle and sweeping curve of track, cut through the world's oldest rock by the shore of the world's largest freshwater sea. Eager to practise his profession for the first time, he quickly found a room on John Street, not far from the station. This was to be Clarence Howe's first base camp for his work across the Canadian West.[1]

The old fort, once the imperial field headquarters of a vast fur-trading domain, was gone, but thanks to the coming of the railways, and to the trade in timber and grain, Fort William was now a raw, rising city.

There never was a more exhilarating time to be alive and young and working in western Canada. The provinces of Saskatchewan and Alberta were but eight years old. New towns were appearing where a generation before there had not been so much as a single tent. Much of the vast prairie was still to be taken up for cultivation or covered with railway branch lines. Tens of thousands of settlers continued to pour in each year. Manitoba No. 1 Hard was the name of the best wheat in the world. John Dafoe's *Manitoba Free Press* was the best newspaper in Canada, and the daily reports of his agricultural correspondent Cora Hind on the condition of the western wheat crop were eagerly awaited in the industrial and financial capitals of Canada. The bleached piles of buffalo bones on the prairie were vanishing and being replaced with the tall, stark forms of the grain elevator, symbol of the promise of the new West.

That promise appeared to be well on its way to fulfilment. A booming economy, a flood of immigrants, and cheap, easy access to markets in Europe stimulated a wheat boom of unprecedented proportions. In 1901 Canadians raised fifty-five million bushels of wheat on four and a quarter million acres of land. By 1913 wheat acreage had more than doubled to eleven million, and wheat production quadrupled to over two hundred and twenty million as the virgin lands of the prairies were brought into production. To hold the wheat, grain companies built country elevators along rail lines across the prairies: by 1913 these private elevators were matched by systems owned by the farmers themselves, highly successful businesses that competed on equal terms with their rivals, first in the country elevator business and then in the more complicated terminal elevators.[2]

Terminal elevators were located at major collection points for the wheat crop – in the larger cities such as Winnipeg and Edmonton, and at the Lakehead and Vancouver where shipments were prepared for the overseas market. These terminal elevators served two functions: they were, like their country cousins, vast storage bins designed to hold the crop until it found a buyer and a shipper; they also served as points where the crop could be graded, mixed and, if necessary, dried. As Grain Commissioner Magill informed Cora Hind, his board's elevators were multipurpose: "If they are not wanted for one thing, they will be for another." And in a wet season like that of 1915, elevators were essential for salvaging what would have been, a few decades earlier, a useless harvest.

Magill had decided to locate the board's first elevator at Port Arthur, the smaller twin city and rival of Fort William, located at the mudflats five miles to the northeast of the mouth of the Kaministikwia River. So Howe, after settling into his boarding house, headed over to Port Arthur to inspect the site. Construction soon began on what Magill proudly described as "one of the best elevators in Canada." It also turned out to be one of the cheapest.

But Port Arthur was only the first. The board had plans for terminal elevators at Saskatoon, Moose Jaw, Calgary, Vancouver and at the southern end of the projected railway to Hudson Bay. Howe packed his bags again, this time to set up an office in Saskatoon. From here for the next couple of years he travelled almost continuously, planning and overseeing the board's engineering work. At the end of 1915, the board estimated, it would have 15.75 million bushels of storage capacity, in Canada's most modern grain terminals.[3]

For Howe it was a revelation. He had never been west before – but discovering the West was an engineer's dream. Everybody was building, everything was new. Nothing was beyond improvement, and the horizons were limitless. As the young engineer crisscrossed the prairies, he learned a great deal about western Canada's economy and society. He learned even more about its politics. The Board of Grain Commissioners was technically divorced from politics, but in a new society, politics was often the only way things ever got done. The board's choice of where it located its elevators – Calgary or Lethbridge, Moose Jaw or Regina – was the subject of intense local rivalry and political manoeuvring. The elevator at Calgary, for example, received the attention of Sir James Lougheed, the leader of Borden's government in the Senate, as well as that of the prosperous lawyer and local M.P., R. B. Bennett. While working at Calgary, Howe met and clashed with the imperious Bennett, who was used to having his way, especially in his own backyard. What they quarrelled about does not survive. Howe undoubtedly dismissed it as of no significance once the storm was past; Bennett left Parliament in 1917 and his political career appeared to be over. That he would be a future Conservative party leader and Howe one of his chief opponents would scarcely have seemed credible to either of them at the time. There were other people to worry about, and other things to do.[4]

The outside world was beginning to impinge on the self-centred, aggressive society of the West. At first it seemed a long way off, a distant assassination of an Austrian prince, and then no more than a Balkan war. When Britain and her empire declared war on Germany on August 4, 1914, there was a stir, but mainly of excitement as a lot of young Canadians tried to discover how to get in on an adventure that was bound to be over by Christmas.

The real effects of the war did not become apparent for some time. Then, toward the end of 1915, they were suddenly obvious. Prices rose, unemployment fell, and the public ear was assaulted by demands for more men, more money, more munitions – and more food. Wheat prices rose abruptly, from $1.13 a bushel in 1915 to an incredible $2.05 in 1916. Supply followed demand. In 1916 Canadian farmers planted fifteen million acres in wheat; that fall they harvested almost four hundred million bushels. The Allies took all the wheat Canada could grow and asked for more.

In the crisis, the Board of Grain Commissioners' elevator system proved its worth. But there was still not enough storage space. Howe, as he travelled from the Lakehead to Vancouver, pondered the situation. It might just be his opportunity. Certainly the private grain company officials and the managers of the farmers' cooperatives thought so: they would be expanding their facilities. It was a chance for an ambitious young engineer to get in on the ground floor.

Howe's forthright presence and pleasant manner stood him in good stead with the westerners he met. His clear, open face sometimes made him appear much younger than his thirty years but there was something very definite about his features that inspired trust: a resolute chin and, beneath the prominent black eyebrows, high forehead and neatly parted hair, the deepset piercing brown eyes. The ears were stuck on rather as an afterthought but, like his good suit, they were neither sleek nor awkward but simply serviceable. His lean but sturdy frame made him seem taller than he really was.

A friend who remembered meeting him for the first time in western Canada recalled that when Clarence was among a group of farmers he became instantly one of them. Some experts were inclined to talk down to the board members of a rural cooperative, "not giving them credit for understanding technicalities. He wasn't that way at all." Howe shared his views of any problem simply and clearly with whatever audience he happened to be with. "It made a great impression."[5]

Howe made many friends in western Canada, but one was to be especially important for his career. Charles Avery Dunning was, like Howe, a recent immigrant to Canada. Born in the same year, Dunning emigrated to Canada from England in 1902 to take up farming in Saskatchewan. After a number of years he became involved in the farmers' movement and prominent in the Saskatchewan Grain Growers' Association. In 1911 he organized the Saskatchewan Cooperative Elevator Company and became its general manager. The next year Dunning entered the Saskatchewan legislature as a Liberal. Capable, intelligent and egotistical, Dunning was going places. So, Howe decided, was his organization, and the other farmers' grain companies with it.

Howe's mind returned to Port Arthur. One or two defects aside, it was an ideal terminus for the grain trade, which still mostly passed it by in favour of its bigger and wealthier rival, Fort William. Port Arthur owed its existence to the mining industry and its name to Sir Garnet Wolseley, who dubbed it Prince Arthur's Landing, after Queen Victoria's son, when he moved his troops through there from Lake Superior on their way to put down the Riel Rebellion of 1870. As the place grew, its name was changed to Port Arthur and its jealousy of Fort William developed after that place was selected as the Canadian Pacific Railway's Lakehead terminal point. When Port Arthur's mayor tried to collect taxes on the railway's right of way in 1885 and seized rolling stock as collateral, the CPR's general manager, William Van Horne, cursed him out and told him he would live to see grass growing on his main street. This ambition was thwarted by the enterprise of Port Arthur's citizens, by the mining and timber economy of northwestern Ontario and by the arrival of a second transcontinental railway, the Canadian Northern. But Port Arthur was still, by 1915, a city of only thirteen thousand, little more than half the size of its rival and still very much the poor relation. Port Arthur had never been a significant grain port because of the marshy land along its waterfront. After he studied the problem, Howe decided to make a virtue of necessity. Fort William's remaining waterfront land was prohibitively expensive. His clients said they would be interested in having elevators of their own on Port Arthur's cheap land if he would undertake the work for them.[6]

Early in 1916 he asked permission of the Port Arthur council to experiment with a hitherto useless section of the waterfront. At his own expense he had piles driven down sixty feet into the bedrock beneath the marsh. He then reported to the Saskatchewan Cooperative Elevator Company that he could build the vast, two-million-bushel storage facility which they required, and sufficient land was picked up for a nominal price. After resigning his government post, Howe asked an engineer with long experience in elevator construction, William Souba of Minneapolis, to join him as a design partner. They hired a young westerner named Ralph Chandler, the city engineer of Saskatoon, who had impressed Howe during his time there, and he too became a partner. Howe's function was to provide the contacts and the ideas, to keep clients happy and to make things work; Souba's was to turn Howe's projects into blueprints, and Chandler's to supervise on-site construction. As senior partner, Howe took 50 per cent of the proceeds, Souba about 30 per cent and Chandler the balance. They hired technical and clerical staff and rented offices in Port Arthur's only skyscraper, the eight-storey Whalen Building. Howe took up residence in Port Arthur, and by mid-year the firm of C. D. Howe and Company was in business.[7]

During his preparation for this new career, Howe was also preparing himself for another major change in his life. Summer 1915 had marked the end of seven years in Canada. All that time he had put aside from his relatively high salary much more money than he spent. He had reached his thirtieth year. At such a time and situation in life it was considered not altogether rash, by the New England custom in which Clarence Howe was brought up, for a young man to contemplate matrimony.

In September of 1915 Miss Alice Worcester of Waltham, Massachusetts, found herself surprised by a young gentleman caller, who arrived with a large bouquet of roses and a proposal of marriage. She remembered Clarence Howe as an acquaintance of her sister Barbara, and as one of the many engineering students who spent their summer vacations from Tech working for her father in the drafting rooms at the back of their house. She had seen Clarence a couple of times during his seven years' labour in Canada because he was in the habit of calling occasionally upon her father during his brief visits home to his parents in Waltham. But young Mr. Howe's proposal, she recalled, "startled the life out of me." She discussed it with her father, who had given Clarence permission to court her, although he did not entirely approve of the idea. But her mother commented, "Why not? He seems a very nice boy." Alice protested that she scarcely knew him.

Mr. Worcester's reservations were professional and financial in nature. He thought anyone who had spent so many years in Canada – and as a professor and civil servant at that – was bound to be a bit of a rolling stone. He wanted to know when and if young Clarence was going to settle down in one spot and begin his own engineering practice. He also did not particularly care for the idea of an engineer who, unlike himself, lacked the benefit of an education in the arts and sciences at Harvard or one of the other Ivy League liberal arts colleges. Such men tended to be only half-educated, he felt, and few of them could even write a civilized letter. But there was no question in his mind that it was his daughter's decision, not his, as to whom she would marry.

Alice Worcester was a handsome and intelligent young woman who had already acquired a good education and a number of firm convictions. She had taken an arts degree at Smith College in 1912, perhaps North America's premier women's college at that time, supplemented by a year of fine arts at Radcliffe. She respected intellectual excellence, integrity of character and, within the bounds of common sense, utter frankness. She was opposed to women's suffrage and remained so sixty years later; she believed the electorate was already sufficiently ignorant and ill-informed without compounding the deficiency. Women, unless well-educated, would be inclined to make political judgments on the basis of mere physical appearance and manners, she felt, and to be at least as ignorant as most male voters.

She had considered the possibility of a career – probably in landscaping if anything – but in fact since graduation she had lived at home and busied herself with such causes as a club for the Waltham factories' working girls. She believed in different roles for the sexes.

She admired men of achievement and distinction, and especially her uncle, Dr. Alfred Worcester, who was renowned in his profession and who had the wisdom and good fortune to marry "a daughter of the President" – that title meaning for a Bostonian of her class, not the President of the United States, but the President of Harvard College. If she decided to marry, Alice would marry out of respect rather than sentiment.

She found herself somewhat puzzled that she should be seriously considering the proposal of a young man who was a virtual stranger to her. And yet, almost from the moment he asked, she recognized "fate – the handwriting was on the wall," and she had a keen instinct that this was to be the person with whom she would share her life. It would just be a matter of getting used to the idea. So she thanked Clarence for the flowers, declined his proposal for the present, and asked if he would be calling at Christmas time.

When Clarence returned to Waltham at Christmas and called on her again she accepted him. It was agreed that they should be married when he was next able to return – at some point in the late summer of 1916. Thus they became engaged one night and the following day he left for Vancouver. For the next eight months they communicated in brief factual letters – "nothing sentimental," she recalled. He told her, for example, about his government work in Saskatoon or his plans to set up his own engineering practice. The actual date of the wedding was eventually left to be determined by the timing of a Saskatchewan provincial election in which a number of his clients were involved, and by whatever day was fixed for the opening of tenders on some of his elevator work. It was finally settled that the wedding would take place on September 16, 1916.

Though both the bride's and the bridegroom's mothers were inclined to attend the Baptist church in Waltham, the Worcesters, like many New Englanders of their status and generation, had Swedenborgian* traditions in the family and the wedding actually took place in the Swedenborgian chapel in Waltham. Alice's own religious preference was Episcopalian (and therefore in Canada, Church of England), following her Uncle Alfred. Since Clarence had no interest in attending any church, Alice became a devout Anglican on her own.

The honeymoon happened in several stages, and mixed business with pleasure. The couple had three days at the Worcester summer home in Rockport, northeast of Boston on the tip of Cape Ann. After uncharacteristically hot weather ("the hottest of my life," Clarence commented), they entrained for the Lakehead only to arrive there thirty-six hours later in snow up to their knees. After one day in Port Arthur, to deposit baggage and attend briefly to business, it was on to Moose Jaw, Saskatchewan. Here Alice was left in a primitive hotel room while Clarence spent the day in the country conferring about elevator contracts with farmers in the district. The evening celebration in the next room, she recalled, was enough to make her think the revolution had come. "I pushed a bureau across the door, but I soon decided it was only cowboys in from the country celebrating their Saturday night."

Next day the Howes went on to Lake Louise in the Canadian Rockies for a further holiday. For Alice this was mercifully brief, since the altitude made her ill. From Lake Louise it was cross-country from Calgary to Saskatoon ("the roughest train ride of my life"), where Clarence had more business to transact.

* A high-minded, vaguely pantheistic movement founded by the eighteenth-century scientist and mystic Emanuel Swedenborg, which found particular favour among well-educated New England Protestants.

She was relieved to settle into their first home at the end of the month when they arrived back at the Lakehead. After their Canadian wedding trip, "Port Arthur seemed calm and civilization itself."[8]

Clarence plunged happily into the complex responsibilities of his job. After final consultations with the directors of the Saskatchewan Cooperative Elevator Company, the construction contract was awarded to F. R. McQueen of Minneapolis, who were experts in the most modern forms of reinforced concrete elevator construction, and the work of building began.

Scarcely two months later disaster struck. One contingency Howe had not allowed for was the unpredictable moods of Lake Superior. Normally the site he had picked would have been safe from the weather. But on December 8, 1916, gale force winds from the south sent huge waves rolling across Thunder Bay and up through a gap in Port Arthur's breakwater. The breakers crashed against the skeleton wooden forms and the machinery and loading scows, hurling them about and reducing them in a matter of hours to tangled wreckage. It appeared to be a debacle from which the C. D. Howe Company could not recover. Most of the contractors' machinery and materials were insured, but Howe's commitment to have the elevator in place to receive the 1917 wheat crop was put gravely into question. Much as they liked him, his clients felt that they should make alternative arrangements with the private grain trade; they doubted the ability of Howe or anyone else to accomplish a miracle.

But after inspecting the underwater foundations of the work and deciding that they were still sound, Howe worked out a schedule that could have the elevators completed and ready to receive the crop by the end of 1917. Port Arthur's civic pride had been stung by the disaster, particularly after some smug comments in the Fort William press and from business and political leaders there. The Port Arthur board of trade and the *News Chronicle* put pressure on the federal Ministry of Public Works to have the breakwater repaired as soon as the ice went out in the spring. The manager of the Port Arthur Bank of Commerce lent Howe sufficient funds to carry on his business for another year. The Saskatchewan directors told Howe to carry on with the contract.

Water was pumped out of the foundation work in the nick of time before freeze-up. The harbour ice was then used to support pile drivers in the early months of 1917 so that the necessary pier could be completed before spring break-up. As the ice floated out of Thunder Bay, a crew of three hundred men moved onto the site. They worked two twelve-hour shifts, six days a week, from May through October. The vast elevator superstructure rose above the harbour at the rate of four feet a day. The concrete work was finished on October 23, 1917, and the interior by year's end. The first railway cars from western Canada unloaded grain early in the new year. It was an astonishing achievement. Not only was the company saved but C. D. Howe's reputation for wizardry in accomplishing the impossible was securely founded.[9]

Since Howe's business was crucial to the Canadian war effort, it is easy to see why the question of joining the Canadian army was not a struggle of conscience for him. He felt a deep loyalty to his adopted country, especially to his friends in Halifax, but like the western farmers for whom he worked, he was quite satisfied that he was doing his bit by staying where he was. Beyond that there was no white feather distribution on the streets of a polyglot community like Port Arthur, and by the time the real conscription crisis came in 1917 Howe was thirty-one years old and already married. In 1918 Clarence's mother died unexpectedly during a routine minor operation. It was a bitter blow to him, but not devastating. Clarence was in fact married to a person very much like her: strong, intelligent, totally committed to him, and infusing his home life with the support and comfort he needed.

With the war's end, business expanded further, not only in Port Arthur but across the West and in Southern Ontario. In one of his brief letters to Alice, which read rather like field reports from the front line, Clarence described how he first became involved in the job of replacing the Port Colborne elevator, which had been destroyed by fire. She was spending the summer with her family at Rockport, Massachusetts, and he wrote her from Toronto during a couple of spare hours between trains at the old Queen's Hotel, on the site of what is now the Royal York:

Dearest,

At Sudbury last night I got a wire from the Deputy Minister of Railways instructing me to go to Port Colborne, so I dropped off the train and took the branch line to

Toronto. . . . Apparently, I am to be the grain elevator expert in charge of reconstruction work. That will suit me first rate. Colonel Montsarrat who designed the last Quebec bridge is chairman of the Board of Engineers. Nothing of interest happened on the trip. It rained all the way down but today is fine. . . . Will write you again from Port Colborne as soon as I know more about the job.

With all my love,

C.

On the Port Colborne job Howe not only undertook the position of consulting engineer but the much more lucrative business of general contracting as well. He spent several months moving rapidly about by train between Ottawa and the various plants of subcontractors in Ontario and the West, besides dropping in to attend to business at Port Arthur.

The profitability of such work led him into another contracting adventure, this time to build a pulp and paper plant at the Lakehead. It proved nearly disastrous, since the 1920-21 recession hurt the pulp and paper industry badly. But he found during this further crisis enthusiastic support once again from the business and professional community in Port Arthur. He resolved to keep out of general contracting in future, and to participate more fully in the civic life of the Lakehead. He joined the Fort William – Port Arthur Industrial Commission, and showed his dislike of the traditional twin cities' rivalry by attempting to get some new industry settled in the five miles of land occupied by marsh and railway tracks between the two communities. On April 27, 1920, he appeared before the Port Arthur council to make what was probably his first speech before a political body. The burden of it was that he and his colleagues were making an industrial survey of the city and actively persuading a number of Canadian firms to settle at the Lakehead, but that they should seek to "do away with all undue publicity" until solid results were achieved.[10]

Howe was not a civic booster in the traditional manner. But he was in a position to practise his old high-school motto, "Deeds not words." In 1922 he introduced nine of the directors of the Saskatchewan Cooperative Elevator Company to the Port Arthur Chamber of Commerce as "the big men of Canada." "They have accomplished something for the whole country." He went on to point out that their company was now also "the largest tax payer in the city, outside of the two railways," and to remind his audience that it was the largest concern of its kind in Canada, marketing one quarter of Saskatchewan's total crop and owning 360 elevators. It was owned by twenty-five thousand shareholders, all of them farmers.

When the managing director replied on behalf of the company, he in turn preached the gospel of direct control of business by the farmers. "Do you not think it a remarkable thing," he proudly asked the assembled businessmen of Port Arthur, "that a company could be composed of men who had no knowledge of the grain business, and I might say of any business?" And he paid tribute to "the talent and personality of our Mr. Howe, or, I might say, your Mr. Howe."[11]

"Your Mr. Howe" was making his name all across the West. By the early 1920s the C. D. Howe Company had the business of the Alberta and Saskatchewan wheat pools and was beginning to branch out. The construction of grain elevators was a highly specialized business; it was also lucrative. There was already a well-established firm in the field, the John S. Metcalf Company, an international firm of consulting engineers, whose Canadian offices were located in Montreal. If the grain industry was truly international, the Metcalf Company was one of its dominant features, as its string of grain elevators from Australia to St. Petersburg, Russia, testified. But by the early twenties Howe was cutting a swath into Metcalf's western Canadian business, and he was beginning to branch out into central Canada as well. In 1926 Howe constructed a two-million-bushel addition to a transfer terminal at Midland, Ontario; in 1928 the Howe Company built a two-million-bushel facility in Toronto; and in 1929 work began on a terminal at Collingwood.

Selling his company's services was, as Howe knew, a very political business. The very success of Howe's contacts with the western farmers' cooperatives made the private grain companies suspicious, to say the least. Of the fifteen million bushels of private terminal capacity built at the Lakehead between 1917 and 1931, not one contract went to Howe. But thanks to the farmers, his company accounted for over twenty-three million bushels of new storage at the Lakehead alone, and Howe was looking for more.[12]

As one of his junior engineers recalled, Howe had one overwhelming factor in his favour: he designed better elevators. The standard design of grain elevators provided a "workhouse," where the drying and mixing and grading took place, at one end of the building. That was inefficient, Howe decided. Time and money would be saved by placing the workhouse in the centre of the terminal, allowing a two-way distribution for both shipments and receipts to the storage part of the elevator. He began to tinker with the possibility of automating the discharge of grain. Eventually, in cooperation with Dominion Engineering of Montreal, he worked out a new system of unloading grain cars: the Dominion-Howe unloader. The unloader was a huge machine which gripped a grain car, opened its doors and, by inserting baffles, directed the flow of grain from the tilted boxcar into a grain pit below. Where it had taken a crew of men twenty minutes to open and unload a boxcar before, two men, operating the Dominion-Howe unloader, could empty eight boxcars in an hour. At a time when grain cars were a scarce commodity and freight rates high, it represented a great saving of money for railway and farmer alike. It was all the more impressive because most people in the business still remembered the time when grain handling was done by wheelbarrow, hand shovel and primitive chutes.

Howe could also build elevators faster and cheaper. On one huge Lakehead terminal, he had a thousand men working day and night in two shifts. Aided by electrically powered building jacks devised by the Howe Company, they completed the pouring of concrete in four months. But he never forgot the need for economy. He had been brought up frugally at home and from his early summers on the farm he knew at first hand of his uncles' struggles to make ends meet. In his father-in-law's business and at MIT he had learned well the lesson that "the dollar is the final term in every engineering equation," as important as the calculations in "feet, minutes, pounds or gallons." Howe would find out the space requirements of his client, and then quote a simple price per bushel. He avoided showering a customer with statistics and charts, but he was prepared to answer almost any question about detail instantly. If he wanted business badly enough, he knew the right moment to propose a 10 per cent discount. To meet the cost targets he set himself was never easy. The construction business was rife with uncertainties: so many elements had to be assembled at precisely the right place and exact time that mistakes were inevitable. Textbook engineering was an exact science; construction in the field was anything but. A successful contractor and engineer had to know who was reliable, who could best handle emergencies, who would be steady and unflappable when everything went wrong. Besides being his own architect, auditor and manager back at the office, Howe learned out in the field to be tough supervisor, pliant diplomat and cheerful politician as the occasion demanded. The story of Howe's triumph over the elements at Port Arthur in 1917 was legendary among engineers. Howe's old client, Charles Dunning, who by 1922 was Premier of Saskatchewan, knew the story well, and never tired of telling it to his friends and cronies. His stories were continually reinforced by others.[13]

One involved a new grain terminal at Collingwood, which Howe designed for E. C. Drury, a former head of the United Farmers of Ontario and former premier of the province. The contract was awarded to the Cape Construction Company. Cape assigned local operations to a young staff engineer, John Stirling. It was Stirling's first meeting with Howe, and he liked him instantly. As work progressed, he grew to like him more. He was, Stirling remembered, steady and reliable, and a man of great integrity. The construction of the elevator was beset by problems. The government's survey of Collingwood harbour described a rocky bottom; in fact, as the Cape engineers discovered, it was silt. They had to haul in bargeload after bargeload of rock to provide a foundation for the terminal. Stirling appealed to Drury for help: the contract must be revised if his company was not to take a serious loss on the project. He pointed out that it was no fault of Cape's that the government's survey had gone awry. The request was reasonable and Drury suggested the matter be arbitrated before a panel headed by a judge, with each side appointing a representative. Stirling promptly agreed. His company had already chosen its representative, he told Drury. It would be C. D. Howe. Drury was astonished. Howe was, for these purposes, Drury's employee: surely Stirling was being unwise. But Stirling stuck to his choice, and finally Drury decided that if Cape trusted Howe, so would he; his own engineer would be the sole arbitrator.

Stirling phoned Howe with the proposition. Howe hesitated. He said he had no objection to being asked, but how in hell was he going to collect his fee from Drury, he wanted to know, if he found against him? Eventually, Howe accepted. Six weeks passed, and the judgment came in: the Cape Company, Howe decided, should be awarded its losses; moreover, he told Drury, it would be appropriate, although not mandatory, if he gave them 6 per cent interest as well. It was everything Stirling could have hoped for, and he phoned Howe to thank him. But, he asked his friend, what had happened to the $70,000 fee that had been worrying him? "Oh, that," Howe chortled. "I got that weeks ago." But regardless of his financial attachments, Howe had sworn to his own possible loss in giving Cape its claim. For future prospects, Howe was relying solely on the fairness of the award and his own good name.[14]

As his business reputation grew and spread so did Howe's reputation and involvement in his own community. Late in 1922, when local Liberals were involved in greeting a carload of CNR nabobs, including the president, Henry Thornton, Howe led the whole party on a tour of "the largest grain-handling plant in the world" and looked on proudly as the automatic car unloaders were demonstrated to the guests. The following year Howe joined a band of Conservative worthies in greeting the Leader of the Opposition and the head of their party, Arthur Meighen, during an evening at the Port Arthur Country Club. His politics were neither Liberal nor Conservative but those of economic initiative and business expansion.

As the man who had done most to bring prosperity to Port Arthur, Howe was several times asked to run for city council as an alderman. He refused, but eventually agreed to go on the local school board in 1921. Unlike the other candidates he did not deign to advertise in the Port Arthur *News Chronicle*, nor to place a thank-you notice afterward, but he headed the polls first time out. In his first two years on the board he was involved in a heated battle with the women teachers' association, who objected to their low wages and an anti-feminist school supervisor. At one point during a meeting attended by militant women teachers, Howe caused an uproar by accusing a labour colleague of his on the school board of having a conflict of interest because he was the father of one of the women teachers.

When Howe was elected chairman of the board in 1924, he managed to defuse labour difficulties, however, by making each local principal responsible for personnel matters. At the same time he centralized academic records and standards, and successfully guided a program of school expansion through both board and city council. He also persuaded Port Arthur to embark on technical education in a serious way for the first time, by using provincial grants which were available for this purpose. After he retired in 1925, even the labour representatives voted to award his firm the engineering contract for Port Arthur's first technical high school.[15]

As a member of the school board, Howe spoke not merely with the authority of a prominent local businessman and as an alumnus of the world's greatest technical institute, but also as a parent. In 1922 Alice bore their first child, William. In 1923, when Clarence was thirty-seven, the Howes moved. They remained within the same comfortable middle-class neighbourhood but left their modest home on Winnipeg Avenue for a grander and more serviceable three-storey house round the corner at 272 Court Street North. It was part Ontario farmhouse and part William Morris in inspiration, and had been solidly and spaciously built some twenty years earlier by a local timber baron. There was ample room for a nursery and live-in help on the top floor, five bedrooms on the second floor and a large hall, study, living room, dining room, kitchen and auxiliary rooms on the first. Four more children arrived in quick order. Elisabeth was born in 1923, John in 1925, Barbara in 1927, and Mary in 1928.[16]

Like his office in the southwest corner of the Whalen Building several blocks away, Howe's home commanded a magnificent view of Thunder Bay, the vast rock formation of the Sleeping Giant and beyond, on a clear day, Isle Royale, sixty miles out in Lake Superior. The house was surrounded by a spacious play yard and by two levels of lawn rising up from the street, so that it stood some thirty feet higher than the roadway. The view was for the family. Howe, apparently, never noticed. Long afterward, back in Port Arthur on political business, a colleague looked out his Port Arthur hotel window and ex-claimed at the beauty of the scene. Was that, he asked Howe, what he used to see every morning? Howe looked blank, and then went over to the window. Puzzled, he said, "Yes, I sup-pose so."[17]

In the household, Alice Howe was absolute ruler. Early in their marriage her husband announced that he did not intend to deal with anything inside the front gate. He would provide for all that was needed as prudently as the condition of business would allow and he would be happy with whatever ar-rangements she made. Almost every year he took out another life insurance policy, with Alice as beneficiary; by their tenth anniversary he had coverage of $100,000, a large sum at that time even for the head of a prosperous household. Alice kept the accounts, paid the bills and decided which of the local charities merited support.* She hired and supervised the help, dealt with the tradesmen and delivery people, and saw that the place was run in an efficient and orderly manner. She was the one who usually had to struggle with the furnace, a monster occupying what seemed to be half the basement, and she stayed up all night stoking it with coal when the mercury hit 30 or 40 degrees below zero on one of Clarence's many trips out of town. A favourite family story is that of his question to her one day when he had walked home for lunch: "Who is the old codger who met me on the way out the gate?" The answer was that it was the furnaceman and he had been coming to attend the furnace for months. When she went downtown, she usually walked or used the new Port Arthur Electric Street Railway. There was a family car but it was reserved chiefly for Sunday outings in the surrounding countryside, or for Clarence when he did not walk to the office.

As for diet, provided Clarence had an occasional meal of baked beans and johnnycake in honour of his New England upbringing, he did not particularly mind or even notice what was on the table. Bacon and eggs for breakfast and the very best cuts of roast beef for dinner was the staple fare. Alice occasionally ventured into something more fancy for dinner guests and was particularly careful about standards of service.

The diet of culture for the whole family was also supervised by Alice. The classic nineteenth-century novels and such American magazines as the *Atlantic Monthly* figured prominently. Clarence would occasionally glance at whatever was on the table in the study and in theory dipped into a classic once in a while, but the newspapers and a mystery story constituted his chief reading matter outside of business reports.

Alice and her brood summered in the Worcester family compound at Rockport, Massachusetts, from June through August. Clarence enjoyed his children, but as far as their early upbringing was concerned he took no responsibility. And it was Alice who dealt with the teachers of the local Port Arthur public

---

* Clarence's own frugal donations were mostly confined to his Alma Mater and to the odd worthy cause back home in Waltham. Without giving the matter serious thought, he was firmly committed to the gospel of self-help.

school which the children attended. Elisabeth recalled that "Daddy was never the last court of appeal" in the small or large crises of childhood. When asked questions while buried behind the evening paper, he was apt to mutter yes to anything and everything. At Rockport as they grew older, he was seen as the "friendly Canadian" who dropped in occasionally. At home the two oldest children were soon considered mature enough to share their father's passion for the local hockey team, the Port Arthur Bear Cats, who eventually won Canada's senior amateur hockey championship and the Allan Cup. The children's nurse-companion in the early 1930s recalls that when their father was in town they would sometimes be allowed to spend the evenings with their parents in family games or in performing the plays or songs they had prepared for the occasion. They looked forward to family picnics and exploring by car the countryside around Port Arthur with their father. The younger boy, John, who scarcely knew his father, yearned to be taken on one of the fishing trips to the bush, but he never was.

To the household staff, their employer was "congenial, down-to-earth and appreciative of any service," though vague about names. If he asked for anything special, which happened rarely, they were happy to please him. Clarence in effect played silent and satisfied shareholder to Alice's chief executive officer so far as the whole sphere of domestic life was concerned.[18]

When in town, Howe frequently lunched at the Shuniah Club which occupied the top floor of the Whalen Building immediately above his office and he would sometimes play a hand of bridge there. His other recreations included at least a couple of fishing weekends every year with local business friends and regular rounds of determined but unskillful golf at the Port Arthur Country Club, to whose annual tournament he donated the C. D. Howe Trophy. His habits on the golf course were typical of his approach to most things. On the green he would always go flat out for the hole: the ball either dropped in or skidded past, so he was down in one putt or, more often, in three or four, but rarely the conventional two. In the rough or on the fairway he loved hacking away, more decisive than calculating.[19]

Whether striding over the golf course or along the street, Howe would shoulder ahead, head down a bit, at a good brisk pace. An astrologer would doubtless make something of the way he seemed to be butting aside every impediment, like the Capricorn he was.*

On board a train or in hotels, Howe was always looking for anyone interested in cards. He loved playing for small stakes, but since his luck still held – that extrasensory control of the deck mingled with keen intuition – he usually came out well ahead. On one long trip he ended up with $2,500 in winnings.[20]

It was during the 1920s that he made his first transatlantic voyage, a business trip to England to arrange the sale of a British grain company in Calgary to Canadian interests. Howe wrote to his old MIT classmates that he was greatly impressed by British businessmen. One may well suspect it was their hospitality and their sublime self-confidence that overwhelmed him, rather than any actual demonstration of efficiency or entrepreneurial skill. He also thought well of their suits, and had himself measured by a Bond Street tailor. The problem was that as his clothes wore out or his weight shifted, he did not bother with further fittings. For the rest of his life, he simply wired over instructions to make another suit of the same sort, with the caution that he was ten pounds heavier or lighter than last time. It was not surprising that his friends and public alike remarked on the baggy, rumpled, strained or shambling character of his clothing – all the more noticeable by contrast to the decisiveness of his gestures and the quick responses in that flat, clipped voice.

Clarence was casual about other matters he had little patience for. His handwriting was firm and his sentence structure simple and clear, but his spelling was apt to be phonetic and full of improvised abbreviations. It was for his secretaries to type up the correct version, but if he could help it he wrote out nothing in longhand; memos and letters were taken by dictation.[21]

His handshake was serviceable but not the bone-crunching grip or prolonged clasp that one might have expected. Associates and employees found his manner genial and warm – except when they had roused his displeasure. Signs of the coming storm were easy to read: a grim mask and an abrupt bark of one's surname, in contrast to the customary cheerful

---

* Capricorns are also described as decisive, practical, self-confident, opinionated and moral to the point of self-righteousness; they are little taken up with theories, dreams, wishful thinking, elaborate explanations or regrets. Whatever its general merit, this description fits Howe perfectly.

first name or "boy!" His anger exploded and ended quickly. He never liked anyone to leave the room on a note of bad feeling and he almost invariably parted with a cheerful remark or a mischievous wink. His smile burst on those severe features like magic. Alice pronounced that the only people who had to fear her husband's continuing wrath were those who were trying to cover up something or skim over their wrongdoing.

His language under pressure was well-laced with hells and damns but no obscenity, unless it was some expression long since admitted to respectable male company: "I'm busier than a whore working two beds" was said to be one. For associates who used a lot of obscenity or got too friendly with the bottle or with other men's wives, his response was pity or mild contempt mingled with amusement. When told of a merger between two companies whose presidents were both notorious womanizers, he mused that they had better install a bedroom next to the board room. For a man who enjoyed female company and also loved dancing, and who was always away from home for at least twenty to thirty weeks a year, some have found it strange that Howe had neither close friends among women nor any extramarital sexual liaisons. His domestic partnership, his love of male company and his work seemed to have been all he wanted.[22]

Prosperity, and the bumper wheat crops of the later 1920s, put the services of the C. D. Howe Company at a premium. They acted as consulting engineers at places as distant as Prince Rupert in northern British Columbia and Prescott on the St. Lawrence River, a major transfer point before the Seaway was built. By the end of the decade the company had built elevators with a storage capacity of forty million bushels and worth over $100 million. The firm had 175 employees, approximately half of them civil, mechanical and electrical engineers, and the rest draughtsmen and secretaries. Their crowning achievement was the construction of the world's largest elevator, with a capacity of seven million bushels: the repeating white silos of Saskatchewan Pool Number 7 rose on the edge of Thunder Bay, a vast Doric temple, matching the dimensions of the Great Lake and the low mountains of its rolling shore. It was completed in October of 1929.[23]

That same month the stock market crashed and Canada was plunged into the Great Depression. The effect on wheat was acute and prolonged. Where it had given the farmer a net return of 78 cents a bushel in 1928-29, wheat provided 47 cents in 1930-31 and 37 cents in 1931-32. The pools' marketing system teetered under the pressure, and then collapsed, leaving the federal government, now headed by R. B. Bennett, to pick up the pieces. Bennett did what he could, appointing a central compulsory wheat marketing agency, the Canadian Wheat Board, to try to rationalize Canada's methods of selling and shipping wheat. But against the forces of worldwide depression and domestic calamity, governments could do little.

The impact of the crash spread outward in widening circles. At first the Howe Company was insulated from the effects: it had contracts for terminals at Prescott and Kingston, Ontario, and Churchill, Manitoba; these would not be completed until 1931; work in Vancouver went on into 1933. But then it stopped. There were no more contracts, no more money, and no prospects. Canada's shrunken wheat exports needed no more terminal space.

As the Howe Company's prospects dwindled, so did its staff. By the end of 1933 only the partners remained, along with a secretary and a junior engineer, Murray Fleming. To meet office costs, the firm took on a new kind of business, acting as consultants for insurance companies in assessing property damages. But that was only keeping the wolf from an increasingly modest door. Howe himself occasionally consulted with governments.

And then, suddenly, the partners were gone too. Souba felt the weight of advancing years more heavily than most. With Howe's blessing, he headed home to retirement in Minnesota. But Ralph Chandler's departure was a blow. On the first working day of 1934 Howe entered the office to find Chandler's desk unoccupied, and a letter from his partner awaiting him. His junior partner, he learned as he read, had taken a job as city engineer of Port Arthur. Howe swore, and not softly. Chandler's ill-timed departure complicated his taxes, and added another burden to the company's precarious state. Though Howe himself was comfortably off – he was worth about $500,000 in 1934 – the prospects of continuing on alone in a business where nobody seemed to want his product any more was truly uninviting. It was, he decided, time to try something new.[24]

CHAPTER FOUR

Going into Politics

I n the late winter of 1933, during one of his regular trips to Ottawa to deal with government construction contracts, C. D. Howe took a detour to visit an old friend, Norman Lambert. Lambert was an Ontarian by birth and a westerner by adoption. Like Howe, he had seen a future in the West and in the grain trade, and for over twenty years he applied his talents in the service of the Grain Growers Grain Company, the Canadian Council of Agriculture, the United Farmers of Manitoba and his own grain business, which he established in Lethbridge. Few people knew the West like Lambert. He early mastered the lesson that to survive on the prairies it was expedient to be ingenious, congenial and adaptable. Adaptable Lambert certainly was: he had been by turns a journalist, a political organizer and a businessman. It was in the last capacity that Howe first met him, in the untroubled days of the late 1920s.

Since then, the grain business had collapsed, and with it Lambert's business career. Farm receipts plumbed new depths every year; by 1932 income from wheat was barely a quarter of what it had been only four years earlier. And the worst was still to come. Lambert let his friends know that he was available for new employment. It came, unexpectedly, in the shape of Vincent Massey, a Toronto millionaire whom Mackenzie King had made president of the National Liberal Federation. The federation was a ghostly organization without even a telephone to its name. But King and Massey knew what they wanted: King a return ticket from the political wilderness, and Massey the Canadian high commissionership in London. Massey's money and King's political skills bound the disparate pair in a close, bickering alliance. To keep the peace and do the actual organizing they needed somebody else: a national secretary who would in fact be the party's national organizer. Lambert was given the job.[1]

When Howe stopped by, Lambert had been at work for almost a year, trying to steer clear of King's quarrels with Massey, scrabbling for money for the party and keeping a weather eye out for suitable recruits to the cause of Liberalism. Howe was not a Liberal, and had no idea of becoming one. He told Lambert he had come to call because some friends had asked him to. They wanted to set up a new kind of Liberal association in Port Arthur. If Lambert could help them, they would be grateful. It was not an unusual request in 1933 when more and more people were beginning to wonder whether they had made a wise choice in putting R. B. Bennett's Conservatives in power at Ottawa. As economic conditions got steadily worse, doubts turned into resolution, and then into action, especially among younger men whose political convictions had not hardened along the lines of their grandfathers. The Liberals exploited the trend by proclaiming their commitment to change and their openness to modern ideas; and to show the value placed on youth in the Liberal party they encouraged the establishment of "Twentieth Century Clubs" for those born since the turn of the century.

Howe's Liberal business friends were addressed by Norman Lambert at a dinner in Port Arthur on April 19, 1933. Howe, still apolitical, was absent; a man who needed contacts and contracts from all parties could risk a lot by attending an overtly partisan function. Most of those present could not remember a time when a Liberal had been elected to Parliament from either Port Arthur or Fort William. The working-class electors of the Lakehead had long scattered their votes among Progressives, Independent Labour, United Farmers of Ontario, Communists, Liberals and Conservatives. The Conservatives usually won.

The most prominent local politician sat for Fort William. Dr. Bob Manion had once been a Liberal but had left the party over conscription, and been elected as a supporter of Borden in 1917. In Bennett's government he was Minister of Railways and Canals, a vital post in a district where so many jobs and lumber contracts depended on the country's two national railways. Honest, hard-working, popular, and palpably devoted to local interests, Manion had an appeal that carried far beyond the lumber barons who made up the backbone of the Conservative party at the Lakehead. Once, when a temporary coalition of left-wing groups seemed to threaten Manion's position, the president of the Fort William Liberal Association urged his members to support Manion as the first cabinet minister the riding had ever had. Even the executive of the local Trades and Labour Congress attacked their president for failing to perceive that duty and advantage lay in supporting Manion. If the Liberals were to win Port Arthur they needed a non-partisan equivalent to Manion, a candidate who could lure both labour and business away from traditional loyalties.

At the end of his dinner meeting with the would-be Liberal ginger group, Lambert asked their leader, a chartered accountant by the name of Harry Black, if he understood the importance of choosing the right candidate. "There is one man," Black replied, "if we can persuade him to stand, who can win in Port Arthur." Clarence Howe is highly regarded in the community, he continued, and he has as many Conservative as Liberal friends. That evening, before taking the midnight train to Ottawa, Lambert called on the Howes. Lambert recalled that "Mrs. Howe was an interested but completely silent listener" to what he told them, and that "her husband had little more to say than she had about the suggestion that he embark on a political career. He intimated that he had not been definitely approached, and would wait further developments."[2]

Ten days later Vincent Massey gave a luncheon in Ottawa in honour of another prospective Liberal candidate, the Toronto lawyer Salter Hayden, who as it turned out was to contest the Toronto riding of St. Paul's in 1935 with a small assist on the platform from none other than C. D. Howe ("I think the worst speaker I ever heard," Hayden later recalled of Howe's performance). Lambert saw to it that Howe was invited to the Ottawa luncheon. Afterward Howe told him privately that he was now willing to consider the Liberal nomination in Port Arthur. Lambert made sure Howe did not feel unwanted. He shared a compartment with him on a western business trip in June, he visited Howe in Port Arthur at the end of that month, and he arranged to meet him in Toronto early in July.[3]

But Howe refused to make any final commitment. He had shown his interest. In his view, it was now up to the head office of the firm in Ottawa to make him an offer. If they had a big project for him to manage there for the next four or five years, he was interested in the job. Meanwhile, he consulted his friends. Harry Black he knew would be favourable. But what about other, more established businessmen, the kind of people he knew through construction and engineering? What did they think? Howe polled some of his business acquaintances across Canada for their reaction to his going into politics as a Liberal. Was the new firm respectable? Was its direction sound? Was it appropriate for him? The answer to all these questions, from Liberal and Conservative friends alike, was yes. If Howe thought he must get into politics, then he should.[4]

During that same summer of 1933 Mackenzie King complained to Lambert of the poverty of material available for his next cabinet, and his distaste for the prospect of dealing with the many unsuitable leftovers from his previous ministry. Even worse, undesirable elements in the Liberal caucus would all be pressing their claims. King's thought, Lambert decided, might dovetail with Howe's need. He eventually arranged for Howe to meet the Leader of the Opposition at King's home, Laurier House, for about half an hour on January 20, 1934. In Lambert's view, Howe and King were suitably impressed with one another. But neither man would make an explicit commitment. Each expected the other to make the first move. Afterward, Lambert grumbled into his diary: "Howe's approach to running in Port Arthur seems to be a desire for a guaranteed cabinet position!"[5]

While Howe waited, there was a Liberal revival of another sort in the provincial elections of June 1934. The flamboyant and headstrong Mitchell Hepburn swept into power at Queen's Park, hurling out a long-established Conservative administration. He had successfully managed to identify it with the Great Depression and with established privilege. During the elections Howe had been absent from Port Arthur on business in the United States. Harry Black and the federal Liberals were annoyed by this, especially since a Hepburn Liberal won in Port Arthur: it showed that Black's group had not been involved in the victory as much as they would have liked it to appear. But Howe felt sure he could easily get their nomination if he sought it. He had no intention at this point of identifying himself with any and every Liberal, or indeed with any other political cause than his own.

Throughout 1934 he kept another prospect in mind. He was

on the verge of a large business venture which would have taken him to South America for the better part of the next three years. In 1933 Great Britain and Argentina signed a commercial treaty which involved, among other things, large shipments of Argentine wheat. Baring Brothers, the London investment bankers, were willing to finance the scheme to insure Britain of a good supply of grain, provided modern storage and shipping facilities could be built in Argentina comparable to those available in Canada. The obvious man to take charge of this operation was C. D. Howe. By this time he was well known in the British grain business and he had acquired a good reputation in London financial circles.[6]

Howe had spent several weeks in Buenos Aires during 1931, and decided that the challenge to duplicate his Canadian feat – or improve on it – was tempting. During visits to Britain in 1933 and 1934 he formed a syndicate with Henry Simon Limited of Manchester which eventually made a deal with the Argentine government. They would build eight huge terminal elevators on the Buenos Aires waterfront, with the prospect of adding a network of country elevators to replace the system of carting bagged wheat by burro or wagon to railway sidings or riverboat docks. A change of government later aborted the grand scheme.

Back in Canada meanwhile, during the fall of 1934, there were rumours of a snap federal election. Liberal headquarters instructed local associations to choose candidates immediately. The convention in Port Arthur was called for November 29, 1934, just after Howe had returned from England. His friends saw to it that they had control of the convention, and without giving up on his Argentine prospects he agreed to stand.[7]

There was only one other candidate in sight, a railwayman from Schreiber named Fred Kelly, who was nominated and seconded by two of his union brothers. After pointing out Howe's good labour record, Kelly withdrew and moved that Howe's nomination be made unanimous. The Liberal Association president (and the Howes' family physician), Dr. J. M. Eakins, spoke to the 130 delegates of his friend Clarence Howe's career. He had close connections with "various government departments in Ottawa," he told them, and he was "a personal friend of the Right Honourable W. L. M. King," "a lifelong Liberal," and "high in the councils of the party." This was probably more of a surprise to the candidate than to anyone else present.

Accepting the nomination, Howe stated that Canada had been "badly governed" during the 1930s and that the government's attempts to remedy the Depression had only made matters worse. "The grain policy of Canada has been desperately bad. [Canada is] begging other countries to join her in a reduction of acreage. . . . Wheat is made to sell and eat. Let us go out and . . . win back our foreign markets." Howe then attacked Prime Minister Bennett for putting the Canadian National Railways in bankruptcy under trustees who did nothing more than lay off its employees and cut services. He pledged himself to job security for railway employees – which could best be gained by good railway management. He praised Mackenzie King as one of Canada's pioneers in social legislation, and pledged himself to support Liberal proposals to bring in unemployment insurance.[8]

As it turned out there was no winter election. Instead Bennett was persuaded by his brother-in-law, William Herridge, the Canadian Minister to Washington, that Franklin Roosevelt's New Deal offered the best way out of the Depression. Early in January of 1935 the millionaire Conservative prime minister stunned the Canadian public with a series of radio addresses on the evils of capitalism – fireside blasts, they might have been called. With a boldness and thoroughness unequalled by any prime minister of Canada before or since, and quite inconsonant with the vague liberal pieties of Mackenzie King, Bennett proclaimed his program of intervention in the economy to protect the disadvantaged, the victims of the capitalist system.* He put an outline of his program before Parliament, defended it in an exhausting series of public speeches over the next few weeks, and then retired to his apartment in the Chateau Laurier Hotel with an apprehended heart attack. He only emerged from convalescence late in April to leave directly for Great Britain and King George V's silver jubilee celebrations.

* In line with his bold new interventionist approach to the Canadian economy, Bennett also prepared a Wheat Board Act that would give the central agency absolute power over the marketing of the western crop. Members of the Winnipeg Grain Exchange lobbied vigorously against this measure. Howe himself was much occupied in February of 1935 with supporting their position in the back rooms of Ottawa. In the end the Conservative government weakened the bill considerably; ironically it was left to a later Liberal government of which Howe was a member to end finally the free market in wheat and place absolute control of wheat sales in the hands of the Canadian Wheat Board.

The parliamentary session of 1935 lasted just long enough to pass Bennett's "New Deal" legislation. An early spring election or a fighting prime minister in the House might have kept his program alive as the major issue before the Canadian people. But in Bennett's absence, its momentum was lost. There were cries of hypocrisy and deathbed repentance from many of its potential supporters. And rumblings of blue ruin from the Montreal business community which had traditionally given Bennett his most solid backing.

Early in 1935 Howe became embroiled in political controversy in the constituency of Fort William. As in Port Arthur earlier, there was an uprising of younger and more active men seeking to control the local Liberal organization and to nominate a promising candidate in the coming election. To meet their challenge, the heads of the old Liberal machine, with help from one of Hepburn's men in Toronto, equipped two hundred unemployed men from a nearby relief camp with voting memberships. One of the trucks bringing them in on the night of the nominating convention was struck by a train and twenty of them were killed or maimed. At the hospital where the victims were taken, their identity was discovered from the Liberal delegate cards in their pockets. The grim news broke up the convention. National headquarters wired Howe for a quick report. He replied tersely that the aspirations of the new group should be recognized and that the candidate for Fort William should be the Reverend Dan McIvor, a social-working padre there, who would probably be nominated by the CCF party if the Liberals failed to get him.[9]

It took Howe, with the expert support of Norman Lambert, a full six months to gain control of the Fort William Liberal Association and swing Liberals of both factions there behind the nomination and election campaign of Dan McIvor. Older Liberals could see no reason why they should exert themselves to replace the great Bob Manion with a left-wing preacher. There is no tenacity like that of a group of party professionals committed to their own permanent incumbency by remaining a small and certain group of losers. Besides, they now had powerful allies at Queen's Park.

Hepburn's 1934 provincial victory had also swept Fort William into the Liberal fold, and the new premier confirmed the old guard in power in the riding, subject to ultimate control from Toronto. Hepburn's Toronto organizers and his new friends among the northern mining promoters, who constituted the single most powerful element around him, were displeased at Ottawa's attempt to take over the party in Fort William. Northern Ontario was a mining frontier which offered one of the few new sources of wealth, patronage and power during the Depression. Its gold production in 1934 actually surpassed the former record high set in 1929. The Hepburn crowd wanted their bailiwick kept in reliable hands. But they eventually backed off rather than risk outright battle with Lambert and Howe. They also convinced themselves that if the Liberals did win the next federal election, Hepburn's own prestige and power in the province would give him a strong voice in all federal decisions affecting Ontario.

McIvor's selection as candidate paid unexpected dividends. A gentle, good-humoured person, the new candidate was immensely popular in Fort William. He was never too busy or too preoccupied to hear a complaint or a problem, and from his social work he knew what to do, whom to see and where to go. If Howe helped him in 1935, he would help Howe in the future.

Howe's part in the affair naturally made a good impression on Mackenzie King and improved his prospects for a cabinet post if the Liberals won. But when he saw King again in Ottawa on June 12, the leader was preoccupied with larger problems. In particular, his two strongest English-speaking colleagues from the last Liberal government, Charles Dunning and J. L. Ralston, were now completely out of public life. They refused to run in 1935. They had thus "lost first place in the Liberal succession," King decided. Worse still, he feared that the expected defeat of Bennett would bring back his mortal enemy Arthur Meighen as Conservative leader. He fretted about failing to have a strong and experienced cabinet.[10]

By the middle of 1935 the prospects for a Liberal victory looked excellent. Seven out of the last eight federal by-elections had gone against Bennett. By July, all five provincial Conservative governments that held power during the Depression had been heavily defeated at the polls. On top of that, Bennett's former Trade Minister, Harry Stevens, had formed a national party to fight for the interests of the little people hurt by the Depression; the Reconstruction Party, as it was called, found pockets of small-business support right across the country. That same summer Social Credit, a protest movement even more populist and right-wing than Stevens', swept to power in Alberta, and prepared to enter the federal field. Altogether, King decided it would be best to occupy the middle ground and commit himself to as little as possible. In the face of Bennett's radical program of 1935, he would offer "not a New Deal but a square deal." In the face of a disintegrating Conservatism and the newly founded socialist CCF, the choice for Canada would be "King or Chaos."

The general election was called for October 14, 1935, and as C. D. Howe faced his first campaign he found the national trend reassuring. It helped too that the sitting Port Arthur Conservative chose to retreat to the safety of a judgeship while his leader still had the power to appoint him. Nevertheless, the Liberals had their work cut out for them. Nobody could gauge the likely size and split of the protest vote, but it promised to be large. The Communist candidate, the Reverend A. E. Smith, had always attracted a solid minority, and while it seemed unlikely that he would gain more than fifteen hundred votes, many of these would otherwise have gone Liberal. The CCF were now clearly the heirs of the old farm-labour element which had once captured the seat provincially and they had a strong candidate in Alderman Alex Gibson, who flaunted resolutions from the United Church of Canada about the un-Christian nature of the capitalist system. The CCF national leader, J. S. Woodsworth, came to the Lakehead and his reception was only surpassed in size by the rally of twenty-five hundred men and women who turned out to hear the Communist leader Tim Buck.[11]

While Howe had an excellent reputation among the business and professional elite of Port Arthur and also in labour circles, he was scarcely known at all in the large and varied ethnic communities of the city, let alone the far-flung rural outposts of the constituency. Half of Port Arthur's electors lived in the city but the riding itself was vast – the largest in Ontario. It stretched from the shores of Lake Superior to those of Hudson Bay, and included a great chunk of the Canadian Shield, as well as a piece of the vast clay belt in the lowlands southwest of James Bay. The riding's most remote poll, Michipicoten Island, was reached in good weather only twice a week by boat out of Sault Ste. Marie. Another of the riding's typical towns lay over three hundred miles to the northwest of Michipicoten Harbour on the main CNR line to Winnipeg. One of the larger towns was White River, best known elsewhere for its record-breaking winter temperatures of 60 and 70 degrees below zero. The riding included the mining camps of Pickle Crow, the timber workers of the northwest frontier's traditional main industry, and, scattered along the main lines of both transcontinental railroads, the railway workers and their families. Some of C. D. Howe's potential constituents, such as the miners in the central Patricia goldfields or the Hudson's Bay Company clerks at Osnaburgh House, would never see the candidates. And some, such as the trappers of Upsala and Quorn, the candidates could hardly find if they tried.[12]

Howe's organization put on a vigorous campaign. The candidate whistle-stopped all the main lines and branch lines. He spoke on the local radio station's Liberal Hour. He sat dutifully on the platforms of town halls, school gymnasia and labour temples. Amid a program advertised as "a worthwhile gathering for young people," Howe delivered a special message to the youth of Port Arthur. He addressed the Italian community of Port Arthur at the Sons of England Hall, in halting Italian coloured by the Spanish he had picked up on his trips to South America. But he was best-off in the ethnic communities when he said little or nothing and let others do the talking for him. "At the Finnish Labour Temple a slight pioneer matriarch Anna Koivu spoke on Howe's behalf before an audience of one thousand. Already well known to them as 'Log Cabin Granny,' the title of her column in the local Finnish newspaper, Mrs. Koivu held her feminine audience easily with homely metaphors about sweeping the Bennett stable clean. Howe's enforced silence on the platform was all the more effective, since constructive work ranked far above the idle talk of women and politicians in the minds of the taciturn bush workers and carpenters in the audience."[13]

In those days election meetings were among the chief forms of entertainment in Port Arthur. The Liberals usually attracted between two hundred and two thousand people to their meetings. At the larger rallies choral and orchestral music was provided along with the roster of speakers. David Croll, the left-leaning provincial cabinet minister, was imported for a visit. So was the president of the National Seamen's Association, to criticize the big corporations like Canada Steamship Line. Mackenzie King called as well, and was rewarded with a large turnout. But Howe's chief allies were necessarily local. The most colourful – and dubious – of them, and the one who most often shared the platform with him, was the mayor of Port Arthur and its provincial MLA, Charles "Call-me-Charlie" Cox. "He was a self-made timber operator and political stuntman who would sometimes race the fastest men in town up Main Street before climbing the platform to speak. On the rostrum, which was often the flat bed of a truck parked among the pines, Cox struck a colourful contrast to the sober dress and measured words of C. D. Howe. His jaunty straw boater, navy blazer, white slacks and shoes were those of a dandy, but his salty language and rugged good looks were those of a seasoned lumberjack."[14]

The support of Cox, of well-known ethnic leaders, and of local Liberals, old and new, all helped boost Howe's stock in the riding. So did the national trend. But right to the end it was the stature of Clarence and Alice Howe as worthy members of the community which provided the clinching argument. Howe reminded the electors of the work he had done in the Lakehead, the jobs he had provided, and of his desire to help bring prosperity back again. Certainly he was a wealthy man, but he stood for no special interests other than those of the working people of the community. If he had not chosen politics, he boasted, he could carry on as an engineer anywhere in the world. But what would that do for his children? He proudly pointed to them as the Five Best Reasons for letting him serve as member of Parliament for Port Arthur. An ad reproducing the letterhead of his firm, with a typed personal note over his signature, appeared in the *News Chronicle* at the end of the campaign. He said he wanted to give his children "the same chance I had to start their productive years under a Liberal government."

October 14 brought decisive victory, not only for Howe but for the party right across Canada. The Liberals elected 173 members, the largest number by far of any party since Confederation. There were but 40 Conservatives returned, the majority of them from Ontario, along with western blocs of 17 Social Crediters and 7 CCFers. Reconstruction elected only its leader, Harry Stevens, but its total popular vote, nearly one-third as large as the Conservatives', reflected just how badly it had cut into traditional Tory support. Vote-splitting, plus the astonishing upsurge of Liberal support in the Lakehead, even brought victory for Howe's Liberal running mate in Fort William, Dan McIvor, over the previously invincible Bob Manion.

In a rash moment, under questioning, Howe had told a campaign meeting that, if elected, he would not move to Ottawa: "I am a citizen of this town, and my stake is here." It was one election promise he could not keep. No sooner were the victory celebrations over than he found himself booking a rail ticket to the capital, to learn what plans the new prime minister had in store for him.[15]

CHAPTER FIVE

Cabinet Making

W hile the returns were coming in to Laurier House on the night of Monday, October 14, 1935, the Leader of the Opposition jotted down some notes, with his stubby pencil, for a victory statement to the Canadian people. It was Mackenzie King's fifth general election as leader of the Liberal party, but for the first time it appeared that he was about to win a decisive, perhaps an overwhelming, victory.

What emerged over the airwaves – not a flattering medium for King – was a turgid and monotonous collection of commonplaces, delivered through his false teeth in his high, sometimes squeaky voice. But, as usual, King got across what he meant to convey: he would do nothing rash, nothing untoward. There would be no chaos.

Even King, who could never be accused of failing to take his own speeches seriously, or of discounting personal flattery, was surprised at the response to his election-night statement. His old friend and confidant, "Holy Joe" Atkinson of the *Toronto Star*, told him in all sincerity that "it was a charter . . . the best statement of Liberalism given by any man at any time." Another observer prophesied that "it would keep the party in power for twenty-five years." His ancient mentor, Sir William Mulock, who had first appointed him in 1900 to the civil service post that later led to his elevation to the Laurier cabinet in 1909, advised King to make sure that every one of his cabinet ministers swore to uphold the principles of that statement as a condition of holding office.

When he arrived from Winnipeg to lunch with King ten days later, John Wesley Dafoe of the *Winnipeg Free Press* had already been consulted by telephone and turned down King's attempt to lure him out of his editor's chair and into a place in the cabinet. But he rejoiced in the "triumph of true Liberalism." He told King that 1935 had been the most important campaign in Canadian history. When he looked over the cabinet that King had chosen, at the Liberal aspirants that had been rejected and at the contrast with the "medieval mercantilism" of R. B. Bennett's Conservative regime, Dafoe pronounced that "no government since Confederation was so promising."[1]

He particularly singled out "the new men, Howe and Rogers and Ilsley," for high praise. The press generally agreed. The Toronto *Globe*'s first headline on the subject read "Young Liberals to be Included in the Cabinet." The *Globe* spoke of a cabinet of "vigorous, forward-looking, progressive young men" like "Charles D. Howe," as it persisted in calling him for the next five months.[2]

At first blush, such effusions seem to border on the preposterous. King's 1935 "charter" of Liberalism is as forgettable as it is now forgotten. Most members of his cabinet were in their fifties and had spent the better part of a lifetime in politics. The group portrait of his new ministers – stiff-kneed, strait-laced, solemn in their spats and stick pins – is about as prepossessing as any newly elected executive of the Oddfellows or a collection of civic worthies from some small-town council. Howe himself had of course spent a term of service in local government, and as a matter of fact, he kept up his Oddfellow association back in Waltham throughout the time of his membership in the King cabinet. The stolid men in that cabinet portrait hardly suggest a radical new departure in the history of Canadian politics.

Among King's fifteen ministers, there were nine lawyers, three farmers, a small-city newspaper proprietor and a former journalist. Nine of them had already been members of his Liberal cabinets in the 1920s. Two of them were former premiers of Saskatchewan. Most came from rural and small-town ridings. There was not a single representative from most of the larger Canadian cities. Excluded entirely were Toronto, Winnipeg, Calgary, Edmonton and Halifax, and there was but one member each from Vancouver and Montreal.

Yet the prophecies about the longevity of the new regime and the comments about its collective ability were not far wide of the mark. And Howe, at least, represented a new phenomenon in Canadian politics. To begin with, he was neither Liberal nor liberal in the manner of Mackenzie King and his friends Dafoe and Atkinson. Government interference in the economy, centralized power and drastic administrative solutions held no terrors for him. To a degree he remained blithely unaware that such things might be a problem for anyone.

Howe was the only cabinet minister of the 1935 group who represented an industrial and working-class riding. He was the only engineer among them, and the first ever to hold office in a Liberal government. He was the only self-made entrepreneur and probably the wealthiest man in the cabinet. With two exceptions he was the only minister whose higher education was not confined to training in law, normal school or agricultural college.

Among his new colleagues, Howe was very much a political neophyte. Unassuming and straightforward at his natural best, dull and prone to cliché when exerting himself to oratory, he was rightly regarded as a poor speaker, and this in a time when a talent for ornate and long-winded rhetoric was still highly prized. But in one sense Howe was the most political of the 1935 ministers, in that he represented the new politics of the National Liberal Federation. To its most active young members Mackenzie King made a good deal of the dubious notion that putting Howe in the cabinet was his own personal reward to them for their help in winning the 1935 election.

Immediately after election day, before consulting anyone, King had pretty well decided to reduce the size of the cabinet from twenty-one members to sixteen. One of these, besides himself, would be the venerable, white-bearded Raoul Dandurand, the government leader in the Senate and a member of that body since Victorian times, who would join the cabinet as Minister without Portfolio. Of the remaining fourteen, if tradition prevailed, three or four would have to come from the West, two or three from the Maritimes, four from Ontario, and four from Quebec, of which one must be a representative of the English-speaking community.

The work of cabinet-making began on October 17 when King's French-Canadian lieutenant and closest political friend, Ernest Lapointe, arrived from Quebec City. King came downstairs to welcome his visitor at the front door of Laurier House. It was just past noon and the sun was shining. King noted in his diary with pleasure that his dog Pat gave Mr. Lapointe "a great welcome also." They quickly got down to business. King said he "was not to have men in the cabinet who drank – that character must be the first essential." To this, Lapointe replied wryly, "You will have a pretty difficult time."[3]

When they had gone over the names of the most essential members, it became clear that King's first problem lay in the fact that there was not a single candidate from Quebec, other than Lapointe himself, who did not fill King with apprehension. P. J. A. Cardin, the other senior Quebec privy councillor, had to be given something. King wished it could be Secretary of State, at that time a minor office where he could do no harm, because King's general impression, as Lapointe agreed, was that "Cardin was a grafter." But Cardin wanted his old post back at Marine, whose potential as a treasury of political patronage – especially in Quebec – was enormous. They deferred a decision and went on to something easier. To represent English-speaking Quebec the obvious candidate was Charles G. "Chubby" Power. Able, astute and popular though Power was, King thought his periodic drinking bouts made him too great a risk. He wondered if there were any other form of recognition Power could be given. Lapointe insisted there was not. Besides, there must be an Irish Catholic in the cabinet or there would be great trouble. King protested that he would rather have trouble outside than within the cabinet. Then it occurred to him that if Power were taken in it might prevent a cabal of "the drinking crowd" on the outside. Much relieved, Lapointe seized on the idea.

In looking over the prospects from Ontario, they immediately agreed on two names: that of the plodding veteran, William Euler, from the old German-Canadian riding of Waterloo North, to return to the cabinet with the portfolio of Trade and Commerce; and that of the Queen's University professor Norman Rogers, Mackenzie King's former private secretary and now the member for Kingston, to be Minister of Labour. King remarked on the utterly "spiritual quality" of both Mr. and Mrs. Rogers.

There was no one from Ontario, however, who could command the confidence of the financial community. Talk turned to the possibility of bringing in Charles Dunning, who had briefly served as King's finance minister in 1930, but had not run in the 1935 election. His presence could be tangible "evidence of stability in the new cabinet," and a pledge to the financial community that the government would not be as dangerously liberal as Dafoe or Atkinson hoped. Though he was an immigrant farm boy and homesteader who had arrived in politics through the Saskatchewan Grain Growers' Association, Dunning, after his defeat in the federal election of 1930, had spent the next five years in business in Montreal.

If Dunning were brought in, by having an Ontario seat opened up for him, that would leave one place for a new man. King mentioned in particular C. D. Howe and Arthur Slaght, the Toronto criminal lawyer who had made a fortune in Kirkland Lake gold and was widely touted in the press as the likely cabinet minister from a northern riding. Slaght was a crony of Ontario's Premier Mitch Hepburn, and since Hepburn had done so much campaigning across the country, he felt entitled to help King choose the Ontario ministers. Slaght was also close to another of Hepburn's friends, the Laura Secord candy tycoon, Frank O'Connor. In spite of the fact that he was distasteful to King (an "Irish Catholic drinking man"), O'Connor had been allowed to raise the largest amounts of money for the federal campaign, including $25,000 from himself, and lesser sums from such mining magnates as Hepburn's friends Jack Bickell and "Sell 'Em Ben" Smith of New York, as well as from various beer and liquor interests.

Next day – Friday the 18th – while King was still wrestling with the problem of the Hepburn influence, the Premier and political boss of Saskatchewan, Jimmy Gardiner, arrived at Laurier House. This presented the Prime Minister with another problem. He badly wanted Gardiner in his cabinet, but Gardiner was opposed to Charles Dunning, his predecessor as Premier of Saskatchewan, joining the government at all. Gardiner complained that Dunning would not stop intriguing against him in his own province. King assured him that if Gardiner entered the cabinet he would have the dominant role in the West. Dunning would only be brought in for an eastern seat. Gardiner remained adamant.

King went to bed that night with nothing further decided. But he woke at four a.m. next morning and did not go back to sleep. In those predawn hours he made two firm decisions: to include Dunning (it was only a matter of what to say to Gardiner) and to "take in Howe from Port Arthur" as the new Minister of Transport, combining the portfolios of Railways and Marine, on the grounds that "he was at the head of the lakes for marine and at a great railway centre." In rejecting the chief alternative, Arthur Slaght, King acknowledged to himself that he was extremely able; famous for his devastating set-piece courtroom speeches, he would be of great political usefulness to the government. But he was a Hepburn man and not quite "straight."

> My feeling is [he wrote in his diary], that Howe would be an infinitely better man from the point of view of character though possibly less effective as a public man. He would represent Northern Ontario, being resident in Port Arthur and Fort William. The winning of these two seats was a great achievement and due largely to him. Being a relative of Joseph Howe was also a factor in his favour, and his family and personal associations were of a kind which would be helpful to the party. Also he is well informed on Western problems. Slaght would really be a Toronto minister representing Algoma. We owe Toronto very little, since she has given us only two members [in the new Parliament]. I cannot be blamed if I take Ontario members from the four corners of the province, other than from Toronto.

King was ready for Jimmy Gardiner when Lapointe escorted him back to Laurier House later that morning. He persuaded him to accept Dunning in the cabinet as a purely eastern minister, arguing that R. B. Bennett would "have only one motive from now on, which would be vengeance and a determination to destroy our party and that we would need men in government who could counter him at every turn." But King also had to fend off Gardiner's demand that the post of railways minister go to the West, either for himself or for the veteran Tom Crerar of Manitoba. King told Gardiner that he wanted to keep the railways portfolio in conjunction with that of marine so that the two could be combined, and suggested that it ought to go to "a centre that connects with the water system." He did not mention that he now had a political newcomer in mind for both posts.

On Monday morning, October 21, King had two visitors. First, old Senator Dandurand dropped in and agreed with him in opposing prominence for Cardin, as a man who was reputed "to have made a lot of money out of dredging contracts." Dandurand was pleased to hear that Chubby Power would be invited to join, even if on King's explicit condition that he and his wife both pledged to stay sober.

The second visitor was Charles Dunning, who accepted the finance portfolio, and readily agreed to keep out of Gardiner's political preserve in the West. But to King's chagrin, Dunning supported Lapointe's view that Cardin would have to be given a significant post in the cabinet. When he heard of King's choice for Transport, Dunning "jumped out of his seat and said Howe is one of the best men on the continent for a post of this kind. His name is well known from one end of Canada to the other."

King's next problem was to persuade Tom Crerar that he should not have the railways post he wanted. Crerar pressed his claim as being the man who could hold Manitoba for the party. But Dunning had already reminded King that Crerar had been particularly weak as railways minister in the last Liberal government – among other things in letting President Thornton of the Canadian National spend a great deal of money on new hotels and a lavish style of living. Crerar was designated minister of what became, after some departmental amalgamations, Mines and Resources.

The next day King called Vincent Massey, the president of the National Liberal Federation, and asked if he would like to be consulted about the make-up of the cabinet. Massey had been roundly attacked by his leader on the last occasion he had presumed to offer some confidential advice, and he quite rightly suspected King had already made up his mind. He declined to make any suggestions. King then told him about his choice of Howe, and reminded him that this was the man Massey had "discovered and brought to see him." Howe was to be the "National Liberal Federation's contribution to the cabinet."

Swearing in was due to take place the following evening. But the Quebec problem was still not settled that morning. Cardin was in a towering rage and threatening to quit politics because he had not got his old ministry of marine back. He told King it was an affront to Quebec for him to be offered the inconsequential post of Secretary of State. He insisted on having one of the largest-spending departments. King finally gave in, no doubt under some pressure from Lapointe who, King sadly mused, was "very weak in resisting forces which could make trouble – with him it is 'who the boys want.'" Public Works was taken from King's original nominee, J. C. Elliott, an upright Ontario veteran whom King had picked as an alternative to a Hepburn man, and given to Cardin. The fourth Quebec minister was to be Fernand Rinfret, a former editor and mayor of Montreal, about whose morals and conduct King was equally unenthusiastic. Elliott became Postmaster General and Rinfret Secretary of State.

In Defence was the witty and affable Ian Mackenzie from British Columbia, who eventually proved that Quebec had no monopoly on the parliamentary drinking championships and who had to be removed from his National Defence portfolio for administrative incompetence when war broke out. The Acadian Joseph Michaud of New Brunswick became Minister of Fisheries, and J. L. Ilsley of Nova Scotia, destined to be one of Canada's great public servants, entered the cabinet as Minister of National Revenue.

By Wednesday afternoon there were still a few prospective cabinet members to be told of their assignments. Howe was summoned to Laurier House at 4:30 p.m., just half an hour before King was due to leave to call on Chief Justice Sir Lyman Duff, acting in the absence of a governor general, to be sworn in as Prime Minister and to present his list of colleagues. King told Howe that he was to be assigned two portfolios. He was to have Railways, because he had no previous involvement in the CN – CP battle and was opposed to amalgamation, and because he had the confidence of the railway employees. At the Ministry of Marine he would probably be required to preside over the abolition of the nation's local harbour commissions and the wholesale political patronage that prevailed within them. Howe said he was pleased at the confidence shown in him. King remarked later on the "quiet and unassuming way in which he made due acknowledgement."

That night Howe and his new colleagues assembled on Parliament Hill, in the Opposition Leader's office. From there King summoned them at 10:00 p.m. to the Prime Minister's quarters in the East Block. They trooped across Parliament Hill, followed by a horde of reporters. King lined them up in order of precedence for the swearing-in. During the ceremony the Prime Minister saw fit to remark on the shocking manner in which ministers of the crown had in the past violated their oaths of office. "It was all part of the declining moral standards in public life," he told the Chief Justice, who ventured to agree, and to reply that he had had trouble himself with judges of the Supreme Court. The new cabinet then walked down the hall to the gothic Privy Council Chamber for their first brief meeting.

Howe's first task was to find an office staff. The usual practice for a new minister was to bring in at least one of his own aides or partisans. But Howe, who had inherited Bob Manion's old portfolio, decided to keep all his predecessor's staff. One of Manion's secretaries, Ruth Thomson, stayed with Howe for the rest of his life, working for him even after his departure from politics. She quickly learned to summarize lengthy documents for him, and to draught most of his routine letters and memos and to handle personal business.

To run the office, Howe wanted Manion's private secretary, Frank Collins. But since Collins at that point was seriously ill, someone else had to be found. Howe remembered a young man who had spoken for him a couple of times during his election campaign. On the weekend after the new cabinet was sworn in, William Bennett, a 23-year-old University of Toronto graduate from a Conservative railroading family in Schreiber, received a long-distance phone call. "Can you come up to Ottawa?" said Mr. Howe. "Right away – I've got a job for you." It turned out to be the most important appointment he ever made.

As private secretary, Bennett organized Howe's office, ran the minister's appointments, produced the right documents at the right time and handled liaison with the constituency. Slim, dark and handsome, Bennett had what a later commentator called "a slightly Mephistophelian appearance" and a "cheerful, unobtrusive way." He was by far the youngest of the ministerial private secretaries in Ottawa. But he had boundless confidence in his own abilities and judgment, and was afraid of no one. His biggest qualification was invisible: he knew Howe's mind, and could sense what his minister would, or would not, approve of. On minor matters at first, and then on more important subjects, Bennett's opinion was often as good as Howe's; if he saw things in a certain way, it was likely that the minister would too, though without any prompting from Bennett. When necessary he could do a perfect replica of the minister's signature. As he grew older he acquired a certain uncanny resemblance to his boss. It was as if he were a slighter, smoother version of the real thing. Bennett made a most effective interceptor between the minister and a host of importunate callers. As Minister of Marine and Railways, Howe was sitting squarely in the middle of a vast assemblage of government patronage. Members of Parliament, party faithful, old friends, new friends, friends of friends, people who remembered him from out West, back in Halifax, on the train – they all appeared at Howe's door as if drawn by gravity. Often they were drawn by Howe's cheery responses to their requests and problems when they met him on the street or in the corridors of Parliament. He liked being useful, he believed there was a way out of every difficulty and he hated saying no, particularly in cordial company. Bennett's task was to free the minister from the trap of the more preposterous misconceptions which Howe's friends and suitors had acquired about what the minister would or could do for them. It would be a familiar enough role for ministerial executive assistants in years to come. But Bennett, thanks to his minister's sanguine style and vast, expanding responsibilities, may well have had as great a job of saying no as anyone who has ever served. And unlike Howe, he became very tough about it.

There was one other new appointment. Manion had run a unilingual office. Howe decided he must have a French-speaking secretary, particularly in view of Marine's presence in Quebec: half its lighthouses, docks, channel buoys, pilotage and dredging operations were located along the shores of the St. Lawrence, its Gulf and its tributaries. Howe asked Ernest Lapointe if he could help out. Lapointe was only too pleased. His daughter Odette had a friend who worked in External Affairs; her health had broken down in her last post in Paris, and she was home on sick leave. Could he send her around? In this way Howe acquired his last recruit, Annette Saint-Denis, a reliable and intelligent young woman from an old Ottawa family. She remained in the minister's office, both as social secretary and in charge of francophone correspondence (Howe never did try reviving his high-school French) until the day he left in 1957.

To head up his two departments, Howe had to make a decision about deputy ministers. There were two, one for Marine and one for Railways. The Marine deputy presented a ticklish problem. R. K. Smith had, until recently, been the Conservative MP for Cumberland. Cashing in his political debts, he had appealed to R. B. Bennett to find him a safer berth than his constituency. Bennett complied, and Smith became a deputy minister. The Liberal victory of 1935 boded ill: with another minister, his career might have been finished. But Howe decided he was competent (a correct guess, as it turned out) and he was told he would stay, no matter what Liberal critics might say. The other deputy was V. I. Smart of the Department of Railways and Canals, a seasoned veteran of the CNR. As senior of the two,

Smart would become the deputy minister of the future combined Department of Transport, and Smith would be head of its marine services.[4]

As Howe's first task at Marine, the Prime Minister asked him to investigate and make recommendations about Canada's ocean ports. He had little more to do than to reread the report of Sir Alexander Gibb, commissioned by Prime Minister Bennett, but not acted upon. One of Gibb's expert witnesses had been none other than C. D. Howe. The harbours, Howe believed, were "perfect sinkholes of wasted public money." Appointments to the local harbour commissions were a major means of political patronage: hundreds of jobs turned over with a change in government. And this led in turn to local decision-making on grounds of partisan advantage rather than proven need. The matter was the most urgent item of business facing the first working session of cabinet on October 28.

Howe recommended that the harbour commissions of Canada's seaports, from Vancouver to Halifax, should immediately be put under the control of a three-man central body in Ottawa: two officers of his department and a new appointee from the outside. For this third position Howe suggested his friend Norman Lambert, secretary of the National Liberal Federation, as a person whose judgment and ability he trusted. This apparently blatant political move stemmed from Howe's utter political innocence rather than his partisanship. Such naîveté, however, which he never entirely lost through the next twenty-two years of his own increasingly fierce partisanship, could in itself be the most infuriating of all forms of political bias.

King, who wanted to keep Lambert working where he was, seized on the impropriety of appointing the party's national organizer to such a sensitive new post, whose very purpose was to end a massive political spoils system. Lambert, much to his disappointment, was to remain where he was, and settle for a place in the Senate three years later. The Prime Minister welcomed the speed with which Howe proposed to act. Other ministers close to the local interests represented by the harbour commissions, with supporters eagerly anticipating appointments as quickly as the Tory appointees could be dismissed, argued for delay or compromise. "When we reached a point," King wrote of the cabinet meeting, "when I saw that if a discussion re-opened nothing would likely be settled for days to come and possibly not at all, I said at once: 'Then we are agreed that all harbour commissions should go . . . and for the present the whole business be managed from the department at Ottawa.'"[5]

Everyone knew that the political pressure to have the decision modified or reversed would be "terrific." Howe said he would be equal to it. Though Ilsley would likely be the most vulnerable of all, he could be counted on to hold firm. He had intended to return to Halifax the next day, however, and in a rare concession to the merely political course of action, he prudently decided to hole up in Ottawa until the worst of the storm was over.

Before the cabinet meeting adjourned, Howe was instructed to draft an announcement about the harbour commissions. Until then the decision was to remain strictly secret. But somebody's tongue was loosened up and the press got hold of the story. The Prime Minister deplored this breach of cabinet secrecy as "outrageous." His colleagues later received a stern lecture, though no suspicion was directed at Howe or his department, where the leak could most readily have occurred.

Howe's first real taste of heavy political weather did not come until he had to defend his bill for a new National Harbours Board in Parliament the following spring. Until then he was increasingly open to public notice and always in a favourable light. Only twenty-four hours after that first Monday cabinet meeting the Prime Minister called an informal press conference. He was gratified that one reporter made a flattering reference both to Howe's stand on the harbour commissions and to his auspicious arrival in public life. King took the opportunity to reply that, yes, the cabinet had its share of "younger men with vision and enthusiasm."

"And innocence," added his faithful servant and chief mandarin O. D. Skelton, who was standing beside them.[6]

CHAPTER SIX

Political Apprentice

The first requirement of a new minister was that he move himself to the capital. So while Clarence was getting to know his officials and exploring the peculiar ways of politicians, Alice was beginning the more painful chore of mobilizing the family, packing the china and furniture, and supervising transportation to Ottawa. She was also saying goodbye to old friends, for the Howe house was up for sale.

Clarence also had to arrange his business affairs. It would be improper to continue to own one of Canada's major engineering firms while simultaneously attempting to carry out the duties of a minister of the crown. The C. D. Howe Company would have to go. But to whom, and for what considerations? The first question was easy to answer. Howe had had his eye on Murray Fleming for some time. Fleming was bright, and he was young – but not too young: just about the same age Howe himself had been when he started out as a consulting engineer. He was capable and well liked in the business. All in all, a fit successor.

So it was arranged. Howe agreed to sell the C. D. Howe Company, lock, stock and reputation, to Fleming and a group of partners for $10,000. The principals were Fleming himself, Bill Peach, a local business friend, and W. H. Carter, the president of Carter-Halls-Aldinger, the construction firm. If any of the partners subsequently wished to sell his shares, Howe had a ninety-day option to repurchase them, an option he kept for well over a decade. The company continued to use the name of its founder, and it stayed in the grain business. Howe kept in touch with Fleming and, through Fleming, with the C. D. Howe Company's fortunes. If his advice was sought, it was freely given; from 1935 on, however, Howe derived no personal profit from the company.*

After several months in a rented place, the Howes moved into what was to be their permanent home at 7 Crescent Road in the suburb of Rockcliffe Park. It was for sale at the very high price, for those days, of $50,000. It had many rooms, enough for the children and servants, and a large garden in which Alice could grow vegetables and tend an abundant variety of shrubs and flowers. Below the garden there was a bridle path and a small woods through which one could glimpse the Ottawa River and the Gatineau Hills.[2]

The Howes were located in the heart of the finest residential area Ottawa had to offer. Rockcliffe Park was a microcosm of Ottawa's elite. Set on picturesque bluffs high above the river, the area was developed about the turn of the century and expanded thereafter. It was attached to Ottawa by a streetcar line, which passed in front of the Governor-General's mansion, Rideau Hall. Rideau Hall was, of course, the centre of the Ottawa Season, such as it was: skating parties in the winter, cricket matches and garden parties in the summer. Visitors to the vice-regal residence could be titillated with the sight of Lord Grey's curious sofa, to which His Excellency had lured susceptible young ladies in the distant, glamorous days before the First World War. But then Lord Grey was a gallant soldier, as well as a lord of high degree and ancient lineage. The current incumbent was of humbler stock, and came complete with a recently minted title: Lord Tweedsmuir. He had been a British MP, but was familiar to his hundreds of thousands of readers around the English-speaking world as John Buchan, the novelist. He would write two books during his stay at Rideau Hall, but regrettably none recording his impressions of the "sub-Arctic lumber village" to which duty and Mackenzie King had called him. Though that description had been coined long ago by an unkind

---

* Howe was comfortably off. He had roughly $500,000 worth of investments in companies not doing business with the Canadian government. In 1935, the only legal, and expected, requirement for a cabinet minister, was that he divest himself of shares in companies seeking government contracts.[1]

critic, Ottawa was still close to its origins. Lumber yards dotted the centre of the city along railway lines that had been built to accommodate wood and its by-products, the Ottawa lumber millionaires. Across from Parliament Hill, along the Hull water-front, the E. B. Eddy Company piled up wood chips and floated lumber booms down the Ottawa River. Just a little way downstream, another lumber company belched out sulphur which, when the wind turned east, gave the entire city the odour of a vast overturned latrine.

Ottawans were usually above noticing such things, or if they did, they accepted them as part of the natural order of creation. They preferred to point out the city's beautiful parks, its fine old houses, the striking neo-Gothic Parliament Buildings and several of the more elegant government edifices built to house the civil servants whose duty it was to run Canada.

Howe's two departments were a study in contrasting accommodation. Railways was definitely the senior: it squatted on Parliament Hill itself in what used to be called the "West Departmental Building," latterly the West Block. The West Block was completed in Alexander Mackenzie's day, in the 1870s. Besides being Prime Minister, that worthy former stonemason was also his own Minister of Public Works. He created an office to his own taste, with beautiful wood panelling, high windows and a lovely view, looking west over the river. The office had a secret staircase so that the Prime Minister could slip out the back way to avoid inconvenient confrontations with the petitioning faithful who thronged the outer office.

The staircase was blocked up when Howe came to occupy Mackenzie's office, but in other ways the spacious and solid Victorian atmosphere evoked the history of the building. Portraits of his predecessors as Minister of Railways and Canals stared down at him from the wall. He also inherited his predecessors' capacious desk, the table behind it by the window, the deep, dark-upholstered armchair and sofa and the ancient carpet. He changed nothing, not even adding family pictures or any personal ornaments to the desk or the walls.

Howe's Marine Department was more modestly accommodated a few blocks south on O'Connor Street, in the Hunter Building, an ugly brick pile erected sometime in the 1910s. Howe rejected his offices there: they were too inconvenient and in any case Marine would soon be absorbed in the new

Transport Department and cease to exist. From the West Block it was only a quick stroll to cabinet meetings in the East Block, or to lunch in the parliamentary restaurant or, if Parliament was not in session, across Wellington Street to the Rideau Club. (All his life he refused to have working lunches in his office, or anywhere else.) Howe enjoyed the club, and its members enjoyed their cheerful new associate. In his terse, utterly frank way, Howe liked to chat; and he loved political gossip: he eventually became one of the better retailers of cabinet secrets. Grant Dexter, the dean of Ottawa newsmen, and a regular inmate of the club, described Howe in 1936 as "good-natured, affable, with a ready sense of humor, but a mind that is razor-edged. . . ."[3]

Howe was good value among the members of the cabinet: more intelligent than most, and more talkative than some, he could always be relied on for an opinion or a story that would enliven the rest of his listener's day until the listener could get home and tell his wife the latest news. Howe never did: his gossiping was something he associated with the man's world at the office. The house and family were Alice's preserve, and the Howes made and kept a tacit agreement never to bring business matters home.

Alice had her worries over the children, and though her husband was no longer away half the year, he gave her little support with the personal crises that arose. Elisabeth's health was delicate and John was desperately unhappy at school. The two younger girls were packed off to attend a private girls' day school in Rockcliffe, and the boys were consigned to Bishop's College School in the Eastern Townships. Neither experiment worked well. In Alice's opinion, the girls learned nothing of value at their school, and were removed and sent to the less exclusive but more intellectually demanding Rockcliffe Public School and Lisgar Collegiate. That was more to their taste, although when their father drove them in on his way to work, they would ask him to let them off a couple of blocks away, so that their classmates would not see them arriving in a chauffeur-driven limousine. (It was a plain Buick: Howe explicitly objected to having the customary ministerial grandeur of a Cadillac.)[4]

Alice had her social obligations as well as Clarence. There were political functions to attend, official dinners to give and necessary entertainments to go to, such as the Prime Minister's dinner parties at Laurier House. On at least one occasion, King startled his guests by seating his Irish terrier, Pat, at the keyboard of his piano, and proceeding to sing and bark.[5]

One of the few cabinet colleagues Howe was close to personally was Ernest Lapointe, who often played golf with him before morning cabinet meetings and taught him a bit about the mysteries of Quebec politics. The veteran and the neophyte developed an affectionate respect for one another, and some years after Lapointe's death, when Ernest's son Hugues joined the cabinet, Howe took him under his wing rather like a favourite nephew. But for Howe, like most of his colleagues, cabinet sociability usually stopped short of the frontiers of personal friendship. For reasons personal and public, the members of the cabinet preferred to relax with less demanding company where they could be themselves at the centre of attention. Ottawa offered a good deal of scope for this: no minister was complete without his dogsbody, running errands, judiciously agreeing, being generally helpful and kind to the children.[6]

In his time as a minister Howe had several. It was not a quality he demanded from his staff: after hours they were free to spend their time as they saw fit. But if someone happened to have the inclination to make the passage of the minister's time easier, Howe was not the man to obstruct him.

In Howe's department the role of companion and fixer was allotted to Commander C. P. Edwards, the Marine Department's director of radio in his professional capacity. In his spare time Edwards was reeve of Rockcliffe Park. As such, he had a splendid opportunity to help out in his neighbours' backyards: dog-catching, paving the streets, and keeping out the riff-raff from Rockcliffe's unlovely neighbour Eastview. Before coming to Ottawa he had worked for Marconi, the British radio firm. He talked well and had an ingratiating manner, which some Ottawans envied and attributed to his English upbringing. When Howe found he was prepared to place himself at his service, he was only too happy to shovel minor preoccupations into Edwards' hands. Edwards was later rewarded with a promotion. Some people, who viewed his sycophantic manner as a camouflage for his lack of ability, felt Edwards had too much influence on Howe. But on major issues in which the minister had any real interest, Howe usually dealt directly with the effective operating head responsible for the matter in question or else left it for Bill Bennett to handle for him personally.

Edwards was one of the few figures associated in the Howe

children's minds with their father's social life. Edwards was licensed to drop by for a drink on Sunday, before or after the rest of the family trooped off to church under Alice's ministering eye. She had long since given up persuading her husband to do his duty by God and the Anglican church: for Clarence, religion stopped at weddings and funerals and the obligatory appearance with the family at Easter and Christmas.

Another regular Sunday visitor was Norman Lambert. Lambert was busy running the National Liberal Federation, now without interference from Vincent Massey, who had been dispatched to his reward as High Commissioner in London. To keep the Liberals fuelled, Lambert drew on the good will and resources of the party's wealthy supporters, and during his Sunday walks with Howe the two men sometimes talked over the technicalities of party finance.

A lot of party finance, it turned out, passed right through Howe's own departments – or department, when the single Department of Transport was created in the fall of 1936. Howe already knew how party finance worked; he could not have survived twenty years around harbours and government contracting without such knowledge. Generous contracts meant that generous contributions to party funds were expected of the contractor, a practice hallowed in Canadian politics under the name ''toll-gating.''

Lambert found the instrumentalities of fund-raising too crude to be reliable and too blatant to be safe. He preferred to collect from a contractor only after (not before) a contract was awarded. Thus an act of grace was rewarded with a token of gratitude, rather than induced with sordid money. Lambert liked to know what contracts were being awarded, and to whom: on those contracts he collected 1½ to 2½ per cent of the total value, although on large contracts the percentage sometimes went higher. Howe saw nothing wrong in the practice: bribery or prior favours were not involved, and he was free to hand out contracts to the best qualified. When, on occasion, Lambert had indicated to someone else that a contract would be forthcoming, Howe gave him neither sympathy nor support, setting off fulminations in his friend's private diary.[7]

But Rockcliffe, the office, the Liberal party, were only a periphery to the main attraction of Ottawa life, Parliament itself. The Parliament Buildings sat grandly on a bluff overlooking the Ottawa River to the north, and the American legation and the Rideau Club to the south. There were no tall hotels and office buildings to compete with the Peace Tower. Members of Parliament and senators occupied offices in the Centre Block, and here too Howe located himself when he had to. Though most work was done down in the old Railways office, when Parliament was in session his office on the Hill became a centre of activity. And it would be in Parliament that Howe would have to show the public how well qualified he really was to govern. If he was to succeed in his new career, if he was to maintain credence at all, let alone change old patterns of government and create the new things the country needed, he would have to do it there before he could do it anywhere else.

In spirit, it was still the House of Commons of Macdonald, Blake and Sir John Bourinot. A score of its members had actually sat there with Laurier, seventeen years before. Such was the simplicity of government in 1935 that the Commons was still the focus for testing not only the major matters of policy but most of the significant details as well.

Howe soon got his baptism of fire. Within the short space of a week, in late March of 1936, he introduced motions in the House of Commons that led not only to the creation of the National Harbours Board but also to the founding of the Canadian Broadcasting Corporation and the modern structure of the Canadian National Railways. The Prime Minister would introduce the bill to create Howe's new Department of Transport. But the minister would be on his own, and very much on his mettle, to put through his three major pieces of legislation.

What sort of opposition did he face?

On the back benches behind him, and spilling round onto benches opposite him, was seated a sizable portion of the huge Liberal majority of 174 MP's. Some of these Liberal members were to give Howe more trouble than anyone from the opposition as far as the Harbours Bill was concerned. Other Liberals, particularly the Ontario and Quebec veterans who had not received their expected reward of a cabinet post, were waiting for the political novice to make mistakes. Others again, such as the colourful and loquacious Jean-François Pouliot, simply felt free to follow their own genius and inclination wherever it led them, no matter how embarrassing for the government. (At one rather delicate point in the history of the Canadian Radio Broadcasting Commission, Pouliot had proposed that its august chairman, Hector Charlesworth, be tied up in his own whiskers.)

Of the splinter parties in the House, the CCF had only seven members. But their share of the western popular vote was large, higher in British Columbia, at 33 per cent, than that of either of the old parties. And they were among the ablest debaters. The youngest of them, T. C. Douglas, spoke no less than sixty times in his freshman session, in contrast to the majority of MP's who hardly spoke at all. Their leader, J. S. Woodsworth, was perhaps the most respected person in the House. Howe's chief criticism of Woodsworth was for straying off the subject under discussion into the exposition of general principles and ideas, things for which Howe had limited concern and even less patience. But the CCF did not concentrate much of their fire on Howe during his first Parliament. After all, he represented a labour riding into which they had made few inroads. And more important, the measures of public control and management he was proposing as Minister of Transport were more or less in line with their own point of view.

By far the most formidable attacks on Howe during his first session were levelled by members of the official opposition. There were just forty Conservatives, the smallest number since Confederation. But they represented established ways, solid wealth and big business. Their strongholds were in Westmount, Rosedale and Calgary West, in Victoria and Vancouver South.

Fully one third of them came from Toronto. All the city's members, except for the Liberals' Sam Factor of the old Jewish garment district, Spadina, and Hugh Plaxton of Trinity, were Conservative. It did not take much of former mayor Tommy Church, the member for Toronto's ultra-British east end and now a caricature of his imperialist and parochial self, to increase Howe's already strong distaste for what he regarded as the smug bigotry of Toronto.

His toughest critics in the House were men like the Montreal MP's, C. H. Cahan, a member of the previous Conservative cabinet, and the perspicacious W. A. Walsh of Mount Royal. There were the elderly knights of the Privy Council Chamber like Sir George Perley. There was R. Smeaton White, who first entered the Commons in 1888 during Sir John A. Macdonald's second last term. There was Howe's fellow engineer, the Honourable Grote Stirling, the first member of the profession to sit in a Canadian cabinet. And above all there was the sleek, immensely imposing presence of the old bruin himself, R. B. Bennett – heavy, deft, relentless, judicious and lofty in manner, neither as brilliant nor as noble a statesman as he wished men to believe, but never to be crossed lightly. He had been brought down but not ruined by virtue of having been the nation's undisputed governor through the five worst years of the Great Depression. He and his front bench were a formidable group. In contrast to their Tory successors in the parliaments of the 1940s, they had the capacity to keep the minister in line. And they used it.

The session opened early in February. The Prime Minister led the House in mourning for King George V, who had died the month before, and with grave private misgivings hailed the accession of the new monarch, Edward VIII, the elderly young playboy Prince of Wales. The Versailles peace settlement also died in 1936, as Mussolini's troops completed the conquest of Ethiopia and Hitler marched into the Rhineland. But in Canada, the running of External Affairs was the Prime Minister's prerogative and rarely a concern of Parliament's even when it was sitting. Such things were not a matter for comment by other ministers like Howe, even had they been interested.

Howe began well. For two weeks he attended Parliament regularly and said nothing. For a month more he spoke pretty much when spoken to, answering questions about departmental estimates, setting the record straight. His first skirmish in the House came over the Hudson Bay Railway terminus at Churchill. The topic suited him perfectly. Various members were impatient with the failure of the new route to attract more business. For years western Canadians had pushed for a railway to connect the granary of Canada by direct ocean route to the markets of Europe. It was to be a fulfilment in modern form of the ancient dream of wealth which had first brought the Hudson's Bay Company into being.

Howe was questioned closely about the matter when his departmental estimates were before Committee of the Whole. Grote Stirling wanted to know what money was being put into dredging at Churchill. M. J. Coldwell of the CCF asked about high insurance rates for these northern waters. Other western MP's observed that not enough was being done to popularize the route. Howe responded briefly and directly to every point. Someone asked about fog. He replied there were no fogs during the shipping season at Churchill that he knew of: the honourable member must be confusing Hudson Bay with the Gulf of St. Lawrence. One MP speculated about better ways for loading grain ships. Howe told him precisely how and why an ocean ship's cargo had to be packed tight before it was safe to sail, adding "My hon. friend is thinking of . . . the great lakes rather than an ocean port."

When ill-informed press criticism was repeated in the House, the minister spoke more personally: "I have spent a good deal of time at Churchill, perhaps more than any of my officials, and more than any hon. member. . . . I have talked with captains who have brought in ships." (The small frostbite scar on his cheek was acquired during one of his visits there.) And he reminded the House that Vancouver, too, had taken time to develop as a port.

Howe's first major test in the House of Commons began on March 19, 1936, when he rose to explain the nature and purpose of his National Harbours Board bill which was to elaborate and establish permanently what he had done immediately after taking office. Although it was generally thought to represent one of the most fundamental political and administrative reforms since Confederation, Howe blithely assumed that there would be no great difficulty in having it passed.[8]

This was understandable in that the previous Conservative government had made the first move to change the system. But Premier Bennett quickly discovered that he would have a first-class rebellion in his own ranks if the sacred and long-entrenched rights of patronage were removed from local party functionaries. And many Liberal MP's, who had done well out of the harbours pork barrel in the 1920s, anticipated their own turn at the public trough again and were not disposed to help Bennett out. So nothing further had been done.

As far as Howe was concerned, the key decision for reform was made at his very first cabinet meeting in October 1935. He reported to the House in March that his centralizing and streamlining measures had, without hurting foreign trade preparations for the coming year, already saved on operating costs. As for capital assets, there was nearly half a billion dollars tied up in government port property – all of it needing reassessment, much of it out of date or useless. At a stroke, Howe's bill would substitute, for over twenty different pieces of legislation, one single act to regulate the whole harbours system, and run it by a single body located in Ottawa and reporting to the minister himself.

After a little preliminary questioning of the minister, a Conservative MP called out "Good legislation!" Then, slowly, the trouble began. Liberal MP's rose to congratulate Howe on his position as new minister and the government on the fine purpose of the bill, and to explain why one or another port should be treated as a special case, and in some way exempted.

McGeer of Vancouver and Isnor of Halifax, Ryan of Saint John and Gariépy of Trois Rivières, told the House that their support for reform was only equalled by their belief in the value of local initiative. Thomas Vien of Montreal, whose Liberal loyalties in House and Senate lasted year in and year out from Laurier to Trudeau, warned of a groundswell of opinion for an independent French republic on the banks of the St. Lawrence: in the light of this threat, he asked, could yet "another slice of local autonomy be centralized in the hands of bureaucratic officials"?

Several Conservatives joined in support of these sentiments, adding a touch about ministerial control being an even more powerful engine of patronage than local control. Lawyers began to deplore the drafting of the bill and indicating amendments that would be necessary in committee.

To get matters back on track, the loquacious R. E. Finn of Halifax exclaimed that Howe brought to his office rare skill, youth and intelligence. And that he graced a government "whose leader I follow with an allegiance amounting almost to a religious belief, because he has followed in the footsteps of that great Canadian, the Right Hon. Sir Wilfrid Laurier." But with equal respect and at much greater length did Finn then recount the history and the problems of the port of Halifax. ("Hark, do you hear the whistle of the Hong Kong train?" his old Liberal uncle had cried out to the crowd from the proscenium of the Halifax Academy of Music. "No, and why? Because it is blowing in Portland, Maine. . . .")

For over a week, Howe bore up through all the mounting chorus of praise, criticism and rhetoric of dubious relevance. Just before his bill's second reading, he briefly thanked members for their kind personal words and for their helpful suggestions, many of which, he assured them, were being examined closely.

A month later, during the committee stage of the bill, Howe made his first serious mistake. By now he was impatient with his chief opposition tormentor, the Montreal lawyer C. H. Cahan. He was further annoyed by an amendment from the Liberal backbencher Ernest Bertrand, who stated that he had received 315 letters of protest. In order to preserve all that was sacred in the Dominion of Canada, Bertrand moved that the proposed National Harbours Board be split into three sections, one for each ocean and one for Quebec. The Leader of the Opposition had just started to demonstrate how unworkable this proposal was, when Howe snatched the opportunity to attack Bertrand away from Bennett and did the job himself. And then, warming to his task, he threw in an attack on the previous Conservative era of harbour boards administration for good measure:

> I have before me a volume which I compiled with some little trouble, going back over five years of harbour commissions. . . . To me it shows the most shocking betrayal of public trust I have ever read in my life. I feel in one way that it should be put in Hansard . . . on the other hand I dislike to do this because it would certainly give the people a very unfortunate idea of how public affairs are conducted.

That did it. The Conservative front bench, already restive over the unqualified praise the new minister had been receiving during his first six months, decided that the honeymoon was over. They took after Howe every chance they got. His gentlest and most perceptive critic, W. A. Walsh, asked him to qualify his wholesale besmirchment of all past harbour commissioners. He should either curb himself or make specific charges against particular individuals. If anything, Howe promptly made matters worse by cheerfully replying, in what he took to be conciliatory fashion: "I am unable to distinguish between . . . harbour boards . . . I may say that it is confined to no particular period and no particular party." At this the Leader of the Opposition exploded. He proceeded to lecture Howe for a good ten minutes. "The minister has said either too much or too little," exclaimed Bennett.

> He has condemned the character of decent Canadians . . . men in Montreal, Halifax, Saint John, who have given their very best to their country. . . . Does he assail Professor Brock whose life is gone? He assails him. . . . The minister says his remark applies to no period and to no particular board. Therefore it is universal. . . . No minister would even think of making a charge of that kind against men who cannot be heard, who are not here, who have not an opportunity to appear, who have wives and families . . . whose honour and good names . . . their children are proud of. . . .

The House joker, Jean-François Pouliot, tried puncturing this balloon flight by earnestly asking Bennett for his estimate of the number of children that had been damaged by the minister's words. But Bennett swatted him aside and charged on. He and Cahan then went after Howe's bill clause by clause, subsection by subsection. At one point Cahan expressed concern about the limited resources of the board for meeting legal judgments. On the contrary, retorted Howe, "the board is dealing in millions of dollars" – his first, though not his most famous, round and general reference in the House to sums of that size.

Finally Cahan dispensed with the details and attacked Howe head on:

> Patronage . . . under his control will lead to evils far greater than those to which he called attention. . . . This bill provides for the honourable gentlemen a system of patronage unprecedented in the administration of any department of the government. . . . I assume that the honourable gentleman thinks that if he were prime minister he would be best qualified to select all the civil servants. . . .

Howe wryly thanked his honourable friend for complimenting him on his prime ministerial aspirations. Pouliot jumped up to defend Howe on a point of order. Finn blasted back at the previous Conservative government for firing everybody working in Halifax harbour in 1930 – right "down to the men who swept the docks. . . ."

"Patronage," he cried, "they had it for five years and their party grew rich on it."

Point of order from the Conservative front bench. Aborted attempt to reiterate from Finn. Interruptions all round.

More hassling, after which the Liberal chairman of the Committee of the Whole found Finn to be in order – "so far" – but restrained him from retracing his steps or going further.

Both sides quieted down for a speech from CCF MP Angus MacInnis of Vancouver East, who praised the bill and the minister, but offered him a suggestion. Howe should go all the way and get full credit for his fine legislation by requiring that harbour appointments be made through the Civil Service Commission, thus eliminating any further opportunity for patronage. "We are not going to get rid of the evils merely by appointing a board."

The CCF leader J. S. Woodsworth wanted to know more about these evils, and kept pressing Howe to explain "the shocking betrayal of public trust" he had mentioned. Could any of the vast sums squandered be got back? He warned that the morale of the civil service would be undermined "in a very subtle way" if the harbours were exempted from the Civil Service Act. Sir George Perley followed Woodsworth, repeating the point.

Howe ignored the two CCFers but turned to answer Perley. His suggestion was "impossible": as an experienced businessman he should know better than to "ask us to place a vast organization like this under the Civil Service Commission. There is a time and place for all things." The crucial matter of appointments – "to the elevator business, the cold storage business, the wharf and warehouse business, the terminal railway business, stevedoring and so on" – should surely be left "to the business heads of enormous undertakings of this kind, allowing them to keep personnel up to the mark by giving them the power of dismissal."

This was the first of many occasions on which Howe made a case for the principle of the independent crown corporation. It was a publicly owned enterprise, but not directly part of the civil service. It was to be managed as efficiently, absolutely and aggressively as if he himself were the private entrepreneur at the head of it, and no nonsense about politicians meddling with the management. Among the opposition speakers, only Walsh appeared to see Howe's point clearly. And he dismissed it as unfit for the real world of Canadian politics: "a pleasant picture . . . not possible under present conditions."

Perley advised Howe to let the clause stand down so he could fix it, and lectured him on what the rules of the House would and would not allow. But "this is the third month of Parliament," cried Howe. "We have debated this one section for nearly two hours."

The plea was ignored. The debate went right on. Bennett and others again warned Howe about political patronage and the need for permanence. By now thoroughly exasperated, Howe gave the House a piece of his mind: "Until this bill is passed and we get our board organized we have very little chance of instituting [any] system that will work. . . . I must say I am getting a bit fed up . . . and my resistance is at a rather low ebb."

At that, Bennett became ever so patient and helpful. He

reminded the neophyte where he was: "The minister will learn by and by that he will get very weary of many things he may have to do. . . . He cannot deal . . . as he would with a design in a drafting room . . . there are 245 members of this house and they all have a right to express their views."

Howe repeated his plea: action first, details to be sorted out later: "We are trying to get the wheels turning. . . . The one important point of which we are apt to lose track is that ports must operate efficiently, the business must be done. I am more afraid of obstructing the wheels of progress . . . than I am of one or two political appointments."

In vain Howe reminded the House that he had spent "a great part of the last twenty years building in harbours." His chief critic, C. H. Cahan, went blithely on picking apart the bill's legal details: "I am not familiar with Saint John Harbour, but I understood that . . . the Navigable Waters Protection Act, chapter 140 . . . section 4, which reads . . ." and so on, and so on. Howe snapped at him. "My honourable friend has spent a great deal of time in the courts of law and has not been out sufficiently in the firing line of business."

A month later, on May 20, Howe was still defending his bill: "We are trying to avoid setting up an inflexible machine to run a . . . highly competitive . . . business." And Bennett was still expressing his appreciation of Howe's point but telling him that he failed to realize that there was too much power to be vested in the minister: "The minister says: Trust me and we will see that it is properly administered, which is the usual excuse made for the exercise of arbitrary power."

Finally, on June 19, 1936, the Harbours bill was given royal assent and Howe's first crown corporation came into being.

Twenty years later in the House of Commons, the opposition was still warning the country about the dangers of absolute power in the hands of one man. Howe, with less patience and little justification, was still telling the opposition they must leave matters to the minister. But this first time he was right. The harbours system had been both a scandal and a deep-rooted tradition of Canadian politics. His board put them on a business footing, free from the drawbacks of both private greed and bureaucratic inertia. A few months later it would be hard to imagine what all the fuss was about – or to credit that anybody could become so exercised about the matter.

One reason Howe's bill took so long to pass was that its drafting did need improvement. In the end Howe accepted some thirty amendments. But another reason for the flurry of opposition criticism had nothing to do with the case. At the same time as the harbours were enduring their stormy weather in the House, Howe was also trying to take the Canadian National Railways out of the hands of the bankruptcy trustees where the Conservatives had placed it in 1932. He was determined to turn it into an efficient modern enterprise able to compete throughout its range of railway, shipping, trucking, telegraph, hotels and other services with the Canadian Pacific or with anyone else.

But the first step in Howe's CNR legislation (unlike that for the harbours) was to demolish rather than to create an arrangement for which the previous Conservative government could take credit. As a result the battle was drawn on party lines. It became very personal and very bitter.[9]

CHAPTER SEVEN

Political Railways and Public Airwaves

There is no such thing as a Minister of Railways now; C. D. Howe was the last. The president of the Canadian National Railways no longer holds court in his private railway car, as the princely Sir Henry Thornton once did. The head of the Canadian Pacific no longer receives a British title upon accession, nor does the Prime Minister call upon him when he arrives in Ottawa; he must wait for an appointment, if he can be fitted in, like the head of any other large corporation. The transcontinental no longer rumbles under Parliament Hill; the steam engines are gone to the scrapyards or to museums or to India; the dull red wayside stations are vanishing; the vast and glorious cathedrals to steam await the developer's hammer or some new life from the restorer's hand.

No nation on earth has been so bound up with the history and politics of railways as Canada. From the first railway age of the 1850s – when Sir Allan MacNab declared "Railways are my politics," and Joseph Howe prophesied to his incredulous listeners that some of them would live to see the six-month Cape Horn voyage from Halifax to Victoria reduced to six days and would hear the whistle of the steam engine in the passes of the Rocky Mountains – down to the 1940s and the crowded coaches and boxcars of the Second World War, the railways were at the heart of Canadian national enterprise and daily life. More than this, railways were, in the beginning, an article of faith. Their chief prophet was the civil engineer Thomas Keefer, who

92

declared that "Poverty, bigotry, the demagoguism of politicians" (probably war and plague too) would all be banished by the "restless, rushing, roaring acidity of the iron civilizer."[1]

It was in the golden summer of the age of such faith that Clarence Howe grew up, chose his profession and practised it. As a boy he constructed an elaborate model railway in the attic in Waltham. Training engineers for the construction of railways was the most important concern of the institute from which he graduated. His first assignment to Dalhousie University civil engineering students was the planning of railways. Both as a civil servant and in his private business, he began his engineering practice at the head of the Great Lakes in the railway junction town of Canada and he spent all his years in politics as its representative in Parliament.

Howe was a familiar figure in the club cars of western Canada and his work brought him east many times a year. For over twenty years he spent a good proportion of his waking and sleeping hours on the railways and in their hotels. He rode the trains of the Grand Trunk Pacific and the Canadian Northern even as the lines were still being built. He had travelled the Canadian Pacific Railway through the Rockies in its first generation, before it cut under the mountains to avoid the perilous grades and weather of the Kicking Horse and the Rogers passes. He saw for himself the changes in bridging and tunnelling that could be accomplished by a courageous and ingenious engineer. By the time he entered politics and became Minister of Railways, however, he also knew well the damage that uncritical faith in railway building had done to his profession and to his adopted country. The great grain elevators he had built were often empty; certainly not all of them were needed in 1934, when western wheat shipments were down to one-eighth of their 1928 level. The operating surplus of the Canadian National fell to almost nothing. The mountainous charges on its debt of some $2.5 billion loomed larger than ever and demoralized all who tried to work in their shadow. As Canada's first Minister of Transport, Howe would find many opportunities for a variety of new ventures, but of all the problems he inherited, that of the national railway system was the greatest.

The CNR was assembled by the wartime and postwar governments of Sir Robert Borden and Arthur Meighen out of the wreckage of four bankrupt systems: the government-owned

Intercolonial, connecting the Maritimes to central Canada; the old pre-Confederation Grand Trunk; and the two extra transcontinentals – the Grand Trunk Pacific and the Canadian Northern – which the Laurier Liberals had allowed their political friends to build and overbuild with little financial commitment of their own but generous government help. The Canadian Northern was cheaply built on a poor roadbed (it was sometimes known as "The Canadian Nowandthen" or "The Wooden Axle"). The Grand Trunk had a reputation for being proverbially late. Its offspring, the Grand Trunk Pacific ("Get There Perhaps"), which Laurier had proclaimed would "roll back the map of Canada," was denounced as "a mad route over granite ranges." As for the old Intercolonial, it seemed to wander through New Brunswick and Nova Scotia according to the pull and whims of local mayors and MP's who wanted to be sure the railroad went through the centre of their town. Even before the last spike on the Canadian Northern transcontinental line had been driven in 1915 the government had had to bail out its backers. The next year it had to take it over entirely. The government had not only to think of the effect of the railroad's bankruptcy on the war effort but also of the probable collapse of the Canadian Bank of Commerce which was deeply involved in its financing. In 1919 the Grand Trunk fell, although it was not until 1923, after long and complex litigation, that the various government systems were put together as the CNR.

By that time the Liberals were back in power. To head the new national railway they appointed Sir Henry Thornton, an American who had had a successful career in England as manager of the famous Great Eastern Railway. When he took charge of the CNR, the disasters of postwar inflation and depression were already past. The mood and the economy of the mid-twenties encouraged him in his own sanguine inclinations. His answer to the problems of the new railway was not retrenchment but attack. He would compete with the CPR on their own terms, and beat them. The CPR had Banff; he would outdo them with the erection of Jasper. They were building the largest hotel in the British Empire in Toronto, he would build the Hotel Vancouver and the Nova Scotian in Halifax. They had the Empire's largest steam engine, he would acquire the world's mightiest oil locomotive. They had a splendid fleet of *Empresses*, he commissioned the construction of five *Lady* boats to cruise the West Indies; and he would serve the west coast of North America from

San Francisco to Alaska, with his *Princes*. The CPR added branch lines to attract more trade in the boom times of the 1920s; he could compete with them there, too. Their headquarters was in Montreal's Windsor Station, so his first act was to move his headquarters from Toronto to the premier city of Canada, and encouraged by Mackenzie King, to commission the outfitting of a private Montreal residence for himself and future presidents of the CNR.

Thornton succeeded in giving a sense of purpose and morale to the railroad. He built a single organization with a definite character out of a demoralized set of individual companies. The CPR might fight back, but Thornton, with the government behind him and the staggering debt charges expected to melt away in the sunshine of prosperous times, could afford to match them in every measure, however sound or however extravagant.

With the arrival of the Depression and a new government in power, Sir Henry Thornton, as the most public of Canadian tycoons, proved to be a scapegoat for both the real and imagined sins of the CNR. He became the target of abuse from several Conservative members of the Commons Railway Committee, who accused the CNR of corruption and extravagance. Thornton refused to reply to his critics. He had responded to the exigencies of the Depression by cutting out railway luxuries and trimming salaries. But he refused to make drastic reductions in staff simply to save money. "You cannot turn people loose and merely transfer the burden of their maintenance from the railway company to the government." CNR revenues held up at a better ratio than almost any other North American railroad but the ancient debt, incurred in the building of the system, loomed larger than ever.

Thornton was asked to resign by the Minister of Railways, Robert Manion. A distinguished international panel of railwaymen and other worthies under the chairmanship of Mr. Justice Lyman Duff of the Supreme Court of Canada, the largest royal commission in Canadian history, was appointed to examine the problem and find a solution. The end result was not a happy one. In 1933 the government replaced the old CNR board of directors with three trustees – Judge C. P. Fullerton and two Conservative businessmen – all of them more suited to eliminating deficits on paper than to running a railroad. They reduced the complement of employees drastically, from some 110,000 to less than 75,000. But little money was saved and no hopeful solutions for the future were in sight by the time the government changed hands again in 1935.[2]

After introducing his CNR reform bill in March, Howe rose in the House on April 27, 1936, to move second reading. He began with a broadside attack on the board of trustees and all their works. He attacked their attempts to save money and balance books in the abstract – "the bankruptcy situation," which was the essence of the position they represented. What little improvement there had been in the CNR since 1933, Howe stated, was the result of economies introduced by Thornton's old board of directors and by small increases in traffic rather than further cuts in staff. The trustees were "laymen inexperienced in railway problems . . . who knew nothing of actual railway practice." Yet they allowed the real operating head of the railway almost no power to run the system as a competitive business. Their labour relations were as bad as their business practice. No wonder there was unrest among the employees. Howe accused the trustees of having "shown a complete lack of understanding of the human element which enters so largely into a successful railway operation."

Yet the trustees were "responsible to no one" in rendering account for this state of affairs. The last government had divested itself of all control and direction over the railway. It had ignored the warnings not only of the Liberal opposition but of the railway unions.

Howe's solution was to make a normal business enterprise of the CNR, publicly owned but independent of political influence upon its operations. He proposed a board of directors which would report to Parliament through the Minister of Railways. But unlike Thornton's original board, it would be independent of government control in its operations and in all but the broadest policy questions. It would not include the deputy minister of the department as a member; its chairman would not be under direct government control like Thornton, nor would he speak with the voice of the government as Thornton had. Whatever contact between the government and the board was necessary would be provided "by conference between the Chairman of the Board and the Minister of Railways direct."

Howe was particularly scornful of the previous government's stupidity in choosing an outsider, and worse still, a lawyer, to run a railroad. He signalled his intentions to appoint as the CNR's new president its chief operating officer, S. J. Hungerford, a railwayman who had risen from the ranks.

Howe ended his speech with an appeal to members on both sides of the House to recognize that "the railway problem is not a party question but a matter of business." As such it was "a matter of vital concern to every Canadian citizen."

The Leader of the Opposition was not pleased. Bennett told the House that Howe's remarks were "of such an acrimonious and political character" that he could scarcely recall himself to his duty, "which far transcends the answering of the speech to which we have just listened." He then launched upon an extensive apologia for his government's appointment of the royal commission on the CNR. He defended the board of trustees and Judge Fullerton. He recalled the sins not only of the Thornton era but of the Laurier Liberals who in the boom times of the 1900s had created the problem in the first place. He went out of his way to attack Howe's proposed new railway chief (whom he had known many years ago in Calgary) as a fine "railway master mechanic," but unfortunately, a weak man who "temperamentally cannot resist pressure" and his own natural inclination to please those in power. For good measure, Bennett also attacked Howe as a man with little experience in the complex politics of the Canadian railway question.

On June 5, while one of his Conservative critics was waxing fulsome in praise of the board of trustees and its chairman, Howe could not resist heckling. He taunted him with the suggestion that Judge Fullerton had been spending more time in the past few months in the offices of opposition members than in discussing the railroad's problems with the government. "As long as this government is responsible for the problems of the CNR," Howe stated, "it wants a management at the head which is loyal to the government."

The press blared this into headlines: FULLERTON DISLOYAL, MINISTER CHARGES. The Conservatives responded gleefully: Howe's slip of the tongue had let out the real truth.

Howe eventually managed to extricate himself and return to his main point that the CNR must be run as much as possible by its board of directors like a private corporation. "We are going to establish the ordinary business set-up of successful business concerns in this country and elsewhere. We are going to restore management by experts in the railway business." The experts would be surrounded by a board recruited for "national service" from among the best businessmen in the country and at small remuneration that could not possibly compensate for their real time and contribution. Unlike the trustees, they would not concentrate upon the debts of the past but upon the expansion of future business.

Howe met a totally different kind of criticism from the left. The CCF was concerned lest the new board continue the trustees' policy of dismissing employees by pooling certain services with the Canadian Pacific. The CCF proposed that for every employee who was downgraded or lost his or her job as a result of the two railways' pooling services, a special tribunal should be set up to review the case and award compensation.

Howe refused the suggestion. It would be unwarranted government interference. The best solution would be to let the railway unions and management work it out, he said, rather than to proliferate judicial tribunals. He challenged Woodsworth to produce a single statement by a railway union showing support for the CCF position. The fact of the matter was that a number of Liberals, like Howe himself, had been elected from railway constituencies on a pledge to oppose further employee dismissals through pooling arrangements and to prevent amalgamation with the CPR. Woodsworth readily admitted that he only had communications from many individual union members and some locals. He did not have the support of any railway union. Having wrung this out of him, Howe settled the matter by replying, "I can take it that the honourable gentleman is speaking for himself and not for the railway organizations of Canada."[3]

In the end, the opposition had no alternative structures or solutions to offer in place of Howe's. The legislation passed in June.

Howe proposed names for appointments to his new board to cabinet on June 7, 1936. Most of them were from Montreal and Hamilton; some were Conservatives; none might be considered a labour representative and there were no westerners among them. His cabinet colleagues objected strongly and King was horrified. In the end, Howe kept his key nominees, the head of Noranda Mines, J. Y. Murdoch, and the western lawyer Herbert Symington, with whom he had worked closely in the grain business during the 1920s. But he had to accept appointments which presented a better picture of balanced national representation, people who were not quite the forerunners of his wartime dollar-a-year men from the ranks of Canadian industry which he originally had in mind.[4]

Howe's first objective for the CNR had been met, however.

One measure of its potential competitive threat was that Sir Edward Beatty of the CPR renewed his public campaign for amalgamation. He complained of the unfairness of his private enterprise trying to compete with a government organization which had the vast treasury of public funds behind it. Public ownership had cost the Canadian people three billion dollars, he told the luncheon circuit. It presented "a charge to Canadian citizens of three dollars a minute from the beginning of the Christian era." Howe saw to it that Beatty was pursued on the campaign trail by senior officers of the CNR best equipped to refute him.

Beatty also counter-attacked when Howe proposed his next railway reform: a change in the capital structure of the company, so that its massive debt would no longer inhibit its operating function. Since large amounts of both Canadian National and Canadian government bonds were still held overseas, the CPR pressed its case in the City of London. John Dafoe spoke of "an organized campaign to damage the credit of Canada on the ground of the railway situation, in the hope that the government can thus be intimidated to yielding to Sir Edward Beatty's demands. I was told that no Canadian can stir about in London without encountering this propaganda." Dafoe was relieved to find Howe unyielding in his intent to proceed with recapitalization at the next session of Parliament.[5]

Finally, to change the economic context in which both the CNR and the CPR operated, Howe introduced a bill in 1937 to set up a Board of Transport Commissioners (replacing the Board of Railway Commissioners), with power to regulate every major form of transportation in Canada. It was vigorously opposed by Great Lakes shipping interests and by various trucking firms, assisted by such advocates of provincial power as Ontario's Minister of Highways. Previously, freight rates in these fields had been unregulated and companies operating in them were able to sell their services cheaply when they could take business away from the railways but to charge whatever price the market would bear otherwise and elsewhere. By contrast, under the Board of Railway Commissioners, the railways had been closely regulated to prevent them from using monopoly positions to take advantage of their customers.

After an effective lobbying campaign against it, Howe's bill was held up by the Conservative majority in the Senate. Eventually he had no alternative but to withdraw it and return to the

1938 session of Parliament with a bill that omitted reference to interprovincial trucking. But its crucial feature remained: both the railways were freed to compete with other forms of transport; they could thus set lower rates, for example, for customers who gave them larger portions of their business. Altogether, Howe's CNR reforms and his new regulatory agency enabled the railways to match other forms of transportation more effectively and made them readier for the pivotal role thrust upon them during the Second World War.

While members of Parliament were scrapping and orating and crying blue ruin over Howe's first railway bill in the spring of 1936, they quietly passed another piece of legislation he introduced, creating the Canadian Broadcasting Corporation, without serious debate and with little dissent or public notice.

It had been the CNR which pioneered network broadcasting in Canada. In 1923 when the first local Canadian and American radio stations were going on the air and a few enthusiasts were assembling wireless sets to tune in, CNR President Thornton grandly announced that the railway would bring the new communications miracle to the whole of Canada. Parlour cars and hotels would be equipped with radio receivers and headphones, with an operator in attendance, and a chain of stations would be established to broadcast news, entertainment and educational material. Early customers actually rode the Calgary-Edmonton train just to hear the Dempsey-Tunney fight broadcast. But the objective was not merely to attract more passengers and tourists for the CNR; it was to bind closer the regions of Canada, to keep outlying settlers in touch with a wider world, and help "create a sense of nationhood." On Canada's fiftieth birthday, Dominion Day, 1927, the first network broadcasts were heard from coast to coast. In 1929 the Toronto Symphony Orchestra was signed up for regular programming – over a year before CBS went on the air with their orchestra in the United States.

Then the Great Depression closed in. CNR revenue plunged, and the railway was put into trusteeship. But radio was booming; local stations in Canada mixed American broadcasts with their own programs like the Neilson Hour and Foster Hewitt's Hockey Night in Canada. Canadians also heard the roar from another sports palace, as the screams of Adolf Hitler roused his Herrenvolk; and they listened to the calming fireside chats of Franklin Roosevelt and the first of King George V's Christmas broadcasts to the Empire.

The Canadian stations in 1935 were commercial and privately

owned – mostly by the manufacturers of radio equipment. In 1929, however, a royal commission, headed by the president of the Bank of Commerce, Sir John Aird, and encouraged by Prime Minister King after his visit to the BBC, had come out strongly in favour of public ownership and control of broadcasting. A wealthy young Canadian named Alan Plaunt, just back from Britain, determined with his fellow Oxonian, Graham Spry, secretary of the Association of Canadian Clubs, that public broadcasting would be the means of reinforcing national identity and countering the cultural onslaught of commercial radio, "with its American ideals, advertising and cheap programmes." Like the churches, the arts and the public school system, radio should first and foremost be a public service, rather than a business enterprise. To achieve their ends Plaunt and Spry organized a powerful and effective lobby. Using the posture and methods of "Machiavelli as well as Sir Galahad," they soon rallied church, farm and labour organizations – along with an impressive list of newspaper publishers, establishment financiers and elder statesmen of the two major political parties – into their Canadian Radio League. The League would do battle with the commercial broadcasters and turn the Aird Report proposals into a reality.

The Bennett government took the first tentative step by setting up the Canadian Radio Broadcasting Commission in 1932. But since the CRBC was short of both money and power, the League began pressuring the Liberals to do better when and if they were returned to office.[6]

When C. D. Howe became Minister of Marine, Alan Plaunt moved in swiftly. After two sessions in Howe's office on December 27 and 29, 1935, Plaunt left with the minister enthusiastically asking him to outline draft legislation for a strong radio authority and to suggest possible personnel for its governing body. Howe had no considered views or principles on the matter, and was an easy mark for a crisply presented brief from someone whom he judged competent. Besides, he knew that both Norman Lambert and Vincent Massey, as well as a couple of his cabinet colleagues, were Radio League members, and that the Prime Minister was already committed to public control of broadcasting.

But in January members of the Canadian Association of Broadcasters, the rival lobby of private enterprisers, began putting pressure on Howe. It did them no harm that one of the people closest to Howe's ear was his general factotum and the ministry's director of radio services, Commander Edwards, with whom they had cultivated good relations for years. Howe backed off from the Radio League proposal, which would essentially give the government body both the power to run its own network and to regulate the activities of the private stations. The latter objected to being regulated by the body which would also be their chief competition, and instead backed Edwards' suggestions to Howe that the regulatory power be placed in the hands of the minister and his department. This appealed to Howe; when asked in Parliamentary committee if that did not open him to the perils of direct political pressure from seekers of broadcast licences, he dismissed his critic with a straight face, and the reply that "a Minister is careful to see that he does not allow himself to get mixed up with politics." (A CBC historian, commenting on this classic Howian utterance, regrets that the record does not show whether at that point anyone burst out laughing.) But the Radio League lobbyists simply went over Howe's head to the Prime Minister and soon had their way. Their brilliant young lawyer Brooke Claxton told Plaunt triumphantly: "The Bill seems to be better than anything we could have hoped for. In fact they have given us practically everything covered in my draft."

Unperturbed, Howe was simply glad to get the matter settled with such little fuss in the Commons, compared to the railway hassle. When his bill to create the Canadian Broadcasting Corporation passed the House on June 19, 1936, he proudly pointed out that it embodied the two principles which had emerged strongest from the years of discussion on broadcasting: "complete coverage by government facilities" of the whole country, and the CBC's "complete control over all forms of broadcasting whether public or private."[7]

When it came to the choosing of the CBC's first general manager, Howe once again found himself on the losing side of a skirmish behind the scenes. The League and the Prime Minister wanted a Canadian from the BBC, Gladstone Murray. Howe had been impressed by a dynamic young man named Reg Brophy, who had moved from the post of sales manager for Canadian Marconi to a senior position with NBC in New York. The private broadcasters pushed hard for Brophy. Brooke Claxton reminded his old friend (and King's closest confidant in cabinet) Norman Rogers that "Brophy is a Marconi production who has always worked against national broadcasting . . . tooth and nail . . . [who would make possible] a sellout to the private and predominantly American interests." Gladstone Murray got the job. Brophy eventually returned to Marconi in Canada, and thence became Howe's deputy minister of defence production.

The intrepid Commander Edwards and the private broadcasters did not give up. They next persuaded Howe to back authorization of high power transmitters to private stations like CFRB, Toronto, and in general to be liberal with the granting of licences in smaller centres. (So much for the argument that the minister would not be open to political pressures from private interests!) They also persuaded Howe to drag his heels on rapid building of the main CBC stations across the country. With the backing of his board and general manager the CBC chairman, Leonard Brockington, reacted with both cunning and fury. Having first consulted Mackenzie King about Howe's resistance to the CBC board's policies, he told the minister that his attitude to the CBC was unacceptable. Referring to Howe's complaints that the CBC was ignoring his wishes, Brockington said his reply to Howe was so strongly worded, "not because your remarks were unheeded but because they were received with attention and astonishment" by the CBC board.

He then in effect offered their resignations if Howe would not accede to their wishes. Once again, Howe gave in. It was probably the boldest and most severe rebuff Howe ever received in public life without his having its donor's head on a platter in return.[8]

By 1939, in time to broadcast the events of the royal tour, the CBC had its powerful transmitters in place from the Prairies to the Maritimes, and 85 per cent of the Canadian people were within reach of the network. It had happened more in spite of the minister than because of him. Two years later the function of reporting to Parliament for the CBC was transferred, to Howe's relief, to the Minister of National Revenue. Of his many projects, it was one in which he had perhaps least interest and concern. He was not unhappy to accept the Prime Minister's overruling hand.

At the same time as he was experiencing the birth pangs of the CBC, Howe had his attention fixed on the creation of another crown corporation which was to be his pride and passion for the rest of his years in power. Though a reluctant godfather to the CBC, he was the true founder and moving spirit of Trans-Canada Airlines.

CHAPTER EIGHT

"My Airline"

In 1935, Canada was ready for bold leadership in the field of air service. Flying had caught the national imagination. During the First World War half the pilots of the Royal Flying Corps, including the Allies' champion air ace, Billy Bishop, V.C., were Canadians. During the following decade Canadian bush pilots, who were mostly war veterans in their early twenties, opened up the north and moved hundreds of communities out of the era of canoe and dogsled into that of wings without passing through the stage of the wheel. "Wop" May aroused the public imagination with his mercy flight to bring anti-diphtheria serum into Fort Vermilion. "Punch" Dickins became famous for his long hops across the barren Arctic tundra. Barnstormers looped the loop over the fall fairs of rural Canada; city dwellers joined flying clubs or planned investments in new airplane manufacturing companies.

It was only fifty years since the completion of the CPR had reduced the span of the continent from five months to five days. In the new air age it now seemed possible that Canadians might cross their country in a matter of hours. Mackenzie King noted with amazement in his diary the adventures of his enterprising young minister: Howe had left Ottawa one afternoon to take a flight that same night from New York which crossed the continent; he landed in Hollywood for breakfast the next morning.

Canada in the early 1930s had some regularly scheduled flights (most of them using pontooned seaplanes) on the west coast, on the St. Lawrence River and down into the Maritimes.

A few people were acquiring the habit of crossing the border to take the new American passenger services between eastern and western points on the continent. Already there was pressure to develop a series of north-south branch lines between adjacent Canadian and American cities. If there was no pan-Canadian airline soon, the branch line service might threaten, as it did in the 1880s with the railway, to become the northern tributary of American private enterprise.

By 1936, even without regular cross-country service, Canadian planes were carrying more air freight (25 million pounds) than those of any country in the world; the Canadian Post Office stood to make more than 100 per cent profit on its new airmail service. In the depths of the Depression, the airways offered hope of dramatic future growth and a way out of despair. They also offered a potential new east-west link for a transcontinental nation, reinforcing that of the railways, and counterbalancing the north-south pull of the highways which first became an economic force in the 1920s. The questions remained as to how the new industry should be organized, who would reap the benefits, and how it would relate to other forms of transportation.[1]

When the new Liberal government took office in 1935, Howe was joined by the Minister of National Defence and the Postmaster General in a cabinet subcommittee to develop air policy. Civil aviation was at that time a branch of the Defence Department. Its capable head, J. A. Wilson, with the encouragement of the army's chief of staff, General A. G. L. McNaughton, had built a series of airfields across the country using unemployed men from the Depression work camps. Minimal navigation, radio communication and safety equipment was installed.

The new government's first decision was to transfer civil aviation, and hence the expansion and supervision of all auxiliary air services, from Defence to the proposed Department of Transport. It also decided to profit from the lessons of Canadian railway history: the disastrously expensive and inefficient results of constructing two extra transcontinental systems must not be repeated. There would be only one major airline connecting the chief cities of Canada from Halifax to Vancouver.

The biggest entrepreneur in the aviation field in Canada was James Richardson, the large-framed, prepossessing Winnipeg grain merchant who had become one of the major forces in

Canadian business. With government blessing he had formed Canadian Airways Limited in 1930 out of a group of smaller companies which operated bits and pieces of local service in various parts of the country. To lend weight and prestige to the new company, the heads of the two national railways, who themselves were interested in the new air service, became its vice-presidents and each of the railways subscribed for a 10-per-cent holding of shares. In 1932 Prime Minister Bennett, who was also his own finance minister, cancelled Canadian Airways' airmail contracts as part of his plan to combat the Depression. It was a serious blow to the new company. Richardson voted Liberal in 1935 – partly as a result of Bennett's drastic government intervention into the grain business. But he confidently expected a reversal in air policy too.

In response to Richardson's inquiries, Howe replied on February 12, 1936, "You are fortunately situated . . . every consideration will be given to the past experience of Canadian Airways when plans for new services are being developed." Howe gave Richardson's general manager, G. A. Thompson, to understand that he intended to "form one large company with Canadian Airways as the backbone." During his first parliamentary session of 1936 Howe was busy trying to reverse the whole thrust of Canadian transport history. But with the session's end in June, he could turn his full attention away from the problems of the past to the exciting new field of the future. He consulted with officials and pilots of British Imperial Airways. He made forays across the border to inspect American air fields, to examine airmail facilities, and to climb aboard the Douglas DC-1's and Ford Trimotors. He asked questions about technology, profits and plans for the future. He basked in the company of the legendary Eddie Rickenbacker, head of Eastern Airlines, and Juan Trippe of Pan American. Clearly these men were already running large, successful North American enterprises. Theirs was the pattern he must bring to Canada. Howe was in no hurry to share his interest with Canadian private enterprise. Throughout the summer and fall of 1936 he kept postponing a serious meeting with Richardson and Thompson on the grounds that he wanted a definite proposal to present to them and also that the civil aviation branch was just about to be transferred from Defence to his new Department of Transport.[2]

He told Richardson on August 25 that he was planning to present to cabinet "a definite programme for flying mail and passengers from Winnipeg to Vancouver commencing on July 1, 1937," and to extend this service to Halifax by July 1, 1938. But by this time Richardson and Thompson were already skeptical about Howe doing anything substantial for them. Thompson wrote to his boss from Saint John, New Brunswick, on September 4 to say that he had been "confidentially advised by a member of the Cabinet" that Howe's transport policies did not have King's approval. Rumour had it among Maritime businessmen who were still fuming over Howe's drastic elimination of local patronage by means of the National Harbours Board, that Howe lacked the political understanding and ability to carry out his plans. Thompson advised that the time of waiting upon Howe was over and that they should use "all the influence at our disposal" to pressure the government into a plan that would involve Canadian Airways as its chief agent. He believed that certain Royal Bank directors and other members of their own board, together with the local New Brunswick cabinet minister, Joseph Michaud, could be counted on to push a favourable scheme through cabinet.[3]

The lobbying became intense that fall. Norman Lambert, who was staying over with Richardson in Winnipeg after a flight from the west coast via Fargo, North Dakota, noted in his diary that Richardson was working closely with Sir Edward Beatty of the CPR to set up a new company. Richardson rather intemperately complained to Lambert that Howe was "definitely in league with the Post Office Department" against the interests of Canadian Airways. The lobbying soon had its effect, but not the one that was desired. Howe told Lambert on one of their Sunday walks in Ottawa that Richardson's word was no good and he doubted that Richardson wanted to work with him at all.[4] Howe was also being pressured by a group of Toronto financiers headed by J. H. Gundy whose chief assets were their financial and political clout, and their reliance on American airline connections and on the executive talents of a young entrepreneurial genius named E. P. Taylor. In November Mackenzie King noted that "Howe is terribly annoyed at the pressure of private interests."[5]

Early in 1936 Howe had given a cheerful but indefinite encouragement to the Toronto group, just as he had allowed Richardson to convince himself that Canadian Airways would be the "keystone of the transcontinental service." Howe hoped that these two groups along with the two railways could let their energies and financial assets and skills be conscripted into a single company. Like the reconstituted Canadian National Railways, this company would be run in the manner of any other big business. But in return for the government guaranteeing payment of its losses and provision of all ground services, the government would nominate some of its directors. The company would also be the chosen instrument of basic government policy vis-à-vis competing airlines, foreign and domestic.

On November 26, 1936, a group of senior cabinet ministers – Lapointe, Dunning, Crerar and Ilsley – met with King and Howe to determine basic policy for shaping a bill to be presented to the next session of Parliament. They rejected two alternatives: they would not hand transcontinental air service over to a private corporation, and they would not make it a purely government-owned, government-run enterprise. They opted for a company whose capital would come from the two railways. Along with directors nominated by the railways, the government would also have representation on the board. The government would lend its full weight to seeking reciprocal privileges for the company over routes which ran between points in Canada and the United States. Northern and other local Canadian routes were to be left to private enterprise.[6]

The 1937 bill to form Trans-Canada Airlines proposed a capital stock of $5 million, equally subscribed to by the CPR and the CNR or by whatever aviation interests they cared to nominate that met the approval of the Minister of Transport. The board would consist of four nominees from each railway and one from the ministry. (This was later amended to three, three and three.) Howe sent Sir Edward Beatty a draft of the bill and Beatty forwarded it to Richardson with a comment that it was unacceptable to him. He regarded the CNR and the government as being in effect identical; his own Canadian Pacific shareholders were being asked to invest in a "politically directed" corporation. Howe replied:

> I cannot agree with your suggestion that the Canadian National Railway is to all intents and purposes a Department of the Government. On the contrary, the Government maintains only one very slight contact with the railway . . . [and] it does not undertake to direct the policies of management.

But he argued that the government must have some representation on the airline's board, since it "is accepting responsibility for all deficits in operation, as well as providing airports, radio services and weather reports."[7]

Upon the withdrawal of the CPR, Howe quickly amended his bill to provide 51-per-cent ownership by the CNR and to offer 49 per cent of the shares to other parties interested in aviation. In sharp contrast to Howe's harbours and railway bills, there were few entrenched local interests and MP's for his TCA bill to offend. It had a relatively swift passage through Parliament during April, and on the 26th Howe met with Richardson to propose that Canadian Airways subscribe for shares. In return, Richardson could expect cooperation from Trans-Canada on Canadian Airways' northern and feeder lines and a position on the board for himself. Richardson replied that this meant his firm was effectively excluded from any managerial role. He said he resented Howe's suggestion in Parliament that his firm was a bush operation and did not have enough experience to run a transcontinental service. He countered with the offer to undertake by contract for Trans-Canada Airlines its Winnipeg-to-Vancouver service. This was flatly rejected.[8]

Howe attended the CNR board meeting on April 23 where he suggested that the CNR should now consider subscribing for all of the Trans-Canada Airlines shares. The CNR agreed to do this and then nominated to the TCA board the CNR president, S. J. Hungerford (who also became TCA president), along with three of Howe's men on the CNR: J. Y. Murdoch, Wilfrid Gagnon and Herbert Symington. Howe also announced that in view of heavy North American demand for the best twin-engine aircraft and the need to start service as soon as possible, his department had placed tentative orders for three existing Lockheed planes and four of the newest Lockheed 14H "twin-engine monoplanes" just being developed. He asked the CNR if they would consider taking over these orders until such time as the Trans-Canada Airlines board was constituted, and could in turn be assigned the aircraft.[9]

This done, Howe nominated three of his departmental officials to join the four CNR directors. Thus constituted, TCA held its first board meeting in May. Howe arranged for himself to be invited. He was full of advice and ideas, and in any case could not bear to miss the launching of his favourite toy and chiefest concern. He advised the board that since American commercial aviation was well out of the pioneer stage and since there was no one available in Canada with the combined technical, operating and executive experience to run a transcontinental service, he had already interviewed a potential candidate to operate Trans-Canada. The heads of leading American airline companies all recommended to him a young man who possessed many years of experience in both aircraft production and airmail service. Philip Johnson was a University of Washington engineering graduate who became president of Boeing Aircraft in Seattle in 1926 at the age of thirty-one. Five years later he became first president of United Airlines, until the inquiries of a U.S. Senate committee investigating airmail contracts led to his resignation. He was eventually exonerated of all charges and returned to Boeing as president to head up the Flying Fortress manufacturing program in the Second World War. But in 1937 Johnson was temporarily unemployed and available for a post in Canada.[10]

While the Trans-Canada board decided they should make the widest possible search for an operating chief, they also instructed their president, S. J. Hungerford, to investigate and make a recommendation about Johnson. They accepted without question Howe's judgment that no Canadian seemed to be qualified for the position. The senior pilot and west coast manager of Canadian Airways, D. R. Maclaren, had already been hired as Trans-Canada's first employee, and others, much to James Richardson's chagrin, followed.

Hungerford duly reported a favourable estimate of Philip Johnson to the next board meeting, and in June 1937, he was hired as TCA's vice-president of operations. He brought with him two technical advisers from United Airlines, each of whom eventually succeeded him in his job as chief operating officer of TCA. Johnson had a free hand, particularly since the president was preoccupied with running his railway, and he performed brilliantly. Like CPR's William Van Horne, that other dynamic American brought to Canada to build a national transportation system, Johnson set about his task with speed and authority.[11]

No sooner had he begun, however, than his minister casually but dramatically upstaged him. The deadline of July 1, 1937, for the first regular long-distance service, to which Howe had publicly committed himself after his transcontinental flight across the United States in 1936, obviously could not be met. But Howe was determined that something significant should be done to mark the new air age in Canada. He told his department to arrange a dawn-to-dusk flight from Montreal to Vancouver – the first ever attempted – on July 30. He brought with him his friend Herbert Symington, and his faithful companion from the Department of Transport, Commander Edwards.

Before daybreak that morning the pilot, Squadron Leader J. H. Tudhope, took the Department of Transport's Lockheed up from St. Hubert Field outside Montreal to have a look at the weather. He found visibility to the west so bad that he returned immediately and put the plane back in the hangar. When Howe arrived he told him to get it out again, they were going to travel anyway. They took off in a thunderstorm. Miraculously the plane got down for the first refuelling stop, near North Bay, but cloud cover over Northern Ontario was so thick that they had to pass by the second one, Kapuskasing, and simply pray that the pilot could somehow find a gap in the clouds at Sioux Lookout, the next fuelling point.

James Richardson got a vivid account of what happened next from his general manager and TCA's Philip Johnson, who were that day both in Winnipeg negotiating for TCA to take over some Canadian Airways' equipment and routes:

> Tudhope was on his knees most of the time with the map, trying to figure out where they were, and just as they were out of gas they found themselves squarely on top of Sioux Lookout. Tudhope was a very relieved man.
>
> Thompson tells me it was a very fine piece of dead reckoning and that very few men in Canada could have done it; on the other hand, Thompson also knows that there was a very large share of unadulterated good luck, because when one is flying without a beam and cannot see the ground, it is quite impossible to make correct allowances for wind drift.

From Winnipeg to Vancouver there was no serious problem, although skimming the Rockies at 12,000 feet was always an adventure in those days. The plane touched down at Sea Island Airport in Vancouver seventeen hours and thirty-four minutes after leaving St. Hubert, the first dawn-to-dusk transcontinental flight in Canadian history. Howe stepped off beaming, the only person aboard who had enjoyed himself – or pretended to – throughout the whole trip. A great deal of favourable publicity for air travel resulted, and in September TCA began its first scheduled flight by taking over Canadian Airways' projected Seattle-to-Vancouver service. Ironically, the new airline seems to have established from that time on its early reputation for efficiency and safety.

Richardson could scarcely believe Howe's luck, and he never

forgave him for it. As he said, it was a miracle that they were not "reading biographies of five gentlemen in the morning papers. . . . This man Howe is the loosest talker of anyone I have ever met holding a responsible position. Why he should wish to advertise his ignorance on so many subjects is a bit difficult to understand." Of the dawn-to-dusk flight he wrote Sir Edward Beatty of the CPR:

It was altogether just a fool piece of business and something that could only be got away with the odd time. Philip Johnson was in Winnipeg when they passed through and he was very annoyed and upset about it. The Minister told him it was not a stunt, and he wanted to know if it wasn't a stunt, what was it. Howe announced in Winnipeg that they had never had an uneasy moment on their trip. If you run into Symington sometime you might ask him how he enjoyed it.[12]

"Howe's sudden acquisition of cabinet rank and power has gone to his head," Beatty replied. "He is not able to deal with ordinary individuals except on the basis of a superior being dealing with inferiors. However, he has undoubtedly been getting the breaks in many ways and as long as his luck holds out, we need not expect much change in him."[13]

Howe's luck with TCA did not change. Philip Johnson and his successors, ably aided by the Department of Transport's J. A. Wilson and his staff, served TCA well. Navigational aids had to be developed, particularly in Northern Ontario: there was not a single control tower in the country and, of course, there were no air traffic controllers. Passenger service sales and ticketing were managed through Canadian National Railway offices. Once passengers had arrived for their flight they never left the vicinity of the plane. They simply stayed nearby until mechanical difficulty or weather or whatever caused any delay cleared up and the pilot decided to take off. The fourteen passengers were strapped in, seven on either side of the narrow aisle. All stewardesses had to be registered nurses.

After a series of experimental flights, airmail routes were established between Winnipeg and Vancouver and finally Montreal during 1938. On April 1, 1939, the first scheduled passenger flights left Vancouver and Montreal simultaneously. They made the many necessary refuelling stops, including a four-hour delay in Lethbridge on the westbound flight, and arrived safely at their destination. The first ticketed passenger on the first leg of the trip between Montreal and Ottawa was the Minister of Transport himself.[14]

Once his airline was well launched, Howe was content to let TCA management develop and run it without interference. But he kept closely informed of its needs and plans. Executive vice-president Johnson dealt directly with the minister rather than reporting through the deputy when he had a major problem. Howe downplayed what little criticism of TCA there was in Parliament, and made it clear to Canadian Pacific and Richardson's Canadian Airways that "his" airline was to be the nation's sole transcontinental carrier. He continued to fight off any attempts by Sir Edward Beatty and his successor President Coleman of the CPR to build up a strong Canadian Pacific Airlines, though a later CPR president, William Neal, a blunt, hard-driving manager who courted Howe as assiduously as Beatty had crossed and countered him, eventually won Howe's blessing for CP Air's proposed routes to the far east.

For the rest of his political career, however, as he moved from one ministry to the next, Howe kept Trans-Canada in his personal portfolio of responsibilities. And whenever he mused about leaving politics, he thought of becoming president of Trans-Canada Airlines. Friends remember him during the 1940s, at a time when he was near-absolute ruler of the whole industrial economy of Canada, wistfully pointing up to a TCA Lockheed over Wellington Street and saying "Now what I would really like is to be head of *that!*"[15]

But Howe's pleasure in presiding over the birth of TCA did more than anything else to confirm him in his good opinion of political life and make him forget for the moment the idea of quitting it. As early as the fall of 1936, after his first transcontinental shopping trip to the American west coast, he had something like a triumphal tour from Vancouver through Calgary, Regina and Winnipeg to Ottawa, telling the local press and luncheon clubs about Canada's great future in aviation. Besides opening up isolated areas and new fields of commerce, he proclaimed, it would bind the country's established businesses together, and in so doing help end the Great Depression.

Howe also found that he liked his job as Minister of Transport at least as much as he had enjoyed conceiving and promoting great engineering projects. It was gratifying that the most important of his responsibilities – the Harbours Board, the

CNR, the CBC and TCA – were bodies that operated directly under the minister, rather than relating to him through his deputy and the civil service. He would become intensely and thoroughly involved with each project in turn until it was well launched or shored up for the moment, then put his mind to something fresh.

Howe's administrative style was established early. When he had picked the man he wanted to run an enterprise, he delegated near total responsibility to him. He expected him to take the initiative and backed him up with absolute trust and support, unless and until he found his confidence misplaced. "Keep out of here and keep out of trouble," he would say. "But if you're in deep, tell me." If one of his people needed help, he learned to provide Howe with a concise summary of the issues and a clear recommendation. This was done verbally, in a brisk one-to-one meeting, or by a brief memo no more than two pages in length. Howe refused to read long policy papers unless absolutely necessary and he did not take patiently to elaborate discussions of principles and weighings of pros and cons. He particularly disliked and avoided departmental meetings or group consultations.

If a subordinate wanted to see him about an important issue, the trick was never to suggest a big agenda or hint at the need for large policy considerations. You simply told Bill Bennett or his assistant, Tommy Bryson, "I have a problem," and if it was not something that Bennett could resolve on the spot, you were quickly inserted into the boss' schedule. You were then expected to say your piece quickly and concisely. Almost never were you told, "I'll get back to you on that tomorrow," or "We'll decide next week." For further information, Howe would seize the phone or send the office messenger scurrying and the necessary was at hand in minutes. If not, he usually gave you a decision anyway. It was either, "That's what you recommend, we'll do it," or "No, let's try this." If in fact you just wanted to talk or explore issues, you found the next appointment harder to get.

Howe loved the personal relationship of leader to his men, and in particular the dual roles of crusty demanding boss and solicitous amiable father. He enjoyed the little drama of damning or praising a performance, then comforting the performer when he was down or cutting him cheerfully to size when he got too pleased with himself. If he failed to meet a staff member's expectations or to follow the prepared script – granting some request too fast, for example, giving away a bargaining counter too easily, or supplying Parliament or the press with the wrong information because he could not resist answering questioners immediately – he was amused to play the penitent or the comforter afterwards. "What've I done wrong now?", "Now young man, it's not all that bad," and "We just changed our policy then, didn't we?" are the kinds of things he would say to staff after the event.

"Howe was soft, you know, he never really fired anybody," a couple of his old associates recall. It was of course difficult to fire either a civil servant or someone you had contracted to work for you. What Howe usually did do was to move certifiable incompetents to places where they could do little harm. He carried his soft-heartedness too far on occasion. One crown corporation head fondly recalled having to fire a man three times over because Howe kept finding a way to give him his job back. But fire people he did, particularly if they refused to be straight with him. The main point was that Howe was loyal to his people, loyal to a fault; they knew it and they responded with a commitment and a standard of performance that often nobody thought they had in them. And the most unlikely men managed to work well together out of love or fear of their boss.

Howe's hiring record was reasonably good, better than it deserved to be, given his penchant for intuitive casual proposals, particularly if the man in question was an engineer or someone he had liked as a Dalhousie student or in the western grain business years before.

To his colleagues Howe was also loyal, though more out of duty than feeling. He never sniped at other members of cabinet behind their backs and religiously defended them in public, whatever his private misgiving and disagreements. He expected the same courtesy in return. On the rare occasions when a colleague appeared to be interfering in his domain he resisted stoutly. The leader's interference or overruling was another matter. Without pretending to understand or even like him, Howe respected "the old man," as he called King. In particular he admired his political judgment and the shrewdness with which he controlled difficult colleagues and conducted a meeting.

"A first-rate second man" was a favourite expression of Howe's for a number of people he knew and valued; and in his first years in Ottawa that more or less was how he saw himself in relation to the Prime Minister. Overall policy was not something he aspired to make or even share in making, except in so far as it impinged directly on his own sphere of interest. Once the policy was settled he would apply it and make it work.[16]

Howe had little time for partisan feuds. His office was as open to opposition MP's as to Liberals, though there were a few people on both sides he refused to see. He often referred scornfully to one of these, or to anyone else who did not measure up as "Our friend So and So." But as yet Howe had few enemies in public life.

There was one fact of political life, the behaviour of the provincial Liberals in Ontario, which Howe found distasteful. Yet it was one which he must face up to directly if he was to continue his career. In the fall of 1937, Mitch Hepburn and his crew of political pirates swept back into office on an anti-communist, union-busting platform. Ontario voters were deeply stirred, and even the working-class Lakehead swung into line behind Mitch and Charlie Cox, now Minister without Portfolio. Even a distressing incident in February 1937 had not dented Charlie's popularity with the voters. At that time Cox, on a trip home, was badly burned when a young woman, whom local gossips dubbed his jilted mistress, threw acid in his face. Port Arthur was agog, but there was less political than physical damage. Cox showed only his good profile to the voters in the ensuing campaign. Beside him on the platform was C. D. Howe, who had been reminded that Cox had supported him in 1935 and that it was his turn to return the favour.

Not everyone was pleased. Lakehead Liberal politics were a wild and woolly affair and the strange alliance in Port Arthur contrasted painfully with chaos in Fort William, where a divided party lost the provincial seat to the Conservatives. Howe hoped that his election help would be enough to preserve the peace in Port Arthur for the next federal contest, expected in the fall of 1939.

Howe was wrong. Relations between the provincial and federal Liberals in Ontario lurched from bad to worse in the wake of Mitch Hepburn's decision to prosecute a feud with Mackenzie King to the bitter end. The Ontario government stubbornly refused to cooperate with Ottawa on constitutional reform and on the building of a St. Lawrence Seaway. Hepburn formed a political alliance with Maurice Duplessis, arch-enemy of everything Liberal (and liberal) in Quebec. Canadian newspapers were enlivened by explosions in Toronto as Hepburn launched one salvo after another at Mackenzie King. Hepburn vowed to himself he would "never be satisfied until King's political heels go through the wringer."[17]

One of the instruments to Hepburn's hand was his MLA from Port Arthur. Charlie Cox was no longer a member of the provincial cabinet (he had exited as mysteriously as he entered) but he did come from the same place as C. D. Howe and he was still mayor of the city. Hepburn liked neither Howe nor the strong federal power he stood for. He had not forgotten that his own candidates for the cabinet in 1935 had been swept aside in favour of Howe and Rogers. It might be as well to return the compliment and show King that while he could appoint men to his cabinet, only Hepburn could get them nominated and elected.

The defence of Howe's Port Arthur bastion was in the hands of Bill Bennett. Bennett paid monthly visits to the riding and early learned who was who in the Port Arthur Liberal association. Bennett, together with Howe's chief political adviser in Port Arthur, Harry Black, decided it would be wise to anticipate the enemy and hold Howe's nominating convention for the next federal election as early as possible. With Howe's enjoyment of his job and his new taste for politics, it was easy to get his agreement. There would be an early convention, in the autumn of 1938, and Howe would be a candidate.

One day, just after he had arrived on one of his regular field trips to Port Arthur, Bennett got an uncharacteristically abrupt call from Howe, instructing him to return to Ottawa right away. Bennett telephoned Howe's junior assistant Tommy Bryson in Ottawa to find out what was wrong. It turned out that the Howes' Port Arthur family doctor, J. M. Eakins, who was also a riding association past president and saw himself as the Liberal senior statesman in Port Arthur, had written to Mrs. Howe and told her that the substitution of Bill Bennett for C. D. Howe's personal presence in the riding was worse than useless. Bennett in fact had been too busy dealing with constituents and with the dozen Liberals who really counted to pay court to Dr. Eakins. The doctor told Alice that her husband had already as good as lost the federal nomination for Liberal candidate next time round to the execrable Charlie Cox.

Without consulting anyone else in Port Arthur about the matter, Howe impulsively called Bennett and summoned him back to Ottawa. He also told his friend Norman Lambert on their

Sunday walk that his career was finished; that he would just have to go back home and take a licking and then find something else to do. Lambert told him to stop talking nonsense. If things were really that bad, the nominating convention must be postponed until its result could be guaranteed.

When Harry Black back in Port Arthur discovered that Howe was recalling Bennett to Ottawa, he phoned Howe, and as usual spoke bluntly to the point: "You want to lose this convention, C. D.? If not, then let Bill Bennett get on with it." The upshot was that Bennett was told to stay, Dr. Eakins' alarms were ignored, and there was no contest for Howe's nomination.[18]

But even without a rival candidate, the convention turned out to be an exciting one. Mitch Hepburn had been escalating his feud with Mackenzie King. Besides verbal abuse, Hepburn was attempting to seize control of all Liberal party fund-raising in Ontario, and was now rumoured to be using his influence with his new ally, Premier Maurice Duplessis, to hamper federal Liberal fund-raising in Quebec.

King remained outwardly serene. He was sure Hepburn would come to a bad end, but he was reluctant to involve himself in a graceless and sordid quarrel merely to gratify Hepburn's wounded psyche and hasten the day of reckoning. Then, in November, Hepburn helped the Conservatives win an Ontario federal by-election and began threatening to do the same thing in other Ontario constituencies unless King resigned. King told his cabinet he must counter-attack decisively, but hinted that his ministers should do it for him. At Howe's Port Arthur nominating convention on Saturday, December 10, Labour Minister Norman Rogers had been invited by Howe to give the main address.

That night Rogers lit into Hepburn. He accused him of plotting to make the federal government "dependent on and largely controlled by the provincial governments at Toronto and Quebec." Howe repeated Rogers' charge of a Hepburn-Duplessis "conspiracy." On Monday morning Hepburn called a press conference and his blistering counter-attack was even more intemperate than King had dared hope for. He ridiculed King and talked of supporting the newly elected leader of the Conservative party, Robert Manion, at the next general election – "at least he's human." He threatened the Ottawa Liberals with "a fight to the limit" on the hustings, "if that's the sort of thing Howe and Rogers are looking for." Unequivocal evidence of party disloyalty was just what King needed. He could now legitimately demand a decisive vote of support from his federal troops, which he got from a special meeting of all Ontario senators, MP's, and defeated Liberal candidates.[19]

Hepburn withdrew into a mood of black depression. Besides being politically outmanoeuvred for the moment, his health was poor and his life of personal dissipation was beginning to catch up with him. He left on a two-month ocean voyage to Australia amid speculation that he might soon resign.[20] King could face 1939 in clear command of his own troops. To Howe and his colleagues the new year offered the prospect of a federal election, and in spite of general relief over the Munich agreement with Hitler, more rumours of approaching war in Europe.

CHAPTER NINE

The Coming of the War

While Trans-Canada Airlines air crews were completing their flight training, the pilots of Hitler's Luftwaffe were gaining experience of another sort in the skies over Spain. At the end of 1938, the year of Munich and the climax of the Spanish Civil War, it was becoming abundantly clear to many Canadians that there was not, nor would be, peace in their time.

Some at least of Canada's military planners were already convinced of the importance of air supremacy in the approaching world war. In 1935 Canada's most respected soldier, General A. G. L. McNaughton, before retiring as chief of general staff to become president of the National Research Council, advised the government that there was "not a single modern anti-aircraft gun of any sort in Canada . . . not one service aircraft of a type fit to employ in active operations, nor one service air bomb." The government of which Howe was a member decided to give priority to the airforce ahead of both the navy and the militia, and did succeed in increasing its manpower. In describing the previous regime's defence budget, Howe once referred to 1934 as "the year they just bought the postage stamps." Yet the new Liberal government's first budget appropriations for the Department of National Defence ($29 million) were actually lower than those of the previous year, and by 1938-39 had reached only $36 million. Even this increase provoked concern in the cabinet and among some Quebec Liberals, as well as outright opposition from the CCF. Prior to the outbreak of war in 1939, the only new undertaking of military significance in Canada was the production of Bren guns – an enterprise which raised a first-class public row even before it was launched. As Minister of Transport Howe had nothing directly to do with the Bren gun affair, but his intervention at the height of the debate in the House of Commons was impressive, and prophetic of his future wartime role in the government of Canada.[1]

The Canadian government wanted the new machine gun and proceeded to place an order with the only person in Canada able to manufacture it, Major James Hahn of the John Inglis Company. But a military publicist, Colonel George Drew, produced a public furor by denouncing the deal savagely in *Maclean's* magazine. When Parliament assembled early in 1939, members demanded to know what a familiar name in the washing machine business had to do with machine guns, unless something peculiar and improper was going on. Because the Inglis plant also made a variety of heavy engineering equipment including industrial boilers, the new Opposition Leader Robert Manion began referring to it as "an old boiler factory." When the Minister of National Defence, Ian Mackenzie, floundered badly in response to criticism, Howe moved in, and for the first time spoke extensively in the Commons on a matter outside his own department. He referred to his past business dealings with the Inglis Company, and to a recent visit he had paid there:

I took enough interest in this matter a short time ago to visit this so-called decrepit and broken-down plant, because I wished to confirm my opinion that it was still capable of efficient production. To my surprise I found that the Bren gun was not being made in the Inglis plant as I knew it. I found that a new plant had been built of the most modern factory construction . . . and with special machinery required to carry out the Bren gun contract . . . This was the broken-down plant that has been referred to so frequently.

Howe then asked whether the contract was a bad one and a matter of private profit at the expense of the Canadian taxpayer:

If any other manufacturer had been approached to manufacture the Bren gun, his first question would have been, "What do I have to do? What kind of equipment is required? What kind of layout do I need? Do I have to build a new factory? What is this all about?" Major Hahn knew the answers to those questions, and as a result he got the order. The contract was drawn up to cover this work. Obviously the work had to be done on a cost plus basis. No factory in Canada would have been able to tender on any other basis, because the production cost of that piece of equipment could not possibly be known to any manufacturer. . . . I have put it to a number of my friends in the manufacturing business, and I have not found one who, when he was pinned down to it, would admit that he would take this contract into his plant.[2]

Howe was proved right. The profit on the initial twelve thousand guns was considerably less than 5 per cent. The plant was ready on time, and when the guns were desperately needed in 1941, it was able to produce ten times the number of units originally planned for. The old boiler factory, before the end of the war, had turned out nearly a quarter of a million Bren guns. But in the meantime, the government backed away from any further arms contract even as safe as the Inglis one, and no Canadian manufacturer in 1939 was interested in being pilloried as a profiteer and "merchant of death" like Major Hahn.

Mackenzie King did not find the international situation so threatening as the summer of 1939 approached, and his mind turned to more important things. Parliament was reaching the end of its fourth year and an election would have to be held soon; September or October might be a good month. Early in August, King sent an inquiry to British Prime Minister Neville Chamberlain, telling him that he was thinking of an early fall election. Was anything likely to interfere with his plans?

Chamberlain's reply gave King pause. There were problems in the east, along the German-Polish border, and Britain had promised to assist Poland. Perhaps it would be better to wait. When, on August 23, 1939, the Soviet Union and Germany signed a non-aggression pact, it was obvious that the waiting would soon be over.

The next day, August 24, King summoned the cabinet. The turn of events was ominous, he told them, and "while we were all still in a calm frame of mind, it was advisable we should decide upon our policy in the event of war breaking out." Before speaking himself, King asked each one of his colleagues to state his own views. None of them felt Canada could avoid joining in, but they differed as to exactly what its participation should be, and whether the cabinet should issue a statement at once. Howe spoke last. He was, King noted later, "of the view that Canada would have to participate and that we should have everything in readiness. War, if it came, could not be a limited operation: Canadian participation would have to be to the limit of our resources." There was, however, no point in anticipating matters by issuing an immediate statement which, Howe thought, could "divide the country."

To King's relief, the cabinet was not divided on the basic issues: when war came, Canada would become a belligerent alongside Britain and France; no minister would resign in protest.[3]

When Hitler's blitzkrieg moved into Poland, and Britain declared war on September 3, 1939, King summoned Parliament. Since he had already agreed with a suggestion of Opposition Leader Manion earlier in 1939 that in the event of war there would be no conscription for service overseas, no serious objection to a formal declaration of war was expected. It was assumed also that Canada's chief contribution to the war would be in the form of "food, raw materials and munitions." The day before Parliament met, King asked for the preparation of an act to create a department of supply.

On the Prime Minister's behalf Howe defended this move in the House and referred to the experience of the Bren contract and his dislike of the principle of public tender as a means of acquiring war material. "The best guarantee that profits on war material will be kept to a minimum," he stated, "is to place men of skill, experience and absolute integrity" in complete charge of purchasing and production. More than that, when some vital commodity was needed immediately the government was not going to wait to acquire it by public tender. Anti-submarine netting, for example, "is not a commodity sold on the ordinary market." The government had ordered some to protect Halifax harbour. Since Howe was speaking just days after the *Athenia* had been torpedoed in the North Atlantic with heavy loss of life, and German submarines had already been sighted in the Gulf of St. Lawrence, his argument was not challenged.[4]

Before adjourning on September 12, Parliament agreed to a Canadian declaration of war on Germany, and passed the bill authorizing a department of supply. But since the department was not set up immediately – King and his colleagues were still uncertain what form Canadian participation in the war would take – a War Supply Board was created in the interim under the chairmanship of Wallace Campbell, president of Ford of

Canada in Windsor. Campbell's board was put under the wing of the new finance minister,* Colonel J. L. Ralston, the highly respected former minister who had come out of retirement in response to King's call to duty. With his thrusting chin and prominent shining dome, his legal wisdom, military record and reputation for rocklike integrity, Ralston was just the man needed to enhance the government's authority in wartime. He was also an appropriate superior for such a self-important industrialist as Campbell.[5]

Ralston quickly perceived that Campbell had little understanding of government and of the ultimate authority of cabinet and Parliament. King agreed, and added that Campbell's "type is in the industrial world what dictators are in the political world." Ralston asked to be rid of responsibility for the War Supply Board. He and King feared that Campbell, with a little help from the opposition or the press, could be a real source of embarrassment to the government. They decided the best man in the cabinet to take it over would be C. D. Howe. Since there was no question of giving up the Department of Transport, Howe readily agreed to the extra job. Thus in November 1939, without realizing where it would lead (he was not yet even a member of the War Committee of cabinet) Howe took on the responsibility for mobilizing Canada's defence production which would last through war and peace for the next seventeen years – until his electoral defeat and retirement from politics.[6]

At first there was little for the War Supply Board to do, mainly because no orders were forthcoming from Britain. A delegation of Canadian businessmen had been over to Britain in August to find out how they might contribute. But British industrialists and public servants feared that their inventories of war material were too large in some areas. One of them told a Canadian reporter that "England was filled up with bombs, shells and so on." After all, it was going to be a short war, and France and Britain would win it by themselves. Their armies massed behind the impenetrable safety of the Maginot Line. The *Star Weekly* displayed the laurel-wreathed *gloire* of General Gamelin's hat and the comforting quiet understatement of Mr. Chamberlain's umbrella.

Throughout the winter of 1939-40 Howe's most significant involvement in the war lay in matters relating to transport.

* Charles Dunning had been forced to leave politics because of ill health.

Canada had agreed to act as host to a major scheme for producing pilots and groundcrew, the British Commonwealth Air Training Plan. Immediately Howe set to work building the dozens of necessary airfields, hangars and supply depots across Canada.

The toughest problem the government faced during the winter of the "phony war" was leadership: who would be in charge of the war effort once hostilities broke out in earnest? What kind of war effort would it be? There was a strong feeling in business circles across Canada, and among most people of Conservative and imperialist persuasion, that Mackenzie King was an inappropriate prime minister to lead Canada in war. No one in his government, except perhaps its other senior statesman, Colonel Ralston, was perceived as fully suited to the task of directing Canada's fight at Britain's side. Certainly C. D. Howe, while enjoying respect and political popularity among many people who knew him, was not thought of as representing in any way the business elite of the country. He was after all a small-town engineer in charge of such "socialist" enterprises as the new government airline and the CBC.

The first serious challenge to King's government came not from the war hawks, however, but from the opposite direction. Premier Maurice Duplessis of Quebec called a provincial election to protest the vastly increased power assumed by Ottawa at the outbreak of war. He was confronted in turn by one of the most daring political moves in all Canadian history. Lapointe and Power persuaded their dubious and hesitant leader, who knew the potential appeal of provincial rights and French-Canadian nationalism as well as they did, that the federal ministers from Quebec should campaign against Duplessis. And they did so boldly. They threatened to resign from the federal cabinet, thus leaving Quebec open to a conscriptionist anglophone regime in Ottawa, if Duplessis was not turned out in favour of the provincial Liberal party. Their dangerous plan worked; Duplessis suffered the only defeat of his long career.

The next challenge to the Prime Minister came in the form of English-Canadian pressure for a truly national government, consisting of the best brains in the country – essentially men from both major parties, as well as senior Canadian businessmen. In the mid-1930s there had been much talk and some action in favour of creating a national government to fight the Depression. Britain had one, after all. A Toronto group was even formed for the purpose, and Sir Edward Beatty of the CPR, it had been rumoured, was willing to put up $3 million for a campaign.

When the idea revived in 1939, Robert Manion opposed it at first, but later in the year reversed himself and supported it as a means of gathering anti-King support behind him in the expected federal election of 1940. Manion was regarded as a radical by the Montreal financial and railway interests who were the traditional backbone of Conservative support. A Roman Catholic himself, with a French-Canadian wife, he was also seen as leaning dangerously to French and Catholic opinion. His position as party leader was not strong. It was even intimated that his job was to beat King and then turn power over to a real Conservative, like former prime ministers Meighen or Bennett, who would head up a wartime coalition.[7]

The showdown with King was eventually provoked, however, not by Manion, but by King's arch-enemy in English Canada, Mitch Hepburn. With the support of George Drew, now Conservative leader in Ontario, Hepburn put a motion through the Legislative Assembly on January 18, 1940, condemning King's conduct of the war. King had not been looking forward to meeting his critics in Parliament, but he had pledged himself to do so before calling an election. He saw Hepburn's move as a golden opportunity to release him from his pledge. Consulting no one but his closest colleague, Ernest Lapointe, and even then only briefly at the last possible moment, King decided to dissolve the House as soon as it reassembled on January 25. Just after noon, less than three hours before the Speech from the Throne was to be read, King sent word of his decision through Lapointe to the morning meeting of cabinet, which he did not attend. It was the first that Howe and his colleagues had heard of it. The Conservatives and the country were also caught by surprise – stunned, in fact.[8]

The Throne Speech brought bitter words from Manion; he had lost the chance to raise election issues as well as funds and candidates during the promised parliamentary session. King then adjourned the House, and went over to Rideau Hall to ask Governor General Tweedsmuir for a dissolution. He rallied the Liberal caucus next day, telling them that national government would be the first step toward dictatorship of the kind Canada was fighting. He invited any member who disagreed with him and could not pledge 100 per cent loyalty to himself and his ministry to leave the room. No one budged.

King next met the press and told them that they had better ask Manion precisely "who the best brains were he intended to take in [to his national government] – that the people were entitled to know in advance." At least, he added, "the personnel of my Government was known."[9] During the election campaign that followed he made it clear that if they were defeated, none of his ministers would serve in a coalition, but would rather become His Majesty's Loyal Opposition. Frustrated by King's tactics and lofty tone, the Conservatives began lashing out wildly at the inadequacy of the government's war effort, and in particular at King's protégé Norman Rogers, who had replaced Ian Mackenzie as Minister of National Defence. Manion denounced Rogers as "an irresponsible little falsifier" and George Drew called him "a standing joke in every military camp since he blossomed forth as our new war lord last September."[10]

Howe steamed into Port Arthur aboard the CPR. As Minister of Transport, his assurances about railway jobs and his opposition to CP-CN amalgamation were convincing. As for his Tory opponent, he was a nice fellow, Howe said, "who is one of the few men who play golf as badly as I do." The campaign passed without incident, except when the chef aboard Howe's campaign train fell ill and had to be flown down to the Lakehead on a Conservative plane. On election day, March 26, Howe consolidated control of his constituency, winning by over five thousand votes. In Fort William, Dan McIvor again defeated Manion. The Conservatives had ceased to be a factor in Lakehead politics; Manion had ceased to be leader of his party. The Conservatives won only forty seats in all Canada, a third of them in Toronto. The Liberals took 184, the largest number in history. Mackenzie King saw his prayers answered. "I have dreaded having to choose the moment for the campaign . . . especially at a time when human lives are being slaughtered," he wrote in his diary. Now, to his profound relief, the political conflict at home was over, "before the worst of the fighting begins in Europe."[11]

CHAPTER TEN

"Howe for Supply"

E arly on the morning of April 9, 1940, German forces invaded Denmark and Norway. Within hours Denmark had surrendered. The Norwegians, luckier in the initial battles, began a valiant but futile resistance. The war now extended from the Balkans to the Arctic. As the battle for Norway continued, it became obvious that the Germans would apply in the West the same tactics that had won them their smashing victory in Poland the previous September. Allied forces sent to help the Norwegians were routed and driven back to Britain.

The news of the German invasion of Norway reached Canadians over breakfast. Mackenzie King, as usual, found a silver lining in the war clouds, and again recorded how he was "thankful that our elections were over before this great offensive began." There was just time to get through another piece of business; before the day was out C. D. Howe was appointed Minister of Munitions and Supply.[1]

Howe was not grateful for the appointment. When it was first mooted, just after the election, he told King that he preferred to stay at Transport. He liked his job, and he had no desire to move to the snake pit of Munitions. The most he would do, Howe told the Prime Minister, was to go in as acting minister and organize a Department of Munitions and Supply, and then turn it over to a suitable successor. But King was persuasive. The crisis did not permit an "acting" anything. Howe must become full minister to underline the government's determination to do something with Canada's chaotic munitions industry.[2]

And so, late in the afternoon of April 9, Howe strolled over to the offices of the War Supply Board to find out what war supply was all about. He found the organization teetering between doubt and jubilation. The board's chairman, Wallace Campbell, had left in a huff; he was persuaded only at the last minute not to publish a press release damning the government. Two members of Campbell's staff, however, were positively delighted. R. A. C. Henry, a Montreal executive drafted into civilian war service, and Henry Borden, the board's counsel, had both threatened to resign unless Campbell went. Even if the new minister was something of an unknown quantity he could hardly be worse than the autocratic and indecisive Campbell.[3]

Campbell's abrupt departure was virtually a routine accomplishment for Henry, who was an old hand around Ottawa. An engineer by profession, he had risen in the twenties to be deputy minister of Railways and Canals; in that capacity one of his clients had been C. D. Howe. Moving to private life as general manager of the Beauharnois Power Company, Henry's reputation was briefly touched by the Beauharnois scandal of 1932, which saw no less a figure than Mackenzie King denounced for accepting dubious favours from special interests. But King had bounced back, and so had Henry. Returning to help in the war effort at Ralston's request, Henry's shock of red hair was once again a familiar sight in Ottawa and the old mandarin was quickly back at the work he enjoyed most, constructing and dissolving constellations of bureaucrats, charming and cursing by turns, but always moving inexorably towards whatever goal Henry had set himself.[4]

Henry's ally in the struggle against Campbell, Henry Borden, was another Ralston appointment. But there the resemblance ended. Although not devoid of personal charm, Borden was an adviser rather than an executor, better known for his quick legal mind than for his ability to talk his way out of political or public problems. A corporation lawyer from Toronto, Borden was also the nephew of the former prime minister, Sir Robert Borden, and a devout Conservative in Sir Robert's mould. A younger man than Henry, Borden was debarred from military service on grounds of doubtful health. Instead of serving in the army, he worked seventy hours a week for the government in Ottawa, returning to Toronto on weekends to try to hold his private law practice together.[5]

There was an absent third from the War Supply Board when Howe first moved in. Gordon Scott, the board's secretary, had resigned rather than serve one minute longer under Campbell. A prominent Montreal accountant, Scott had briefly served as Treasurer of the Province of Quebec and remained a member of that province's Legislative Council. To Campbell, Scott was little more than an advanced stenographer, and so Scott had retired to Montreal to await better days. These came with Howe's arrival and Scott quickly returned to the scene of action.[6]

Scott, Borden and Henry formed the nucleus of Howe's administrative apparatus. They were a self-constituted leadership group, and Howe recognized their function by appointing them to be his department's executive committee, a kind of departmental cabinet, to advise him on broad policy. An executive committee was an unheard-of departure from ordinary civil service procedure in Ottawa, where permanent civil service heads – the deputy ministers – were assumed to be the natural chief advisers of their ministers. An executive committee divided the deputy minister's authority; equally important, it allowed the minister, the political head, a larger role in the direct running of his department. That was the way Howe preferred it.

But the new department still needed a deputy minister, and one was found in the person of the office manager of the War Supply Board, G. Kingsley Sheils. A 46-year-old New Brunswicker, Sheils had spent thirty years working his way up the office ladder. In Borden's opinion, he would be the perfect office manager for the Munitions and Supply Department. Over lunch, Borden and Henry played on Sheils' patriotic responsibility. He was, they told him, the perfect man for the job. "Bless his heart," Borden chortled, "he had to agree and he did."[7]

Sheils remained Howe's deputy minister until the end of the war. Systematic, orderly and predictable, he proved to be a virtuoso of the filing cabinet. Forms moved, files swelled, regulations marched in proper form from Sheils' tidy desk. The deputy minister did not ask to make decisions, nor was he allowed to. In Munitions and Supply it was the minister, not the deputy, who was "executive head."

There was one more appointment to complete Howe's executive team, and in some ways it was the most unusual one of all. Edward Plunkett Taylor was thirty-nine in 1940. A poor boy from Ottawa with large ambitions, he had clambered quickly to dizzying heights in the financial world of Toronto. Henry Borden sauntered over to "Eddie" Taylor's table at the Rideau Club in April 1940 and asked him to come over and meet the minister. Taylor knew little about Howe, but Howe already knew enough about Taylor. Would Taylor care to join his department? Flabbergasted, Taylor asked for a few days to put his business affairs in order. He would report for duty at the end of the month.[8]

Borden, Henry, Scott and Taylor were the first of Howe's "boys," the dollar-a-year men who came to Ottawa to work for the government for free while the war was on (their firms picked up their salaries as a patriotic duty). Under normal circumstances, the government could not have afforded any of them, but the magnetism of war drew them to the biggest task any of them had ever known. War service was its own reward.

The minister, his deputy and his executive committee – his boys – moved into the Munitions and Supply Department's new quarters on Ottawa's Wellington Street. There, baking winter and summer in a rambling, overheated pile of colonial clapboard, Howe stayed for the rest of his political career. Around him, above him and below him, his executives clustered. Scott and Borden proposed, and Borden drafted; Henry organized and Taylor implemented; and Sheils kept the records. Howe depended on them; but they depended on his commitment and his enthusiasm to turn Munitions and Supply into a reality.

C. D. Howe at fifty-four was at the height of his powers. Only his grizzled hair indicated the passage of time; the dark brown eyes still penetrated, and the abrupt bark still dominated any room he entered. The war made no difference to Howe's routines. Except on his House of Commons "duty days" his car picked him up at the office door and swept him away to Crescent Road where he presided, genially but obliviously, at the dinner table. After a few hours with a detective novel (the chauffeur was periodically sent out to buy them) Howe disappeared to bed and a full eight hours' sleep. He would, he reasoned, be no use to the war effort if he came to work exhausted. When he walked in the office door the next morning at nine, he was fresh and ready to tackle whatever problems the day might bring.[9]

Bill Bennett was always at the office before the minister,

organizing Howe's schedule, advising what letters would have to be answered immediately and which could be put off to "letter day" on Saturday, and ready with drafts of Howe's speeches, should any be required. Then it was the deputy minister's turn. Minister and deputy treated one another with a reserve born of incomprehension; Howe did not care for Sheils' passion for filing and moving paper, and Sheils never understood Howe's ability to dispense with such matters. But the forms of politeness were observed. Next came the members of the executive committee, if they happened to have any problems that required Howe's scrutiny. All other callers had first to pass by Bill Bennett. No one entered without first being approved, and then summoned. There would be no lines of mad inventors or patronage-hungry politicians outside Howe's door. Not in this war.

Independent of his departmental duties, Howe's political importance was growing. One of Mackenzie King's first acts after the 1940 election was to "promote" his Minister of Trade and Commerce, W. D. Euler, to the Senate. Euler had been the senior Ontario Liberal. Now, suddenly, Howe and Norman Rogers stood at the head of the federal party in that province.

On May 10, Germany invaded Holland, Belgium, Luxembourg and France. The Germans outmanoeuvred the British and French armies, and split them in two, the northern half being forced to evacuate France through Dunkirk. Strewn along the beaches and roads of Belgium were hundreds of tanks and thousands of trucks and guns, abandoned to the enemy. After pausing to regroup, Hitler's armies marched south, taking Paris on June 14. The French sued for peace on June 17, and on June 24 fighting ceased. The French were out of the war, and the British Commonwealth was left to fight on alone.

The battles of May and June 1940 were an unqualified disaster for British war plans. The British had severely limited reserves of gold and foreign exchange with which to buy supplies abroad. They had hoped to use their own resources and to husband their existing equipment, drawing on British factories for most of their military supplies. Now, suddenly, the British cupboard was bare.

Howe knew that the British would order most Canadian supplies reluctantly, if at all. "British manufacturers," he once exclaimed, "[do] not want to see Canadian sources of supply established." But in May and June 1940 Howe understood that this was changing. He moved into action on two fronts, bombarding King, and through King the British government, with demands for orders for Canada's factories. To his executive committee, Howe's message was more positive. He ignored the fact that there were no firm British orders, and his executives were told to "take such steps as we felt proper in the interest of getting on with the war effort and that he would stand behind us in every way." What Howe meant was pithily summarized. "We have no idea of the cost," the minister admitted, "but before the war is over everything will be needed so let's go ahead anyway. If we lose the war nothing will matter. . . .If we win the war the cost will still have been of no consequence and will have been forgotten." Howe's cabinet colleagues backed him up. The need was dire, and for the moment the dollar sign was off.[10]

But what could Howe buy, and what could Canada produce? Some crude estimates existed from prewar industrial surveys. There was undoubtedly industrial capacity to spare in a general sense, but it took time, money and tools to ready a factory for war. Tools came from abroad, and with British supply blocked by Britain's own desperate needs, the only place to find them was the United States. But not only tools must be imported. Raw materials, such as silk and rubber, had to come from the Far East, and in Asia the Japanese empire was dangerously threatening. Something would have to be done, and quickly, to secure Canada's vital supplies from abroad.

The solution was Gordon Scott's. Let the government buy machine tools, rubber and silk, not on its own account (that might stimulate speculation) but through government-owned corporations whose real ownership would, for the moment, be kept quiet. Henry, Borden and Scott discussed the matter one night, then phoned the minister. Could Howe stop by that night on his way home from the House of Commons? Howe could. Sitting with a drink in his hand, he listened as Scott explained their idea. Scott struck the right note. Government ownership was no novelty; that was the way Trans-Canada Air Lines was run. And Howe was not afraid of novelty in any case. A crown corporation was a good idea, and he knew it would work. Let Borden draft the necessary documents. From the evening's discussion emerged three new crown companies: Fairmont (rubber), Plateau (silk) and Citadel Merchandising (machine tools). The Munitions and Supply Act was amended to permit the minister to set up crown companies using the existing Companies Act. Overnight, C. D. Howe became an industrial tycoon.[11]

Howe's next step was to by-pass the bottleneck of British bureaucracy. The British Supply Mission in Ottawa was wound up, and a Munitions and Supply office in London opened, and put in the charge of Charles Banks, a mining engineer and mineowner. In future, the British would place their orders directly with Howe, and Banks would cope with any remaining details. Howe thereby eliminated not only a bottleneck, but a rival supply authority. In Ottawa there would be no one but Howe in charge of military supply.[12]

To complete Howe's authority, King brought him into the War Committee, the small group of senior cabinet ministers charged with running the war from day to day. There Howe joined King himself, Ernest Lapointe, Raoul Dandurand, T. A. Crerar, Ralston, Rogers and Chubby Power, who in May 1940 was placed in charge of the air force. In June, however, the defence minister, Rogers, was killed in a plane crash.

After a hasty and unfruitful exploration of the possibilities of a bi-partisan cabinet, King turned back to his existing stock. Ralston, a colonel in the First World War and defence minister in the twenties, returned to his old portfolio. J. L. Ilsley, the granitic, red-haired revenue minister, like Ralston a Nova Scotian Baptist, became Minister of Finance. Finally, King appointed the Premier of Nova Scotia, Angus L. Macdonald, Minister of National Defence for Naval Services. The three Nova Scotians were a sub-cabinet in themselves – "the three musketeers." They had more in common than their origin: all three were dedicated supporters of a total war effort, whatever that might involve.

While King was shuffling politicians, Howe was coming to grips with his department. The Munitions and Supply Act gave him large powers, and the emergency legislation of the War Measures Act gave him still more. The minister could buy and repair, mobilize and construct, requisition and order anything he felt necessary to the production of munitions. There was no barrier to his powers, not even a constitutional one, for in wartime the provinces were forced to concede their jurisdiction over provincial resources to the central government. Canada passed in the twinkling of a pen from a free enterprise system regulated by ten jealously competing sovereignties to a centrally directed economy regulated by the government's perception of the needs of the war.

These needs were great. Howe had to produce munitions, but first he had to secure the supplies to produce them, the transport to carry them, and the power and fuel to make Canada's factories hum. On June 24 Howe took his first steps. A War Industries Control Board was set up, to consist of economic controllers who would regulate the most essential sectors of the economy to ensure that Howe's supplies got through. That same day, the first of the controllers was appointed: H. R. MacMillan, the British Columbia lumber baron. MacMillan, appropriately enough, was to run Timber Control. He joined Hugh Scully, the Commissioner of Customs, who became Steel Controller and chairman of the WICB.[13]

MacMillan's selection was significant. Timber control was first proposed by the British Columbia government, which thoughtfully nominated its own Minister of Lands and Forests for the job. Howe firmly refused the offer. His department could not tolerate the presence of two serving politicians. Faithful to his principle of a single, central authority in munitions, he wanted someone from outside, someone who would not pose an obvious political threat. But MacMillan was a powerful man in his own right, and one used to getting his own way. Howe's task would not be easy with him.[14]

Other controls and controllers followed. George Cottrelle, a banker specializing in industrial reorganization – the chairman of Union Gas – became Oil Controller. George Bateman, a mining engineer, became Metals Controller. In August a Machine Tools Controller was appointed, and in September, to complete the roster, Howe's friend from the TCA board, Herbert Symington of Montreal, took over Power Control. Each controller was armed with an order-in-council passed under the War Measures Act, establishing broad powers for action and, if need be, coercion.

But first Howe tried persuasion. Steel was one of his first targets. On July 4 Howe met the managing heads of Canada's four great steel companies, Stelco, Dosco, Dofasco and Algoma, to introduce them to Hugh Scully. Scully's powers were formidable, and Howe's were even more so. Every aspect of steel, its foreign and domestic sales, its profits, and its supplies and production, now came under Howe's jurisdiction. Even large corporations, commanded by men many times richer than Howe, were no more than "small cogs in your wheel," as one steel president wrote to the minister.[15]

The real reason for steel control, in Howe's mind, was the scarcity of steel supply. Control was essential to provide coherence. But before brandishing the stick of his emergency powers, Howe dangled the carrot of cooperation. The steel managers got the point, and before they emerged from Howe's office they had conceded a freeze on the prices of their raw materials and their finished products. Steel control would be run on the basis of a calculated cooperation between industry and government. Those who cooperated could count on all the help in Howe's power. Those who refused to adapt, or who failed to understand what was demanded of them, could always be coerced. Or, worse still, they could be ignored.

Problems affecting the entire control program were taken up by the controllers at a weekly meeting in Ottawa. Howe intended these meetings to be strictly technical; larger questions of policy were his prerogative, or the business of his executive committee. But the executive committee had its mind on bigger things.

Taylor had spent his first month in Ottawa fruitlessly seeking directions and orders from the Canadian military. Following the Dunkirk evacuation, what was an absurd task became an impossible one. At Howe's direction the executive committee drew up a list of what it thought Canada would require in the way of war production; only a few of the items on its list were even on order. Getting ready to produce the equipment required by a modern army was a complicated, time-consuming and expensive business, the executive committee wrote to Howe on June 24. It was necessary to learn now, without a moment's further delay, what the Department of National Defence required from the Department of Munitions and Supply. That evening, Howe and Ralston and their advisers met. When the meeting was over, Howe had his list of military requirements. This, added to the new British orders, gave Munitions and Supply a framework for its production program.[16]

Canada undertook to produce ships, trucks, shells, rifles and ammunition, artillery, aircraft, and even tanks. Given the state of British and Canadian stocks, all these supplies were needed yesterday. Howe and his advisers knew it would take time, though how much time nobody could guess.

Its task done, the executive committee disbanded. It was encouraged to do so by the unwanted addition of two senior ex-members of the War Supply Board, W. A. Harrison and Billy Woodward. For them, Howe invented the title of "executive assistant," which he also bestowed on Bill Bennett (Bennett was later raised to the rank of chief executive assistant, to distinguish his useful functions from those of his nominal peers). Woodward cheerily roamed the corridors of power, looking for something to do, until Howe sent him packing back to British Columbia, to become that province's lieutenant-governor. In any case, the committee's functions were virtually complete; Howe needed its members as individuals, but he no longer needed their collective advice. Howe, and his department, were finding their feet.[17]

To organize production, Howe made calls across Canada, recruiting anybody who knew how to run a business, and who combined common sense and determination with an absolute refusal to be cowed. There were plenty of men in their late thirties or forties, just over military age and often just below the top in their own companies. Chance impressions of years before were now translated into the surprising offer of a job.

Typical was Ralph Bell, the head of a Halifax fishing and shipping firm. Howe had met Bell several times while the Minister of Transport, and from their conversations he remembered that Bell was an enthusiastic amateur pilot. Howe sent out a call for Bell. The summons found Bell perched on the end of a dock in Prince Edward Island, quietly fishing. No, Bell told the minister, he would not drop his vacation to come to Ottawa for the next day. But the following morning, Bell was sitting in Howe's office, while the minister explained to the astounded fishpacker that he expected him to take on Canada's brand-new aircraft production program. Bell pleaded ignorance: he knew how to fly planes, not build them. "I didn't ask you that," Howe snapped back. "I said I wanted you to take charge." Bell walked out of Howe's office vested with the title of Director-General of Aircraft Production.[18]

Bell had little more than a title to begin with. There was a vestigial Canadian aircraft industry, subsisting on a couple of British educational contracts, "making string and stick machines," as Bell later recalled. Out of this unpromising material, Bell was to construct trainers, fighters and bombers.

The first decision was a basic one. On British advice, it was decided not to try to build aircraft engines in Canada, but to construct airframes only. The engines would come from the United States.

To gear up the first program, the vital British Commonwealth Air Training Program, Canada needed trainers. The British had promised a training aircraft, the Anson; now they could no longer deliver. So the Anson must be built in Canada, and Henry Borden was pressed into service to procure a suitable engine in the United States. One was found, manufactured by the Jacobs Company of Philadelphia, and duly paid for by a cheque signed by the government's New York bankers – the Jacobs Company had little faith in Canadian credit that disastrous summer.[19]

Next, a crown company was chartered to handle Anson production. Borden, Scott and Henry set to work, and within an hour Bell found himself president of a new corporation, complete with a board of directors. Howe's executives specialized in this kind of exercise; to Bell, it seemed that they were "making the thunder roll and the lightning play." Bell, however, found himself torn between his duties as Director-General of Aircraft Production, and his responsibilities as president of the new company, Federal Aircraft. Howe therefore decided to divide the responsibility, selecting Ray Lawson, the crusty and dynamic head of a large printing company, to assume control of Federal. Lawson had a good business reputation, and he was forceful and energetic. As far as Howe was concerned, he had as many qualifications as Bell. But Howe had forgotten that likes do not attract. Bell continued to regard Federal as "his," and when Lawson refused to follow his advice, decided that his successor was incompetent and pig-headed. Soon each loathed the other and an epic confrontation was in the making.[20]

The Bell-Lawson feud could not have come at a worse time. The opposition was clamouring for action, demanding to know what results the government was getting for its money. In particular, when was the air training program going to get off the ground? Howe assured Parliament, on the strength of word from Bell, that planes would be rolling off the production line by the end of the year. That promise would return to haunt him.

Some planes were flying in the summer of 1940. They were American planes bought with Canadian funds, and flown by their pilots to the designated place of delivery, a field along the

North Dakota-Manitoba border. The Americans had a neutrality act forbidding the export of war materials to belligerents, but there was nothing to prevent Canada buying U.S. planes on American soil. Once the sale was complete, a rope was thrown across the border, and the plane towed across.

Howe himself spent the summer in other dealings with the American government, travelling back and forth between Ottawa, New York and Washington, trying to secure vital materials for his factories, and learning just how Washington worked. It was a new experience, but a successful one. And Howe got to know one of the most powerful of President Roosevelt's advisers when Treasury Secretary Henry Morgenthau came up to Ottawa in August. One consequence of Morgenthau's visit was the confirmation of Munitions and Supply's role as sole purchasing agent for Canadian war supplies in the United States.[21]

Howe secured not only official cooperation from the United States, but unofficial. Canada was in the unique position of making munitions to British specifications using Canadian or American components and North American machinery. Sometimes the effort to merge British design and North American parts stumbled; and there were problems, too, in organizing and training a work force. The British had few experts to spare, so Howe turned to the United States. In one case, when production of 25-pounder artillery at Sorel, Quebec, was jeopardized, Howe brought in executives from Chrysler of Canada, which sent one of its American vice-presidents to be general manager. But Howe stipulated that the arrangement was to be temporary; French-language replacements were to be trained to take the places of the outside consultants – an unusually sensible decision for the period.[22]

Throughout the summer Howe turned from one crisis to another without losing his temper or becoming overwhelmed by complexities. As his daily schedule rolled on, from one half-hour appointment to another, Howe effortlessly turned his mind from one set of problems in Vancouver to another in Montreal. Facts were recorded and stored away in the minister's prodigious memory, each cross-referenced with its appropriate personalities. That summer and fall, Howe was present at the creation of one factory after another, whether in person or in spirit – and usually by cheque. Increasingly he knew the men who ran them: if they had problems they came to his office. At the end of the summer, the American minister shrewdly commented, King had two ministers, and two ministers only, who were "at home with, and consequently able to deal, without a sense of inferiority, with the representatives of 'money'!" They were Ralston and Howe.[23]

Howe had met enough moneyed men to be impressed by personal qualities, not wealth. Those wealthy enough to come to Ottawa and to stay without an invitation were allowed to hang around as glorified office boys. Those who combined talent with wealth were put to work. But Howe chose the line of command, and ultimate authority for dispensation and retribution was his alone. So many and so complicated were the lines that passed through his office that the minister was compared to the ringmaster "not of a three ring circus, but of a thirty ring circus, with Mr. Howe playing a vital role in each ring." The main event was yet to come.[24]

The most unpopular man and one of the most powerful in any government is the minister of finance. The head of the treasury tells other ministers how much they can spend; his consent is necessary for any program involving the spending of the people's money. Mackenzie King's minister of finance, James Lorimer Ilsley, might have been selected by central casting for the job. Honest, upright, seething with integrity, Ilsley had entered the King cabinet along with Howe in 1935. Spectators and reporters were reminded of "those earnest and unsmiling young men you might meet at the neighbourhood tabernacle, who will give you a grip of the hand and ask if you are saved." Many of Ilsley's colleagues had the same feeling as the minister pored over their spending, and asked if they *had* saved. If they had not saved enough, they were sent back to their departments to try harder.[25]

Howe first felt Ilsley's cold breath in the autumn of 1940. Ilsley had been warned by his deputy minister, Dr. Clifford Clark, that Canada would soon run completely out of gold and American dollars. When Clark spoke, ministers listened: they knew and valued his ability and his industry as well as his foresight. As Ilsley looked around to see what was causing the drainage of Canadian assets, one department stood out: Munitions and Supply. Ilsley raised the question of Howe's spending in the cabinet. Was Howe spending the money as wisely as he might? Could not some system be devised to regulate and systematize Munitions and Supply's purchasing and production priorities? How much money had been committed? Howe returned indefinite answers. He was confident that his department was doing well, and had just said so in Parliament, but he did not have up-to-date figures, nor could he rank his department's expenditures in order of priority. In the rush to control the economy and set up production, the statisticians had been left behind. Eventually the cabinet agreed that Ilsley had a point. Howe's accounting left something to be desired. A committee was established to find out what to do. To head the committee, called the Wartime Requirements Board, the cabinet appointed Howe's Timber Controller, H. R. MacMillan. MacMillan had the brains and the experience to find out; but his imperious temper made his knowledge dangerous.[26]

That fall Howe had other things on his mind besides MacMillan. Part of his difficulty in answering Ilsley derived from his uncertainty about what he should produce for next year's war effort. Gradually the answer seeped through: the British did not know. The head of the British Supply Council in North America, Arthur Purvis, later recalled that as late as September 1940 British estimates were "haphazard." This was a blow to Purvis. He once believed that secreted in the bowels of Whitehall there was a master plan for the British war effort. Could it be that there was none? Investigation confirmed his worst suspicions. London was uncertain what the next year would bring, and only after great pressure was applied would British ministers allow their departments' requirements for the next year to be set down on paper. "One of the most difficult men he had to deal with" in that respect, Purvis added, was the Minister of Aircraft Production, Lord Beaverbrook.

This was the first time that Beaverbrook had crossed Howe's horizon. He knew, as everyone else knew, that "the Beaver" had started out as a business buccaneer in Canada, and that he still held substantial investments here. But Canadian money was not enough. Beaverbrook craved power, position, and the friendship of the great. Migrating to England, he achieved all three, buying a great newspaper and using it to promote his favourite causes. He was rewarded with a title, but his eccentric politics kept him out of power for almost twenty years. Churchill appointed Beaverbrook to his cabinet in 1940 with the task of securing, in any way possible, the airplanes necessary to defend Britain against invasion. Beaverbrook and his agents set to work with a will. Wherever the Beaver put his hand, a state of chaos in motion resulted. Out of it flew Britain's aircraft, as promised. Left behind in the debris were other people's plans and priorities, which Beaverbrook ruthlessly overrode.

Howe's plans for aircraft engine purchases were among the casualties. Beaverbrook's men, scrambling for planes for Britain, broke his American contracts and disrupted his priorities. Production schedules fluctuated wildly as Canadian officials tried to discover whether they would have enough engines, or airframes, to put in the air. To make matters worse, in October an emissary of the British government, Sir Walter Layton, arrived to discover what was going on. He did not like what he found. Much of Canada's munitions program, he told Howe's officials, was superfluous. Canada was producing ammunition and shells when it should be making more aircraft (especially aircraft engines), guns, rifles and tanks. This contradicted the British advice in June.[27]

Layton's observations were novel and unwelcome. It was obvious that the Canadians and the British were working at cross-purposes in the same cause. It seemed to Howe that it would be a good idea to set matters to rest with a personal visit. When he broached the idea to Mackenzie King, the Prime Minister was pleased. A restful sea voyage was just what Howe needed.

Howe prepared to leave in mid-November. He left behind R. A. C. Henry as a member of MacMillan's Wartime Requirements Board, with instructions to watch for knives. Besides protecting himself and his department from MacMillan, Howe also had to protect two of his friends from each other. He wrote to Ray Lawson, the embattled president of Federal Aircraft, "Please understand that you are in complete charge of our Anson program. . . ." In Howe's absence, no one but Sheils or the acting minister, Angus Macdonald, had any authority over Lawson. The Anson program was to have first priority in supplies, regardless of what anybody else (meaning either MacMillan or Ralph Bell) might say.[28]

After bucking up Lawson, Howe wrote a second letter. It was to his eldest daughter Elisabeth, at school in South Carolina. "Am leaving today for England to spend Christmas with Bill," he told her, "and to do some work on munitions. I am looking forward to a good holiday." Howe's ship, the *Western Prince*, steamed out of New York harbour on December 6. The holiday turned into the nightmare of torpedoing and survival.[29]

By the time Howe and his bedraggled party reached England

much had happened. The minister was a minor hero, having braved the dangers of the deep and survived. Howe immediately set down to consult with his opposite numbers, the British Minister of Supply, Sir Andrew Duncan, and Beaverbrook, Minister of Aircraft Production. "I must say," Billy Woodward wrote, "C. D. handles himself damn well with these people. He is very diplomatic but he is also very firm and correct in his dealings." Howe liked Duncan: he was an efficient, hard-headed businessman. He was less certain about Beaverbrook. This time, however, the Beaver aimed to please. He and Howe were soon calling each other Max and Clarence; the Canadian was treated to Christmas at Beaverbrook's country estate. Howe was no stranger to charm, but Beaverbrook was a past master at the art, and the two men began a guarded friendship that lasted many years.

It was with Duncan that most of Howe's outstanding business was transacted. The two men agreed to coordinate their demands on the limited machine tool supplies from the United States. As for aircraft, it now appeared that the British wanted long-range bombers instead of fighters. Howe sent the revised list to Sheils along with New Year's greetings. A week later, almost as an afterthought, he sent his deputy another message: "Assist Lawson every possible way." The best news came from Arthur Purvis. Finally, he reported, a "master sheet of actual military requirements for the British during the years of 1941 and 1942" was established. Canadian production could follow.[30]

With British needs as certain as the vagaries of war could make them, Howe decided to return home. This time the British decided to make sure he would get there. He travelled in style on the battleship *King George V*, in company with Lord Halifax, the new British ambassador to the United States. Landing at Norfolk, Virginia, he arrived in Washington on January 25, to be greeted by a solicitous phone call from Mackenzie King. The next day, Sunday, the cabinet turned out in force to meet Howe at Ottawa's Union Station. The first to greet the returning hero was his daughter Elisabeth, who rushed into his arms; then the rest of the family, and finally, at a sedate distance, Mackenzie King and Ralston. Howe looked "a little older," King recorded, "but was very cheerful."[31]

Howe needed to be. While he was in England, factions in his department battled for power. It was, the American minister reported, "the absence of the skipper from the helm" that precipitated matters, as the two most vociferous and fractious personalities of Munitions and Supply, Bell and MacMillan, unwittingly converged.

Bell pursued his feud with Lawson, recruiting the manufacturers of Anson components in support. He also talked freely to the press, which was only too happy to publicize his complaints. The appearance of an aircraft "crisis" added a new importance to MacMillan's Wartime Requirements Board.

MacMillan, when he was appointed to head the board in November 1940, had been in Ottawa for five months as Timber Controller. A self-made millionaire lumber baron from British Columbia, MacMillan was both intelligent and politically minded. He had only reluctantly come to Ottawa, believing that the King government was a mediocre collection of second-rate hacks and time-servers with an infirm and temporary grasp on power. "He gradually grew somewhat discursive," Herbert Symington, the Power Controller, reported, "and had a faculty for coming in with complaints which he had heard here, there and everywhere, and always had a remedy for everything whether policy was involved or not."[32]

MacMillan's new position gave him an unprecedented opportunity. The board included representatives of all the important wartime departments, as well as from Munitions and Supply itself. It also included Clifford Clark, a master of bureaucratic manoeuvre, whose presence on the board indicated his expectation that it would become a powerful, if not decisive, factor in Canadian war planning.

While Howe was absent in December and January MacMillan was very active. He passed on whatever of Bell's complaints about Lawson that Bell himself had not already retailed to an eager press corps. Bell's embittered comments were used to sustain MacMillan's thesis that Munitions and Supply was out of control. When he visited Toronto just before Christmas, he chatted with Mitchell Hepburn about the prospects of the King government. Hepburn informed him that these were not great. Indeed, there would soon be "disastrous resentment against present federal administration." As Senator Lambert recorded in his diary, MacMillan "predicted upheaval very soon against Govt.'s failure to arouse the country."[33]

Bad as the King government was, he believed Munitions and Supply was positively hopeless. In mid-January he told a reporter that Howe's organization was deplorable. The absent minister had consistently appointed the wrong people, Mac-Millan said, and he cited E. P. Taylor, Frank Ross (Director-General of Naval Armaments) and W. F. Drysdale (Director-General of Munitions Production) as prime examples. Mac-Millan decided that he had better make an appointment on his own: he called in Harry Carmichael, vice-president of General Motors of Canada, to become assistant chairman of the War-time Requirements Board. Meanwhile the *Financial Post*, whose Ottawa correspondent was well briefed on Munitions and Supply's problems, began to run editorials demanding the speedy appointment of an "industrial statesman" to clear up Canada's munitions muddle. MacMillan began to prepare for the cabinet a report which, he believed, would give the *coup de grâce* to the muddle.[34]

Not everyone on his board was prepared to follow Mac-Millan's lead. R. A. C. Henry, of course, was looking out for Howe's interests; mysteriously, Henry's assignments from Mac-Millan never seemed to get done. Clark too had his doubts. He wanted to bring expenditure under control, but he was not willing to meddle in politics above the waterline separating the bureaucracy from the politicians.

MacMillan, however, had no such qualms. He believed that Howe's position was very weak, and that if he was rash enough to defend himself he would surely be destroyed. It was a widely shared view. Some of King's advisers advised their master to run for cover as the press barrage intensified. Walter Turnbull and J. W. Pickersgill, the Prime Minister's two principal secretaries, urged King to divide Munitions and Supply into two new departments: "Construction," which Howe understood and could handle, and "Production," under some other minister, possibly the *Financial Post*'s "industrial statesman." King put off any action until Howe's return; but once his minister was back he was anxious to hear his response to the allegations made against his administration of Canada's war production.[35]

Howe's first task, therefore, was to convince his leader that any political problems associated with munitions production could be contained, and mastered. Howe first checked his dispositions. On January 27 he met with MacMillan, Carmichael and Henry. Henry reported that it was not a pleasant meeting. Howe informed MacMillan that he would not fire Taylor and Drysdale. There might be some room for changes in personnel – Carmichael had favourably impressed the minister – but there would be no butchery. Howe had never abandoned a friend, far less consented to humiliate one. The minister then turned to the question of the Wartime Requirements Board. Its prospects, he told MacMillan, were nil. When MacMillan protested that war production demanded a general manager, Howe snorted: "You want my job, and I'm not ready to turn it over to you yet." If MacMillan wished, Howe would appoint him director-general of priorities, to adjudicate disputes referred to him by the other directors-general. The meeting thereupon broke up. MacMillan was disgruntled by the rejection of his advice and confused by Howe's apparent freedom to do so. He decided to bide his time and see what developed. Howe immediately appointed Carmichael to help Drysdale in gun production.

Howe next went to see King. At a meeting of the War Committee on January 29, the Prime Minister brought up the complaints about aircraft and, particularly, the Anson program. Howe conceded that there were real difficulties. But there was no reason to panic. Bell's charges against Lawson were exaggerated. No one could have anticipated the troubles that had plagued the Anson's production – certainly not Ralph Bell. Lawson might have contributed to some of his own difficulties, but he was neither culpable nor negligent, and Howe would not let him resign under fire.

Howe's matter-of-fact defence impressed King. He knew that the government could not escape being blamed, and he simply wanted to know whether it could defend itself. Howe persuaded him that it could and that he could take on the job. With the Anson affair out of the way, the ministers turned their attention to the MacMillan difficulties. King spoke to Howe, Ilsley and Norman Lambert, to whom MacMillan had confided Mitch Hepburn's views on the King government. The Prime Minister concluded that MacMillan was "a rather dangerous man to have on the job." Other ministers went further. Jimmy Gardiner, who despite his abrasive temper never turned his back on a fellow Liberal, was blunter. "[T]he civil service clique centred about Finance [was] responsible for starting campaign vs. himself and Howe," he told Lambert.[36]

Too late, MacMillan realized that he was in serious trouble. When he met with his board on January 30 he protested that he was not responsible for the "recent publicity relating to his activities" and that he had not granted an interview with the press "for some time." MacMillan's words echoed hollowly among the other members; Clifford Clark began to absent himself from board meetings.

The War Committee of the cabinet had given Howe a free hand to find a way out of the difficulties, and if that included disposing of H. R. MacMillan, so much the better. MacMillan's only defence was to go ahead and publicize the contents of his report. The *Financial Post* ran a version on February 8. "The basic argument," the *Post* told its readers, "is that the lack of [production] figures reflects weakness in the set-up of the department and that reorganization of the supply effort and personnel is the only way to correct this." It was not a bad argument, as far as it went, but it was not the political dynamite needed to blow Howe out of Munitions and Supply. MacMillan was perhaps the only man in Ottawa who could not understand his report's feeble impact.

MacMillan next thought of resigning, but allowed Graham Towers, Governor of the Bank of Canada, and Clifford Clark to talk him out of it. Instead he decided on a short vacation, and caught the train to attend his daughter's wedding in Vancouver. En route to Vancouver he stopped off in Toronto; from there the news quickly reached Ottawa that he had visited "the York Club, where he related to quite a number of people his troubles and his criticisms." "This," in the opinion of Howe's friend Symington, "was unpardonable." Continuing west, MacMillan broke his journey in Winnipeg to consult with the venerable Liberal sachem J. W. Dafoe. According to Dafoe, MacMillan did not press his complaints against individuals, and confined his comments to general criticisms of the Munitions and Supply department.[37]

Weeks passed. MacMillan's report gathered dust on Howe's desk. MacMillan refused to retract or resign, and he also refused suggestions that he take another job. But he also refused to go to the opposition with the specifics of his charge, and as usual the Conservatives were the last to know what was really going on.

When Parliament met on February 26, Howe could go over to the attack. Responding to taunts from R. B. Hanson, the Leader of the Opposition, that he was covering up the Mac-Millan report, Howe boldly laid it on the table of the House. He then tackled his critics. His department had been unjustly slandered. Munitions and Supply could stand any comparison and the facts would show that its production was not only on schedule but ahead of schedule. Some people said that Mac-Millan had exposed scandal and incompetence. If they said that, Howe charged, they had not read the report. He then quoted whole sections of the report in support of his contentions.

Howe kept his heaviest ammunition until the last. There had been, he told the House, some mention of MacMillan's name in connection with rumours about Munitions and Supply. He was sure that there was no foundation to these stories. MacMillan had, after all, taken an oath of official secrecy and his position was the same as that of any other civil servant. He had not resigned, and therefore must be presumed to agree with the policies of his minister. The responsibility for policy, of course, lay with the minister, where it should. "I am the head of the department," Howe affirmed, "and as long as I have the responsibility I am going to assume the authority." There was only one culprit in the whole storm over H. R. MacMillan and that was the press: "The number one saboteur in Canada since the beginning of the war is the *Financial Post* of Toronto."

The Liberals were delighted with Howe's counter-attack. The backbenchers had always liked him, and they appreciated a strong partisan lead. So did Mackenzie King, who thought Howe's tactics splendid. By appearing to defend MacMillan he had in fact neutralized his tormentor. King by now had no doubts at all about the B.C. lumber king: he was "a traitor, by violating his oath of secrecy, and a conspirator and a cat's paw in the hands of those playing a Tory game in bringing about a Union Government." But MacMillan had not been anybody's cat's paw, far less a conspirator with the Tories. The Conservative leader in the Senate summed up his party's frustrations when he wrote to a friend that MacMillan's "silence under these conditions I really cannot understand."[38]

MacMillan was no longer a threat to Howe's control of Munitions and Supply, and Howe was disposed to forgive and forget. Let MacMillan go down to Montreal and become Director-General of Shipbuilding. Otherwise, as T. A. Crerar warned, "he will be finished and Howe will let him go." MacMillan cut his losses and took the job. Like Howe, he held no grudges, and despite their differences he came to admire Howe greatly. Shortly after the end of the war, he sponsored a banquet for his minister in Vancouver. Howe, he told the audience, was "the greatest organizer Canada has ever seen."[39]

Had MacMillan not embarrassed the government with his

leaks to the press and associated himself with the demand for an "industrial statesman," it is likely that his analysis of Munitions and Supply would have been treated with considerable respect. For many of his criticisms were perfectly true. W. F. Drysdale, the target of some of MacMillan's most scathing criticism, was a case in point. Drysdale, an engineer from Montreal, had been hired because of his presumed experience in locomotive production – the closest Canada could come to heavy war equipment. But Drysdale's experience had a serious flaw: he was the nominal president of an American branch plant – adept at taking orders. It showed: "He collects men around him that no one can work with, with the result that he has gotten out of sorts with all the other Directors General." Eventually Drysdale was eased out, receiving the title of Director-General of Industrial Planning and Engineering, a position which Howe hoped would allow him to "function in a field of his own without causing friction."[40]

E. P. Taylor ("Eddie" to Howe) was another problem child, but of a different sort. Howe had a high regard for Taylor's talents as a business manipulator and believed that, properly employed, he would be an invaluable asset to the department. Yet in some circles within the department Taylor was obviously unpopular – perhaps because he was an operator; with the dissolution of the executive committee he had lost his free-wheeling status as Howe's jack-of-all-trades. Soon after their return from Britain Howe looked for a new, spacious field for Taylor.[41]

That field was the United States. The Americans held the key to Canadian war production. They had the tools, and sold the supplies from which Howe's industrial machine had been constructed. Increasingly, Canadian industry relied on American designs and American parts to produce equipment for the British and Canadian armies. By the end of 1940, however, there was a formidable competitor: the U.S. government itself. During 1940 the Roosevelt administration began a vast rearmament program; the American armed services were buying up and requisitioning as much as they could. Canada's sources of supply were beginning to dry up. Even if the Canadians had been able to compete, another threat loomed: Canada's reserves of American dollars were dwindling. Once they were gone, the Canadian munitions program would grind to a halt.

Taylor began scouting the American defence agencies as soon as he arrived in Washington. He had two tasks: to insure Canadian supplies, and to sniff out orders for Canada. But as he made his contacts and settled in to guard Canada's interests more bad news arrived in Ottawa.[42]

On February 3, Mackenzie King invited Howe to dinner at Laurier House. The only other guest was Arthur Purvis, who handled all the British government's purchasing in the United States. What Purvis told King was intensely disturbing. Britain, King later reported, was "in an appalling condition . . . she is a bankrupt country. . . . He had not conceived that England could ever be bankrupt . . . but that was where she was now." This meant that the British had no more money to invest in Canada, and that Canada must not expect payment for war material exported to Britain. Not, at any rate, in dollars.

The long-run implications were far worse. Canada's own trade deficit with the United States, largely incurred in order to produce war supplies for Britain, was out of control. It would be necessary to make some arrangement with the United States. The trouble was that the British had got there first.

The Roosevelt administration had conceived a scheme to "eliminate the dollar sign" from American exports of war material to Britain. In return for an unspecified future consideration in trade, and certain other things, the British were to receive, free of charge, the necessary supplies to keep them going in the struggle against Hitler. This proposal, called lend-lease, was winding its way through the American Congress, and its passage was anticipated some time in March. After that, the British would no longer have to worry about paying for their ships, guns and airplanes in the United States; and that, without any doubt at all, would make the American supplier preferable to the Canadian, especially when British financial requirements in Canada were estimated at between $1,200 and $1,500 million a year.*

As an ex-officio member of the British Supply Council, and as a friend of Purvis, Howe was fully up to date on British plans for purchases in the United States once lend-lease began. Meeting with the cabinet War Committee on February 18, he

* By September 1941 the Department of Munitions and Supply had awarded contracts totalling $2.6 billion, of which just over $1 billion were on British account.

predicted that there would soon be "considerable transfers of United Kingdom purchases from Canada to the United States."[43]

In London, where it was received doctrine that Canada was not sacrificing enough for the war effort, the newly appointed British High Commissioner to Ottawa, Malcolm MacDonald, was instructed to tell the Canadian government that the British would place their future munitions orders in the United States if they were unable to pay for them in Canada. The uncertain situation frayed the nerves of Canadian ministers; there was, American Assistant Secretary of State Adolf Berle reported, "a steadily growing distrust between the Canadian and the British officials."[44]

But what could the Canadians do about it? Canada itself could qualify for lend-lease, but only on condition that Canadian assets in the United States were used up first. This, Howe believed, would do great harm to Canada's position in international trade and would leave the country unable to finance its American trade when the war was over. Moreover, acceptance of the lend-lease terms would put Canada in the position of a moral debtor at the very least; future American administrations might not take the same generous view of their allies as Roosevelt's. Accordingly, Howe told King "that it is in the best interests of future relations between Canada and the United States that Canada shall not come under the provisions of the 'lend-lease' bill, except as a last resort."[45]

In the first week of April several British war orders were cancelled. Under this strong pressure the Canadian government hastily guaranteed all British purchases in Canada. This could be only a temporary expedient; the cost of importing parts and materials from the United States would speedily use up all of Canada's foreign exchange, and then production would inexorably grind to a halt. Howe and Clark were sent to Washington; after they had laid the ground work, King would arrive on April 16 for talks with Secretary of State Cordell Hull and Secretary of the Treasury Henry Morgenthau. For his discussions with Morgenthau, King went armed with what he described as "a splendid summary by Howe," listing the materials that Canada could make for the United States. As Howe now knew, the Americans' rearmament program had outrun the capacities of their industry. But thanks to Canada's pell-mell rearmament of 1940, instigated by Howe, Canada had capacity to spare. It was the minister's impression that Canada's need for cash and the United States' need for arms could be happily mated. It was King's job to persuade Morgenthau that it was the secretary's own idea. Having sown these seeds, King left on a short vacation while Howe and Clark carried on in Washington.

Soon King learned that his two negotiators had made "splendid progress" – so splendid that King was informed that the following Monday, April 21, he and Morgenthau could go to Roosevelt with "all the programme of production outlined and get the President's agreement to it." But King decided not to wait. Summoning Clark and Taylor to meet him at the Harvard Club in New York, he worked out with them a draft agreement. Then, on Sunday April 20, King climbed on a train for Hyde Park, Roosevelt's nearby estate on the Hudson River. There King found the President and his friend and adviser, the head of the lend-lease program, Harry Hopkins. King set to work and within hours he had Roosevelt's agreement to a declaration promising Canada between $200 and $300 million in war contracts over the next year, as well as the inclusion in British lend-lease of American components shipped to Canada for inclusion in Canadian production for Britain.

It was a "grand Sunday" for the President and the Prime Minister, and also for Howe. In his discussions with Roosevelt and Hopkins, King learned that Howe had made a splendid impression on his American hosts. Howe's detailed outline of Canadian productive capacity was convincing, and he himself had persuaded Hopkins that Munitions and Supply was the best source of supply. All American orders in Canada, Hopkins told King, would be placed through Howe. Howe's war production program, the source of many of Canada's American dollar problems, now produced its dividend. What had been built with American equipment and paid for with scarce American currency, could now earn back American dollars. It was an entirely satisfactory arrangement.[46]

Only a few officials in Ottawa understood what a close shave it had been. Howe did, and told the Prime Minister that he thought him "the greatest negotiator the country had." King had saved crucial weeks, weeks Canada very probably could not have afforded. Now, assured of a flow of American dollars, Canada could stick by its reluctant guarantee of British purchases in Canada, while piling up unconvertible balances of British sterling in London.[47]

In order to sell to the Americans, Howe created a new crown company, War Supplies Limited, and made Taylor its president. Since American industry had not yet mobilized for war production, Taylor had a ready-made sellers' market. It proved easier to fit Canadian production and Canadian requirements into an incomplete American war economy than it would have been if American industry was fully prepared. Howe and Taylor had another advantage in dealing with the Americans: speaking the same language, sharing the same attitudes and feeling the same urgency, they soon got to know Roosevelt's production chiefs. The Americans learned that Howe's word was his bond and, at the same time, found he could be a wily negotiator. "What a quarterback C. D. Howe would have made," Roosevelt enthused. "If one play fails, he always has another up his sleeve." Taylor positively thrived in the Byzantine atmosphere of wartime Washington, where achievement depended on putting together bizarre coalitions of antagonistic personalities and competing agencies; Taylor was an old hand at that.[48]

Relations with the British were less certain. Howe liked Purvis; he found that they shared a distrust of Beaverbrook and his methods. Over dinner in February Howe told King that Beaverbrook had been a "colossal failure" as Minister of Aircraft Production, and Purvis, who loathed Beaverbrook, added that the Churchill government might fall because of the Beaver's phenomenal unpopularity.

It was not Beaverbrook, however, but Purvis who became a casualty of war. Summoned to England in August to confer with Beaverbrook, he discovered when he arrived that his quarry was in America. Munitions and Supply's London office received an urgent message from Howe to Purvis: "Beaver in Washington. Better get back." Purvis had already left. His plane crashed on takeoff from Prestwick airport in Scotland.[49]

First Gordon Scott had perished at sea; now Purvis was dead. Howe learned that there might be a third. R. A. C. Henry, his right-hand man, suffered a heart attack and lay between life and death for months, forbidden to move from his bed. Eventually, in the fall of 1941, Henry left for Connecticut to recuperate. From his sickbed he sent Howe advice and appreciation. "I am sure you are having 'at least one crisis every day,'" he wrote, "but you have always been able to meet such crises with the least amount of expenditure of nervous energy of anyone I have ever seen. . . ." Henry was glad that Borden was still in Ottawa; but late in 1941 Henry Borden too was sent away on doctor's orders.[50]

The new strong man of Munitions was Harry Carmichael, whom Howe had promoted at H. R. MacMillan's instigation. Born in the United States of Canadian parents, he had returned to Canada at the age of twenty-one, in 1912, to play baseball for the McKinnon Industries team in St. Catharines. Some "sort of occupation was found for him in order to get him into the plant," Henry Borden explained. It was a fortunate choice for McKinnon and for Carmichael; he was president and general manager when the company was taken over in 1929 by General Motors. Carmichael had worked his way up from the shop floor; he understood production technology and was thoroughly versed in mass production. He used this knowledge to clean up Howe's Munitions Production Branch, and was then asked to apply his techniques to the whole department. Carmichael found that there were not enough engineers or production managers in government service to do the job properly. So, just as Howe had recruited men from Chrysler, Carmichael turned directly to industry for his recruits: General Motors, General Electric and Westinghouse supplied the backbone of his production army.[51]

Carmichael liked Howe. He had all the talents of the first-class executive: decisiveness, intelligence and loyalty. Howe, he said, was a man "who when he entered onto a project never stopped until he finished." It was a quality that Howe recognized in Carmichael himself when he gave him the job that Mac-Millan had once coveted. "Harry Carmichael is proving to be invaluable," Howe told Henry in the fall of 1941, "and he has brought some excellent men into the Department." Better still, Carmichael had improved the organization of the production divisions and had brought production to the point where some plants were producing "at an astonishing rate." C. J. Mackenzie, Howe's old student, and now President of the National Research Council, was even more positive. He called Carmichael "the best man I have seen around Munitions and Supply."[52]

It was a strong end to a year that had begun shakily. By late November 1941 Howe was satisfied with the progress of his department. Even Federal Aircraft was turning out "a substantial number of planes" (88 by the end of 1941, but 1,432 in 1942), while Simard Industries in Sorel were producing forty-one 25-pounder guns a month and were about to christen their first naval gun. Tank production, which had caused endless problems because no one knew quite how to manufacture one, was moving at the rate of three a day. Other plants that had "looked the worst" in the spring were "now among our best." To Howe's surprise, an experimental crown company* which designed and manufactured high technology products such as optical equipment and radar had taken on $90 million worth of orders. Cautiously, he kept his "fingers crossed on their being able to meet delivery dates."[53]

Production was booming. When many large plants reached the limits of their capacity in the summer of 1941, Munitions and Supply came up with a new program on the principle of a jig-saw puzzle. Work was subcontracted wherever there was a spare machine. "[M]illions of dollars' worth of bits and pieces are already being manufactured," Howe told the House of Commons in November. In one factory, more than 82,000 bits and pieces had been supplied by sixty-three subcontractors within two months. Howe was finding that in Canada at war nothing was impossible: "this is a great country."[54]

Canada prospered, but the allied cause did not. At the beginning of 1941 Howe told the cabinet War Committee that while the British might not lose, he did not see how they could hope to win. Hitler's attack on Russia in June changed that, although the monotonous succession of Russian defeats and retreats cast long shadows during the summer and fall. Worsening relations between Britain and the United States, on one side, and Japan on the other, jeopardized allied positions in the Far East. In September, Howe agreed with the rest of the War Committee to reinforce the British garrison at Hong Kong. There, in the afternoon of December 7, Canadian time, they were attacked by the Imperial Japanese Army. At the same moment the Japanese struck at the American naval base at Pearl Harbor. It was an American defeat, but perceptive Canadians, listening to the news, understood that the turning point of the war had come: the United States' long neutrality was over, and with American resources, industry and manpower behind them the allies could not now fail.

* Research Enterprises Limited, under Eric Phillips.

CHAPTER ELEVEN

"You Can't Sink a Howe"

By the beginning of 1942 the Department of Munitions and Supply had spread out from its modest quarters in Number One Temporary Building on the cliffs above the Ottawa River. Its four thousand employees now occupied a whole series of "temporary buildings," Virginian colonial structures adapted to withstand the Ottawa winter and therefore impervious to any imaginable calamity. Howe liked the hot, stuffy buildings. They were functional, and they were solid. He even adopted the engineer responsible for building them, Emmett Murphy, into his bureaucratic family, and the two men remained friends until Howe's death.[1]

In Number One Temporary, the centre of his wartime empire, the minister received and dispensed, barked and threatened, cajoled and charmed. Visitors arrived at Howe's office to be ushered into a modestly furnished room with a magnificent view of the river. But it was the visitor who got the view, not Howe. Only one feature of the sparsely furnished office was out of the ordinary: a bright red phone. It was not, as the visitor might have imagined, connected to the Prime Minister or the chiefs of staff; it was just a gift from a friend. But when Howe used it, the colour seemed appropriate.

Outwardly, the man inside the office had altered. After two years of war, Howe's hair had turned white. His throat bothered him, but, as one reporter admiringly noted, "he refuses to take time from his tremendous responsibilities for an operation." Howe was also afraid of doctors and what they might do to him; it took over a year for his family to persuade him to take time off and let a cousin operate on him for tonsillitis.[2]

Visitors to Howe's office usually left under the impression that the minister must work incredible hours to have been prepared to receive them and to deal knowledgeably with their problems. But Howe was simply blessed with an unusual memory, an efficient staff and an ability to make quick decisions. Because so little time was set aside during the day for diversion or pointless activity, Howe was able to sail by with a mixture of good briefing and abundant common sense.

The family saw little difference. Howe at home was still an amiable background figure, intruding as little as possible on the functioning of the household under the resident commander-in-chief. But Alice and the children missed him, particularly when business took Clarence across the Atlantic or to Washington or to some exotic munitions plant to unveil the ten thousandth truck produced. One night, when Howe returned from one of his trips, the whole family stood when he entered the living room. "Children," Alice intoned, "I'd like you to meet your father. You may not remember him."[3]

One Howe was never home. Bill had been in England since 1940 and had qualified as an officer in the Royal Navy. Posted to HMS *Devonshire*, Bill was sent off to the Indian Ocean, where his ship was torpedoed. At home in Ottawa, the family anxiously waited for news. Long afterward, Howe's children remembered it as the only time their father was really shaken. But his routine had to go on. One night he attended a banquet in Montreal and took along Elisabeth, now studying at McGill. She could hardly bear to face the evening, but her father patted her on the back. "Don't worry, Sis," he said, "you can't sink a Howe." If Clarence was unsinkable, so was Bill. And so it proved when Bill was rescued. His proud father collected the admiring comments of shipmates and commanders and stored them away in the office.[4]

Howe decided that the war demanded some variation in routine. He experimented with the family Newfoundland, Danny. After some time he convinced Danny that he could bring in the morning paper (the *Ottawa Citizen*), sparing his master a trip down the stairs in the morning chill. Howe was immensely proud of his achievement. He forgot that Danny couldn't open the front door. Eventually a separate dog entrance was carved out; thereafter Danny carried out his duties efficiently.

The war imposed strains greater than occasional absences. Howe never brought work home from the office, nor did he gossip with his family about the events or personalities of the day. Sometimes this bothered them. It was a longstanding promise that the Howes would buy a second car, and it was agreed that 1942 would be the year. But when Alice speculated on the model she would choose, Clarence grew silent. A few days later she found out why: new cars were discontinued for the duration. On another occasion Alice found herself directly victimized. She was to fly to Montreal to visit Elisabeth for a few days and she and Clarence said goodbye on the morning of her departure. Returning home that evening, Howe was surprised to find his wife still there. Then he remembered. He had had to get one of his officials down to Montreal on the first available plane, and he ordered that a seat be found. It was found, and Alice stayed home.[5]

For Howe, home was an oasis of calm every night. Not everybody was as lucky. "C. D.," one of his officials recalled, "would be fresh in the morning, fresh as a daisy, when the rest of us felt like hell." Howe once compared his executives to a team of huskies; like huskies, he said, they responded well to the occasional crack of the whip. It was his job to estimate when they needed it. To most people Howe displayed a calm and quiet manner. He never made idle threats, but simply asked that a given task be carried out quickly and quietly. Mistakes, he knew, were possible and forgivable; but if you made a second mistake, you did not survive to make a third.[6]

Production was surpassing all previous records. In 1941, Howe proudly told an engineers' convention, Canada had produced more armaments than during the five years of the First World War. The target for 1942, he announced, would be 250 per cent of 1941's production. Howe's executives shuddered. In this third year of the war it was impossible to estimate how many more resources the war production program should be permitted to consume. What was obvious was that, with conversion to war production virtually complete, with every possible Canadian producer contracted to work for Howe's department, with unemployment unknown, the Canadian economy was straining at its seams. It would, some thought, be fortunate indeed if Munitions and Supply maintained its production levels.[7]

There was another new factor to be considered. American entry into the war had little direct, immediate effect on Howe's supply programs (the American economy was already on a wartime basis and cooperating with Howe's department through joint war production committees) but it did mean trouble down the road. The Americans, Howe speculated, might be more retentive of their own supplies, and less willing to hand over scarce materials, now that they would actually be needed for American fighting men. Canada, he told his controllers in his only appearance at a War Industries Control Board meeting, would have to look out for itself. That meant that more of everything would have to be produced, and produced in Canada. A list of scarce products was immediately drawn up, while factories feeding the civilian economy were scrutinized to see if they too could not be converted to war purposes.[8]

One obvious shortage was rubber. Canada had a stockpile, thanks to the stocks accumulated by Fairmont Limited, but that supply allowed only a breathing space. What Canada needed was an independent source of rubber – artificial rubber. A process for making artificial rubber had been developed, ironically by the Germans. As Howe's officials speculated on the possibilities, Howe, on a visit to Washington, learned that there would be an American meeting on the subject the next day, December 27, 1941. Howe instructed the relevant officials to pack their bags and get down to Washington. Within days, an arrangement was worked out. Canada was allotted a specific quota of rubber production, and the American owners of the German patents for the process agreed that Canada could use it – provided that their property rights in the patents were respected. A phone call to Norman McLarty, the Secretary of State and the minister in charge of enemy property, fixed that. It mattered very little to Howe what technicalities were involved; if Canada could use German technology to beat the Germans, so much the better.[9]

Canadian rubber production was organized into a new crown corporation, Polymer Limited. Construction of Polymer's plant was assigned to Douglas Ambridge, the Director-General of Shipbuilding. Like any good engineer, Ambridge was versatile and resourceful; with an assist from the oil companies and Ontario Hydro, Polymer's facilities were soon rising over the St. Clair River at Sarnia, Ontario. Howe turned over Polymer's administration to J. R. Nicholson, a young British Columbia lawyer who had been on the spot when the first key decision for rubber production was taken. Howe followed the new company's progress anxiously, but with growing pride. Polymer, he wrote in August 1942, was so promising that it might be kept operating after the end of the war – as a government enterprise. A year later, speaking to the House of Commons, Howe was more positive. Polymer would certainly survive the war, and as long as it turned a profit the government would not sell it: "It should be operated by the government during the war and during the peace."[10]

Howe may have been surprised by Polymer's quick success (its rubber quota was soon doubled, and its unit costs were lower than those of its American counterparts) but he was not surprised that Canada could, out of virtually nothing, create a complicated new chemical industry. It was all a matter of good management. What Canada lacked, Howe believed, was not money or resources, but "managerial skill" – Canada's basic shortage, Howe told a reporter early in 1942. But Howe had been conducting a school for managers for two and a half years, training men to think for themselves, decide for themselves, and create for themselves, without referring to a distant head office or waiting for orders from a telephone. If it worked in war, Howe was beginning to think, it would work in peace as well.

Once a good managerial team was in place, Howe believed, it was up to him to back it up, not to badger it or undermine it by allowing appeals to his authority. Howe's controllers and directors-general could rely upon their minister to support them, even when what they did was exceedingly unpopular. The extreme case was that of oil control, which included gasoline rationing. Oil control was the domain of George Cottrelle, who reigned imperturbably over Canada's petroleum rationing system from June 1940 until the end of 1945. The task would have exhausted a lesser man, but Cottrelle reduced his worries by applying a simple maxim: no exceptions. Cottrelle's inspectors spread out over the country, investigating, justifying and occasionally prosecuting, sustained by widespread public approval and a considerable network of private information. Those who violated the law were hauled in to explain themselves; those who wasted gas found their rations suddenly reduced.[11]

Even Howe sometimes found dealing with his oil potentate trying. One day, Bill Bennett and a visitor paused to listen to the shouts from the minister's office. That, Bennett casually remarked, was nothing unusual – just Cottrelle paying a visit. "He's still there but he's resigned four times," Bennett added.

Through the controllers and the directors-general Howe got

160

his impressions of how the economy was working. It was, in general, enough to know that a plant or an industry was in good hands. But it occasionally became necessary to know more, especially when production figures dropped, labour trouble broke out, management changed, or costs rose. And sometimes it was necessary to know a great deal. Under Howe's various programs, private companies were responsible for the proper use of a lot of government money which might have been granted directly, through crown-owned tools or buildings, or indirectly, through accelerated depreciation. The latter device permitted a company to write off a new investment within a very few years, so as not to be left with a potentially useless burden at the end of the war. It was a means of channelling private money into investments that might well prove to be uneconomic once wartime demand lapsed and it was, on the whole, very successful.[12]

Munitions and Supply's largest investment in steel was at Algoma Steel, in Sault Ste. Marie. Its owner, the eccentric Sir James Dunn, usually held himself at arm's length from Algoma's day-to-day management, and kept aloof from his company's dealings with the government. That he left to T. F. Rahilly, his competent general manager. When Dunn and Rahilly finally disagreed, there was only one way out from the steel magnate's point of view: Rahilly was dismissed. Rahilly's departure provoked uneasiness in Ottawa; the Steel Controller complained to Howe, and Howe was soon making discreet inquiries to discover what Dunn was about. Only when Howe learned that Dunn had in mind a competent successor for Rahilly did his concern abate.[13]

Other companies were not so lucky as Algoma. The owners of the National Steel Car Company plant at Malton, Ontario, had accumulated a record of extravagance and inefficiency. In October 1942, the company fired its general manager, the man on whom production depended. Howe decided to give National Steel Car until midnight that day to reappoint him or face the consequences. At midnight a government controller simply walked into the plant and took over. Reorganized as Victory Aircraft, the Malton factory was run as a crown company for the duration of the war. In this case and in others, "continuity of operational management" was Howe's criterion.[14]

Howe's admitted strong points were in management and production. But production depended on manpower. By the end of

1941 there was not enough of that commodity, and Howe did not know how to handle what he had. Labour took Howe into strange and dangerous by-ways that he and his executives hardly understood – though some believed that they understood it all too well.

Howe never synthesized his philosophy of labour relations. He believed in the enlightened self-interest of employers. If an industrialist were intelligent, and attentive to the proper management of his plant, he would look out for his workers. He would avoid, above all, stirring up trouble through unfair labour practices. He ought to be ready to sit down and talk things over if problems developed.

These views were more liberal than the average in Canadian business. Early in the war, American officials were sent north to study Canada's industrial relations. They were surprised at what they found. Howe, they reported to Washington, was reputed to be "'a strong man' closely allied to industry." Many of his war executives were "known to be antilabor." For the first two years of the war, King even had a corporation lawyer (McLarty) as Minister of Labour. But the real problem was with Howe's executives: "Canadian industrialists, especially in Toronto, have preserved a strength and an arrogance surprising to an American." These were the men who surrounded Howe.[15]

Where labour was concerned, the Canadian business community was subject to periodic panics. In May 1941 the Canadian Manufacturers' Association warned that "groups of dangerous men [were] trying to seize control of the key war industries of this country, in order to control the workers . . . and to obstruct and restrict the output of munitions which are so sorely needed in the war." Howe was not much impressed. He raked the CMA over the coals when it proved unable to substantiate its accusations against labour. In June he urged both sides to give impartial labour-management tribunals a fair chance.

Some of Howe's officers took the rumours of communist infiltration more seriously than their minister. In July George Bateman, the Metals Controller, warned his colleagues that "agitators from abroad" were making progress in Ontario's mines. The controllers responded by asking the minister to help combat the red peril. Two weeks later, on July 24, news came that seemed to confirm the controllers' worst fears. There was a work stoppage at the Aluminum Company of Canada's Arvida smelter. If work was not resumed in a matter of hours, Howe learned, the pots used to smelt the aluminum would freeze, and it would be virtually impossible to repair them. Canada's aluminum industry would be shut down for months while new pots were installed. Production of anything requiring aluminum would be delayed. If an enemy agent wanted to interrupt the allied war effort, Arvida was almost the perfect spot. Naturally, Alcan executives told Howe, an enemy alien *was* leading the work stoppage.

Howe was frantic. Without aluminum, airplane production would grind to a halt. If an enemy alien were involved, it became a job for the army. Fortunately, he learned there already were troops at Arvida. Picking up the telephone, the minister asked the chief of the general staff, General Harry Crerar, to order them into action to save the plant. Crerar refused. He and his troops had no powers in a civil dispute, nor could they determine for themselves when they should take a hand in a civilian matter. If there was a danger to public order, it was up to the Attorney General of Quebec to decide what to do, and not Howe. Only the province could ask for troops to aid the civil power. The rest of the day passed in frustration. Ralston, whom Howe tried to reach next, was in Prince Edward Island, and unavailable. The Minister of Justice was on vacation. P. J. A. Cardin, acting Minister of Justice, was ill. The Attorney General of Quebec could not be found. Meanwhile the pots froze.

Further attempts to get Crerar to arrest the "enemy alien" were unavailing. Finally Howe decided he had had enough. He had, he told Crerar, "reached the end of his endurance and could no longer carry on." Hanging up on the general, Howe called in his secretary and dictated a letter to King. When the Prime Minister received the letter, he was astonished to learn that the Alcan plant "had been seized by a group of men led by an enemy alien and was now in the control of 400 men." Now it was up to King to deal with this alarming situation, because Howe himself was resigning, effective the following Monday, July 28.

King was perturbed, and grew alarmed while his staff tried to locate Howe. No one, it seemed, knew where he was. Finally, late Sunday afternoon, Howe turned up at home. He had simply gone to the country club and stayed overnight in order to recuperate. He was still angry, but he was no longer exhausted, and he was prepared to listen while the Prime Minister promised over the phone to find a way out of this dilemma. What he wanted, he told King, was "a real showdown with his colleagues, to know whether he was going to get the co-operation he needed for these situations." The two men arranged to meet the following morning.

After seeing Howe on the morning of July 28, King took up the Arvida strike with the cabinet in the afternoon. Howe told his colleagues that he must have the powers necessary to deal with emergency situations, including the authority to call out troops if necessary. If he could not get that authority, he would not stay as minister. After discussing the matter, the cabinet agreed to pass an order allowing the Minister of Munitions and Supply to call out the army in cases of sabotage in war plants. There the matter should have rested.

Unfortunately, Howe also decided to air his grievances with the press. He described the situation in Arvida in lurid terms, and the word flashed across the country. It was a "rebellion against constituted authority," fumed a Conservative leader. It was nothing of the kind, Ernest Lapointe told King. "What I was afraid might be the case is unfortunately so," he wrote to King. "Howe has allowed himself to be deceived by the Aluminum Company, and his statements have precipitated a storm in Quebec." The cabinet appointed a royal commission to investigate.[16]

When the royal commission reported, it became obvious that Howe's information and his public statements were wildly exaggerated. The main problems were the weather and the language barrier. It was hot in Arvida, and temperatures in the pot room had gone over 100 degrees Fahrenheit. There were problems with pay deductions as well and the workers were uneasy with management's explanations. In fact, it was difficult for management either to explain its position to the workers or to understand what was happening: all but one of the management personnel were English. An army officer later reported that the culprits at Arvida were "bigotry and intellectual sloth." There was no enemy alien.[17]

During the war and after, Howe would have denied that he was "anti-labour." He appointed a railway union official, Howard Chase, to be his labour adviser; in one labour dispute he even appointed Chase controller of a factory to put an end to labour strife. But Chase's views were close to Howe's own: they represented the old-fashioned craft unions, not the aggressive industrial unions that Howe's managers had to contend with. Production was important to Howe, and jobs to labour. It was, he thought, a fair swap. If someone wanted to work in one of Howe's factories, that was his right, and he ought not to be forced to join a union for the privilege. As the American observers had reported, these views were not uncommon, but they were old-fashioned by American standards. They were, moreover, at variance with the labour policy of the Canadian government, which encouraged unions and collective bargaining – but not strikes.[18]

By the last years of the war, Howe was more conciliatory to labour. Where labour representatives had been conspicuously absent, as on the boards of crown companies, they were appointed. Howe's department was able to reject union complaints of under-representation by early 1944; it reported that "Boards of older companies [were] being progressively overhauled to give labour representation, sometimes not without resistance, e.g. Victory Aircraft at Malton where the whole board had to be replaced." Distrust of unions died hard among Canadian businessmen, but Howe, impelled by his commitment to industrial peace and war production, was willing to do what the times demanded. Yet he would not have agreed with a Gallup Poll result in February 1944. When asked whom they would prefer to dominate government, big business or the unions, Canadians replied by 65 per cent to 35, "labour unions." Americans, when asked the same question, replied in almost precisely opposite proportions.[19]

Labour problems, though occasionally acute, were not a perpetual cause of concern. Howard Chase was sufficient for most purposes, and when Chase failed, Howe or the government could invoke the services of Carl Goldenberg, Howe's Director-General of Economics and Statistics. Though an economist by training, Goldenberg had a natural gift of mediation, which he struggled to put to use in bringing management and unions together. But Goldenberg's main contribution to Munitions and Supply lay elsewhere.

During the fall of 1941 the cabinet's attention was increasingly drawn to the question of the allocation of Canada's manpower reserves. No question was more volatile, or more likely to provoke dissension. Between 1919 and 1939 the Liberals, and latterly the Conservatives too, had promised that there would be no repetition of the conscription crisis of the First World War.

On that understanding Mackenzie King's French-Canadian colleagues, led by Ernest Lapointe, supported Canada's entry into the Second World War. King's promise was repeated during the 1940 election. And though conscription for home service was adopted in June 1940, only volunteers proceeded abroad.

Howe stayed aloof from the politics of conscription. His concern was economic, not political; his worry was that military recruitment would dry up his own labour force and oblige him to reduce Canadian production just when the war was entering a crucial new phase. And since for Howe the war was being fought and won on the shop floor and production line, there was no question that production must come first, now that the defence of Canada and Britain was assured. This perspective clashed fundamentally with that of the military, and it became a component of the conscription crisis of 1942.

The first act of that crisis was played out in February 1942. Ernest Lapointe had died in November, and to fill his seat and three other vacancies, by-elections were scheduled for February 4. For Howe the key races were in Ontario, where he was the senior responsible Liberal. Most important for Howe's immediate purposes was Welland, where the new Minister of Labour, Humphrey Mitchell, an old friend of Howe's and a sometime labour leader, was running. Even Harry Carmichael, who came from that area, took to the air waves in Mitchell's support. But Mitchell's election was easy. More controversial was the contest in York South, where Arthur Meighen, the old Conservative warhorse and former prime minister, was running on a platform demanding conscription now. The Liberals ran no candidate there, leaving the field clear for the CCF, and Howe remained cheerily unperturbed about it. When Howe told King that he believed Meighen would lose, King confided to his diary that Howe's prediction was "sheer nonsense." But Meighen did lose.[20]

The other new recruit to the cabinet, Louis St. Laurent, did not lose in Lapointe's old seat of Quebec East. St. Laurent, a sixty-year-old corporation lawyer, was a man of considerable talents who quickly made his impact felt in cabinet. For the most immediate future, however, St. Laurent was important for one thing: he was not pledged to oppose conscription under any or all circumstances.

And so, when King decided to hold a plebiscite to decide whether the government should be released from its election pledge to oppose conscription, its principal Quebec member was not bound to disapprove. A united cabinet asked Canadians to vote yes to its question, and Howe along with the other ministers took to the campaign trail. It was an easy election, at least in Ontario; for Howe, its only notable incident was the offer of a $5,000 campaign contribution from Sir James Dunn of Algoma Steel. It was refused.[21]

The result of the plebiscite was never in doubt. The government won overwhelmingly in Ontario and lost by an equal margin in Quebec. The King government then introduced Bill 80 into Parliament to authorize conscription as and when the cabinet considered it necessary. Howe, like a loyal soldier, accepted King's lead.* At that point Cardin resigned, but no other French-Canadian ministers followed his lead. As the battle over conscription subsided, the struggle over manpower began.

The protagonists in the struggle for Canada's manpower were, inevitably, Howe and Ralston. Howe informed his colleagues that war production could not stand the continual leaching away of essential workers. Nor were women workers likely to be able to help, because the worst shortages occurred in primary industry, in the mines and forestry. So acrimonious had the dispute become by the end of May 1942 that it was reported that Howe had "acquired complete contempt for Ralston as a business man. He just plows Ralston under." But ploughed under or not, Ralston did not give up. In June Howe went public with his complaints, telling the House of Commons that "our whole war effort is being distorted at the present time by the undue emphasis now being placed on men for the army overseas." If "every physically fit man" were sent abroad to fight, then war production would have to be curtailed. A reporter aptly commented after the end of Howe's speech that "our ministers now do their fighting in the House and not in the cabinet."[22]

The reporter was wrong about the cabinet. Through the summer Howe strove to impress on his colleagues that Ralston was asking too much of the country. If Ralston had his way, Canada would have mobilized proportionately more men than had

* Howe summoned a meeting of Ontario ministers to his office to proffer advice to the Prime Minister. King, who feared even the possibility of an Ontario cabal, reacted violently – so violently that he later apologized to Howe when the latter's innocent intentions became apparent. But Howe never again assembled the Ontario ministers.

frontline Britain. When Ralston again raised the suggestion that women take men's places, Howe sarcastically asked how he intended to apply that principle to the mines and lumber camps. By September Howe's dire predictions were borne out when the War Industries Control Board reported "a serious decline in the production of vital materials." The situation failed to improve thereafter; in 1943 Howe grumbled to Beaverbrook that lumbering, base metals and coal mining were all suffering from labour shortages. When employment in war industry reached its peak of 848,000 in July 1943 it was far short of the 910,000 Howe thought he needed. Though the cabinet approved some palliatives to ease the worst of the labour shortages, Howe's manpower program had reached its definitive limits. He would, for the rest of the war, have to make do with what he already had.[23]

War production, under the capable direction of Harry Carmichael, nevertheless worked miracles. H. R. MacMillan, working happily on shipbuilding, reported that he had not only successfully adapted the basic American cargo-ship design, but had improved on it. Unit costs had been reduced to the point where ships built in Canadian yards were actually cheaper than their American counterparts built only a few hundred miles away. A specialized crown corporation, Research Enterprises Limited, headed by Eric Phillips, was so successful with its optical equipment that Howe made a point of distributing its prized binoculars among high-ranking allied officers. Any advertising was good advertising.[24]

One new industry received no publicity at all. In June 1942 Howe received an unusual delegation consisting of the British High Commissioner, Malcolm MacDonald, and two British scientists. With the president of the National Research Council, C. J. Mackenzie, at his side to advise him, they conferred for about two hours. The British explained to their Canadian hosts that the possibility existed of a new super-weapon, utilizing the power of the atom, and that Canada possessed quantities of a mineral essential to building it. The mineral was uranium, mined by the Eldorado Gold Mines Company at Great Bear Lake. It might be necessary, the British explained, to assume control over the mine. Howe agreed. He knew the mine's owner, Gilbert LaBine, and he was confident that he could assume control. Within weeks, Howe had his mine, and Canada was launched into the atomic age.[25]

Howe assigned responsibility for Canada's atomic interests to

168

Mackenzie. LaBine became responsible for deliveries of uranium to Canada's British and American allies. But uranium was not to be Canada's only atomic contribution. In August 1942 the British offered to send a nuclear research team to Canada, to collaborate with Canadian scientists on atomic matters. Mackenzie found the prospect exciting: in a single bound Canada would share in some of the most advanced scientific research anywhere in the world. On Mackenzie's advice, Howe consented to the British proposal. Thus were founded the Montreal Laboratory (in an unused building on the University of Montreal's campus) and Canada's future atomic industry. In August 1943 there was more: Howe became a member of an Anglo-American-Canadian Combined Policy Committee, a liaison group which was intended to coordinate exchanges of information among the three allies. For the next two years, as the Americans steadily progressed with their work on the super-bomb, Howe, King and Mackenzie sat on top of one of the allies' most vital secrets, the "Manhattan" project.

Atomic cooperation was not achieved without its quota of inter-allied discord. British and American quarrelling several times threatened to disrupt the entire Canadian atomic program, while Howe at one point bore the wrath of no less a personage than Winston Churchill for selling all his uranium – and with it the British Empire – down the river to the Americans. Howe and Mackenzie reacted angrily, explaining to the equally angry British that there was no alternative to cooperation with the Americans, and on the Americans' terms if no better could be had. The British subsided.

It was a lesson in inter-allied diplomacy. Canada's uranium deposits, and its geographical proximity to the United States, were a limited ticket of admission to a technology of unimaginable opportunities and dangers. But there was always an implied condition. The Americans could, if they wished, go it alone, and they would, if provoked by delays and interference.[26]

If that was true in atomic energy, it was much more so in other questions of supply. Here, Canada offered supplies to an American war economy bulging at the seams. Canadian salesmen were a familiar sight around Washington by the fall of 1941; and they represented not the Department of External Affairs, official custodian of Canada's external virtue, but the Department of Munitions and Supply.

It was a reminder that in war production the two countries

had moved very close together. By the time the United States entered the war Howe had established a tightly knit production and sale organization that acted as the sole agent in Canada for purchases by the British and American military. It was a straightforward business relationship. Canada produced materials for the allies using standard designs furnished by them. Because Howe's organization was vertically integrated and hierarchically controlled, there was little duplication and interdepartmental squabbling. Munitions production was firmly under civilian control.

Some members of the Canadian military disliked this situation. Howe was producing equipment for them as well, but as a sideline, a bonus on top of production for the allies. Delays in production fed the suspicion that the supply for Canada's armed services was running a bad third in Howe's priorities while his factories worked overtime to fill the more lucrative orders of the British and Americans. There was no doubt that the production organization sometimes failed to respond properly to military requirements. The design and production of military equipment depended on specifications furnished by the soldiers themselves, and the troops' lives were at stake. It would be more satisfactory, some soldiers thought, if munitions purchasing were restored to the military, just as it was before the Bren gun affair.

There was some justice in the military complaints. Managers on the production line wearied of incessant design changes demanded from overseas. In the case of the Anson trainer, the specification changes were such a drag on production because of the retooling involved that the president of Federal Aircraft ordered his executives to ignore all requests for design changes that did not bear directly on the safety of the aircraft.

Britain and the United States organized their war production differently. There, military requirements came under military jurisdiction and so, when the two countries gave thought to establishing combined organizations to plan and run the war more efficiently, it was natural that the combined boards established to run war production should have a distinctively military flavour. But combined or separate, their relations with Munitions and Supply remained the same: they were large and valued customers whose orders sustained the Canadian war economy and made production for Canada's own armed forces technically and financially possible.

When, therefore, Howe first learned of the new Anglo-American arrangements in January 1942 he was unperturbed. So was the chief of Munitions and Supply's Washington bureau, J. B. Carswell. There was no danger in what Canada's allies had done, he advised his minister. To be sure, Canada was not represented on their chief Munitions assignment organization, the Munitions Assignment Board (MAB), but its absence was at worst a minor inconvenience for those people who wished to do practical business. Indeed, business would go on as usual.[27]

If Howe's reaction was calm, Ralston's was quite otherwise. Canada's exclusion from the combined boards, he told his colleagues, posed a grave danger to Canadian supplies. What Canada produced could now be dispensed by a distant committee in Washington without a thought for Canada's own military needs. Ralston demanded, and got, his colleagues' support for a campaign to open the MAB and other crucial joint bodies to Canadian representation.[28]

Howe did not share his colleague's enthusiasm for Canadian representation. For one thing, Canadian representatives on the MAB would be military, not civilian. They would represent the Department of National Defence, not the Department of Munitions and Supply. They would mean interference by the military with his own smoothly functioning organization. It followed that Ralston's efforts were to be ignored if possible, and resisted if necessary.

Howe had his own fish to fry. He wanted Canadian representation on two civilian boards, the Combined Raw Materials Board (CRMB) and the Combined Production and Resources Board (CPRB). These boards dealt with matters closer to Howe's heart: the availability and distribution of scarce raw materials, and questions of combined production. Given the vagueness of these boards' terms of reference and the uncertainty of their powers, there was no predicting what they might do. It would be wise to join them and find out. Using his friendship with the British and American members on the CPRB, Howe at first suggested that Canada had been omitted only by an oversight. Although that produced a friendly response, no positive action was forthcoming. And so Howe played his second card. If there were no hope for Canadian membership in a tripartite body, perhaps Canada could join a bilateral one. On a fishing trip in July 1942 with Donald Nelson, the American War Production

Board chairman, Howe suggested that Canada and the United States set up a Combined Production and Resources Board of their own. That produced an anguished reaction from London. Canadian economic integration with the United States, already "naturally pronounced," would go too far to be reversed. In October, Canada was formally offered membership on the CPRB.[29]

Howe's cheerful announcement of this fact to the War Committee of the cabinet on October 28 provoked anything but a joyful reaction. Ralston condemned membership on the CPRB as a betrayal of Canada's larger interest in securing membership on the MAB. Howe was unperturbed. "Mr. Ralston," he told the committee, "has a wholly erroneous view of the work of the CPRB." Its work closely duplicated that of Munitions and Supply, and it was natural that Canada should join it. Besides it was already too late. The British Minister of Production was en route to Canada to tie up the final details. The War Committee surrendered, grumbling. Canada was represented, by and through civilians from Howe's department, on civilian production agencies. It was *not* represented by the military.[30]

Howe's reasoning during this minor diplomatic confrontation was, of course, self-interested. He knew that by accepting the pooling of munitions as proposed by the British and Americans, Canada stood to gain, not lose. Supplies to the United States, or for that matter to the British, would be unaffected by accepting the exclusion of Canada from the Munitions Assignment Board. "[The] only thing that will lead to a cessation of U.S. orders in Canada is the termination of the war," the Canadians were told. Rather than disrupt his existing contacts and contracts for the sake of an abstract gain in national prestige, Howe plumped for the tangible benefit of production for an assured, rich market. Munitions and Supply continued to run its own show, without interference from Ralston and his generals.

Howe and Ralston had now clashed on two serious issues. Howe knew that his colleague was an outstanding public servant. Ralston had helped to create the munitions machinery that Howe now ran, and the men Ralston had recruited were the backbone of Munitions and Supply. But Ralston was not, Howe decided, a capable manager of men. He was what his legal training had made him, a master of his own brief. The Minister of National Defence laboured long hours on behalf of his client, the army, just as he had in private life. It did not matter to him that his client was now a large government department, too complex for any one man to administer in detail. Ralston refused to compromise; with the help of his generals he would overcome his opponents through mastery of detail. Not surprisingly, it was the details, and the generals, which mastered the minister. For Howe, it was clear that Ralston's ideas of organization were still at the cottage industry stage. There was more than a trace of professional arrogance in his attitude: engineers, according to their own self-image, "do what lawyers talk about."[31]

At least there could be effective opposition to Howe's policies within the cabinet. There, Howe and his colleagues bartered with counters of real power, and on a theoretical basis of equality. Outside it was different. The Liberal caucus followed tamely where its masters led. Some members, including some ministers, resented their divorce from war patronage and even more that Howe gave contracts and authority to Conservative firms and prominent Tories like Henry Borden. The minister replied innocently: If it was the cabinet's desire to award contracts as patronage they had only to instruct him. No more was heard on that score. Members grumbled that the restrictions Howe's department imposed were intolerable. This constituent or that might need an extra gas ration; a church might need a new copper roof; someone might want one of the strictly controlled supply of new trucks. Howe refused to interfere.

Where his own constituency and region were concerned, Howe made no exceptions either, but he kept up his interest. He travelled, as before, three times a year up to Port Arthur to make his presence known and to point out that the war had brought money and employment to the Lakehead. Ordinary patronage was not suspended for the war, nor were his duties as the political chief of staff of the Liberals of Northern Ontario. His friends were the federal Liberals, of course. When the provincial Liberals went down to disaster in the Ontario election of August 1943, Howe refused to interfere. It was a consolation that Charlie Cox sank with the provincial ship. His ability to make trouble would from now on be strictly limited. But this relief was at the price of electing a CCFer in Port Arthur.[32]

With his home base secure from Cox's interference, Howe's political battles were confined to Ottawa. The burden of daily criticism of government actions fell on a few members on the Conservative side: R. B. Hanson, the official Leader of the Opposition, Gordon Graydon, Grote Stirling, Howe's fellow engineer, and John Diefenbaker, a newcomer elected on his third try in 1940. Their chief opportunity to flail away at Howe was the annual war appropriations debate, when the government's estimates of the cost of the conflict were brought into the House and examined, department by department. Howe always took advantage of these occasions to expound in careful detail – the details were always prepared beforehand – on his department's achievements. His officials gazed, shuddering, from the House gallery to see whether they had given Howe enough information to prepare him for any eventuality. Usually they had: with Bill Bennett sitting in front of him and handing him the answers Howe could repel anything the ill-informed opposition threw at him.

It was, however, difficult to handle both parliamentary business and the administration of a huge wartime department. King, after pondering the question, agreed that the most hard-pressed ministers should have extra help. On April 1, 1943, he appointed Lionel Chevrier to assist Howe.

Chevrier was first elected to Parliament in 1935 for the riding of Stormont, around Cornwall, Ontario. He was a very popular member and an accomplished orator. He was also, as Howe stressed to King, "bilingual, [and] a conscientious workman."* Chevrier had been chairman of the War Expenditures Sub-Committee on Supply, and therefore knew something of Munitions and Supply's work. As long as Chevrier entered into "the spirit of the arrangement," Howe would like to have him. By this, Howe meant that his assistant's role would be to take the information he needed from the department, and to do the routine parliamentary business that Howe could no longer afford the time for. Chevrier was agreeable, and the two men began a long and happy alliance – with Howe as senior partner.[33]

The Committee on War Expenditures, on which Chevrier served, was supposed to be Parliament's watchdog on the spending of public money in the war. It had the customary heavy majority from the government side, eighteen Liberals to four Conservatives, with one member each from the CCF and Social Credit parties. It served a purpose, though perhaps not its ostensible one. As J. F. Pouliot put it, ". . . the purpose of nearly all committees is to keep members out of mischief." And, as he might have added, to keep them feeling useful. The experience of the War Expenditures Committee was frustrating.

* Howe was not bilingual. He always mispronounced Chevrier as "Che-vree-ur."

Its American counterpart, the senatorial Truman Committee, regularly made headlines with its revelations of government waste and private corruption. The Canadian committee often languished in the shadows, meeting in camera and occasionally issuing toothless reports.

Opposition criticism of the Munitions and Supply program was innocuous, partly because of the non-political nature of its administration. As it turned out, it was easier for the opposition to seek and demand answers from old friends in Howe's department than it was to raise questions in the House, and the Conservatives, once they were persuaded that business was behind Howe, muted their tones.[34]

That did not apply to the CCF. For them, the war was an object lesson in the benefits of planning and state direction of the economy. They recognized and applauded Howe's ability to get things done, but they loudly condemned his cooperation with business. And in one of Howe's wartime arrangements the CCF thought it had found the perfect target.

Through a combination of British and American government loans, and with the help of a Canadian depreciation allowance, the Aluminum Company of Canada (Alcan) had expanded its plant to meet wartime demand. To the CCF, it appeared that Alcan had received a quarter of a billion dollars of actual or potential public funds to create a permanent expansion of its facilities. M. J. Coldwell, the CCF's scholarly leader, aired his charges in Parliament. He promised to make them stick in hearings before the Wartime Expenditures Committee.

Howe handed Munitions and Supply's case to the department's financial adviser, Frank Brown. Brown, with the assistance of Alcan's Ottawa representative, Fraser Bruce, laboured to give the committee the real facts on Alcan. "Entirely British and United States money has gone into creating those ingot facilities and these power facilities [for Alcan]," Brown rumbled at Coldwell. "It was not our arrangement at all, it was not our money; all we have said is that we would not queer the deal by the application of our tax situation." As for Alcan's profits, they were not unusual. Coldwell, crestfallen but unconvinced, stalked out of the committee room. "I didn't come here to be laughed at," he exclaimed to his jeering colleagues. But he had failed to convince them, and the Alcan affair died a quiet death.[35]

What the Alcan investigation did illuminate, however, was

175

the system of profit control and special grants by which Munitions and Supply regulated Canadian industry. Accelerated depreciation was merely the newest and the most unfamiliar. For companies it provided both tax relief and a hedge against the future. Investment for war production could be a disaster when peace returned and markets dried up. If a company was to risk its own money in building factories it had to be protected against what reasonable men assumed would likely happen: a return to the depressed conditions of the thirties. Accelerated depreciation was a new idea for Howe. When the concept was first explored, he spent an evening at the Rideau Club arguing it out with officials from the Finance Department and Alcan. Finally, satisfied that it would work, the minister yawned and looked at his watch . . . and left. The rest of the meeting worked on through the night settling the details and presented them to a well-rested minister in the morning.[36]

Between 1940 and 1945 special depreciation privileges totalling $514 million were granted. Of that sum over $300 million was spent on machinery and equipment, and the rest on the construction of buildings. At the end of the war, with their investment paid off, the companies were free to make what they could of their depreciated property. As they then discovered, their accelerated rates of depreciation meant exactly what the economists said they would: "Plants built during the war, but now idle," the president of Alcan wrote to Howe in 1948, "can become costly for owners and 'profitable' for municipalities and school boards." Howe had no sympathy. "The taxes you are now paying," he replied, "as contrasted with those of 1938, represent the other side of the medal of accelerated depreciation and perhaps explain why we were so willing to grant accelerated depreciation during the war years."[37]

The Wartime Expenditures Committee scrutinized other aspects of Howe's financial policies as well. What concerned government and opposition members both was the word "profit." Was there profiteering, influence-peddling or other skulduggery at Munitions and Supply? How much were Canadian businessmen making out of the war? Would there be a scandal of the kind that had disfigured munitions production in the First World War?

The answers to these questions were complex, but revealing. The first lesson learned from the war was that peacetime financial controls could not support the heavy load of war contracts.

Good financial practice meant calling bids on contracts and receiving tenders. This practice could, and did, take months. Howe short-circuited the system. Any company that could do the work got the contract, and sometimes started work with nothing more than Howe's word of mouth that it was authorized to do so. The contracts, Howe decided, could be written later. In any case, with virtually every firm occupied with war production, there was no point in seeking tenders from companies that could bid only with prior government permission.

Often contracts were for unknown quantities never before made in Canada. In such cases, the department and its contractors made an educated guess. They aimed at 5-per-cent profit on costs, rather than 5 per cent on capital invested, as Parliament had wanted before the war. In fact, Howe told Parliament years later, his officials were able to keep most profits down to 2 or 3 per cent. Using Frank Brown's considerable talents and energy, Howe established a special division whose task it was to evaluate performance on contracts. With 5 per cent as a guideline and 10 per cent as a reward for exceptional performance, Brown and his men started calling in the lucky businessmen who had done well enough to reach 25- to 50-per-cent profit on their costs. Under wartime tax legislation, they would lose it all to the government; but they would get some of it back after the war. Howe determined that they would get none of it back.[38]

That, Brown remembered, "was a real problem because many of the manufacturers thought the war was a wonderful opportunity to make a fortune." The worst case, he recalled, was in shipbuilding. As usual, when contract figures were received and audited, they were sent to Howe's office. Soon a call came for Brown. "Frank," Howe said, "here's a job for you. I want you to go out to the West Coast . . . and see if you can get those shipbuilders to refund a considerable portion of their profits." Howe knew, and Brown knew, that the profits were legally earned; the shipbuilders had simply managed to reduce their costs without cheating the government. No one, Howe knew, would believe that. "We'll have a major scandal on our hands," the minister told Brown, unless the shipbuilders voluntarily refunded some of their profits.

It was just as well to cooperate with Howe's emissaries when they called. When one company, Link Manufacturing, refused to make a refund, Howe promptly issued an order requiring the company to return "an unreasonable profit of some

$2,000,000." A financial controller was appointed to see that the order was properly carried out and to prevent any dissipation of the company's assets in the meantime. The review of contracts was soon a well-established practice. Howe made sure that it was well reported too: "Bigger Firms Hit By Contract Review," the *Financial Post* headlined in June 1944. As always, Howe was concerned to make sure that the public knew that his department was saving public money. When pictures appeared showing ships sliding down the slipway he wanted the viewer to know that the vessels were honestly built. And so, it turned out, they were. Howe's accounting systems and careful cost control steered Canadian war industry clear of charges of profiteering. At the same time his accelerated depreciation program insured that the companies did not fear economic disaster at war's end and were not tempted to make huge profits while Hitler held out.[39]

That, it began to appear, would not be long. Nineteen forty-two was the worst year for the allied cause, with a succession of Japanese victories in the Pacific and German offensives in Africa and Russia. But before the end of the year the Germans and Japanese were halted, and in 1943 allies started to advance. In July Canadian troops landed in Sicily in the first allied seaborne invasion of Hitler's Fortress Europe.

As the war expanded and fluctuated, so did military requirements. Munitions production depended on what the combined chiefs of staff decided would be useful for the coming year's offensives. Sometimes the abrupt switches in allied orders, and even the cancellation of some, inadvertently rescued some other part of Canada's munitions program. When, in 1943, British orders decreased, Howe was grateful for the relief; he now had thirty thousand men he could put to work somewhere else. Howe's busy legal division added contract cancellation to its repertoire of skills.[40]

What Howe's department was quietly doing, out of the public eye, was completing the reconstruction of the Canadian economy. Howe's accelerated depreciation programs, his government grants and his crown corporations had renewed Canada's capital investment after eleven years of depression. In the new factories, workers were learning the techniques of cheap mass production and applying them to a range of products undreamt of in prewar Canada. There was absolutely nothing, as Howe said later, which could not be produced in Canada; the war had proved that.

Most remarkable of all, Howe's complicated war production regulations had stood the Canadian economy on its head. The lines of authority were held in Ottawa. Companies that had once depended on provincial grants and bounties found that Ottawa was now doing the job, and doing it better. Anyone who could demonstrate that his firm had the capacity to meet the department's needs could benefit from Howe's programs. Even the steel magnate Sir James Dunn, who had protested against the shift of power from the provincial to the federal level, learned to like his new situation. Writing to the Steel Controller in August 1944, Dunn explained that he was "strongly in favour of continuing Steel Control when the war is over as far into the future as I can see. I feel that Steel Control has done a splendid job for the country." For Dunn and men like him, the war had transformed the world. The federal government was now an ally, not a distant enemy. From Victoria to Halifax, businessmen were reaching the same conclusion: business had found a capital and a home – and the head of the household was C. D. Howe.[41]

CHAPTER TWELVE

Minister of Reconstruction

I n the fourth year of the war, the popular mind began to speculate on what the postwar future might hold. Hitler was no longer a factor in that future; the Germans were on the run, though there was fight in them yet. The Japanese had been stopped and were slowly being rolled back. The outcome of the war, if not yet in sight, could be confidently predicted. But what would follow? Canadians were not optimistic. People thought of the postwar period with "something akin to dread," the Wartime Information Board told the cabinet, after conducting an opinion survey. Peace would mean a return to normalcy, and normalcy meant the appalling depression and unemployment of the thirties. Public opinion favoured great changes – almost anything to prevent the return of poverty and insecurity – in particular, jobs created and guaranteed by government.[1]

The armed forces and munitions factories had brought about employment for everyone. This had happened in the First World War too, and both during that war and in the postwar period the economy had been released into a frantic cycle of boom and bust, with inflation, strikes and ultimately mass unemployment as the consequences. The lessons of the past were now combined with the experience of the present. Canada's economic performance in the Second World War was good. Inflation had been kept within bounds, the dislocations in production reduced to a minimum. The undercurrent of public nervousness, however, could not be ignored.

The Liberals were slow to grasp the political consequences. The Conservatives, following the American and British examples, by 1943 were preaching the message of full employment; the CCF was ready to reap the benefits of years of its propaganda for social security. But the government hesitated. It had enacted unemployment insurance at the beginning of the war, and set in motion a succession of studies of social security. Throughout the country, public-spirited citizens discussed and wrote about what shoud be done by government after the war, while in Ottawa civil servants dusted off their schemes for a more perfectly governed country. Reform – whether it meant health insurance, comprehensive social security, or merely larger old age pensions – was in the air.

The reform spirit stopped short at the door of Number One Temporary Building. Most people in the Department of Munitions and Supply were too busy to notice. While committees sat and scholarly reports deluged a bewildered public, Howe was indifferent. He would, he told Norman Lambert, speak to the House of Commons Committee on Social Security if it wanted to hear him, and he volunteered the services of his officers if the politicians wanted information on the state of the economy. At bottom, however, he opposed "undue haste on reconstruction," particularly haste to do the bidding of what he called "high pressure groups," who preferred theories to facts and did not understand what had happened to Canada since 1939. Howe thought he did.

The minister did not share the bleak pessimism of the exponents of salvation through government planning and spending. In the winter of 1943, when the president of the Canadian Construction Association, John Stirling, came to Ottawa to publicize his organization's views on how government could best plan reconstruction – through large-scale public works projects – Howe shook his head in disgust. "John," he said, "I'm sorry to see that you've joined the security brigade." Taken aback, his visitor asked what Howe meant. "John," the minister replied, "when this war is over, which I hope will be soon, this country is going to have the greatest era of prosperity it's ever seen." In Howe's view, the prosperity need owe nothing to the government or its plans. The one precondition was that the government get out of the way. When the war ended, fifteen years of deferred demand and five years of accumulated savings would be released. His industrial machine would fill the demand and in its turn create more. Decontrol, not rigid planning by a corps of state experts, would be enough.[2]

The September 1943 meeting of the National Liberal Federation must have given Howe food for thought. It was held in the aftermath of the Liberals' disastrous defeat in an Ontario provincial election, and just as a Gallup poll placed the party equal with the Conservatives and one point *behind* the CCF in public favour. The Liberal assembly responded by plumping for full employment, and an expansion of private and public enterprise to make it possible. Publicly, Howe joined the chorus of approval. His own thoughts, however, were rather different.[3]

That fall Howe began to publicize his views. Speaking in November, he argued that ". . . there need be no fear of unemployment of those willing and able to work. . . . [A] surprising number of [war plants] can be converted without difficulty. Many new types of production that have been organized for war can be continued in peace." What the government should do, he added, was to ease the industrial transition through tax incentives, financial inducements, and research facilities – the very kind of programs that Munitions and Supply had already developed to help out its own contractors when their contracts were terminated.[4]

Howe amplified these opinions in a letter to the Prime Minister on November 17. The key to the government's policy for peace, he told King, should be Canada's experience during the war. The country's productive capacity had doubled. National income had jumped from $4.5 to $9 billions. A working partnership between government, industry and labour had been established; the same partnership should guide conversion to a peacetime economy. In fact, the problem of reconversion was simpler than the original problem of establishing war industry. The plants existed, and many could be converted quickly and easily to peacetime production. Howe cited the example of a large explosives plant, which was already converted to producing fertilizer. The production of civilian goods had been dammed back for four years, so that the rush to buy them would guarantee a bonanza of sales for Canadian factories. The housing shortage would keep the construction industry busy for years. All this, together with new technological developments such as television, improved airplanes and synthetic rubber would be "new sources of employment that will absorb any number of workers" from the war plants and the armed forces. It might be necessary to adjust the work force by retiring some workers early, but that could be eased by larger old-age pensions and bolstered if possible by health insurance. Howe even coined a slogan: "Full employment rather than hand outs from the Government." Fundamentally, Howe was proposing full employment through private enterprise, helped and guided by government only where absolutely necessary.[5]

King weighed Howe's proposals carefully. The program made economic sense, but politically it lacked appeal. The Prime Minister needed a positive and attractive legislative program for the new session of Parliament to bring straying Liberal voters back to the fold. But the voters would not come back unless they were confident that a Liberal government would protect them against economic disaster.

Parliament met on January 27, 1944. In the Speech from the Throne that opened the session, the King government presented one of the most ambitious domestic programs since the building of the CPR. It promised that "social security and human welfare" would be the cornerstones of its legislation. There would be "useful employment for all who are willing to work," old age pensions were to be reformed "on a more generous basis," children's allowances would be established (a proposal Howe had fought in cabinet) and veterans would be retrained at government expense and re-established in civilian life. New government departments would administer these new programs. And to guide the economy there would be another: a Department of Reconstruction.[6]

Such a department had been in the wind for several months. Howe, when King asked his opinion, was in favour and argued that a businessman should head it up. Chubby Power, whom King also consulted, agreed that the government should take it up immediately. But Power, who distrusted big business, did not agree that reconstruction should be placed under a businessman. King then secured general consent from cabinet and set his staff to work to define the future department. One possibility was to turn reconstruction over to a board of economic wizards from the Finance Department. Howe dismissed the idea. A reconstruction department, as he conceived it, would be remarkably similar to Munitions and Supply – a strong executive department, with plenty of power and lots of money.[7]

Howe was disappointed when the draft Reconstruction Bill

reached cabinet early in January. The future department, the cabinet was told, would plan and coordinate the activities of other departments. It would have no budget or powers of its own. The cabinet was doubtful, and referred the bill to a special cabinet committee, including Howe and Power. But the bill, when it returned to the cabinet late in March, was not greatly changed. Howe remained unimpressed. "If that was all there was to the bill," Howe told his colleagues, "there was nothing to it." And, King recorded, Howe warned the Prime Minister to "make sure, before going ahead with it, as to the man I could get to administer it." Howe, King acidly remarked, "seemed to think the only purpose of a Reconstruction Bill was a reconversion of industry." The Prime Minister ignored Howe's objections and the bill went forward.[8]

While the Reconstruction Bill passed through the House of Commons, Howe remained silent, except for one minor interjection. It passed third reading on June 23. King now had his department, but no minister.

King's rejection of Howe's suggestions for industrial reconversion profoundly irritated his minister. Howe was confident that he had both the program and the experience necessary to make a success of reconstruction. King disregarded both, preferring to create a phantom department without a budget. Without a budget, Howe knew, the reconstruction minister would languish impotently while his busier colleagues pursued their own priorities, not his.

As the summer of 1944 wore on, Howe kept himself busy. Munitions and Supply had $900 million worth of new contracts in 1944, and there were plenty of matters requiring ministerial attention. But there were no long-term goals, no new mandate to pursue. It seemed to Howe that with the end of the war his usefulness would be spent. He was still under sixty, and it was possible to pick up the threads of a private career, whether by going back to Port Arthur or by striking out in some new direction. One afternoon, sitting in his office, the minister broached the idea to Bill Bennett. Bennett had managed his political affairs for so long he knew them better than Howe himself: it would be natural, Howe remarked, if Bennett prepared to replace him as the Liberal candidate for Port Arthur in the next general election. Bennett, however, had other ideas about his future, and he let the matter drop.[9]

While Howe brooded, King procrastinated. When the war

ended, he could hold a snap election with a good chance of success – possibly in October or November. The war, however, did not end, and it became necessary to prepare for another meeting of Parliament. The legislation to set up three new departments lay ready, authorized, and inert: Veterans' Affairs, National Health and Welfare, and Reconstruction, all enacted but unproclaimed. Early in September the Prime Minister decided that a Minister of Reconstruction there must be, and that it must be Howe. He invited Howe to take the job. Howe refused, and "spoke pretty feelingly" on the matter, as King recorded. Power, who was asked next, also refused. King returned to Howe, but it was obvious that there would now have to be substantial inducements. Howe would mistrust any offer that came directly from King; in order to entice his minister, King would have to use a go-between. The Prime Minister's eye fell on Louis St. Laurent, the Minister of Justice. He was already a dominant figure in the cabinet, and King knew Howe respected St. Laurent's quick mind and sound judgment. King persuaded St. Laurent to try his hand, telling Power and Ian Mackenzie that he would "insist" on Howe taking the job.[10]

On October 5 King and Howe met again. Howe brought his terms with him. He said he was prepared to reconsider only because St. Laurent had persuaded him to do so, but he was still doubtful. His fundamental condition was that King promise to accept his resignation without delay or complaint if his new office turned out to be powerless. To prevent that eventuality, King must agree to transfer responsibility for scientific research to Reconstruction, along with jurisdiction over air policy. Industrial reconversion was also to move, eventually, from Munitions and Supply to Reconstruction. Howe required an influential and capable deputy minister, and finally there must be a separate appropriation for Reconstruction to spend on its own without hindrance from other departments or agencies. King agreed; the only point he insisted on was that there must still be a cabinet committee on reconstruction. Howe accepted it with an ill grace.[11]

For deputy minister, Howe considered Sandy Skelton, a brilliant economist with the Bank of Canada, and the great Queen's economist W. A. Mackintosh, special wartime assistant to the deputy minister of finance. Finally he settled on his old friend R. A. C. Henry, who had recovered his health. On October 14, the Reconstruction Act was officially proclaimed and Howe's appointment as minister announced. With "grave misgivings" Howe added the title of Minister of Reconstruction to that of Minister of Munitions and Supply.[12]

Howe had been ruminating about the new department with two of his trusted advisers, C. J. Mackenzie of the National Research Council and John Baldwin of the Privy Council Office, who was also advising him on aviation policy. Mackenzie suggested the inclusion of a division of industrial research in the new department, and it was with this in mind that Howe had insisted King add the National Research Council to his responsibilities. Along with war surplus disposal and industrial reconversion, Howe classified scientific research as requiring "intensive action," that is, action solely within the purview of Howe's departments. Intensive action, presumably, would receive immediate attention. Other matters such as social security, labour policy and full employment, public works and housing were grouped together under the heading "extensive action." Extensive action would mean prolonged consideration. Yet it was in terms of these other matters that most people understood the word "reconstruction" – if they understood it at all. That part of reconstruction would be left to the workings of the cabinet committee and to other departments of government. And as Howe told Baldwin: "Until our course is fairly clear, I am not disposed to interfere with the workings of other departments of government." Nor, he presumed, would other departments wish to interfere with his.[13]

Howe wanted Baldwin to join his staff, but could not extract him from the clutches of Mackenzie King. He had more success in the Finance Department, where he lured away W. A. Mackintosh and a small group of economists. Mackintosh was happy enough to leave Finance, and he liked Howe, but his future in Reconstruction under Howe's "extensive action" scheme was cloudy.

The real business of reconstruction proceeded as before, inside the Department of Munitions and Supply. The real planning for reconstruction also continued to be done, as before, by the statisticians and economists of the wartime department, under the general guidance of Howe's production chief, Harry Carmichael. Since he took leave of General Motors in 1941, Carmichael had been Howe's right-hand man; in 1945 Howe described him as invaluable, a distinction he did not bestow lightly. The two men agreed that fears for the economy's future were, to say the least, exaggerated. Carmichael knew that Canadian industry had done very well during the war if its unit costs were set against those of the United States and Great Britain. And Howe later explained to a business lunch what the war meant to Canadian businessmen: "The Canadian manufacturer had acquired such confidence by his experience during the war," an American observer reported, "that he no longer had any fear of his ability to compete with his American neighbor, provided he has access to an equally large market."[14]

There was more than a touch of wishful thinking in Howe's assessment of the Canadian manufacturer's self-confidence. Canadian businessmen had enjoyed the guaranteed markets of war and were happy to pay the price of regulation in return for assured profits. What government had done for business and the economy in war it could, should, and must do in peace. Howe was determined to resist such easy arguments. Writing in October 1944, he condemned attempts by Canada's copper producers to secure a government-sponsored contract with Britain. "I am strongly of the opinion," Howe wrote, "that our copper producers should be placed in the same position that we found them in prior to the war, that is, in private business enterprise." If private buyers could not be found, copper producers or anyone else should not expect government to take up the slack: that would lead to the perpetuation of uneconomic and uncompetitive enterprises. The folly of the tariff would be perpetuated on a grand scale.[15]

The future, Howe told Canadian manufacturers, was theirs to seize. Government was getting out of business, and his officials were busy concocting the means. And high time too, for as he informed Mackenzie King in August 1944, war production must soon wind down. The European war was drawing to a close, and Canada's allies were showing clear signs of nervousness about their future purchases. And though the Pacific war was expected to continue for some time that was an American war; the Americans would reserve Pacific procurement to themselves. In Howe's world, contract cancellation loomed larger and larger, as his officials prepared to draw up their final balance sheets. While one group of officials pored over accounts and computed what government and business owed one another, another group prepared to help businessmen convert to peacetime production. Where businessmen failed to take the hint, Howe personally swung into action. "The way C. D. used to get on the telephone and bulldoze industrialists to convert to new peacetime lines was really something to behold," Brooke Claxton remembered.[16]

An obvious incentive was accelerated depreciation, the fiscal expedient that had proved so helpful in stimulating private investment during the war. The cost of the reconversion of plants would add to the cost of the product, and inhibit trade. The solution was to award double depreciation to companies planning to convert their facilities to peacetime purposes approved by the minister. The effect was to lower the tax rates of companies in order to provide the capital necessary for their expansion. A board within the Reconstruction Department made the appropriate recommendations, Howe passed on them, and exemptions were issued by the Department of National Revenue. This program began operations in November 1944; by January 1946 almost a quarter of a billion dollars had been awarded.

The main thing was to return to a civilian economy. The economy Howe envisaged was not quite the same as the prewar one. The government, for one thing, now had vastly more information about the functioning of the economy. Passing over Howe's desk was a stream of reports, interpretations and predictions from some of the most competent economists in Canada. They told him that civilian saving was at an all-time high, and that shortages of consumer goods were growing daily more severe. Howe hardly needed to be told that: his old Buick, the shabby streetcars, the mouldering rolling stock of the railways, all testified to the sacrifices the civilian economy had made to win the war. All this would have to be replaced.

Howe's Department of Munitions and Supply held billions of dollars' worth of investment across Canada. Most of it would serve no purpose when the war ended, as far as the government was concerned. But most of it could, happily, be reused for some other purpose: at least $2.2 billion out of $3.2 billion was salvageable, Howe's economists reported. The problem was to transfer that $2.2 billion to Canadian businessmen who would use it to open factories and create jobs. To do that Howe set up in 1943 the War Assets Corporation, whose function it would be to sell off whatever the government had, at the best possible price, to the best possible buyer. If there was a conflict between these two criteria, it was the buyer who won out. By 1947, $107 million worth of war plants were sold or leased to private businessmen who guaranteed to keep them operating at prevailing levels of employment for five years. When customers were slow in coming forward, Howe was not above jogging his friends' memories. He had an entire communications system in the Yukon to sell, he wrote to the president of B.C. Telephone. "We are prepared to take a realistic view of its value," he added, "provided we can arrange for disposal when the time comes."[17]

More difficult was the problem of disposing of war equipment when the war ended. No matter what its nominal value, or the total of labour and raw materials it absorbed, a weapon without any prospect of a target was a piece of junk. Howe knew this, but it was difficult to reorient Canadians' perspective to accept that what they had been slaving for five years to produce was now worth no more than its scrap value. If it cost more to store than its drastically reduced value, it made sense to destroy it. In one spectacular example, a field full of Anson trainers near Calgary was simply burned. Howe was undisturbed. He believed, as he later told Parliament, that Canada's record in the speedy disposition of war surplus compared favourably with that of any other country.[18]

Some of the government's planners were excessively optimistic. Anticipating the end of the war, and correctly assessing the scale of civilian demand, the Wartime Prices and Trade Board gave permission for sixty thousand new washing machines to be produced in 1945. Howe's department was doubtful; there could well be a steel shortage, and the government could be left with egg on its face. So it proved. There was indeed a steel shortage and a shortfall in the production of washing machines – a 90 per cent shortfall, as it turned out. Howe urged private industry to be more realistic. The automobile companies, for example, were told to plan for themselves so that civilian production could resume in an orderly manner.[19]

In some cases, Howe's disposal policies were guided by his instinct about postwar demand. Technological advance had accelerated during the war and Canada, thanks to its war production, had kept abreast of it. New industries were encouraged to take advantage of the newly trained manpower available to them. If that meant selling surplus property to a foreign firm with a record of success in the field, it was better than having no industry left at all. In one case, the Research Enterprises Limited plant in Leaside, a suburb of Toronto, was sold off to

Corning Glass of the United States at 30 cents on the dollar. What was notable about the sale, as far as many businessmen and Howe's officials were concerned, was that it brought Corning into Canada for the first time and created permanent jobs for skilled Canadian workers.[20]

Howe's determination to bring Canada into newer technology irritated Ralph Bell, his Director-General for Aircraft Production. Howe saw no reason why Canada could not continue producing aircraft after the war. There were plenty of plants, with lots of skilled workers, and no one could doubt that aviation would expand after the war. Bell disagreed. There were plenty of factories and workers, admittedly, but there were no engine plants and no guarantee of a market for what they produced. Howe persevered. After the war was over, Victory Aircraft at Malton was leased by the A. V. Roe Company of Britain, while Canadair Limited near Montreal was sold to the Electric Boat Company (later General Dynamics) of the United States. With foreign investment, Canada would be able to continue in the aviation field.[21]

Canada was well placed to do so. The development of longer-range aircraft placed Canada (and Newfoundland) at the crossroads of world aviation. Airplanes crossing the Atlantic were bound to cross over Canada and stop and refuel at Gander in Newfoundland. The war showed how many could do so, and some of the many were Canadian. Alongside the bomber ferry, there was already a fledgling civilian service – for "war purposes" – operated by TCA, Howe's very own airline.

TCA had played a small but important role in the war effort. When time meant money and opportunity, TCA ferried key personnel across Canada and across the Atlantic. It ended the war in the black, with every prospect of continuing its expansion. Howe was determined that it should, but he also realized that TCA had two sets of difficulties to contend with. Domestically, there was Canadian Pacific Airlines; abroad, there was Lord Beaverbrook, Britain's aviation minister. Canadian Pacific Airlines was the less formidable. Howe simply reiterated the government's position: TCA was Canada's national airline and CPA was not. CPA must not expect either trans-Canada flights or transatlantic service. And the CPR, in an added fillip, was instructed to get out of the airline business entirely, after the end of the war.*

* The order was rescinded in 1946.

It remained to deal with Beaverbrook. The Beaver had visions of a Commonwealth air route around the world, in which British airlines would play a dominant role. He was prepared to deal with anybody to secure his object: with the other members of the Commonwealth, or, if they would not cooperate, with the Americans. Either way, Britain must get what the Beaver thought was owing, a worldwide split of air traffic. Beaverbrook's air plans left little room for TCA as an independent entity, and attempts by Canada to work within or alongside Beaverbrook's policy were largely fruitless. But it was the Americans who held the key, and they, luckily for Howe and Canada, were not disposed to go along with Beaverbrook.[22]

The final confrontation took place in November 1944 at an international aviation conference in Chicago. Canada attended with a formidable and finely drafted proposal for a charter providing for basic air freedoms. The British, hamstrung by an excessively rigid set of instructions, failed to reach agreement with the Americans, while the Canadians, led by Howe and Symington, did what they could to secure at least a provisional agreement.

The British failure was, from the Canadian point of view, the most important result of the Chicago conference. Canada, and TCA, were free to secure what terms they could in postwar aviation, and they did. A Provisional International Civil Aviation Organization was established, and took up residence in Montreal. Howe and Symington returned to Canada, satisfied.[23]*

Aviation was, for Howe, the transport of the future. It would expand and it would be an important feature of his reconstruction program, a splendid example of "intensive action" under his direction. But other parts of his industrial reconversion program languished – the "extensive action" side of the Reconstruction Department. In the fall of 1944 Howe had carefully stocked his new department with expert economists. Now, the experts discovered, they had little or nothing to do. But Howe appreciated both their techniques and their advice. The war, with its floods of paper and statistics, had taught him how valuable economic forecasting and analysis could be; as he remarked many years later, when he was reorganizing Ogilvie

* Howe was forced to return home early, in order to be present at the rebirth of the perennial conscription crisis; he was so annoyed and frustrated by the government's failure to bury the subject that he supported the pro-conscription forces in this last important manpower battle.

Flour, ". . . we need a well-trained business economist in this organization, which is presently made up of men who started in the organization as office boys." Howe, as a professional, respected other professionals. But in the early days of the Reconstruction Department he was not entirely certain what he wanted from them.[24]

In the view of W. A. Mackintosh, who had joined the department with visions of a carefully planned and directed reconstruction program in his mind, Howe wanted nothing at all. After one meeting between them in the winter of 1945, the economist burst into frustrated rage. He was convinced, he told a reporter, "that there is no such thing as an open-minded minister. All hopeless. Why waste time in trying to reason with them? . . . [It is] an intellectual form of volley ball – bouncing ideas off Mr. Howe's battleship steel headpiece." Mackintosh gradually learned there was no point in conducting a theoretical seminar with Howe. What the minister wanted, what he had time for, was practical advice: information about the economy, national and regional, and advice on its problem areas. These things Mackintosh and his staff could get for him, and what they produced agreed with Howe's own optimistic instincts.[25]

Because Mackintosh and Howe had no fundamental disagreement, cooperation was possible. Howe listened willingly to his economist, day after day, and he could not, in the long run, deny that Mackintosh had a point. What Canadians were getting from the reconstruction program was not what they were expecting.

It was late December 1944 before faint stirrings were heard in the Reconstruction Department. The immediate cause was the circulation around Ottawa of John Baldwin's draft manual on reconstruction. Designed to help businessmen understand and adjust to the department's various programs, it showed clearly what Reconstruction's priorities were – and what they were not. Baldwin's draft fell into the hands of several Liberal politicians, who were disturbed by what they saw. Was this the reconstruction program they would have to defend in an election? Where were the large ideas and spacious phrases?[26]

Something more was needed, fast. Baldwin and Mackintosh talked over the situation. Because Mackintosh was at loose ends, he volunteered to try his hand at a more comprehensive explanation of the reconstruction program, including the "extensive action" that Howe (and Baldwin) had ignored. Perhaps,

Mackintosh suggested, it could be presented to Parliament and the public as a white paper. It was a novel idea. White papers, general presentations of official policy, were commonplace in Britain, where governments assumed there was a literate public requiring more in the way of information than partisan harangues in the House of Commons. In Canada the government had never operated on such a principle; in Mackintosh's view it was high time that it did.

Mackintosh was in an unusually strong position. An academic economist, he had been heavily involved in the thirties in the debates and studies on Canada's economic crisis. Like many of his friends, Mackintosh thought that the only hope for a rational government in Canada was a strong federal – a strong *national* – government. Like Howe, he believed that the central government had demonstrated that it could handle the job of running a diverse, disunited and disparate country like Canada, but only if it stressed the common, national interests: transportation, foreign trade, defence, communications and the mutual responsibility of the different levels of government. Only the national government could concentrate enough economic power through its control of taxation and its predominance in spending it. This was especially true of a country like Canada, where vast distances and a tiny population made a division of economic authority a wasteful and dangerous luxury. Mackintosh's secular faith was reinforced by new economic doctrine. The teachings of John Maynard Keynes had filtered into the Canadian Finance Department just before and during the war. Deputy Minister Clifford Clark and his economists were familiar with Keynes' views on the desirability of using fiscal measures such as tax relief, subsidy and government public works to offset hard times by putting spending power into the consumer's pockets. Using that power, the government should function as the balance wheel of the economy, skimming off the peaks of prosperity and levelling up the troughs of depression. The white paper gave Mackintosh a chance simultaneously to educate the public and commit the government.[27]

First, of course, he had to win the government's consent, and before that, Howe's. Baldwin's cooperation was readily given. The support of the deputy minister, R. A. C. Henry, was also forthcoming. Then Henry and Mackintosh together set to work on the minister. Howe was suspicious. White papers might be a dangerous innovation, exposing too much and raising false expectations. Eventually, Howe's attitude softened, and Mackintosh received permission to go ahead. Over a weekend he produced the first draft of what became the *White Paper on Employment and Income*.

When Mackintosh's draft reached Howe's desk, the minister was uneasy. He and his officials discussed the matter at length (he sought, in particular, the advice of Henry and Carmichael) and he phoned round to other executives and friends in private business to discover what they thought. Their views tended to reinforce one another. Mackintosh's draft made sense and, with some alterations, it ought to go forward. Before it did, Howe asked for one important change. Mackintosh in his draft spoke of "full employment" as the government's goal. That, said Howe, must go. Full employment was an impossible goal. If the words were taken literally, the government would be a sitting duck. A circumlocution was called for: "a high and stable level of employment." It had less punch, but it was much, much safer. It was safely unoriginal: "a high and stable level of employment" had already been discussed in cabinet in January 1945.[28]

A special cabinet committee composed of Howe, Ilsley and St. Laurent was assigned the duty of assessing the white paper. For the ministers, it meant a turn in Dr. Mackintosh's financial school so that he could expound to them his understanding of the best economic policy. It was not a strict professional exercise. Mackintosh was a past master of the art of presenting the unpalatable to public men. He did not, however, make the mistake of under-estimating their intelligence. In fact, his personal style was remarkably compatible with Howe's: down to earth and generally laconic. He could give quick answers to pointed questions. Mackintosh presented the ministers with a multi-coloured, underlined version of his white paper, to highlight the different kinds of policies it proposed. By the end of a long day of questions and answers, the schoolmaster and his ministerial pupils were satisfied that they understood one another and the paper. The white paper was sent on to cabinet with the ministers' recommendation and was formally approved.[29]

On April 12, 1945, Howe rose in the House of Commons to present the *White Paper on Employment and Income*. He introduced the subject by ticking off the many responsibilities of his department. But to summarize the white paper, he added, "would be an invitation to honourable members to avoid giving study to the document itself. Therefore, I will not attempt such a summary." Each member of Parliament would get his own copy to take away and ponder.[30]

Remarkably, many did. The press gallery picked up the white paper and circulated its proposals to newspaper readers across the country; by the end of April, the document was at least well known, if not well read. It was not entirely Mackintosh's; Howe had added two paragraphs of his own, and the cabinet had fiddled with bits and pieces of the wording. But the central concept had survived. The country somehow received the impression that the cabinet had promised to implement policies which would create and maintain full employment – which in fact it had not done in so many words. Howe publicly congratulated his economist on the "excellent reception" given to his paper.[31]

Howe had good reason to be pleased. The white paper listed all the projects which the departments of Reconstruction and Munitions and Supply were pursuing – Howe's "intensive" program. The basic problem, Mackintosh explained, was to maintain a high level of economic activity, and there Howe's program was certainly helping. To keep the economy moving, the government was promoting Canada's export trade through multilateral tariff reductions and through incentives to exporters via the Export Credits Insurance Act. Canadian contributions to United Nations relief received honourable mention. Even if most importing countries were unable, for the present, to afford Canadian goods, the government was willing to help them with credits until they could.

Next to exports, private investment was the most important stimulus to national income and employment. Industrial reconversion and decontrol would facilitate such investment, and tax credits would, it was hoped, do the rest. Once the war was over, taxes would be reduced as quickly as possible to put money in the hands of investors. Where financing was difficult, the government's new Industrial Development Bank would help out. Where possible, labour and materials were to be released from war enterprises for the satisfaction of deferred consumption. Pensions and family allowance payments would, it was hoped, help keep consumption at a high level.

If the worst should occur, and the economy slid into recession – something neither Mackintosh nor Howe thought likely – the government would supplement the efforts of the private sector with public investment, carefully planned in advance to provide a "shelf" of public projects in every area for every contingency. Naturally, the white paper added, the government's plans for the expansion of aviation, that apple of Howe's eye, would help greatly in providing outlets for public investment. Scientific and industrial research, another of Howe's "intensive" projects, would keep Canadian industry abreast of international developments. Then there followed a list of the other projects dear to Howe's heart: the disposal of crown assets, the settlement of war contracts, and specific regional studies to identify special local needs.

The white paper concluded with a ringing definition of government concern for the economy. The Canadian government officially committed itself to securing "a high and stable level of employment and income, and thereby higher standards of living." It could only be achieved on the largest scale – "a great national objective" – and therefore it must transcend merely local or provincial concerns. It was the watchword of a generation that remembered the futile jurisdictional quarrels of the thirties and the mean-spirited attempts of the federal government and the provinces to shift responsibility for the eonomy from one level to another. The war showed that matters could be managed differently, and better.[32]

The symbol of that management was C. D. Howe. It was utterly appropriate that Howe should be the man to grasp the white paper and to fling it down before the opposition parties. Then, on April 16, 1945, four days after the white paper was tabled, Parliament was dissolved and a general election called for June 11.

CHAPTER THIRTEEN

"The Right Honourable C. D."

O ur best work," Howe wrote to Lord Beaverbrook in August 1943, "will be needed to keep the Government out of the hands of the socialists." On that, both men were firmly agreed. The King government had much to recoup. In an amazing feat of political sleight of hand, it managed to do it. The parliamentary session of 1944 was a brilliant success. Advanced social legislation now burdened the statute books: reconstruction, veterans' re-establishment, family allowances, new housing legislation, incentives for exports, all highly visible and popular.[1]

Late in 1943 Mackenzie King abandoned the wartime political truce, and turned his attention back to his party. It was, he noted, in a sadly neglected state. Its life-blood had been sapped by the non-partisan war effort. Patronage had been cut off and, in some cases, actually turned over to professed Conservatives. Some ministers blamed Howe's controllers and officials who conducted themselves with entire disregard for the damage they were doing to the party in power.

As the party computed its electoral assets, King's eyes turned doubtfully toward Howe. He was one of the two or three most prominent ministers. His standing inside Parliament and with the press was high. He had an obvious, broad public appeal, to Liberals and Conservatives. But could he also attract, or at least not repel, the vast numbers of voters who would be inclined to support the CCF? A partial answer was furnished by Howe's reactions to the government's parliamentary program. He opposed family allowances, but only in the cabinet sanctum. Outside, it was solidarity as usual. As King knew, Howe was even prepared to contemplate extending social security to include more unemployment insurance and health insurance, two items that figured among the possibilities for 1945. Extending social security was not an immediate prospect, however, because provincial consent would be required. King knew that it would not easily be granted; it would be better to postpone the matter until after the next election.

Howe carried heavy political responsibilities. He was senior minister for Ontario, an honour that gave him the burden of fund raising for those ridings (the majority) that needed help from the central party coffers. He was, besides, the regional minister for eastern and northern Ontario, responsible for the care and feeding of the party in over twenty ridings, most of them already Liberal. Howe was determined that they should stay that way, especially in northwestern Ontario, where he drew on the talents and energies of Bill Bennett to supplement his own efforts.[2]

The largest responsibility was for fund-raising. By 1943 it was Howe rather than any other minister who had the closest knowledge of and connections with the business community. He became the Liberals' chief fund-raiser in Toronto – one of the two centres of Liberal finance. The largely autonomous Quebec region drew on Montreal and grudgingly shared the surplus with the rest of the country. The Toronto fund-raiser was, therefore, the chief support and resource for eight provincial organizations, as well as for the national campaign. The arrangement was ratified by the appointment of a trinity of ministers in 1943 to reconstitute the finances of the National Liberal Federation: Gardiner, to look after practical politics and the West; Chubby Power to represent Quebec; and Howe.[3]

Howe's increased importance was recognized in other ways. In May 1944, presumably with King's approval (the Prime Minister was attending a Commonwealth conference in England), Howe and the cabinet selected J. Gordon Fogo, a Nova Scotian lawyer and a partner in Ralston's old firm, to be the chief party organizer at a salary of $15,000 a year. Fogo, who was employed in Munitions and Supply, moved his offices from the Temporary Buildings to a suite on Wellington Street overlooking the Parliament Buildings, and set to work. Eight months later, in January 1945, Fogo was placed in charge of the organization of the election campaign that everyone knew must come within months. Howe's influence in party organization was increasing – something that perturbed more populist Liberals such as Power, who had little liking for the managerial style of Howe and his appointees.[4]

As the deadline for calling an election neared, King cast his eye over his cabinet, shrewdly pinpointing the party's liabilities. First on the list was T. A. Crerar, who, in King's opinion, was long past his prime and a political liability in his home province of Manitoba. Then there was the Secretary of State, Norman McLarty from Windsor, who had compiled an undistinguished record in three successive portfolios. General LaFlèche, brought in in 1942 to help the Liberals in Quebec, was a disaster as a politician and an irritation in cabinet discussions. Power, who was no liability, had resigned amid the conscription crisis, and was licking his wounds on the sidelines. Finally, Angus L. Macdonald resigned to return to provincial politics in Nova Scotia.[5]

King had his eye on a group of younger replacements, members of the parliamentary classes of 1935 and 1940. There were many good men among them, but the most notable was Brooke Claxton, a Montrealer and King's own parliamentary assistant. Claxton was rewarded for his energy and devotion in that thankless job by promotion to Minister of National Health and Welfare in October 1944. Besides organizing the system for distributing the new family allowances, Claxton was to look out for the Liberal party's own health and welfare. King saw in the tall, owlish, young Montrealer the closest thing to a real intellectual in the cabinet, and was reminded of his own reforming convictions – dormant for many years – and his own political sensitivities. Second only to those of his master, Claxton's political instincts were virtually infallible, and Claxton always did what his instinct told him. His appointment was easy. Ian Mackenzie, whom he partially replaced, was shifted over to the new Department of Veterans' Affairs. The real cabinet shuffle was postponed until spring.

The slaughter of the elderly and the incompetent occurred on April 17, 1945, just after the end of the session. King consulted first with his remaining senior colleagues. Howe, when asked his advice, sensibly approved most of King's plans. One of King's choices was a welcome surprise to Howe. Lionel Chevrier was under consideration for the cabinet. Howe's astonishment,

King reflected in his diary, was no doubt owing to a selfish desire to keep his parliamentary assistant. That, in fact, was unlikely. Howe approved Chevrier's promotion, although he warned King that his former assistant would find the Department of Transport a heavy burden. The other appointments were to be expected. Douglas Abbott, Ilsley's assistant and then McNaughton's at National Defence, was appointed to succeed Angus Macdonald in Naval Services; the left-leaning young Windsor politician, Paul Martin, was given McLarty's old job as Secretary of State, and the Roman Catholic doctor from the Ottawa valley, J. J. McCann, became Minister of National War Services, replacing the garrulous LaFlèche.[6]

Howe was gratified by most of the changes. Abbott he knew and admired for his pleasant personality and his parliamentary skills. Chevrier was an able parliamentarian as well as a personal favourite. Martin was already known as a coming man, possibly a future prime minister, and to Howe ambition was a spur to better performance. As for LaFlèche, he was a deadweight, and no loss to the government. It was only too bad that Ian Mackenzie, whose drinking Howe despised, had not joined him in retirement.[7]

The most important new recruit, however, was Claxton. He was an enthusiast for the CBC, an able lawyer in his own right, and a defender of unpopular causes. "[W]hen I entered the cabinet," Claxton later wrote, "I guessed that [Howe] had not been my most active supporter." It was true. As Howe liked to say, describing a circle in the air above his head, "Brooke's mind operates on a very lofty plane." He doubted that Claxton had much aptitude for administration or business, and he may have sensed that his new colleague had not much respect for the intelligence of the average Canadian businessman. But Howe buried his feelings, and he soon found that Claxton was an able and energetic colleague. It was important that the two men got along, for in the campaign of 1945 Claxton became the Liberals' chief tactician while Howe was their quartermaster general.[8]

Fund-raising is among the most private and the most delicate of political activities. Howe, like most of his contemporaries, believed and argued that business, like any other interest group, ought to support its political friends. He reminded his business friends that free enterprise was at stake in the 1945 election, and he expected that they would respond appropriately to his hints. Liberal collectors referred to lists of contractors, but Howe needed no lists. He knew who could afford to contribute, and he no doubt appealed to business's sense of its larger self-interest. But Howe's lists of contracts awarded were printed documents, equally available to Henry Borden and the Conservatives. There is no reason to believe that he mined his wartime business contacts for special party considerations. The technique was simple: Howe approached a potential contributor, whether an individual or a business, with a reminder that the King government and the Liberal party had been good for business – as evidenced by the particular prosperity of the source he was tapping. The party fund-raiser would follow close behind.[9]

"Lunch with Howe," Norman Lambert wrote in his diary on May 16, "who said he was going to Hamilton . . . and wanted someone to follow up fast on his footsteps." In Hamilton Frank Sherman of Dofasco was the contact for "the small fry," as Lambert called them; Howe presumably was after bigger game. Once the money was received, or promised, it went to the party treasurer, Peter Campbell, in Toronto. Campbell, a marine lawyer, knew Howe from the thirties when he was Minister of Transport; in reward for his party services (and in anticipation of more) he was made a senator in 1944.[10]

For Howe, fund-raising was a simple and straightforward business. The party needed money, and he knew men who had money. For Campbell, however, fund-raising occasionally raised the sordid question of rewards. Not all contributors regarded their donations as tokens of public duty, money well spent in a noble cause. If, after the election, they chose to come to Ottawa, it was up to Campbell to get them in to see Howe. But Howe refused to see them, and despite Campbell's pleading, he never budged.

But in 1945 the Howe-Campbell team was new and fresh, and its reputation, in the eyes of contributors, unstained by failure to meet their exaggerated expectations. The sums Howe raised were impressive, but not overwhelming. On May 25 Campbell told Lambert that he had received and disbursed over $700,000 since October 1943. With two weeks to go before the election, Campbell estimated that he would spend over $160,000 more. But Campbell had only $63,000 on hand, and the Liberals were short of cash. In the end, the money was raised, but the hand-to-mouth finale of the Liberal campaign indicated that Howe's canvassing had not produced a cornucopia of business contributions.[11]

In fact, Howe was beaten in the race for funds by his old

Conservative friend Henry Borden. Perhaps businessmen simply thought that the Conservatives had a better chance of defeating the CCF. The simultaneous Ontario election helped mobilize business sentiment around the militantly anti-socialist Conservative George Drew; contributions for the provincial party could easily spill over to its federal counterpart. The record of fund-raising in the 1945 election puts to rest the notion that Howe circulated in business circles with a magic list of contributors made up from munitions contractors. If he had such a list, it worked the wrong kind of magic.[12]

It is indisputable, however, that without Howe's efforts the Liberals would have done a good deal worse, perhaps disastrously so, in both their fund-raising and their campaigning. When it came to raising votes, it became clear that Howe was an equally potent asset. Claxton and the Liberals hired the services of an advertising agency, Cockfield, Brown of Montreal, to popularize the party's message for the voters. As befitted a party headed by Canada's elder statesman, Mackenzie King, his achievements and his principles dominated Liberal advertisements. The party's recent legislative record came next. "LIBERAL POLICIES," one ad trumpeted, "will create post-war OPPORTUNITIES for all." Then came C. D. Howe. "The Liberal Government has the man – the Hon. C. D. Howe – under whose direction Canadians have done a great job in the war, and are ready to do it again in the peace."[13]

Howe crossed the country with his message. He was much in demand, speaking in Halifax, Winnipeg and Vancouver. Even when he stayed in the office, he made news. "Canada's Gasoline Rationing to End Soon," the *Ottawa Journal* headlined on May 25: "Howe Sees Ban Off After Three Months." For a gas-starved, travel-famished electorate, the invitation to resume the national romance with the automobile, courtesy of C. D. Howe, was a tangible sign of the government's good-will and thoughtfulness. On nationwide radio on June 3, Howe repeated the promises of the white paper, though with a slightly different emphasis than his officials were used to: there would be high and stable employment, and in case of difficulty, there would be "a vast program of public undertaking to take up the slack."[14]

Howe left the Lakehead campaign in Bill Bennett's reliable hands. And he expected that all of northern Ontario would be solid for the Liberals, as he had told the Prime Minister the previous autumn. There was no reason to change that estimate.

Because Ontario's provincial election was to be held on June 4, it allowed Charlie Cox to furnish one more embarrassment. Cox had been defeated in the 1943 provincial election; his hold on the provincial Liberals' allegiances was slipping. At the end of April 1945, they jettisoned Cox, choosing instead Major Bert Styffe as their candidate for the provincial election on June 4. Nothing daunted, Cox ran as an independent. When the dust cleared, Cox and Styffe were both beaten and the CCF candidate re-elected. The Liberals took cold comfort in the fact that the combined total for Styffe and Cox outnumbered the CCF's.

Howe's campaign literature bore the heading, "This Man Howe." There was almost no need to explain any more who "this" was; everybody knew, not just in Port Arthur, but all across the country. Howe's personal reputation and his personal political coat-tails were a major asset for his party. Returning to his constituency after a spell of duty in Ottawa, Howe found the signs encouraging. "The electoral campaign is going very well indeed," he wrote to Billy Woodward at the end of May. "I will be surprised if we are not returned with a clear majority." The election, Bennett told Norman Lambert, had been a tonic for his minister: "C. D. H. was enjoying the campaign immensely; a contrast with office work."[15]

Election day, June 11, was no surprise. An hour and fifteen minutes after the polls were closed, Howe was declared elected. He took all but two polls in the city of Port Arthur, and most of the rural polls as well. His Conservative and Labour Progressive (Communist) opponents lost their deposits, while the CCF, though running second, was far behind. Howe's vote, as predicted, was just over half the total votes cast. Results in other ridings of Northern Ontario gave the Liberals every seat.[16]

Every seat would be needed. Across the country the Liberals secured just under 41 per cent of the vote and a bare majority (125 out of 245 seats) in the House of Commons. One hundred and twenty Liberal candidates bit the dust, and among the fallen were the Minister of National Revenue, D. L. MacLaren, the Minister of National Defence, General McNaughton, and the Prime Minister.

Mackenzie King took his own defeat badly, but he was in no danger of losing office as a result of it. After a quick by-election in a safe riding he returned to Parliament, bruised but unbowed. The two defeated ministers, MacLaren and McNaughton, quickly resigned.

The business of government resumed. Returning to the

capital, Howe found that he had become an unwilling member of the cabinet Committee on Dominion-Provincial Relations, preparing the government's program for a dominion-provincial conference scheduled for the first week of August. Reconstruction would be a large and prominent part of the federal government's package, and Howe's selection was natural. Nevertheless, the task was irksome. It was a hot summer, and he was very tired. Constitutional arguments left the Minister of Reconstruction cold. He knew how reconstruction must work, and how it was already working. Grandiose schemes and fine phrases he left to others, except when he found it desirable to deflate them.

In the centralized schemes put before the ministers, Howe's department had responsibility for a large-scale program of public works. Many of its aspects lay within provincial jurisdiction; but the civil servants urged that the provinces surrender their control over such matters in return for central planning and finance. Howe was unimpressed. His objection was not constitutional nor even ideological. Public investment on the scale contemplated by the bureaucrats, he told his colleagues, was simply inconceivable. There were not enough planners, engineers and managers in the country to design and run the huge public works "shelf" which the economists thought necessary to combat depression. If such a vast program were promised, it would interfere with necessary private investment and possibly work against economic recovery. It would be far better to jettison the whole idea of central planning and provide cheap money to municipalities in return for central control of the timing of public works. That might not be particularly desirable, in Howe's opinion, but at least it was possible.[17]

Howe had not reckoned with the certitudes of the government's economists. Control of timing, the acting deputy minister of finance, W. A. Mackintosh, told the ministers, meant control of planning. The government could hardly be expected to spend money on minor local projects without knowing what it was paying for. The central government must have the power to review, and approve, local projects. Despite misgivings, the ministers were swept along. It was decided to offer 20 per cent of the cost of any public project under provincial jurisdiction, provided that a province agreed to register and store its project on the federal "shelf" until Ottawa decided it was needed.

Control over public investment was only part, although a very important part, of Ottawa's reconstruction proposals. Taxation was to remain centrally directed and central control of fiscal policy would give Ottawa more power to offset adverse economic trends. Howe found this idea attractive, perhaps because it promised more certainty in the management of economic conditions across the country, and perhaps because he judged it well within the capacity of the federal government to handle.

When the dominion-provincial conference met in Ottawa on August 6, Howe was in possession of two carefully guarded secrets. The first, as expected, was the federal program for reconstruction. The second was the knowledge that soon, possibly very soon, the war would end. The Americans had just successfully tested an atomic bomb. It would now be dropped on the Japanese. Howe, who was among the handful of Canadians with advance warning, prepared a statement explaining to the Canadian people what the atomic bomb was. As the opening session of the conference droned on, he received word that the bomb had been dropped. Howe then passed the news on to King, who announced it to the dumbfounded provincial premiers.[18]

The dropping of the bomb and the surrender of Japan drove the news of the dominion-provincial conference off Canadian front pages. It was just as well, for the August meetings were inconclusive. After a few bursts of oratory, the provinces retired to study the federal proposals. Special committees met through the winter to revise the federal package to meet provincial demands, especially those from Ontario. That province's Conservative premier, George Drew, cherished a deep mistrust of federal encroachments on Ontario's riches. He combined the mistrust with a loathing of Mackenzie King and all his works. Few of King's ministers had escaped tangling with Drew who, as a militia colonel, also claimed to be an expert on armaments, on the army, and on war in general. Drew was not gentle with Howe, and Howe returned the compliment, with interest. "I never heard such a misstatement in my life," Howe growled, after one particularly outrageous Drew sally during the conference.[19]

It was Drew, followed by Maurice Duplessis of Quebec, who finally derailed the dominion-provincial conference on reconstruction. At the last session in April, Drew "literally boomed defiance,'' the British High Commission reported to London. In ''a blustering and even at times truculent speech'' Drew told his fellow premiers and the federal ministers that Ontario would never surrender its rights to any central authority. Drew conveyed, accurately enough, the impression that Ontario would ''make few concessions to meet the general interest,'' certainly not as long as the detested Liberals stayed in power. The conference broke up in confusion.[20]

The failure to reach agreement on reconstruction did not look quite so serious by the spring of 1946 as the economists had predicted. Howe disbanded his reconstruction councils but otherwise proceeded as before. The end of the war produced a decline in production and a rise in unemployment. But unemployment did not rise very much (3 per cent in December), nor did production fall very far. Wartime wages did not collapse, as the unions feared and some employers hoped. A rash of strikes reminded business that labour was both scarce and militant; as controls on prices were removed and the effects of price rises in the United States were felt, inflation succeeded unemployment as the most prominent public issue.

Howe was not surprised. ''I am convinced,'' he wrote in September 1945, ''that there are jobs for all, which is all that concerns me.'' Some labour leaders did not find Howe's laissez-faire attitude reassuring. War contracts were cancelled as soon as hostilities ended, and war plants were closed. Attempts by Carl Goldenberg to bring Howe and labour leaders closer together through government-sponsored labour committees did not produce a meeting of minds. Howe insisted on treating labour's fears of large-scale unemployment as irrational. ''There's plenty of employment in this country,'' he told a Trades and Labor Congress delegation in August. There was no need to keep government plants operating in order to prevent a non-existent danger. When a group of Research Enterprises Limited employees, laid off at the end of the war, caught up with the minister on a golf course near Toronto, Howe put his attitude to them quickly and succinctly: ''R.E.L.,'' he is quoted as saying, ''was a war-time plant. The war is through, the Plant is through and your Union . . . what happens to your Union is up to you. Get the hell off the course.''[21]

Most industry was released from control by the fall of 1945. The exceptions, however, were large and critical: steel, coal and building materials. There was not, Howe learned, enough steel to go around. Leaving distribution to the market would create

206

shortages in essential production; so steel continued to go where controllers sent it, on subsidized transportation where necessary. Coal was in an even worse situation. Shortages of anthracite coal from the United States kept fuel under strict controls for several years as officials wrestled with the problem of declining production in Canadian coalfields. Year after year Howe patiently explained to maritime MP's that their region produced neither enough coal, nor the right kind for most purposes. A declining labour force in the coalfields only made matters worse.

The greatest problems were in construction. In 1943 Howe had assured his fellow engineer John Stirling that no "security brigade" would be necessary to rescue construction from a slump. Howe's prediction considerably understated the situation. Far from there being excess capacity, everything was in shortage: lumber, plumbing supplies, bricks, nails, electrical fixtures. Canada's veterans were coming home to a country which promised and gave them jobs, an education, family allowances and government mortgages. Thousands married and started families. There was only one flaw: there was nowhere to live.[22]

Responsibility for housing was divided among several federal agencies. During the war, Howe set up a crown company, Wartime Housing Limited, to build accommodation for war workers. Then, in 1944, the government revised the National Housing Act to provide loans for housing as a prelude to reconstruction; the Finance Department administered the Act. The National Housing Act brought the possibility of home ownership within the reach of the middle and lower-middle classes, who could now qualify for mortgages for the first time. But what they could afford they could not buy.

While Finance provided mortgages, the Reconstruction Department handled controls over building materials, and Veterans' Affairs looked after veterans' housing. Wartime Housing Limited was still flourishing, and still building houses. In a final complication, the federal government was not, strictly speaking, responsible for housing and urban development: that was the domain of the provinces. It was, Howe explained to Parliament, only because the government had promised housing for veterans that Ottawa was still involved in the whole mess. Meanwhile, officials in competing departments attacked one another in private, and through press leaks.

The first step in finding a solution to the country's housing shortage was to untangle the divided jurisdictions on the subject. The federal side was easy. Howe and Ilsley met to discuss a developing feud between officials in Reconstruction and those in Finance over housing, and devised an amicable solution. There would be a new housing agency, Central Mortgage and Housing Corporation (CMHC), presided over by a Finance Department official, David Mansur. The corporation was then turned over to Howe – a welcome relief for the overburdened Ilsley, because now the opposition's fire would be concentrated on Howe.[23]

"I am completely frustrated by shortages," Howe groused in the spring of 1946. "Every industry in Canada is trying to expand and everyone wants a house, but no one can get materials; for this I seem to be the goat." In 1946 sixty thousand new homes were built, but one hundred thousand new families were established. Howe hoped for a solution when CMHC opened its doors on January 1, 1947; he optimistically promised that in 1947 there would be eighty thousand new homes in Canada. The real total, seventy-one thousand, was creditable, but embarrassingly short of the official mark.[24]

The abuse heaped on Howe as a consequence was a novel experience. Criticism in Parliament was constant. Every member had a housing crisis in his own constituency, and each and every politician in the country seemed anxious to tell the Minister of Reconstruction (after January 1, 1946, the Minister of Reconstruction and Supply) about it. No matter how much progress was made, individual cases were always cropping up to show that the government had neglected its responsibilities, ignored local needs, or callously disregarded the housing needs of the young, the middle-aged, or the elderly.

Caustic attacks on the government's war surplus disposal also took up Parliament's attention. Howe's surplus disposal policy looked fine in the abstract; it was the envy of the Americans, who tried to imitate it. But the opposition hammered away at two simple facts: the government had spent a lot of money on equipment during the war; it was selling it off for a good deal less, when it wasn't squandering it altogether. Two years after the war's end, Howe was patiently (and sometimes not so patiently) explaining that the value of an obsolete fighter plane in peacetime was very close to nil. *Maclean's* magazine in the summer of 1946 gave sensational publicity to charges of favouritism, neglect and incompetence, and that did not lighten Howe's burden. Despite minor difficulties, he told Parliament, he was pleased at the War Assets' Corporation performance: in 1946 they sold off equipment at the rate of $20 million a month, and before they were through he hoped that $450 millions would be realized from the sales of crown assets.[25]

The quibbling debates, the detailed questions and answers were a marked contrast with the spacious days of the war. It was a salutary reintroduction to peacetime politics, but for Howe there was little to do except fret. Parliament, and politics, were getting on his nerves. There were diversions, of course. In the fall of 1945 he led a Canadian delegation to an aviation conference with the British and Americans in Bermuda. He hoped that it would relax him, but when the minister returned to Ottawa his staff was alarmed: Howe's face was grey from exhaustion. The winter of 1945-46 was punctuated by colds, flu and bad temper. Another vacation, this time in Cuba, did little good. It was a sour Christmas.[26]

What Howe heard on New Year's Day made it even sourer. In 1945 there were five living Canadian "Right Honourables," members of the British Privy Council. The title was awarded only for great political distinction, conferring prestige and status in a country that had done away with other titles. King was the only serving politician to be "Right Honourable," but in the past other ministers had, from time to time, acquired the honour. In 1945 the British government asked King if he had any nominations. "Undoubtedly," King replied, he would suggest Ilsley, Minister of Finance, and St. Laurent, Minister of Justice. Malcolm MacDonald agreed with King, and passed on the advice. The good news was announced on New Year's Day, 1946. When Howe returned, tired and irritable from Cuba, his friends commiserated with him on his absence from the list.[27]

He immediately requested an interview with the Prime Minister; it took place on January 15. It was not, King recorded in his diary, a happy occasion. Howe felt slighted, he told his leader, that his war service was not appreciated; he, and not St. Laurent or Ilsley, had "carried the heaviest load in the war effort." St. Laurent had only entered the cabinet in 1941. It was obviously time to go, Howe said; he was very tired "and the work of the office irritated him." That was true enough, as King could see. The immediate solution was obvious. Instead of resigning, Howe should go off on another vacation. After all, King later observed, "His loss would be a real one to the Ministry."[28]

Howe always found it difficult to resist King's blandishments.

Instead of resigning, he went back to his office to brood. It was there that Jack Pickersgill, King's principal assistant, found him. Pickersgill had been sent to make peace, and to present King's elaborate excuses. The British Privy Councillorship was none of King's doing; it was all British Prime Minister Attlee's idea; King was blameless. Howe glared at Pickersgill. "Jack," he said finally, "that's a God-damn lie." That ended the matter, but only as far as Howe personally was concerned. "I admit," Howe incautiously told one of his friends, "I really would have liked that degree!"[29]

King and Howe went their separate ways, each privately fuming. Unluckily, a commemorative banquet for officers of Munitions and Supply was scheduled some days later. Howe was to be the guest of honour. King, who was asked to attend, refused; he did not, at the best of times, feel at home with Howe's boys. Now he was doubly annoyed by Howe's disregard for his explanations. Howe's dinner therefore unfolded without the presence of the Prime Minister. It was a success anyway, and it was reported as such in the papers – more coals heaped on King's conscience. But when the two men met the next day at a cabinet meeting, the topic was avoided, by mutual consent.[30]

Howe's mood remained bleak. He dipped into a novel, *The Late George Apley*, about social recognition in far-away Boston, pondered his own lack of recognition, and told King that he thought he should drop out of politics to become president of Trans-Canada Airlines. Despite their quarrels, King still thought Howe irreplaceable. Finally Howe decided to take a proper vacation and to drop the subject until he returned. Alice, children and staff unanimously approved: the vacation must be immediate. With Alice and with Tommy Bryson, his assistant secretary, in tow, Howe chugged out of Ottawa by train on February 15 for a golfing vacation in Victoria.[31]

He returned, relaxed, on St. Patrick's Day. Golf and sea air had worked wonders; Howe could face work again. The office also relaxed. Things were back to normal. Or nearly so: the marks of the war and the winter were permanent. "His work at Ottawa has taken years off his life," one of his friends commented in 1947. "His hair is white, his shoulders are stooped."[32]

While Howe was growing visibly older, his family was growing up. Bill, back from the wars, decided to stay in the navy. When the Howes went west for their winter vacation, it was partly to see Bill, now stationed on the Pacific coast. For the girls there were marriages. Elisabeth went first. She had met a young engineering student, Bob Stedman. The two were to be married in the summer of 1946, and Howe had to nerve himself to visit the parish church – his first religious exposure in years. "I do, I do, I do," he mumbled as he and Elisabeth got in the car. "Just rehearsing my lines." Barbara was next, in December: she married Lieutenant John Stewart, of the navy. This time Mackenzie King was the honoured guest, and made "brief remarks" for the happy occasion. "The whole affair was exceedingly pleasant," wrote the Prime Minister, ordinarily a connoisseur of funerals.[33]

King and Howe had finally resolved their ceremonial dispute; in June Howe became a Right Honourable member of His Majesty's British Privy Council. King, Ilsley and St. Laurent rejoiced; it was Jimmy Gardiner's turn to resent the obvious slight to his agricultural services. Ian Mackenzie, senior to all of them in cabinet, had threatened to resign in January, and again tendered his resignation. There was only one solution: two more British Privy Councillorships in the 1947 New Year's honours list. There it ended. The distinction was thereafter reserved for prime ministers and chief justices; eventually it was moved to Canada and became a purely domestic affair.

Howe's friends were pleased. "Better late than never," Grattan O'Leary wrote in the *Ottawa Journal* – a notable compliment from the Conservative sage. In 1947 it was the Americans' turn: the Medal of Merit, an event which made the hometown paper in Waltham.[34]

Christmas 1946 also brought cabinet changes. Ilsley, at the end of his tether after six years of Finance, moved to the more serene atmosphere of Justice. Abbott moved from National Defence to Finance, and Claxton from Health and Welfare to National Defence. Paul Martin became Minister of National Health and Welfare. Another sign of the times: Mackenzie King abandoned one of his portfolios, External Affairs, and turned it over to Louis St. Laurent. He was, he told himself, too busy to give it the attention it deserved. He was also, as he and his colleagues knew, too old and too tired. King was now within measurable distance of retiring. Who would succeed him?

There was one change King did not make in the cabinet shuffle: Howe stayed at Reconstruction. It was dull work, he wrote to Frank Covert, a former Munitions and Supply executive who had returned to legal practice in Halifax. It was, however, bearable as long as some of his old friends stayed on. But they were filtering away. R. A. C. Henry went first, and with him Harry Carmichael, his reconversion job done. Henry's heart condition and Carmichael's ulcers were permanent souvenirs of wartime service. To replace Henry, Howe called on his man in charge of Victory Aircraft, V. W. (Bill) Scully, who had just moved to Ottawa to become vice-president of the National Research Council. Scully was a dark, powerfully built Irishman who before the war had been the protégé of Colonel Lockhart Gordon, dean of Toronto's accounting fraternity. C. J. Mackenzie, who had expected Scully to report for work, was surprised to get a call informing him that Scully had another job entirely. Howe knew that Scully had an excellent production record; but it was Scully's tough and decisive character that counted. In any case, Scully, as an accountant, was heaven-sent to clear up the backlog of contract renegotiations and terminations left over from the war.[35]

There was little, apart from parliamentary business, that Scully could not handle by himself. The department's staff list shrank. In June 1946 it was over 2,000; in December it was 750; by March 1947 it reached 538. The conversion of industry, Howe told Arnold Heeney, the cabinet secretary, was "nearly completed." Twenty-two crown corporations had been wound up, and more were in their final stages. Reconstruction kept churning out its economic surveys, but these told Howe what he already knew: the economy was booming. It was, Howe decided, time to move on. "I understand," a worried Arnold Heeney reported to King, "that [Howe] has also given instructions to his departmental officials to have matters so arranged that, over the next few months, the whole department could be wound up . . . should the government so desire, and remaining functions transferred to other departments."[36]

Not everything was dismantled. Howe kept TCA, of course, and to it he added a new favourite: his wartime crown corporation, Polymer. The company was a roaring success; even after the rubber-producing regions of Asia were liberated from the Japanese, Polymer was still able to compete. American and British attempts to get Howe to sell out or shut down were unavailing: Polymer would be sold for a good price, if it was sold at all; in the meantime it would make a profit.[37]

The news from another crown corporation, Eldorado, was

not as pleasant. In order to meet its wartime delivery commitments, Eldorado had mined most of its high-grade ores. With the decline in the grade, there had been a substantial increase in production costs and this was not reflected in Eldorado's current contract with the Manhattan project.* As a consequence, the company was encountering heavy losses. There was also some evidence that the company had incurred losses as a result of a sales agency agreement. While the management of the company had been kept in place following the government's acquisition of control in 1942, Howe decided that the time had come for new management. He asked Bill Bennett to take on this assignment although at the time Bennett had made plans to leave Ottawa at the end of 1945. As Howe knew, Bennett was tough and able. He became vice-president of Eldorado in 1946 and president in 1947. His instructions were to put the company on a sound business footing.[38]

The contract with the Manhattan project was renegotiated and the problems relating to the sales agency agreement were resolved satisfactorily. While this cleared up Eldorado's current financial difficulties, the company was still faced with the prospect of closing its mine at Port Radium following the completion of deliveries on its wartime contracts.

The situation changed almost overnight with the rejection by the USSR of the U.S. proposal for the international control of atomic weapons which was submitted to the United Nations in late 1946. The United States decided to launch a large-scale program for the production of atomic weapons, and on Howe's recommendation, the government agreed to participate in that program by supplying uranium. In 1947 Eldorado began an extensive exploration program which resulted in the discovery of a new mine in northern Saskatchewan. In 1948 Howe announced that the government would purchase uranium produced by other mining companies and that Eldorado would be its agent for this purpose. The arrangement with the United States provided that the U.S. Atomic Energy Commission would contract with Eldorado for the purchase of its own production and any other uranium that might be purchased by Eldorado from other producers. Bennett was able to develop with the Atomic Energy Commission a pricing formula which guaranteed a full return of total investment plus a substantial profit over the five-year life

* The American agency which manufactured the first atomic bomb.

of its own contracts and those entered into with other mining companies. This was the beginning of the rapid build-up of the domestic uranium industry which occurred in the mid-1950s.[39]

Under the direction of C. J. Mackenzie, Canada's other program in atomic energy – the development of a nuclear reactor technology – was well advanced by the war's end. The first Canadian nuclear reactor, the NRX, located at Chalk River, was commissioned in 1947. The successful operation of this reactor proved beyond question that the technology developed in Canada offered good promise for the development of nuclear power at an acceptable cost. This became the principal objective of the postwar program at Chalk River. Fortunately, Mackenzie was able to secure the services of W. B. Lewis, one of England's outstanding nuclear physicists, as scientific director of the project. Like TCA, atomic energy became a Howe trademark, a program he took with him from department to department. The next move would, he hoped, be very soon.[40]

King was not pleased at the prospect of moving Howe. When Howe came to see him in February 1947 and told him that his department could very well be wound up by the end of March, King put him off. "I said that if he was thinking of some other Dept. to let me know," he wrote. "I hoped he would stay on where he was."[41]

The year had begun with an event that echoed on for years afterward, and helped make Howe's pro-American reputation. Howe brought to the cabinet a proposal to sell one of the government's surplus factories. During the war, the government had constructed an aircraft plant at Cartierville, near Montreal. It later turned the operation of the plant over to a group of its executives who incorporated themselves as Canadair Limited. When its production program was cancelled at the end of 1944, Howe made an arrangement with Douglas Aircraft of the United States and Rolls Royce of Britain to produce a new plane using designs from each: the DC-4 airplane and the Merlin engine. The hybrid was called the North Star. The North Star, efficient in flight and economical over distances, but deafening and teeth-rattling for its passengers, put Canada and Canadair on the aviation map. Then, in 1947, the Electric Boat Company, an American company, bought Canadair; it followed this up with an offer to lease the Cartierville plant from the government.

The company agreed to invest $2 million immediately in

Canadair, and to continue producing the North Star. These were then to be bought by the RCAF and TCA. Howe, in presenting the scheme to the cabinet, recommended that the government take the Electric Boat Company's offer. The sale made sense to him. It brought a major aircraft company to Canada, and in addition Canada got continuing jobs and access to American technology. The Canadian government would not have to pay in order to duplicate what the Americans were already doing. In any case, as Howe told the cabinet, the government could not run the plant indefinitely on faith: there were no buyers for the planes Canadair was making. The sale was announced, and explained, to Parliament on March 20, 1947.[42]

Howe was back in form. In February he flew to Vancouver to sort out a housing problem that baffled his officials. In half an hour, the minister and Vancouver's aldermen reached an agreement. Next, anticipating a coal shortage, Howe imported ten million tons just before an American coal strike. Then, when a lack of shipping threatened to disrupt Canada's immigration program in the summer of 1947, Howe agreed to go to Europe and examine matters at first hand.[43]

Howe flew to Europe in one of the new North Stars. In London, he attended the formal betrothal of Princess Elizabeth to Philip Mountbatten; as an Imperial Privy Councillor his formal assent to the marriage was requested. Howe toured around England, visited old friends from the war – largely Tories who were only too happy to let him know at first hand about the performance of Britain's postwar Labour government. Labour was not doing at all well, they told him. Initiative was flagging under state control. But if conditions in Britain were grim at least everyone had food and shelter. The continent was worse.[44]

Knowing that Germany had been devastated in the last stages of the war, Howe's party landed at Frankfurt, headquarters of the American occupation zone. From their undamaged hotel outside the city, the Canadian group then drove into Frankfurt. It was like visiting the surface of the moon. "Life in the city," one of Howe's party reported, "scarcely seems to move." There were no cars except those of the American army, and almost no open shops. The refugee camps the Canadians visited were orderly and clean but apathetic and depressing. They were packed with people from all over eastern and central Europe who would go to Canada if they could, and if the government would let them. Howe remained silent during the tour. The refugees had nothing to do but wait in their cheerless barracks. Human dignity was the most desperately needed commodity, and the most frequent casualty of camp life. The meaning of refugee life was brought home in one camp, where the American camp director was used to tours. The commandant barged ahead, showing off barracks as though they were barns, poking and sneering at his charges. Howe waited until they returned to the camp office. Then he dressed down the startled official. "Never do that again," he snapped, then turned and left.[45]

It was a sobering experience, and Howe returned to Canada shaken. It helped that Canada could liberalize its immigration laws and admit refugees, but that was a drop in the bucket. Europe obviously had a very long way to go before recovery was complete – if it could ever be. Hopes for the restoration of a normal world were sheer folly for the foreseeable future. Attempts by the United States and Canada to shore up the economies of western Europe had been inadequate and ineffective. Howe had supported Canadian loans to Britain and to Europe; like other ministers he underestimated the damage the war had done to Europe's economy. It was now clear that whatever Canada could do, or had done, was not enough.

It was Canada's turn to feel the pinch. In 1946 Canada owned over $1.6 billion in reserves of American currency and gold. Over the next two years, Canadians spent freely in the United States: capital goods needed to repair the wear and tear of the war, new machine tools for new factories, and scarce luxuries. At the same time, they could not sell their own goods to Europe, except through credits furnished by the government. These credits in their turn helped to draw down Canadian reserves of American currency. By November 1947 Canada's foreign exchange reserves were down to less than $500 million.[46]

The slowness of Britain's recovery narrowed Canadian trade options. Despite the successful conclusion of a series of agreements at Geneva (collectively known as the General Agreement on Tariffs and Trade, or GATT) in November 1947, it was impossible to benefit from them as long as the world was divided into hard currencies (those interchangeable with the American dollar) and soft (those that were not). Until the European economies recovered, GATT would remain a virtually dead letter. If Britain's and Europe's recovery were prolonged, there was no hope of using a trade surplus with overseas countries to balance Canada's trade deficit with the United States.

It was therefore to the specific issue of trade and economic relations with the United States that Canadian ministers and officials turned their attention in 1947. Canada's trade deficit could not be allowed to grow. After the cabinet received the joyful news of an imminent agreement at Geneva, they were confronted with Finance Minister Abbott's report on the desperate position of Canada's foreign-exchange reserves, and the measures he proposed to adopt to cope with the crisis. The cabinet agreed reluctantly to Abbott's proposals. The Prime Minister then departed for England where, on November 17, he broadcast a speech announcing the successful conclusion of the GATT agreements. As soon as King finished speaking, Canadian radio listeners were treated to a second broadcast by Abbott announcing immediate restrictions on imports from the United States. Canadian imports from that country were divided into three categories. Luxury imports were banned outright, while certain consumer goods were to be restricted or heavily taxed. Essential imports would still be permitted, in order not to cripple Canadian industry and to allow industrial development to go forward. It was hoped that watching "imports today would save American dollars tomorrow." It was natural to place the new import controls in the hands of the Minister of Reconstruction and Supply who, more than anyone else, was familiar with the needs of Canadian industry. To meet the emergency, Howe's discretionary authority was broadly defined. Three days after controls were announced Howe informed a radio audience that the controls would not last long; in one of his famous bursts of optimism, he forecast their disappearance "in a matter of months."[47]

Though Howe seemed the natural choice to direct import control, his selection was not automatic. King was reluctant to make the choice. Howe's experience, of course, counted for much and so did his restlessness in the barren Reconstruction portfolio. But the key consideration had little to do with either of these factors. Some months earlier Howe had discussed political prospects with St. Laurent, whom King was pressing to stay in politics and seek the Liberal leadership in succession to himself. Howe urged St. Laurent to stay, and added that if he did, he too would remain. St. Laurent in turn asked King whether he could not do something for Howe, such as giving

217

him the direction of industrial development along with control over natural resources. King agreed in principle; but as he had told Howe in the spring, it was a question of finding the right department to engage his minister's talents. And so the question was postponed, until the foreign-exchange crisis forced King's hand.

At the root of King's reluctance to transfer Howe was a distrust of his minister's political style. It was not that Howe was not energetic, dynamic or effective – King knew that he was all three – but that he tended to concentrate power in his own hands. If King was worried, the opposition was furious. When the emergency import controls came up for debate in Parliament on December 16, King secretly sympathized with the Conservatives' suggestion that Howe's new array of powers was far too sweeping. Howe alone had a veto over the importation of a vast range of commodities; in effect, he had the right to decide whether individual companies would flourish or perish. J. M. Macdonnell of the Conservatives stressed this point when, in a long-remembered phrase, he dubbed Howe "our new dictator." Taunted by Howe, who was outraged at the insinuation that he would misuse his authority, Macdonnell pressed his attack:

> The Minister of Reconstruction and Supply is quite a conundrum to me, because I think he believes in energy, private initiative and all that kind of thing. What I am troubled about is that I think he still believes far more in his own personal power. . . . The Minister got his training in wartime, and I do not believe that kind of mentality is necessarily good for this kind of job.

Howe replied the next day. There could be, he told the House, no question of the urgency of the situation or the necessity for drastic measures of the kind he had outlined. Where urgency and necessity combined, it was in the public interest to take speedy action. With a wealth of examples, Howe appealed to the wartime spirit to carry the program to success. His speech had considerable effect, but it did not defuse the charge that he was "our dictator."[48]

Swallowing his mistrust of Howe's political ineptness, King finally gave his minister all he wanted. Early in January 1948 he reluctantly informed James MacKinnon, the Minister of Trade and Commerce, that he must move over and make room for Howe. When MacKinnon returned from his interview with the

Prime Minister, one of his staff tried to console him: "At least," one said, "he can't have made you Minister of Fisheries." MacKinnon, from the land-locked province of Alberta, groaned: "That's exactly what he's made me." Howe became Minister of Trade and Commerce on January 19, 1948. At the same time Ian Mackenzie, Howe's *bête noire* in the cabinet, departed for the quieter atmosphere of the Senate.[49]

King's prolonged reluctance to make the appointment betokened a mistrust not only of Howe's political style but also of his political judgment. From late 1947 King, Abbott, St. Laurent and Howe shared a secret: negotiations were being conducted between Canadian and American officials on the perennial problem of Canadian trade relations with the United States. Early in 1948 a bold solution was suggested: why not solve the problem permanently by abolishing the customs frontier between the two countries? Each country would then admit the other's goods free of duty. The ministers, studying the civil servants' reports, were intrigued. Even King was initially enchanted with such a simple, bold policy.

The Prime Minister quickly had second thoughts. Commercial union with the United States had defeated the Liberal party twice in his lifetime, in 1891 and 1911. Nor was King certain that commercial union would be strictly commercial. If Canada's economic sovereignty were compromised by a customs union with the Americans, what freedom of action would be left in other spheres? King concluded that no reciprocity policy could be entertained.

In the middle of April, the Americans were suddenly informed that reciprocity with Canada had been indefinitely postponed. To the Americans it seemed a curious decision, since Canada's economic difficulties had not noticeably diminished. When a Canadian minister visited Washington soon after King's refusal to proceed, he was naturally asked for an explanation of this strange turn of events. The minister happened to be Howe. After the American Under-Secretary of State, Robert Lovett, raised the subject, Howe observed that "the responsible ministers in Ottawa were still greatly attracted by the proposals and would be prepared to conclude an agreement on this basis when our domestic considerations made this possible."[50]

In Howe's opinion there was no sense in pursuing the matter until King retired. At that time the new Liberal government, presumably under St. Laurent, could take up the issue and bring negotiations to fruition early in the new year of 1949. Reciprocity would then be the issue on which the Liberals could appeal to the people. Howe knew that this could well be unpopular, but opposition would be silenced if another clause were added to the reciprocity agreement, inviting the United Kingdom to join. As was customary, minutes of the conversation were drafted by Hume Wrong, the Canadian ambassador to the United States, and were forwarded to the under secretary in Ottawa, Lester Pearson.

Pearson was delighted. He supported the reciprocity project, and was glad to learn that it was not dead as far as one powerful minister was concerned. He immediately sent Howe's remarks on to King with the comment that he found them "very satisfactory." Mackenzie King did not. He had, he believed, laid down a definitive policy: there would be no reciprocity with the United States, now or in the future. Nor did he enjoy the intimation that his colleagues were only bearing with him until his retirement. He summoned Howe to his office to explain himself. The Prime Minister was gratified to learn that Wrong's minutes were not, after all, completely accurate. There had been no commitment.

King accepted Howe's denial because, as he told his diary, "in matters of this kind, Howe is almost an innocent abroad." What Howe was after, the Prime Minister shrewdly guessed, was export of Canadian manufactured goods to the United States, an idea that King found "absurd." Absurd or not, King made sure that the Americans knew that Howe's musings on reciprocity were not to be taken at face value. He instructed Pearson, who instructed Wrong, that the official version of the Howe-Lovett conversation be amended to convey the true intentions of the Canadian government: no reciprocity.[51]

Howe accepted King's rebuke because he did not expect the Prime Minister would be around long enough to make his prejudices count. Howe was convinced that Canadian industry would do well if allowed to enter the vast American market; it had flourished during the war and there was no good reason why it should not prosper under free trade with the United States. If the reciprocity agreement could be revived after King was gone, well and good: it was a good idea, if it were politically saleable.

King announced his approaching retirement in January. A Liberal convention was scheduled to take place in Ottawa in the first week of August 1948, the twenty-ninth anniversary of Mackenzie King's election to the Liberal leadership.

There were only two serious candidates, Louis St. Laurent and Jimmy Gardiner. Chubby Power decided late in the day to throw his hat in the ring, but apart from Sir James Dunn, who was annoyed at Howe's control program and hoped to strike a blow at him through Power, he had no significant supporters. Power marvelled at the naïveté of the rich man who imagined that an outcast cabinet minister could actually rally enough votes to overcome the candidate supported by the Prime Minister and by every cabinet minister except Gardiner.

That candidate was Louis St. Laurent. He was King's choice, and Howe's as well. King's regard for St. Laurent was natural enough. He appreciated St. Laurent's competence and intelligence as a minister, and he was grateful for the Minister of External Affairs' loyalty to party and country in the dark hours of the 1944 conscription crisis, when St. Laurent had agreed to conscription rather than risk the break-up of the government. St. Laurent, he hoped, was a new Laurier who would repair, symbolically, the rifts between French and English Canada. His selection would atone for the English Liberals' disloyalty to Laurier thirty years before.

Howe's admiration for St. Laurent was less complex. He had no prejudices against French Canadians, and he dismissed as unworthy arguments that St. Laurent's Frenchness or Catholicism were disqualifications for leading the party. It was true that St. Laurent was a lawyer – not Howe's favourite profession – but he was quick in thought, and decisive in action, a different kind of lawyer from the minutia-ridden, agonizing Ralston. As Howe learned during the war, his own right-wing views and those of St. Laurent on social and economic policy coincided more often than not. When they did not, he was prepared to concede that St. Laurent had reason on his side.

Howe put his political influence at St. Laurent's service. Behind him were all the Ontario ministers except Paul Martin, whose isolated base in Windsor gave him a certain independence. Martin's followers launched an unauthorized boomlet for Windsor's hero, but it accomplished little except noise and confusion. Each of the Ontario ministers, a Manitoba MP, Ralph Maybank, observed, "has special reasons for backing Howe" in whatever choice he made. Over the years, Howe had recommended first one, and then another of his colleagues for office; Humphrey Mitchell, Minister of Labour, and Lionel Chevrier, Minister of Transport, were especially close allies. "All Ottawa," Maybank continued, "is full of people who owe their places to him. Also there is a large number of people around the country whom he has done favors."[52]

Howe cashed in the favours for St. Laurent. St. Laurent was "generally accepted as successor to Mr. King," Howe wrote to Senator Armand Daigle, the Liberal fund-raiser in Montreal. Senator McKeen, Daigle's British Columbia counterpart, helped on the west coast. Howe's domination of the Ontario provincial Liberals helped as well. In April 1948 Maybank commented that Howe was effectively St. Laurent's campaign manager. Gardiner, against whom most of Howe's efforts were concentrated, nevertheless stated afterward that Howe was "absolutely fair about the whole thing."

Mackenzie King was not. Nothing in his political life was ever left to chance, and he was determined that this, the last act, should proceed exactly as ordained. Accordingly, King called in the ministers supporting St. Laurent and informed them that they were to be actors in a political charade he had devised. They were to be nominated for the leadership, and then decline it. And so Howe, St. Laurent's campaign manager, found his name put in nomination before the convention so that he could later withdraw because of his colleague's superior qualifications.[53]

Although one observer found the Liberal convention "singularly dignified and almost dull" compared to the lively American variant, for Howe it was exhilarating. Some delegates found it remarkable that it was the exuberant Howe who shepherded a bewildered and uncomfortable St. Laurent from hotel to hotel to meet his potential supporters. As far as Howe was concerned, it was a splendid chance to socialize, make friends and win votes. This was politics and business as he always practised them.[54]

The great day, the opening of the first national Liberal convention since 1919, was set for August 5. As in 1919, it took place in the Coliseum, Ottawa's cow palace. Outside in the parking lot, the Liberal dignitaries lined up behind their leader and at a signal marched, single file, into the auditorium. The assembled faithful rose and cheered, and business got under way. Mackenzie King made a moving farewell to his political legions. Some minor disputes broke out over the platform, and the Young Liberals threatened to stage a public revolt. Their incipient disturbance was hushed in the overwhelming atmosphere of loyalty and propriety. St. Laurent was elected by 848 votes to Gardiner's 323 and Power's 56. Howe, who would have resigned rather than serve under anyone but St. Laurent, went home happy.[55]

CHAPTER FOURTEEN

Minister of Trade and Commerce

On the afternoon of Monday, November 15, 1948, Prime Minister Louis St. Laurent took the oath of office. The rest of the cabinet, and Mackenzie King, watched approvingly. They were mostly old faces: Gardiner in Agriculture, Claxton at National Defence, Abbott at Finance, Chevrier at Transport, and Martin in National Health and Welfare. As befitted a new administration, however, there were some new men as well. Lester Pearson, who became Minister of External Affairs in the last days of the King government, naturally stayed on. There was a new Minister of Justice, Stuart Garson, the former premier of Manitoba, replacing J. L. Ilsley who had retired to private practice. Garson had a national reputation for moderation and statesmanship based on his performance at dominion-provincial conferences. The third and least prominent of the new ministers was Robert Winters, the young member for Queen's-Lunenburg in Nova Scotia.

Winters was an engineer, educated at MIT; people who listened to his flat, down-East accent were reminded of that other MIT graduate, C. D. Howe. Howe liked Winters, and had sponsored his promotion to the cabinet. There were those who thought that the parallel with Howe had occurred to Winters: there is no question that he had Howe's ambition but most colleagues thought he lacked the talent.

Following the ceremony the cabinet departed for the Privy Council chamber in the East Block, leaving behind their former chief. The old leader of the herd, as Claxton called him, entered semi-retirement as a private member of Parliament. Two years later, in 1950, he died.

When the cabinet seated itself around the table it was C. D. Howe who sat on the Prime Minister's right hand. Other members of the cabinet, gazing at the two of them, found the association of the scholarly Quebec corporation lawyer and the Port Arthur engineer peculiarly appropriate. St. Laurent, with his quality for quickly mastering the information set before him and his faculty for making quick decisions, appealed to Howe's conception of leadership. Then too, St. Laurent understood the vagaries of life; he was not a man to waste time with idle reproaches when things went awry. Propriety and efficiency were what he wanted. Howe, who demanded the same qualities from his own subordinates, rendered both to his leader.

Part of the strength of the political friendship between Howe and St. Laurent derived from the fact that Howe was known to be beyond political ambition. The Minister of Trade and Commerce was sixty-two, only four years younger than St. Laurent himself, and too old to serve as anybody's plausible candidate for the leadership. When the next leader came, he would be from a newer, younger generation. To be prime minister, Howe remarked in 1958, "wasn't my line of country. I was strong on departmental administration rather than policy direction." The policy direction, Howe expected, would come from St. Laurent.[1]

In St. Laurent's cabinet that principle was well understood. The new Prime Minister was more polite and more considerate than King had been, and he hesitated to dictate departmental policy to his ministers. But, like King, he understood how to squeeze a consensus out of a reluctant and fragmented cabinet. Where King preferred to wear down his ministers until they gave in, St. Laurent had the knack of persuading his colleagues that they were really men of like mind united in a common cause. None of the intra-cabinet battles of the King regime disfigured the harmony of the St. Laurent cabinet. In a government of strong men this was no mean feat, but the agility of St. Laurent's mind and his detailed familiarity with the items brought before cabinet gave him a clear advantage over his colleagues; in reserve were his Irish temper and the "black opacity" of his disapproving stare. Few men ventured to trifle with the Prime Minister's good nature.[2]

Though Howe, as senior minister, now sat on St. Laurent's right hand, on his left sat the Minister of Finance, the breezy and affable MP for Westmount. Douglas Abbott was entering his third year as Finance Minister (he would last for another six) and it was generally conceded that he added both strength and grace to the government. Strong in the House of Commons, Abbott also rode herd on his free-spending colleagues in cabinet. "I am the Minister of Finance," he once told a group of Liberals, "and so long as I am, I will do what I think is right."[3]

Abbott's electoral neighbour, the member for St. Lawrence-St. George in downtown Montreal, was Brooke Claxton, the Minister of National Defence. In private, Claxton was a pillar of strength in the party and government, where his natural exuberance and inexhaustible energy were politically invaluable. What the public saw, however, was an awkward and tedious orator with a grating, nasal voice, whose principal asset seemed to be his ability to lull an audience to sleep. Claxton believed that as Minister of National Defence he was wasting his time and his talents – precious resources he would need if he were ever to become prime minister. The government owed much to Claxton: he was its organizer, its link with the esoteric worlds of advertising and academe, its spirit and its conscience. But Claxton, most of his colleagues knew, would never be prime minister.[4]

Never far from the centre of any cabinet storm was the diminutive Minister of Agriculture, Jimmy Gardiner. Gardiner's portfolio intersected the responsibilities of many of his colleagues, from Public Works to Finance, and there were few ministers who had not crossed swords with Saskatchewan's representative in the cabinet. Gardiner, even more than Claxton, was a professional politician; but to Claxton and the other ministers he breathed the partisan air of an earlier age – embarrassing to his smoother and more reticent colleagues. In Gardiner's world, Liberal red filled the sphere of heaven; Tory blue was reserved for the damned. The CCF, who had displaced the Liberals as the government of Saskatchewan in 1944, would wander forever in the wilderness if Gardiner had anything to do with it. How St. Laurent had ever become leader of the Liberal party was a mystery to the Minister of Agriculture. "I don't think Mr. St. Laurent was a politician at all," he later explained to an interviewer. "He was a lawyer's lawyer . . . but that isn't politics."[5]

Gardiner respected the political finesse of Paul Martin, the Minister of National Health and Welfare. It was Martin's job to salvage what he could from the fiasco of the dominion-provincial conference on reconstruction; when the government's elaborate social welfare schemes were scrapped for lack of provincial cooperation, National Health and Welfare was left on the beach. Martin's officials were busily at work in 1948 trying to put together a package of health insurance that the minister could sell to his colleagues. But the cabinet was doubtful and reluctant – as befitted more prosperous and conservative times. None was more reluctant than C. D. Howe.[6]

Mike Pearson was another matter. Technically he was a Howe protégé, because the Minister of Trade and Commerce had helped him find a seat in Algoma East. Ambitious without seeming to be, Pearson managed to steer foreign affairs outside the realm of partisan controversy, charming the opposition with his cheerful smile and daunting them with his obvious mastery of the subject. Politically, Pearson was an asset on the national scale; locally, his region continued to be managed by C. D. Howe.

Abbott, Claxton, Martin and Pearson were the cabinet's political pension plan, its guarantee against hard times for the next decade. All were potential leaders, each had notable political skills and strengths. Together with their seniors in government, and helped by the less ambitious or more regionally oriented ministers, they gave the Liberal party an aura of unlimited promise and indefinite continuity. In the meantime, they provided a gloss of administrative competence that compared favourably with that of any previous government.

The early years of the St. Laurent government passed peacefully. When St. Laurent was travelling, Howe substituted for him, sitting relaxed in the Prime Minister's place. Of course, only the routine or the most urgent matters were considered while St. Laurent was away. But the atmosphere was easier because Howe was outwardly friendlier with his colleagues (they called him Clarence or C. D.), and he was apt to sum up an issue with a quip and a wry grin.[7]

When St. Laurent was present, Howe knew his place. It was a senior place, to be sure, but its limits were narrowly defined. He would speak and advise on the economy, on investment, on business – and on TCA, which he continued to cherish for his very own. And there was occasionally an item which overlapped

Abbott's jurisdiction, where a Finance matter affected the climate of business or the overall prospects of the economy. Only once did Abbott and Howe seriously clash. In September 1949 Abbott informed his colleagues that it was necessary to devalue the Canadian dollar forthwith. Howe, with his eye on his own industrial development program, protested that devaluation would impair Canada's capital goods imports. Abbott stuck to his guns, and after an anxious twenty-four hours Howe gave way. It was after all Abbott's responsibility, not his.[8]

The core of Abbott's responsibilities was the making of the budget. That was a secret process, confined to the minister and his officials in order to protect them from external pressures and undue influence. The rest of the cabinet was informed, rather than consulted. As Howe explained to a business friend, "The making of the Budget is not a matter for the Cabinet. I know that Mr. Abbott understands the [taxation] problem . . . but I have no idea as to what he will do. . . ." That did not prevent Howe from drawing his colleague's attention to the requirements of Canadian corporations, and occasionally Howe could be "reasonably sure," as he once wrote to the chairman of Chrysler's finance committee, that Abbott would "take care of your Canadian shareholders when his budget resolutions are brought down. . . ." Howe was right, and Chrysler expressed itself "deeply appreciative." But there was no magical certainty to Howe's touch. "We will make a real effort next year," Howe consoled E. P. Taylor, after one unsuccessful approach.[9]

As Minister of Trade and Commerce Howe had plenty to keep him busy. He had, first of all, his own programs, brought with him from Reconstruction. He had his economic analysis group and his industrial reconversion program, both directed by Sandy Skelton, who came over to Trade and Commerce from the Bank of Canada. Reconversion now went by another name, Industrial Development, and was intended to promote the establishment of new firms and new products in Canada.

Then there were the regular programs of the Department of Trade and Commerce. Although one of the older departments (founded in 1893), it was not one of the most important or effective. Its task was to promote Canadian trade, and to that end it maintained a trade commissioner service abroad, distinct from the functions of the Department of External Affairs. In the thirties, with Canadian trade at a low ebb, Trade and Commerce languished. During the war its functions were submerged by that other trade department, Munitions and Supply. By 1945, Norman Robertson reported, Trade and Commerce had become utterly insignificant. It even lacked a deputy minister: the previous one had left in 1943, and no replacement was appointed.[10]

The reconstruction of Trade and Commerce began, on Heeney's recommendation, in 1945. Maxwell W. (Max) Mackenzie, a partner in a large Montreal accounting firm, was chosen to be deputy minister. Tall, young, strikingly handsome, Mackenzie had made his reputation in Ottawa as Donald Gordon's deputy at the Wartime Prices and Trade Board. Mackenzie had to grapple with the problem of promoting Canadian exports in a world whose trading patterns were completely disrupted by shortages of everything from food to shipping. The British were the key to postwar trade, but Mackenzie had the greatest difficulty persuading them to part with any of their hard-earned foreign exchange to keep the prewar pattern of Canadian exports to Britain alive. The British, after all, had to keep themselves alive first. One problem, Mackenzie found, was his minister. "Gentleman Jim" MacKinnon was one of the nicest people in Ottawa, but he had neither stamina nor guts. Trade and Commerce proposals regularly returned tattered from cabinet maulings.[11]

Howe's arrival in 1948 was a relief. Mackenzie knew the minister by reputation and welcomed him. On his first day, Howe arrived promptly at nine and called his deputy in. This, he explained, would be his routine: Mackenzie, as his deputy, would have first call on his time at the beginning of every day. Except for emergencies, the day's problems were to be worked out then and there, for as long as it took, but the day's problems did not include administration. That, in Howe's view, was Mackenzie's responsibility. Policy was his own: "Keep the hell out of my business and I'll keep out of yours."

Policy at Trade and Commerce meant the development of industry and the promotion of exports. An incident early in Howe's tenure illustrated Mackenzie's administrative style. Tenders were received for ship machinery from three different suppliers. The bids, in Mackenzie's opinion, were equally good; under the circumstances, he asked Howe at their morning meeting if he had any preference among the bidders. The minister looked up sharply:

"Are you the deputy minister in this department?"

"Yes."

"Can you make up your own mind?"

Mackenzie took the point; Howe, having made it, dismissed the incident from his mind.[12]

The department developed its own routine. Mackenzie got on with his trade promotion; the economists made their forecasts and sent them to the minister; Howe regulated capital investments in Canadian industry through his emergency powers. These were all familiar tasks. But there was one task that Howe found even more familiar, and congenial.

Since its foundation in 1935 the Canadian Wheat Board had reported to Trade and Commerce. The Minister of Trade and Commerce in turn consulted the Wheat Committee of the cabinet, whose chairman he was, and then he set policy. The Wheat Committee numbered both the ministers of Finance and Agriculture among its members. As long as MacKinnon was minister, the effective director of Canada's wheat policy was the Minister of Agriculture, Jimmy Gardiner, to whom the timid Minister of Trade and Commerce deferred on all occasions. Gardiner relished the power. Wheat was king in his Saskatchewan constituency, and he viewed its omission from his jurisdiction as a lamentable oversight. As long as MacKinnon was the responsible minister, however, he could rest easily. MacKinnon, an Edmonton businessman, was happy to listen to someone so knowledgeable; a tolerant and easy-going man, he did not resent Gardiner's harangues or his domination of the interminable cabinet Wheat Committee meetings. Howe's arrival in Gardiner's domain was bound to bring change. Years later, Howe told a journalist that he had particularly wanted the Trade and Commerce post because he liked "to be associated with wheat," and because of his own "associations with the West." In assuming wheat policy, Howe was returning to his Canadian roots and, in a sense, to his own constituency. Howe knew grain men from Winnipeg to Vancouver. Port Arthur was a wheat port, and to it the railways moved the wheat crop. Wheat brought Howe back in time and it brought him directly into conflict with Gardiner.[13]

When the Canadian Wheat Board officials trekked east from their Winnipeg headquarters for their annual bout with the Wheat Committee, their chairman, George McIvor, brought along the usual armload of material to keep the committee happy for the several days it took to transact its business. It was mainly an occasion for Gardiner to ramble and philosophize about the grain trade. When the officials entered the committee room, they became aware that the atmosphere had changed. Howe, as committee chairman, glanced at the agenda. "Item one," he read. "What does that mean?" Briefly, McIvor explained. Howe was satisfied. Without glancing around he barked out, "Item two." After another twenty minutes, the astonished Wheat Board officials staggered out: four days had been compressed into half an hour. After that, Wheat Board business was conducted directly between McIvor and Howe; the committee meetings, as Howe intended, dwindled to a formality.[14]

It helped considerably that McIvor and Howe had known each other for years. It helped, too, that Howe knew more about wheat than he did about chemicals, or trade fairs, or even import controls. He had his own ideas about the proper way to handle the grain business, including a strong preference for the free market where it still existed. Sometimes Howe's ideas ran athwart McIvor's, and on one notable occasion, early in 1948, they clashed. The Wheat Board chairman believed that the board's controls should be extended still further, to cover marketing of the coarse grains, oats and barley. Howe resisted, and advanced his own private enterprise schemes. McIvor refused to budge. When he marched into Howe's office for the final decision he found the minister ready to do battle.

"What's wrong with my plan?" Howe asked.

"Nothing," McIvor shot back. "The only thing wrong with your plan is that it won't work." Howe argued his point, but suddenly looked up and shrugged. "Go ahead."

McIvor returned to the capital a month later on other business. Since it was a Sunday, Howe invited him round in the evening for a drink. As the minister poured a whiskey for his guest, he turned round and grinned. "You know, George," he said, "that damn scheme of mine would never have worked."[15]

Wheat policy was the crucial concern of the three prairie provinces, whose federal members serenaded the House of Commons with endless speeches on the tribulations of the wheat farmer and his importance to the country. Because most of the prairie members in the 1945 Parliament were also members of the opposition (CCFers, Social Crediters or Conservatives), they had a tendency to dwell on the inadequacies of the government's wheat policy in debates that took on the quality of an endless tribal rite. Ian Mackenzie, while still the government's

House leader, summed up the stupefying wheat debate in verse:

> To the mating bird, the dearest word
> > is tweet, tweet, tweet;
> To the orphan lamb the saddest word
> > is bleat, bleat, bleat;
> To the maid in love, the dearest word
> > is sweet, sweet, sweet;
> But the blank-damnedest word I yet have heard
> > is wheat, wheat, wheat.[16]

The main issue in the wheat debates of the late forties was the British wheat contract. Britain was traditionally the best market for Canadian wheat. But after the war the same exchange difficulties that afflicted other Canadian exports to Britain also affected wheat. The British were short of dollars to buy Canadian wheat, and they might choose to look elsewhere where dollars were not required for trade. To induce the British to keep their eyes trained on Canada, the Canadian government approved a $1.25 billion loan to Britain early in 1946. To make sure that the Canadian wheat market was kept safe for Britain and secure for Canada's wheat growers, the Minister of Agriculture then recommended that his colleagues accept a wheat contract, guaranteeing British purchases of Canadian wheat at a previously agreed price.

Gardiner's logic was compelling. There was no prospect of an immediate agreement among the world's wheat-exporting and wheat-consuming nations. Canadian farmers were anxious for guaranteed markets which would afford them some of the same security the government was busy promising to city workers with its social security program. If he could get a good price for Canadian wheat years in advance and wheat prices then fell, the Canadian farmer would not only be secure but subsidized, and at British expense. It was Gardiner's instinct that wheat prices would fall. Many farm leaders agreed with him; and so, against the Wheat Board's advice, did the cabinet. A wheat agreement with Britain was concluded in July 1946. It guaranteed wheat prices beginning at $1.55 per bushel minimum in the first year of the contract, fluctuating downward to a minimum price of $1.00 in the fourth and last year, the crop year of 1949-50 (a crop year runs from August through July). In each year the British agreed to buy a minimum of three hundred thousand tons.

Had Gardiner's premonition been correct, and the world

wheat price dropped, his contract would have been acclaimed as a triumph of agricultural statesmanship. Unfortunately the world wheat price rose, and continued to rise. Howe had thought it might, gloomily agreeing with an old friend from the British grain trade that it would have been better to allow the forces of the market to take their course. Whether the market rose or fell, the wheat contract would create the impression that one side or the other was the victim of sharp practice.

Gardiner believed that he had provided against that eventuality as well – at least as far as Canada was concerned. The contract contained a vague clause that promised that in the last two years of the contract the price paid by the British would "have regard to" any differences between world wheat prices and the price paid in the first two years. Gardiner expected that this would mean that Canadian farmers would be repaid any putative losses they might suffer under the contract. To the British it meant no such thing.[17]

Howe had kept a distant, disapproving eye on the wheat contract from his base in Reconstruction. Now, suddenly, as Minister of Trade and Commerce, he was responsible for it. The absurdity of Gardiner's expectations was demonstrated within months. For the crop year 1948-49 the British agreed to a wheat price of $2.00 a bushel – well over the $1.25 minimum for the year promised by the contract, but still below the world wheat price. Negotiations the next year produced the same result: $2.00 a bushel. Canadian wheat growers suddenly realized that for the sake of a stable market they had been subsidizing British wheat consumers. They were not pleased. The western press bubbled with indignation and demands for action.[18]

Gardiner sought satisfaction from the British and Howe took the Canadian case for better treatment to Britain in the spring of 1950. He was not surprised to return empty-handed. As far as he was concerned, the affair of the contract ended there. Canada had taken a not very well-calculated risk, and had lost. It was too bad, but there was nothing else to be done.

The cabinet agreed, but later in 1950, under pressure from Gardiner, St. Laurent reopened the issue. Still the British refused to make any further payment. In Howe's view, none was owing, either to Canada or to Canadian farmers. St. Laurent, for once, took the other side. Wheat farmers had rightly or wrongly been led to believe that more money would be forthcoming, and it was up to the Canadian government to find it for them. There happened to be $65 million left of the 1946 British loan which the British did not wish to use. It should, therefore, be turned over to the wheat farmers. This solution was, on balance, a fair compromise, but it did not satisfy Gardiner, who publicly implied that the British had welshed on their agreement; nor did it console Howe, who believed that wheat farmers had got something for nothing.[19]

The differences between the two men became startlingly obvious when, on March 12, 1951, each gave to the House of Commons his own version of the conclusion of the wheat contract. Gardiner spoke first, producing a long and incoherent justification of his own conduct since 1946. Howe followed. "Personally," he told the House, "I think it was a mistake that there should have been included in the agreement such a loosely worded have-regard-to clause." The British had not been legally bound to pay any more than they had, and any suggestion to the contrary was erroneous. The British, Howe asserted, had "played fair with the Canadian people."

Now the gap yawning between Howe and Gardiner was plain to all. Even the opposition noticed, and demanded to know which minister spoke for the government. St. Laurent hastily rose to smoothe over the differences. The real root of the matter, he argued, was the conclusion of the cabinet. That conclusion had been announced: the government was making an extra payment to the wheat farmers. That was St. Laurent's, and the government's, last word on the matter. Howe bowed to the Prime Minister's will, and said nothing more.[20]

Prospects elsewhere were much brighter. In 1947 the United States made a far-reaching set of proposals to solve Europe's economic crisis. The Marshall Plan promised to put American dollars at the disposal of European governments to finance their essential purchases in the United States and elsewhere. This was good news in Ottawa, especially when the multi-billion-dollar magnitude of the American proposals became apparent. But what particularly stirred the Canadian government's imagination was the magic word "elsewhere." The possibility that European countries, armed with U.S. dollars, would descend on the Canadian supermarket was almost too much to hope for. But it was true or at least would become true, as soon as the Marshall Plan was put into effect in April 1948.[21]

No restrictions initially were placed on the commodities on which the Europeans could spend their money; it could be used, for example, to finance British purchases of Canadian wheat under the wheat contract. Between April 1948 and June 1950,

$1,155 million of Marshall Plan funds were spent in Canada. The total might have been larger, but for another happy fact. Canada's economic troubles were financial, not industrial. There was little prospect of increasing Canadian production; the economy was already going full blast, and it was simply not possible to produce much more. But if the plan helped the Europeans pay for what they were already buying, so much the better.

Under Howe's emergency import program, imports from the United States fell sharply, even in the area of capital goods. At the same time, imports from countries in dollar difficulties, such as Britain, increased. Companies in Canada, or moving to Canada, were encouraged to produce new lines of goods. Exports to the United States rose at the same time, though principally in agricultural commodities. As a result, Canada's foreign trade deficit shrank, and then vanished; there was a net trade surplus in 1948 of $235 million.[22]

Howe naturally claimed some of the credit. As he told the House of Commons, his import program was designed to stimulate investment wherever American dollars could be earned. He also cautioned over-enthusiastic MP's against crowing too loudly over Canadian earnings under the Marshall Plan.

In a world of economic chaos and poverty, Canadians were doing well. The Americans proved remarkably cooperative and understanding, perhaps because they could contemplate a situation in which only the United States and Canada were left solvent in a ruined world. It was not a pleasant contemplation, and although American officials recognized that the Canadian economy was considerably smaller than their own, they wondered from time to time whether Canada should not take a more active part in helping Europe. Canadian diplomats and Howe's own officials fought a continuous delaying action to persuade the Americans that Canada was already doing enough and could hardly afford to do more. Even the wheat contract, so disastrous domestically, was invoked to prove that Canada was generously handing out subsidized food.[23]

Howe found that the devaluation of the Canadian dollar in September 1949 had complicated Canada's trade. Because Canada did not devalue as much as the British, Canadian exports to Britain and Europe became comparatively unattractive; but the Americans had not devalued at all, and so Canadian exports to the United States became considerably more attractive.

The flourishing state of Canadian trade with the United

States did not go unnoticed by those who hoped to see Europe balance America in Canada's foreign relations. The Department of External Affairs was so concerned by April 1950 that it drafted a memorandum, which Pearson signed, calling attention to the dangers of over-reliance on the United States; when "a small country gets too heavily dependent on a much larger one," the External Affairs memorandum warned, it "always runs the risk of political pressure – a vague risk, a rock below the surface, but none the less real." Pearson, who in 1948 and 1949 had favoured a much closer economic relationship with the United States, now marched to a different drum.[24]

Howe's reply was characteristic. The state of Canada's exports, the distribution of Canada's trade, depended on the market, or at any rate on forces well beyond Canada's control. "Our best policy," he explained, was simple: "to sell as much as possible wherever possible." Canadian sales to the United States were the sum of thousands of independent transactions, not the creation of government policy on either side. As long as exports kept Canada prosperous, there was no danger to Canadian independence. On the contrary: "The surest way to lose our sovereignty would be to get into financial insolvency. . . . Selling our goods to the Americans is a much better alternative." "In spite of our best efforts," Howe continued, trade with Europe could not equal trade with the United States. After two years of preference for European and British imports, the figures spoke for themselves. Europe could not begin to replace the United States in the Canadian economy.

The crux, of course, was Great Britain. Much of Canada's aid and trade policy since 1945, and even before that, was designed to restore Britain to its pre-eminent place in Canada's export trade. What was the result? "The United Kingdom is the 'sick man' of the postwar world." This was "tragic indeed" for Canada, which had paid a heavy price, and perhaps should pay it again, to restore Britain's trade. But there was little that Canada alone could do; the cure lay in "the initiative of the British themselves."[25]

Initiative in Canada was pointing the way to self-sufficiency. Every new mine, every ton of exported pulpwood, contributed to Canadian prosperity and helped the country to pay its own way in the world. The discovery of a huge oilfield in Alberta in 1947 meant that imports of American oil (and expenditure of scarce foreign exchange) could be reduced. The expansion of the iron ore mine at Steep Rock and the opening of new deposits in Labrador helped as well. The flow of American investment into Canada ($66 million in 1947, $79 million in 1948, and $114 million in 1949) brought jobs, prosperity, and lessened the dependence of Canada on special treatment from another government, even one as friendly as the American.

Howe explained the rationale of his foreign trade and domestic development programs in a statement to the House of Commons in March 1949:

> The end we pursue may be put very simply. It is to maintain a high level of employment and income as the most practical means of assuring the welfare and security of the people of Canada. . . . The joint effect of our trade development and of our domestic development has been to provide a greater degree of economic welfare and economic security for the average individual.

New plants, subsidiaries of British and American firms, were helping to supply the domestic market and thereby to correct the imbalance in foreign exchange.[26]

First among the industries Howe hoped to encourage was iron and steel. Steel remained under control because of a domestic steel shortage; between 1946 and 1948 steel production increased from 2,327,000 to 3,200,000 tons, and pig iron production increased from 1,406,000 to 2,126,000 tons. Complaints that the benefits of Howe's program were unevenly distributed were firmly rejected by his officials. Sandy Skelton, reviewing the demographic impact of Howe's industrialization, admitted that one effect might well be to attract labour away from the farms of the West to the factories of central Canada. The same, he conceded, was true of the Maritimes. But there was little that government could or should do to arrest the trend: "Was not mobility of labour a good thing?"[27]

Inducements to new investments were not limited to import permits and trade promotion. Until late in 1947 Howe had granted accelerated depreciation, handing out tax abatement in return for approved investment. After a year's suspension, this device was revived, in a slightly different form, in a scheme of capital-cost allowances and embodied in the government's new income tax act. A later study concluded that between 1946 and 1960 over $1.1 billion in deferred taxes were granted to foreign-controlled enterprises alone, presenting "a substantial incentive to the United States investor."[28]

Finally, there was Trade and Commerce's Industrial Development Branch. It was supposed, first, to identify imported products which might be manufactured in this country, then to seek a domestic manufacturer for the product, and finally, if no Canadian firm was interested, to try to interest the foreign manufacturer in locating a plant on Canadian soil. But while the idea of an Industrial Development Branch was plausible, there was some doubt, even in Trade and Commerce, of its real effectiveness.[29]

The impact of Howe's policies could be seen all over the Canadian economy. His department's activities were conspicuous, and they were politically unassailable, given a universal commitment to development, investment, jobs and prosperity. But the minister, the opposition had learned, was not invulnerable, however popular his programs might be.

The parliamentary sessions of 1948 and 1949 were difficult ones for the government and for Howe. There was a new Leader of the Opposition, George Drew, who had resigned as premier of Ontario to be crowned federal leader. A Tory MP resigned to make way for the leader's early entrance to Parliament. The Conservatives were tired of the high-minded, bumbling tedium of their former leader, John Bracken; in choosing Drew they selected a man diametrically opposed in personality. Journalist, lawyer and professional politician, Drew cut a wide swath in Ontario politics. Handsome and arrogant, he looked like a prime minister and believed that he was destined to be one. He was impelled by personal righteousness to do his utmost to turn the socializing, centralizing Liberals out. Under Drew the opposition would be more aggressive than it had been for years.

Drew's accession to the Conservative leadership coincided with a deterioration in Howe's relations with the House of Commons. Two members of the opposition led the attack, Howard Green and James M. Macdonnell. Green was a veteran in the Commons, elected in the face of the Liberal sweep in 1935 in Vancouver. Macdonnell, a Toronto financier, had long been active in Conservative politics. Grey, lean, upright, Macdonnell was a favourite with the press. He was the first to raise the concentration of emergency powers in Howe's hands as an issue worthy of scrutiny. In February 1948, when Howe's power to restrict imports was being debated, Macdonnell observed in the House that he was not particularly worried that businessmen seeking import permits would not be able to see the minister. "Most of them," he added, "know the minister personally, and

I have no doubt they find him a very personable man to do business with. I think he treats them far differently from the way he treats us in the House of Commons."

"They are much more intelligent," Howe shot back.[30]

Howard Green took a less lofty tone than Macdonnell but he had an equally telling effect. In committee of the whole, when departmental estimates were scrutinized, he was the most persistent of Howe's interrogators. It became a popular indoor sport to listen to Green's nasal tones sapping Howe's patience and undermining his defences. Being lectured was even worse. "It used to drive C. D. wild," one of his officials remembers, "to see Green up on his feet wagging his finger at him." At one point, provoked beyond endurance, Howe fired off his own interpretation of Green's censorious character: "He wanders through the halls of Parliament," Howe fumed, "with a Bible in one hand and a stiletto in the other."[31]

Much of the time, Howe and Green cultivated happier relations. Green was interested in Howe's secret atomic energy program and wanted to know more. In 1947 and 1948 he repeatedly urged Howe to give the House at least some information. Howe finally agreed and in 1949 a special House committee was established to examine what was happening in atomic energy. Green, gratified, moved on to another issue: he became interested in pipelines.[32]

Another frequent antagonist was John Diefenbaker, then at the summit of his debating form. Diefenbaker bombarded his opponents with scorn and suspicion. On one occasion, in February 1948, Diefenbaker demanded that Howe table a copy of his regulations for import permits. "Unless there is something of a definite rule," Diefenbaker explained, "the minister might very well find, however he might back up and be adverse to this being considered, that political fitness would become the qualification for the issuing of permits." It was a specious argument; the House of Commons had neither the time nor the capacity to examine detailed regulations. There was nothing in Howe's record to show that he would abuse his powers. Macdonnell had kept his criticism on a loftier plane; but this was vintage Diefenbaker, calculated to enrage the minister and by enraging him to draw blood. Howe replied immediately: "My honourable friend is taking that from the sewer of his own mind." It took five minutes to persuade Howe to retract his characterization of Diefenbaker; never, he angrily told the House, had he ever used his power to punish his enemies or reward his friends, and he repudiated any such insinuation. But Diefenbaker's point was not what Howe *had* done – there he was on shaky ground – but what he *might* do. That harpoon found its target.[33]

Diefenbaker's tactics were calculated to show Howe in a bad light by getting him hopping mad in the House of Commons, staging the spectacle of an angry, elderly man performing a series of tantrums. The tantrums were remembered by politicians and the press, who forgot the provocation. Diefenbaker's master-stroke was to pin on Howe the phrase everlastingly associated with him: "What's a million?"

The exchange arose from a 1945 debate on Howe's war estimates. The estimates debates had a tendency to drag along while the opposition probed for some politically useful weakness in the government's case. The estimates under discussion totalled $1,365 million. When replying to a question about that sum, Howe exclaimed to the House, "I dare say my honourable friend could cut a million dollars . . . but a million dollars from the War Appropriations Bill would not be a very important matter."

Diefenbaker spoke the next day. His version of Howe's remarks was different: "We may save a million dollars, but what of it?" Howe jumped to his feet. He had said no such thing; Diefenbaker was "a past master of distortion." Diefenbaker was incensed at the slur on his reputation. Howe was guilty of bad manners and must withdraw his remarks. Eventually, after much bellowing back and forth across the floor of the House, Howe retracted his epithet, which was promptly forgotten. But Diefenbaker's was refined and sharpened, until it finally emerged as "What's a million?" – the epitome of Liberal arrogance and condescension toward Parliament. Even those who knew that Howe had not said it argued that he might have. Some Liberals agreed.[34]

But Howe remained popular with the Liberal backbenchers. As in the past, Howe let it be known that he was accessible to members of the Liberal caucus. But this time, it was George McIlraith, Chevrier's replacement as parliamentary secretary, who screened MP's who wanted to see the minister. McIlraith, a bespectacled, talkative and diligent Ottawa lawyer, substituted for Howe in routine debates.

Because he lived in Ottawa, Howe was able to volunteer for

the unpopular parliamentary duty days, Thursdays and Fridays, which his out-of-town colleagues preferred to shun. As a result, Alice and the family saw Clarence more often. It was a shrinking nest, however: the youngest, Mary, was married in September 1948 to a young man, James Dodge, whom she met while studying at Radcliffe College. John by now was out of school, out of the house and out of town; inevitably he trained as an engineer and joined his brother-in-law, Bob Stedman, in working for Murray Fleming at the C. D. Howe Company. Both young men started at the bottom.

After a Christmas rest, Howe was ready for a strenuous parliamentary session, the first of St. Laurent's prime ministership. Parliament met on January 29, 1949. The galleries were unusually crowded in the days that followed, as Drew's attack on the government unfolded. "I watched the debate from the gallery with growing misgivings," J. W. Pickersgill, St. Laurent's assistant, later wrote. "It was clear that Drew's manner and his speech impressed the House and the press gallery." Drew hammered at the government throughout the winter, picking up steam in a by-election victory in the Quebec riding of Nicolet-Yamaska in February 1949. Drew's candidate won with some help from the provincial Union Nationale organization of Premier Maurice Duplessis; the latter saw it as a heaven-sent chance to stage-manage an electoral humiliation for the Liberals on the issue of provincial rights. Worse still, the Liberals' margin in the national public opinion polls began to shrink.[35]

The target of Conservative oratory, Howe refused to take Drew seriously or to acknowledge that Drew could possibly be making an impression on the public. When Drew solemnly informed the House that Howe was "the Number One Marxist in Canada," Howe shot back: "And you're the Number One Comedian." Abbott added, "Groucho, not Karl." Drew's attempts to continue were drowned in laughter. Eventually, Howe decided, people would see through Drew and his charges, and the tide would turn. "It is becoming more and more apparent," he wrote to Frank Ross in February, "that [Drew] is a child compared to St. Laurent." "I look," he added, "for him to blow a fuse in due course." In March Howe detected a trend back to the government; he was "more and more convinced," he wrote, "that the Tories have again selected a 'Morning glory.' "[36]

After an initial period of uncertainty, the Liberal caucus took heart. When the Prime Minister explained to the caucus his strategy for a quick dissolution of Parliament and a June election, the backbenchers were "extremely enthusiastic." Ralph Maybank, the habitually disgruntled Winnipeg Liberal, reported that he had never known "such straight talk about tactics and strategy from a leader." Howe's fund-raising machine was grinding away, and the party war chest was full. Claxton, the tactician, and Howe, the quartermaster, gave the signal for action. On April 30 Parliament was dissolved and an election called for June 27.[37]

Prospects were good. "I look for large gains in Ontario and Saskatchewan," Howe wrote to Frank Ross, "while we should at least hold our own in the rest of Canada." Howe did not leave everything to public opinion. Corporate contributors and individual donors were tapped for funds: the CPR, Canada Packers, Eaton's, Swift's, and the wine and liquor companies. Chubby Power was amazed at the Liberals' affluence; he estimated that the party spent $3 million nationally and another $3 million in the constituencies. Drew, whose magisterial good looks and ample double-breasted suits helped the Liberals caricature him as the very embodiment of big business, did worse than Bracken had in raising campaign funds.[38]

With the money against him, Drew had to turn to the issues. These were not promising. The Conservative leader was in favour of dealing harshly with communists, he told his audiences. He made vague promises to reduce expenditure and damned the government for extravagance; but Abbott had just brought in an election budget reducing income taxes for many and abolishing them altogether for some.

The Conservatives had only one card left to play: damning their opponents' records and characters. Howe featured in the demonology that Drew paraded before election crowds. Howe was arrogant and power-hungry. He sold out Canada by peddling crown companies – the property of the Canadian people – for a song. The sale of Canadair to the Electric Boat Company was a case in point, Drew informed a Fort William audience. They were nothing more than a bunch of "international armaments racketeers," and Howe was their friend. It was bad tactics; Drew won no votes, and he alienated many of his own supporters in the business community.[39]

One of these, Henry Borden, wrote to Howe late in July: "I have no sympathy for that sort of thing, and wholeheartedly condemn it.'' Howe's reply was serene: the only effect of Drew's intervention "was to give me a record majority in Port Arthur!'' The rest of the country followed Port Arthur, giving the Liberals almost 50 per cent of the popular vote and 193 seats in the House of Commons. Drew's Conservatives, who in fact marginally increased their popular vote, eked out a mere 41 seats, down from 67 in the previous election. It was a chastened George Drew who crept back to Parliament in the fall, insecure in the knowledge that his own home province of Ontario had given the Liberals 56 seats to his own 25. As usual, Liberal candidates won every seat in Northern Ontario.

"For you,'' Henry Borden wrote to Howe, "it means that you must stay in public life – Canada is the better off for that and I am glad that you have the clear and undisputed right to continue your great work.''[40]

CHAPTER FIFTEEN

War in a Minor Key

The new Parliament opened in a blaze of pageantry on September 15, 1949. Problems were few. Behind the scenes, Abbott's devaluation of the dollar preoccupied the cabinet, but even Howe recognized a silver lining in this cloud: now Canadian exports would increase. The Speech from the Throne promised the abolition of appeals for the Supreme Court of Canada to the Privy Council in London; in future Canadian law would be decided in Canada. The government would seek an amendment to the British North America Act to place the amendment of the exclusively federal aspects of the constitution in the hands of the Parliament of Canada, and provincial consent would be sought to bring the rest of the constitution home to Canada. These were projects dear to St. Laurent's heart. There would also be a Trans-Canada highway, a project closer to Howe's.

A Trans-Canada highway, like all national transportation projects, interested the Minister of Trade and Commerce, but it was relatively uncontroversial. He did not expect that the autumn session would be strenuous. The opposition had been taught a lesson. Drew's belligerence was transmuted into sweet reason and political fireworks were few. At the end of October, Howe celebrated inter-party harmony by moving the establishment of a special committee on atomic energy, a project that interested Howard Green who promptly hailed the happy occasion. But only a few days later the idyll came to an end.

On November 2, M. J. Coldwell, the leader of the CCF, put three innocent-sounding questions to the Minister of Justice,

Stuart Garson. Had the minister received a report under the Combines Investigation Act, and, if so, would he table it? Garson hesitated, and then promised that he would reply tomorrow. Coldwell rose again, with a supplementary question. Had the commissioner under the Combines Investigation Act, F. A. McGregor, resigned? Garson again asked for time; he would reply to that too tomorrow.[1]

The next day, Garson's reply was ready. The answer to all three questions, he told the House, was yes. Yes, he had received the report, yes, he would table it, and yes, its author, F. A. McGregor, the commissioner under the act, had resigned. Once again there was a supplementary question, this time from Stanley Knowles, the CCF's parliamentary tactician. He wanted to know when Garson had received McGregor's report. The Minister of Justice hesitated: it would be tabled the following Monday, the seventh. That, unfortunately, was not the question, so Knowles pursued it.

"When did the minister receive the report?"

"Some time ago," Garson mumbled.

"In other words," Knowles concluded, "the minister did not keep the law." Knowles knew what most MP's did not, that the Combines Investigation Act stipulated that reports of investigations of combines in restraint of trade (conspiracies by business to fix prices or terms of trade) were to be presented expeditiously to the Minister of Justice and tabled by the minister in the House of Commons within fifteen days of their receipt. Garson had received a report from McGregor on December 29, 1948. After eleven months it was still not public. When Diefenbaker demanded to know why it was not, Garson evaded the question: the answer, he claimed, would be found in his letter to McGregor accepting his resignation; he would not repeat it in the House.[2]

The reason why Garson had not tabled the report was sitting a few seats away. When the Minister of Justice received the report in question, on a combine in the flour-milling industry, he showed it to his colleague, the Minister of Trade and Commerce. Howe took it back to the office to read; then he exploded. It seemed to him, he later stated, that the flour millers were being condemned for "carrying out policies that were obviously those of the Wartime Prices and Trade Board." Max Mackenzie, his deputy and a former member of the WPTB, was consulted and agreed.

Howe phoned Garson. The problem, he told the Minister of

Justice, was that there was an official price ceiling on flour during the war. There was, however, no price ceiling on wheat. The government undertook to make up any losses the flour companies incurred through this anomaly; if they made less than "standard profits" (computed on a prewar base) the government made up the difference. Retrospectively, McGregor found this arrangement not to his liking: the flour companies had sold their product at the price ceiling when in fact they could have sold under the ceiling. The trouble with that reasoning, Howe argued, was that their profits would have diminished and the public treasury would have been called on to bail out the companies. In any case, it was not the WPTB's policy to allow companies observing the price ceiling to suffer from price-cutting competition. If anyone had tried it, they would have been stopped. Cooperation did not end in 1945. When, after the war, flour was "de-controlled" and allowed to find its own price level, the government was understandably nervous. At a time of high inflation, it was politically dangerous to release another commodity to skyrocket in price. Abbott accordingly warned the millers that if prices did not remain at a level he considered reasonable, he would reimpose controls. The millers agreed and obeyed. But McGregor was denouncing this too.[3]

Under the circumstances, Howe advised Garson not to table and publish the combines commissioner's report. If he did, the government would be pillorying the very people it had relied on to carry out its policy. In any case, McGregor himself had been a member of the Wartime Prices and Trade Board; he had not resigned from the board to protest its policy. McGregor, however, was unconvinced by the two ministers' arguments, even though they were reinforced by those of his former chief, Donald Gordon. After waiting a year, he resigned, and with his resignation he exploded a political bomb.[4]

By coincidence, amendments to the Combines Investigation Act were due to be introduced by the Minister of Justice in the House of Commons on November 7. The government, the House and the press waited for Garson to defend himself in his opening statement. But to the astonishment of the opposition, it was not Garson who rose to open the debate, but Howe. The Minister of Trade and Commerce sketched out for the House the story of what he had done, and presented the government's version of the *affaire McGregor*. In keeping with the procedure of the House, Howe could not be followed by the Minister of

Justice, but by Diefenbaker, Coldwell and Solon Low, the leader of the Social Credit Party. Replying to Howe, they forcefully presented McGregor's side of the case.

Garson did not speak until evening. He presented the House with the details of the difficulties arising from the enforcement of the Combines Investigation Act; but though he dealt with the facts, he skirted the issue. The issue, plainly, was not the wisdom or even the truth of McGregor's allegations against the flour-milling companies, but whether Garson had fulfilled his statutory duty. That he had not done, in the eyes of many observers. Ironically, Garson had a plausible excuse, which his earlier statements ignored. If he had pointed out that it was not McGregor's report that he had received eleven months earlier, but merely its preliminary draft, he might have escaped censure. But he did not, and he consequently bore the blame.

According to Pickersgill, a friendly observer, Garson never wholly recovered. "Great damage had been done to Garson's self-confidence and prestige," he wrote. Garson's reputation suddenly collapsed. Even worse, he knew it. From an aspirant to the Liberal leadership after St. Laurent, he descended to a bumbling and ineffective regional minister.[5]

Garson was, government supporters concluded, tragically out of his depth in the national arena. Even his performance as a prairie minister suffered; he often seemed to be overshadowed by the powerful ministers who represented the regions on either side of Manitoba – Gardiner in Saskatchewan and Howe in northwestern Ontario. Now more than ever the western Liberals would have to depend on Howe's leadership and his performance as the minister in charge of wheat.

Apart from the British wheat contract, the prospects for wheat marketing were bright. Early in 1949 Canada, the United States and Australia managed to come to an understanding with the wheat-consuming nations on wheat prices and supply. The three large wheat producers agreed to supply to the wheat-consuming nations (the largest being Britain) a given amount of wheat at a set price. Canadian farmers were promised security for the immediate future, once the British contract expired; unfortunately, world wheat prices would be lower, since the immediate postwar shortage of food was finally being relieved. Good news, in this case, could well be followed by bad. But for the moment, Howe could assure the House, Canada's agricultural exports were in good shape.

And so, Howe told the House of Commons on December 1, was the Canadian economy. There were, he admitted, some troublesome areas: exports to the United States were never enough, and imports too high, and some exports to Europe were not as great as hoped. But the year 1949 had been a good one for Canada, because of domestic prosperity and high levels of consumption, and large investments that offset a decline in overseas markets. These trends, he told the House, would level off in 1950. One postwar illusion, massive Canadian exports, was not doing as well as expected, but private investment, unanticipated by anyone but Howe in 1945, was replacing it as the motor of the economy.[6]

The House prorogued before Christmas. The Howes spent the holidays at home, but it was not a happy Christmas. Howe was tired and drawn, and the round of Christmas entertainments was a strain. One night at a party, he suddenly keeled over. The next week was spent confined to his home. The radio broadcast the news, so Howe's various friends deluged the minister with helpful advice. Bill Neal, an old friend and ex-president of the CPR, who had suffered a breakdown himself and was forced to retire, drew on his own experience to urge Howe to rest before it was too late.

Howe recognized the force of Neal's advice. "I am very tired indeed," he wrote to Carswell on December 27; it was high time to have a vacation. Parliament would not reconvene until February, and at St. Laurent's urging the minister decided that he could afford to spend January and February in Europe. "I feel rather guilty about leaving the ship," Howe wrote to the Prime Minister, "but I think that in the long run it was the wisest thing to do." He could combine his rest with business, reassessing Europe's economic conditions; it might even be possible to discover new markets. But the trip would be primarily pleasure. Howe would pay for it himself, and Alice would accompany him.

The Howes sailed on January 12. They landed at Cap d'Ail, where a car and chauffeur, courtesy of the Quebec shipbuilder and old friend, Joe Simard, were waiting. Then it was on to Paris, to the Riviera and Italy, and then back to Paris again. It was a busman's holiday: the local trade commissioners entertained the Howes, and brought their minister up to date on the local situations in France, Italy, Belgium and the Netherlands. In Paris, Howe called on Averell Harriman, the U.S. administrator of the European Recovery Plan. It was, Howe later told the House of Commons, an enlightening visit. Harriman's officials in Paris, the various European governments, and private businessmen all told him the same thing: Europe was doing better than anyone had expected. Soon, it was hoped, European currencies might return to convertibility.[7]

Howe was greatly encouraged. Not only was Marshall Aid having its intended effect, but it was working sooner than he had hoped. Already the European economies were less dependent on American subsidy; perhaps the long-awaited rebirth of a true international trading economy was not far off. Matching the economic recovery was greater political stability, and that alone furnished a refreshing contrast to Howe's previous visit in 1947. "I came back from that earlier visit," Howe observed, "feeling that there was a possibility that communism would sweep western Europe. . . . I came back this time with a very strong feeling that that would not happen."[8]

If communism swept Europe, it would not be provoked by revolution, but by intervention. The possibility of internal disruption supplemented by invasion from the Soviet Union haunted western defence planners and democratic politicians. In April 1949 Canada, the United States, Britain, and most of the countries of western Europe had signed the North Atlantic Treaty, establishing a common defence against external aggression by the Soviet Union and its allies. The new defence organization, NATO, was headquartered in Paris, and for the next year ministers and generals scurried across and around the Atlantic trying to give its commander, General Eisenhower, something to command. It was not easy, for the western countries were, for the most part, disarmed and broke.

Canada was not exactly broke, but it did meet the other, informal characteristic of NATO membership: the country was practically disarmed. Canada's tiny armed forces totalled under fifty thousand, spread among three services. Most were armed with Second World War equipment. Munitions and Supply, of course, was abolished. In its place, the Canadian Commercial Corporation, a crown company reporting to Howe, supplied the military with everything from bread to bombers. An advisory committee of businessmen, veterans of Munitions and Supply, drew up a mobilization scheme for industry and kept a skeleton supply organization in a subdued half-life.

Maintaining munitions production in peacetime was even more difficult than maintaining a military force. For one thing, it was vastly more expensive. Simply keeping Canadian Arsenals

Limited alive, in default of orders, was costing over $2 million a year. By selling off war stocks, the government's arsenals in Lindsay and Quebec City managed to stave off a deficit, but by 1950 that expedient had a limited future.

The problem would have been solved if Canada had been able to produce armaments for others, as in the Second World War. But after 1945 that was no easy prescription. Everyone was in the same boat, recently demobilized, armed forces disorganized, fully equipped with expensive, recent-vintage stocks of weapons that governments could not bear to dispose of. As for ongoing weapons research, that was reserved and guarded for local firms in each country.

The United States was the principal market for Canadian armaments, as for everything else Canada produced. Ostensibly, Canadian-American defence purchases were regulated by the Hyde Park Agreement, which had been renewed by Howe in 1945. In fact, American purchases of Canadian defence equipment came under the Buy-American Act of 1937, which instructed American military purchasers to buy in the United States first, and outside only when there was no comparable American source of supply.[9]

Howe had recognized the inevitable long before. His reconstruction program assigned virtually no resources to defence production. As the West's relations with the Soviet Union worsened in the late forties, he set up an industrial preparedness committee and a Joint Mobilization Committee with the United States to plan against any emergency, but emergencies were slow in coming.

It was Canada's potential, rather than Canada's performance, that interested the Americans. American defence plans took account of Canadian resources and facilities: the nickel of Sudbury, the aluminum refineries of the Saguenay, the iron ore of Labrador and Northern Ontario. The Americans continued to purchase Canadian uranium at a steady rate, a small but useful item in the Canadian balance of payments. The depletion of high-grade iron ore reserves in the American Mesabi Range showed that the Americans would soon have to start importing ore on a large scale; Howe hoped, naturally, that it would be from Canada. Responding to objections in the House of Commons, Howe commented that in the past Canada had imported large amounts of American iron ore for Canadian steel mills, and there was no prospect of damaging Canadian steel capacity by exporting to the United States when, in fact, that capacity was growing rapidly.[10]

Attempts by Howe to secure some larger share of the American defence market were unavailing. Personal diplomacy and feelers through the Permanent Joint Board on Defence met with no success. The most Howe could squeeze from the reluctant Americans was a promise to buy $25 million worth of equipment in Canada. The Americans, it was clear, would buy only what they could not make for themselves. Against that barrier Howe struggled in vain.[11]

There matters rested in June 1950. June was a dull month in Ottawa. The hot season was impending, and members and ministers were anxious to wind up their business before Dominion Day, July 1. Howe's departmental estimates were scheduled for June 26, so that the minister's personal itinerary would be clear for a long summer vacation. The last weekend before the parliamentary recess, June 24-25, was almost a dry run for the longer vacation. Most of the cabinet opened up their summer cottages, and St. Laurent fled as far as his summer place at St. Patrice, down the St. Lawrence from Quebec City.

Most ministers were, therefore, out of Ottawa when, on June 25, the CBC started to broadcast news of a distant war. It was, it appeared, in Korea. There had been border skirmishes and local guerrilla actions for months and the reports were not at first taken seriously. By afternoon, the reports were getting more attention. It looked like an invasion, not a skirmish. Mike Pearson's secretary rowed across a lake in the Gatineau to notify the Minister of External Affairs; St. Laurent was informed and started back to Ottawa.

By Monday, the 26th, events were becoming clearer. North Korea had invaded South Korea in great strength. Contrary to American reports, the South Korean army was no match for the well-equipped and well-trained northern soldiers. The South Korean capital of Seoul was lost in a day, and the South's forces were in full retreat. Because Korea was a peninsula, the outcome of the war could not be long in doubt, unless something else happened to relieve the situation.

With the South Koreans facing annihilation, the United States was faced with a painful decision. It could let a friendly country be overrun by Communist invaders, and take a beating in international esteem. On the other hand, the Americans could send in troops and become involved in a side-show war on the mainland of Asia, perilously close to the Soviet Union – and to China. There was, too, the question of Korea being a conscious attempt to divert American strength to an unimportant theatre as a prelude to a major Communist attack elsewhere, perhaps in Europe.

The Truman administration decided to respond immediately by sending in troops, planes and ships. It appealed to the United Nations to condemn the North Korean aggression and to send aid to the South Koreans. And before a week was out, the United Nations had agreed to do just that. A United Nations army was constituted out of the remaining scraps of the South Korean army and the odd American unit that could make it to Korea on short notice. The army was placed under American command.

The Canadian cabinet was sympathetic but slow to react. Most cabinet members were inclined to let Pearson handle it and to confine Canadian assistance to minor items. It was, Howe assured a friend in mid-July, too late to do anything about Korea. Howe had no liking for a war in Asia. By then Howe and Gardiner were the only survivors of the cabinet that had sent Canadian troops to imprisonment and death in the forlorn defence of Hong Kong against the Japanese in 1941 and Howe was reluctant to repeat the experience.

But the pressure of events was too great to withstand. On August 6 St. Laurent and Claxton addressed the Canadian people on a nationwide radio broadcast. Claxton issued a call for volunteers (it would be a voluntary war, without a breath of conscription) and began organizing a special army brigade for Korean service. Howe was unenthusiastic. He had no quarrel with helping to defeat aggression, but believed it a terrible waste to send troops trained for Arctic warfare to fight in Asia. Pearson, who thought the war a heaven-sent opportunity to promote the ideals of the United Nations, later recalled that "C. D. was not antagonistic but unable to see the big principles at stake." But the principle, as far as Howe was concerned, was that it was the wrong war, in the wrong place.[12]

Instead of going on vacation, Howe stayed at his desk through July. A tentative mobilization had to be considered, just in case, which meant that all the recently abolished controls had to be dusted off and examined to see which ones might fit the new crisis. There was little in the way of surplus capacity for the government to use, and there was considerable danger of a rearmament program chasing too few goods with too much money. "How the Government can move into the present inflated situation and control prices is beyond me," Howe wrote in August. "I think we will have to be satisfied with allocation controls for the time being." These were a familiar postwar expedient, particularly with scarce steel.[13]

Before much could be done to ready the economy for war production, it ground to a complete halt. A national rail strike began on August 22. Rail was the essential transport for people and goods; without railway service most of Canada's business would simply sit idle. The government decided it could not afford to let the strike continue and, after futile efforts at mediation, summoned Parliament for August 29 to legislate an end. When Parliament met, the assembled members were informed that the government proposed to use the opportunity to put through some special measures to meet Canada's international obligations during the Korean crisis.

Howe had prepared an Essential Materials (Defence) Bill. It allowed him to "direct the distribution of essential materials, such as steel, and essential services, such as electric power," along the lines he had predicted. If there were a conflict between military needs and civilian demand, Howe would have the power to resolve it – in favour of the military. He explained to the House that the bill was precautionary; even steel might not have to be controlled under its provisions. The new bill set the stage for another emergency powers debate. J. M. Macdonnell again sallied forth, asserting stoutly that the real reason for the bill was that Howe had "an enormous appetite for power." It was a familiar charge, but this time it provoked no great concern. Under the circumstances, even Conservative newspapers like the *Ottawa Journal* were urging passage of the bill. And passed it was, on September 12.[14]

Parliament adjourned on September 15. "We got rid of Parliament this morning," Howe happily wrote, and now he could get on with real business. There was, he noted, "a great accumulation of work associated with getting the war programme working."[15]

Much of this work concerned the prospect of sales to the United States. It was next to impossible to get the Americans to promise anything, and difficult enough to discover who *could* promise anything. A meeting in early August with Stuart Symington, head of the United States munitions program, stimulated lavish good-will and plenty of assurances – and then, as time passed, disappointment for promises not kept. When Howe spoke to the Vancouver board of trade in early October, he told them of progress in aircraft, munitions and ship-building, all for the Canadian armed forces. There was no progress in negotiations with the Americans.[16]

Howe travelled to Boston a few weeks later, on October 16, to speak on "Joint Resources and Common Purposes." There would soon be, he hoped, "machinery for closer integration in the production of armaments"; he visited Washington a few weeks later to try to get action on such a program. All that came out of the Washington talks was the publication of a "Statement of Principles of Economic Co-operation," agreed on in Ottawa the previous August. Howe blithely told reporters it was a commitment to gear the Canadian war effort to the American. "Howe's announcement made all the Canadian officials turn a faint green," noted Bruce Hutchison, who was there. But it was only Canada's number one optimist at work, putting the best face on unproductive negotiations.[17]

Late October was not, from the Canadian standpoint, the best time to extract economic concessions from the Americans. The United States were riding high. United Nations forces had soundly defeated Communist troops in Korea, and were pursuing them into North Korea. The United Nations commander, General MacArthur, promised victory by Christmas. With the war so nearly over, there was no urgency in securing an agreement with Canada on munitions production.

Two months later, Howe returned to a different Washington. United Nations forces in North Korea had been surprised and soundly defeated, and were still retreating from the Communist Chinese. The atmosphere had consequently changed abruptly. "It seems to me," Howe reported on his return to Ottawa, "that our friends in the United States are suffering from hysteria in a very advanced stage." Although the Americans were much more forthcoming, their war production priorities remained confused.[18]

The worst case was aluminum. Canada had plenty of cheap aluminum, thanks to the wartime expansion of Alcan's facilities on the Saguenay. After the war, much of that capacity was shut down for lack of markets. The biggest market, of course, was in the United States, a country of high-cost aluminum with low manufacturing capacity, and several domestic aluminum companies who wanted to keep it that way.[19] Repeated Canadian efforts to peddle domestic aluminum were frustrated by the opposition of American aluminum companies. An attempt by Howe to negotiate a three-year contract for one billion pounds of aluminum from the proposed Kitimat smelter also failed. "I must say," Howe wrote to his friend, R. E. Powell, the president of Alcan, "I find it impossible to get to the bottom of the situation." The bottom, of course, was U.S. domestic politics. Even Charles Wilson, a particular friend and a senior official in the American defence program, became evasive when Howe broached the subject. Alcan was distressed, but not crippled by the news: there was an alternative market in Britain which was also rearming and needed aluminum. Meanwhile, Howe took pleasure in spiking one American project: power for any contemplated American smelter in Alaska would have to come from Canada, and he was the man who licensed power exports. There would be no such exports, but there would be a huge smelter on the Canadian side of the line, at Kitimat, making Canadian production even cheaper and more competitive.[20]

The United Nations' failure to win the war by Christmas prolonged the conflict in Asia for two more years. Now the Canadian cabinet concluded that it would be a good idea to embark on an extensive rearmament program and to set up appropriate machinery to run it. The Canadian Commercial Corporation, it also decided, was just not big enough, or authoritative enough, for the job. Howe would have to do it.

Howe spent Christmas 1950 drawing up plans for the new department. "I am getting back into the business of war munitions much against my better judgment," he wrote in mid-December. An act had to be drafted, and Max Mackenzie and Kenneth Palmer, a lawyer-veteran of Munitions and Supply, obliged. Mackenzie, who had been planning to return to private business, relented at Howe's insistence: he would stay for another year to get the new department on its feet as its first deputy minister. The cabinet agreed on the form of the bill in mid-January. St. Laurent chose the title: the new department was baptized under the innocuous name of "Defence Production" – it was less likely to excite the opposition.[21]

St. Laurent also profited from the lessons of past debates: he himself introduced the Defence Production Bill to the House of

Commons in a strong speech. The actual piloting and defence of the bill were left to Howe. As Howe explained it to the House on March 2, 1951, he would recover most of the powers he had exercised as Minister of Munitions and Supply. He could, if he had to, force manufacturers to make what he wanted, at prices set by himself. He could seize a manufacturer's premises and operate his business for him. This time there was a difference: contract disputes could be appealed to the Exchequer Court, so that the final determination of money owing was not left to Howe and his officials. Even with this qualification these were extensive powers. They were granted for five years only because, as Howe pointed out, they were powers "which should not be of a continuing nature." Only the "need for speed" forced the government to resort to them.[22]

The opposition was not mollified. There was no war emergency; Korea was far away, and speed was hardly a sufficient reason to give away such sweeping powers. Speaker after speaker rose to bait the minister; he would, they knew, rise to it. After a day of unequal struggle – Howe's sarcasm and obvious bad temper were making the government look silly – St. Laurent decided that he had better take a hand. There was not much that was new in the act, he argued; most of its provisions were already present in the Essential Materials Act, passed the previous session. With some difficulty, he steered the debate back on course.[23]

It was a brief respite. Although the discussion at this stage was supposed to centre on the principle of emergency powers, George Hees, the Conservative member for Broadview, decided to investigate the details of defence production. Howe's remonstrances failed to budge Hees, who demanded answers to his questions. Finally Howe gave up. "Perhaps," he said, "the quickest way is to make this the children's hour and discuss these things." He then replied to Hees' questions. The opposition was off on its favourite talking point, Howe the dictator, and on that ground it could score. Howe's bad temper, his impatience, his demand that the opposition get back to the subjects at hand could easily be portrayed as the impatience of an imperially minded dictator ignorant of, or hostile to, basic freedoms. "What is parliamentary government coming to in this country?"[24]

Finally, on March 9, the bill passed. The Department of Defence Production was officially constituted on April 1 and

Howe, who had been recruiting staff for months, could assume his new functions. The department was a miniature version of Munitions and Supply. It possessed many of the same functions and many of the statutory powers of its predecessor, but it did not have much occasion to use them. What Howe had escaped in the Second World War – dependence on the Canadian military's orders only – had come to pass. Between April and December the new department placed almost $1.5 billion worth of defence orders. Of that, only just over $100 million was for foreign customers. Where Munitions and Supply had been a free-wheeling agency largely independent of Canadian requirements, Defence Production was strictly a subordinate purchasing agency for the Canadian armed forces.[25]

That was nevertheless a considerable task. On February 5, 1951, Claxton revealed the extent of the government's plans for national defence. Over three years Canada would spend $5 billion to rebuild and re-equip its armed forces. The generals, admirals and air marshals were hard at work deciding what they wanted; when they found it, they passed the word to Claxton, who passed it on to Howe. In one of his less fortunate phrases, Howe explained the situation to the House of Commons: "If the army decides they want a gold-plated piano, . . . we buy the gold-plated piano."[26]

It was not, in practice, always that straightforward. Air Vice-Marshal Frank McGill, a retired airforce officer whom Howe appointed his chief of aircraft procurement, complained that there was entirely too much civilian interference in Defence Production. When the Department of National Defence handed in its requirements for equipment and its specifications, McGill fumed, they ought to be accepted at face value. Instead, Defence Production wasted valuable time and money by checking them. "They say," he wrote, "that some civil servant in the Treasury Board, who never had any army, navy or air force experience could question the necessity of procuring the war material and equipment concerned." But for Howe and the cabinet the principle of civilian control, especially over money, was all-important.[27]

Once the first frantic months were past, Defence Production settled down to a quiet routine. It was really a large procurement agency with certain specialized skills and functions. It spent large amounts of money, and because of that, it was a significant factor in the Canadian economy. The department was never called upon to use its emergency powers, which slumbered peacefully. It worked by inducements and incentives, Howe's other more powerful weapons. And it was in the economic power of Defence Production, with its arsenal of subsidies and tax concessions – all remarkably similar to those perfected during the Second World War and reconstruction – that the department's importance lay. It extended – some said perpetuated – Howe's economic power. It gave the Minister of Trade and Commerce, wearing his national defence emergency hat, the authority to dole out tax relief to hundreds of well-deserving industries across the country. And it guaranteed that the Minister of Everything, as some now called him, would remain in the centre of businessmen's thoughts.

Yet Defence Production was not entirely to Howe's taste. He could not take its mission, the preparation of Canada for war, completely seriously. He did not believe that war was imminent, and he stumbled when he was called on to defend his authority in terms of an anticipated, but improbable, crisis. J. M. Macdonnell's comment during the Defence Production debate of 1951 that Howe was returning to tried and true methods because he had used them, and knew they worked, was close to the mark. Defence Production, more than any other of Howe's ministerial creations, was routine: unexciting to its staff (it had three deputy ministers in quick succession under Howe), it was boring to its minister. At the moment of the department's creation in April 1951, Howe could only regret to a friend that he could not "revive the old enthusiasm of the last war."[28]

Howe knew all too well that something was wrong. Unknown to his wife and his family, he sought medical advice on his irritation and fatigue, and on bothersome chest pains. The diagnosis was simple. Howe had heart disease, angina, the clogging of arteries by small accumulations of fatty deposits. It caused great pain; untreated, it could be fatal. But the advice and the treatment were familiar: palliatives to ease the pain, advice to avoid strain, and the suggestion of a regular drink before dinner to help him relax. But Howe could not avoid strain, fatigue, pain – and irritation.[29]

Howe had another secret. In the spring of 1950 he and St. Laurent discussed the governor generalship. The office was occupied, as it had always been, by a British peer, Viscount Alexander. It was a tangible link with the British Commonwealth, and with the hoary traditions incorporated in it. Many Canadians basked in the idea that somewhere in the country there was an oasis of social prestige presided over by a genuine lord who was the embodiment of regal dignity, as well as a useful adornment to Canada's horse shows. Rideau Hall, the vice-regal residence, was a comfortable enough place, with a small court of its own, located in the middle of gardens and cricket pitches.

Canadian nationalists took a different view. Admirable though the individual British governors general were, they were nonetheless British, and their office was a survival of the times when Canada was a genuine British colony and the governor general a real colonial administrator. It rankled St. Laurent, who had been known to ask whether there was no Canadian who could not fill the highest office in his own country with as much appropriateness as a British-born subject of the king. Because he considered Howe to be a most distinguished citizen, it was natural to propose his appointment to Canada's highest office. There was no one more popular from coast to coast, more universally esteemed, and with a better record of public service. Howe it must be. If Alexander served out his term, he would leave in 1953, plenty of time to allow Howe to drop out of the cabinet, occupy himself with purifying good works for a year, and then, all partisanship spent, step forward at the appropriate moment and become the king's representative in Canada. Howe agreed. It would be a nice diversion, and he was tired of politics; his health too would benefit from the relaxing atmosphere at Rideau Hall. It was, all in all, a splendid idea – a long way to come for a poor boy from Waltham.

But St. Laurent's scheme did not work out. A Conservative government returned to power in Great Britain under Winston Churchill, and Churchill picked Alexander to be his Minister of Defence. Though he was prepared to wait until a proper successor was selected in Canada, Alexander's departure was fixed. Howe was taken aback. He did not want to leave politics just yet; even in a boring department he had much to do. And he had begun to worry about exchanging real power for the trappings of royalty. As governor general he might rule over pine and pelt, but he would not rule over people. As Dean Acheson commented, "Public life is not only a powerful stimulant but a habit-forming one." And Howe refused to kick the habit.[30]

It was, therefore, to be Vincent Massey, Canada's former high commissioner in Britain, who was selected. Massey was the opposite of Howe. Rich by birth, well-bred by profession, a patron of the arts, twenty years a diplomat, he practised the vice-regal arts on a small scale at his country estate outside Port Hope, Ontario. He was well known and kindly regarded by King George VI, who was charmed by the idea of a Canadian governor general and grateful that it was to be Massey who would represent him. One wonders what George VI would have thought of being represented by Howe.

Massey, however, would never represent George VI on Canadian soil. Just before he took office, the King died, and was succeeded by his daughter, Elizabeth II. According to custom, the Queen's coronation took place the year following her accession; the event was set for June 2, 1953.

It was a grand and gala occasion, the greatest social event since 1939. White ties, tails and tiaras were taken out of storage. Privy councillors, their friends, acquaintances and allies vied for positions at the coronation. The Howes, of course, would go, and so would much of the cabinet, the provincial premiers, and various bewildered representatives of dignified institutions in the mainstream of Canadian life.

There was little doubt that 1952 was a better year than 1951, and that 1953 would be better than either. After some anxious moments and political doldrums, the Liberals in Ottawa had recovered their momentum. St. Laurent, after prolonged consideration, told his colleagues that he would stay for another election. The popularity polls were rosy with a very Liberal hue. It would be, Howe decided, a very good time to stay in politics.

CHAPTER SIXTEEN

A Businessman's Country

Canada, *Fortune* magazine proclaimed in August 1952, was a happy land. It had riches, it had resources, it had a future – and it had C. D. Howe. Howe was a man who understood and appreciated businessmen, knew their language, asked their opinions, shared their values. Under his leadership and patronage Canada had become a "businessman's country." This was news indeed for American businessmen, who imagined themselves to be groaning under the weight of twenty years of Democratic party rule. That, fortunately, was coming to an end that fall, but before the Republicans reoccupied the seat so untimely vacated by Herbert Hoover, perhaps they could learn a thing or two from a country whose most powerful minister was enjoying a "sensational" career in politics simply by "behaving like a businessman."[1]

Fortune's reaction was not unique or even unusual. It was easy to be enthusiastic about Canada and its prospects in the summer of 1952. Almost every discernible trend was up. Since 1939 Canada's population had grown by 21 per cent to fourteen million people. Investment was up by 53 per cent, and the gross national product had doubled. Average individual income was up 50 per cent – a greater increase, observers noted, than in the United States. More Canadians were at work, eight hundred thousand more than in 1945, while unemployment had bottomed out at 2.9 per cent. More people were coming to share in the bonanza: "1951 Biggest Immigration Year since 1913," the *Financial Post* trumpeted to its readers. "From Coast to Coast,

Dynamic Growth.'' Investment was up too: $225 million in 1950, $325 million in 1951 and $360 million in 1952. Rising as well was the total of Canadian industry owned outside the country, from $7.5 billion in 1948 to $17.5 billion in 1957. Soon people would start worrying, but not just yet. It was still a proud testimony to Canada's high standing and great achievements.[2]

Howe's name went hand in hand with the Canadian economic miracle. He always seemed to have been there – the *Fortune* article's "stocky, candid, unpretentious 'engineering-type' executive" who ran the nation's business. Prosperity meant Howe.

It was hard for anybody to forget, or ignore, what Howe had done and could do. Throughout 1951 and 1952 newspapers carried almost daily reports of contracts awarded, at an average rate of $10 million a week, from the Department of Defence Production alone. Through Howe's unpretentious offices in Number One Temporary Building passed lines of economic control that stretched from Halifax to Victoria, from the Newfoundland fishery to the aluminum smelter at Kitimat (being constructed in 1952 at a cost of $350 million), and from the auto parts factories of St. Catharines to the uranium mines of Great Bear Lake. Every day, over the phone, by letter and in person, Howe was informed of what was happening or what was about to happen everywhere in Canada. To Canadian business, Howe was synonymous with "Ottawa." If Ottawa wanted something done, as likely as not it was Howe who was stirring things up, and if Howe lifted his finger it was axiomatic that he must have a good reason. Howe was, in short, the leader of a national business community as well as a party leader and a minister of the crown.[3]

Yet Howe was much more than the Canadian business representative in government. His real function was, perhaps, the other way around: he was the government's emissary to the board rooms, the watchdog of business as well as its patron and prophet. Howe saw no contradiction in the role; it was his job to enforce the public interest, and the public interest was, ultimately, business's interest. Even if businessmen could not immediately see the point, they would come round to Howe's point of view, as they had before. Millionaires were Howe's lieutenants – indispensable men through whom he worked to safeguard the national prosperity and build a stronger country.

Howe's unique position in the government was pointed up by the painful adjustment some of his departed colleagues made to private life. Charlie Dunning, it was true, had shaken the dust of politics from his feet and found fulfilment as Canada's leading company director and chairman of the board of Ogilvie Flour in Montreal, but Dunning was a lucky exception. J. L. Ilsley, the former Minister of Finance, had a harder time, trying to practise corporate law in Montreal only to discover that representing his business clients meant pleading their causes before officials he himself had appointed. Ilsley quickly fled to the quieter haven of the Nova Scotia Supreme Court.[4]

Howe must have contemplated Ilsley's descent to the seemly obscurity of the bench with misgivings. He could several times have left politics to enrich himself in private business, but he always refused. The real business was in Ottawa, and his real interest was in power, not wealth. "I cannot," he wrote in April 1952, "think of any other occupation as interesting." Where else, Howe liked to say, would he be at the centre of things?[5]

If Howe's attitude to office was changing and becoming more settled, so was his view of the tools of office. His emergency powers and his vast spending programs were a tonic to him; regularly applied, they produced fifteen to twenty visitors a day sitting in rows in his outer office, sometimes offering Tony Pelletier, his reception clerk, bribes of $50 to let them in without an appointment. Because of his extensive contacts, Howe automatically had more information than anybody else. It was a self-reinforcing process: in seeking approval from the minister, his businessmen-clients provided him with his intelligence. That, added to the reports his deputies made each morning, allowed Howe to be a jump ahead, and to stay ahead. "Seldom," Howe's deputy minister later wrote, "was I able to tell Mr. Howe anything about which he had not already heard or surmised."[6]

But it was a reciprocal relationship. Howe had confidence in what he called "the judgment of the industry" to make the right decisions. To make sure he retained that confidence, normally tight-lipped business tycoons found it convenient to keep the minister posted on their most private plans. In July 1950, to take one example, Sir James Dunn found time to have his private railway car hauled to Ottawa for lunch with Howe, at which he "went over most things relating to Algoma." Others imitated his example.[7]

Where personal contact would not suffice, there was the long-distance phone and, for the older members of Howe's fraternity, the letter. From Vancouver, Alan Williamson, a Munitions veteran now in the investment business, reported both on business and party prospects (Williamson was a fervent Liberal). Frank Ross, a Vancouverite by recent adoption, was another connection, advising on some of Howe's personal investments. In Toronto, Henry Borden, Harry Carmichael, Douglas Ambridge (who had built Polymer) and Gerry Godsoe, the vice-president of BA Oil, kept Howe's flame burning bright before their balance sheets. Borden in particular posted Howe on the accomplishments of his company, Brazilian Traction, proudly reporting its sizeable purchases in Canada. Eddie Taylor, another Torontonian, kept in touch as well. He and his partner in Argus Corporation, Eric Phillips, were astonishing the staid world of Canadian business by gobbling up corporations for fun and profit. In the calmer atmosphere of Montreal, Howe stayed in close contact with H. J. Symington (who had retired as TCA president in 1947 to become the head of Price Brothers, a pulp and paper firm), R. E. Powell, the president of Alcan, and Scotty Bruce, Powell's vice-president, sales manager and eventual successor.[8]

Powell and men like him expected, and got, easy access to and considerate treatment from Howe. That was only natural, in Howe's opinion. Powell spoke for a multi-million-dollar enterprise which earned millions in foreign exchange and provided jobs for thousands of Canadians. As Minister of Trade and Commerce, Howe promoted Powell's products abroad, just as he would those of a firm he personally owned. Canadian sales abroad were a barometer of how well the minister was doing his job.

There was another dimension to Howe's work, equally aimed at increasing Canada's economic strength and, eventually, Canadian exports. The import restrictions of 1947 had forced Canadian producers to replace costly or superfluous imports. Where initiative was lacking, Howe sometimes suggested a proper direction and, if he could, added sweeteners in the form of grants or accelerated depreciation. That, of course, was an emergency measure conceded by the government to meet an emergency. When accelerated depreciation was terminated in 1955, Howe mourned, and explained to his friend Frank Sherman of Dofasco that he only "reluctantly" concurred. "Imports of steel and steel products," Howe added in a letter the next year, "are still about the largest items in our too large list of imports."[9]

Howe's contacts with Canadian business were not confined to his friendships with corporate directors, or to his ability to stimulate and coerce businessmen to do what he wanted. As Minister of Trade and Commerce, or as Minister of Defence Production, he was a major business actor in his own right. At Defence Production, Howe presided over Canadian Arsenals Limited, making ammunition for Canada's armed forces. He represented Polymer before Parliament, and watched with satisfaction as its profits grew from 7.8 per cent in 1951 to 8.2 per cent in 1952 to 19.5 per cent in 1956. Another Howe corporation, Trans-Canada Airlines, continued to be the minister's pride and joy. But these were, by 1952, established, going concerns.[10]

Other crown companies were less in the public eye. Production from Eldorado's new mine in northern Saskatchewan began in 1953. At Port Hope, Ontario, the company had installed a new refining capacity which enabled it to sell highly processed uranium to the United States. Much to Howe's delight, the company began to pay substantial dividends to its shareholders. Eldorado's procurement and pricing policies had also resulted in the development of a number of new mines by other producers. By the 1950s Eldorado's American contracts totalled $1.5 billion for deliveries stretching into the early 1960s. Canada's dependence on such a large and exclusive foreign market was cause for concern for Howe and for anyone who remembered the collapse of wheat markets in the early 1930s. However, a tour of the major American atomic-energy installations convinced Howe that the U.S. need for uranium was still urgent.[11]

At Chalk River, a second and larger research and experimental reactor, the NRU, was under construction. In 1952 a new crown company, Atomic Energy of Canada Limited, with C. J. Mackenzie as its president, was established to take over the responsibility for the Chalk River project from the National Research Council. Bill Bennett became president of the company in July 1953 on Mackenzie's retirement. He continued as president of Eldorado. In 1954 the company commissioned a study of Canada's future energy requirements in collaboration with all of the Canadian power utilities. This study showed conclusively that there would soon be a need in Canada for a new source of power to supplement conventional sources. In 1955 the board of Atomic Energy of Canada recommended to Howe that a demonstration nuclear-power station, known as the NPD, should be designed and constructed using the technology pioneered in the NRX reactor. Howe approved the recommendation on condition that the program provide for the participation of one or more of the Canadian power utilities. Ontario Hydro became a partner in the project and this was the beginning of its extensive commitment to nuclear power. Howe and Leslie Frost broke the sod for the NPD power station in 1956. By the time the station came into operation Howe had long since passed from the scene, but atomic energy was to be a lasting and far-sighted bequest to the nation. The Candu reactor, the successor to the NPD, proved to be one of the world's most successful and economic nuclear-power stations. The development of large uranium resources not only guaranteed that Canada would have sufficient uranium to meet its foreseeable domestic requirements, but also that it would have a substantial surplus which could be sold in export markets.[12]

While nuclear technology promised results, another branch of Canadian technology was giving trouble. Canada's aircraft business was apparently prospering. The contracts dispensed by the Department of Defence Production ensured that it would be even more prosperous, and as far as the public was concerned, the Canadian-designed and produced CF-100 fighters rolling off A. V. Roe's production line at Malton were a signal of Canada's industrial prowess. Only a few officials had a different impression. Aviation technology was costly, Howe learned, as well as slow and quirky. The headaches connected with the production of the CF-100 even caused Howe to dispatch one of his Defence Production officials, Crawford Gordon, to Malton to see if he could straighten out the mess. He could not; instead of a solution, the heavy-drinking Gordon became in Howe's eyes part of the problem.[13]

The problem would soon get worse. Production of the CF-100 was past worrying about: its principal costs were already spent. But the next generation of fighter aircraft posed another, more expensive problem. The airforce wanted a supersonic jet interceptor; A. V. Roe obliged with a design. The new plane would be called the CF-105 – the Arrow.

Howe could not bear to contemplate another five years of A. V. Roe, Crawford Gordon, and trouble. "I must say," he wrote to Defence Minister Claxton on December 19, 1952, "I am frightened for the first time in my defence production experience." He had no confidence in the A. V. Roe Company, either in its management or in its ability to stay within agreed costs. If the airforce had to have a new supersonic fighter, let the government contract the work "to a British firm which has the personnel, equipment and experience that qualifies them to do work of this kind." It went without saying that such work would be performed "for a fraction of the cost" of A. V. Roe's product.[14]

But Claxton did not agree. Placing a higher (as it turned out, much higher) value on Canadian technology than did Howe, Claxton launched the Arrow development program. Howe, who had once promised to deliver gold-plated pianos if the military wanted them, could only gnash his teeth as he presented periodic, embarrassed reports to the House of Commons. Howe's attitude toward the CF-105 was anything but lighthearted. "I can now say," he told the House of Commons in June 1955, "that we have started on a program of development that gives me the shudders." As the cost of the CF-105 climbed from $1.5 or $2 million per aircraft to a possible $8 million, Howe's shudders increased. Attempts to sell the CF-105 to the Americans and British were unavailing; both Canada's allies expressed interest, admiration – and polite regret. But it was not until the spring of 1957 that the cabinet's Defence Committee bowed to the obvious: the Arrow would be cancelled – after the next election.[15]

But problems could normally be mastered by analysis, followed by firm decisions. If something had to be put off for the morrow, it would nonetheless ultimately be solved: there were limitless possibilities, unlimited opportunities and, as the phrase went, an ever-expanding economy. What was impossible today (too soon, too expensive) would not be so tomorrow. It might require a little direction from the top, but Howe was in a good position to provide that direction, prodding businessmen here, advising them there, handing out incentives where they were most needed. The trend was most definitely up.

Howe did not produce his economic auguries by himself. He relied, as always, on an expert staff to advise him, and to handle routine matters that might distract his attention to unimportant things. Mackintosh, his reconstruction adviser, went back to Queen's University in 1946, and was replaced by Sandy Skelton, his brilliant protégé. Skelton became assistant deputy minister of trade and commerce, and died tragically in an accident at sea. It was a sad loss. Skelton, many of his friends agreed, showed a better mind drunk than most of the dismal profession did sober.

As a partial replacement, Howe turned to another economist, O. J. Firestone, a product of the London School of Economics and the University of Vienna. Firestone had worked under both Mackintosh and Skelton; he produced Howe's economic surveys and shared the responsibility for Howe's speeches.[16]

The principal speech-writer was a newer recruit, Mitchell Sharp, a lean, red-headed Winnipeg economist who, like Howe, had got his start in the grain trade. Sharp moved to Ottawa in 1942, to become one of Dr. Clark's brains trust in the Finance Department. From time to time the new recruit was called on to represent Finance's point of view before cabinet committees, and so it was not long before Sharp found himself performing before C. D. Howe. It was not, he later recalled, a happy experience. Sharp's views, Howe growled out, were rubbish. Sharp returned despondently to his office, sure that he had made a powerful enemy. But time passed, Howe and Sharp met again, and the minister began to admire the younger man's plausible intelligence.[17]

In 1950, when Abbott told the cabinet that Sharp was about to leave his department to join Central Mortgage and Housing as vice-president, Howe looked up. Did that mean that Sharp was available? Yes, certainly, said Abbott. Good, Howe replied. Within days, CMHC was looking for another vice-president, and Sharp was settling into his desk as assistant deputy minister of Trade and Commerce. Max Mackenzie would soon be leaving, Howe explained, and when that happened he would make Sharp associate deputy minister, responsible for economic policy and wheat.

Sharp shared the title of deputy minister with a Trade and Commerce veteran, Fred Bull, a tall, stocky man whose placid personality belied his physique. Bull had joined the department in 1929 and reluctantly stayed with it at Max Mackenzie's urging in 1945. Their respective duties reflected their contrasting strengths: Sharp on the intellectual and policy side of the department, Bull on the line side. Bull's duties included reorganizing and strengthening the trade commissioner service, handling trade fairs at home and abroad, and keeping the department's employees in order. It was, generally speaking, a happy partnership.[18]

Howe's relations with Sharp were settled right at the beginning. His new deputy was a past master of speech writing. But his first effort for Howe disappeared into the minister's office without trace; when it returned, days later, it was a barbaric parody of Sharp's carefully sculpted original. Disconcerted, the new boy asked the chief of the old boys, Max Mackenzie, for his advice. Should he leave now, or wait until fired? Mackenzie soothed the bruised bureaucrat. Howe, he explained, was a particular speaker. He had a natural style, developed over many years. Howe was not, Sharp would learn, an illiterate, and he would soon find a compromise that would preserve a speaking style that Howe felt at ease in. This he did, and Howe came to rely on him for the rest of his career.

Ability in selecting personnel, Howe once informed the American Institute of Consulting Engineers, was just another necessary skill he had picked up in the course of his own career as a consulting engineer. He had used it in his private business, and had honed it in the war years and during reconstruction. He put it to good use for his own department and his crown corporations, and he was prepared to put it to use in the service of Canadian business at large. Executives soon learned that Howe's knowledge of the personalities of the Canadian business world was extensive, and his advice usually good. The mere fact that Howe picked someone to be one of his senior advisers attracted attention; Max Mackenzie compared the experience as Howe's deputy to being on display in a shop window.[19]

Howe's approval was sparingly dispensed. When Sam Bronfman asked the minister for his recommendations for the post of financial adviser, Howe sent back two names. The first, Frank Brown, had been his financial lieutenant during the war: he was rated as "an aggressive man with a most able and ingenious mind." The other, Wallace McCutcheon of Argus, was dismissed in a phrase: "very able although, for me, lacking in personality." Howe nominated J. V. Clyne, already a judge in British Columbia and known to Howe through his service on the Canadian Maritime Commission, to be president of Canada Steamships, which Sir James Dunn had just acquired. When Clyne refused, Dunn was consoled with another Howe favourite, Rodgie McLagan, a veteran of wartime service with Canadian Vickers.[20]

Howe's personnel bureau did not operate only within his old-boy network. When the Celanese Corporation established a Canadian branch in 1952, its president asked Howe for nominations to the Canadian board of directors. Howe obliged, pointedly adding that Celanese should discuss his list "with whatever Canadian you select to head your Canadian operation." That Canadian turned out to be Max Mackenzie. Howe was gratified by the appointment, and by Celanese's decision to list its shares on Canadian stock markets, a piece of investment etiquette of which Howe highly approved.[21]

Mastery of personalities made Howe formidable; compatibility of beliefs made him congenial. Howe not only understood but sympathized with businessmen's preoccupations and prejudices. They were, on the whole, preferable to those he found among the politicians, as he told the House of Commons. Howe had ready-made ideas on proper and improper business conduct. A good businessman would play straight, since a man was only as good as his reputation. As long as businessmen played straight, the public interest would not interfere with business. But, as his conduct during the flour-milling inquiry indicated, Howe had no patience and little sympathy with attempts to break up workable business combinations in the name of an abstract principle of competition. If it worked, and it worked well, the public was not endangered. If the public interest was affected, then there would be time to prosecute and pillory the offenders – but not until then. Howe relied on his own judgment to tell him when a business transgressed the unwritten, as well as the written, law.

Howe believed that the market would settle most economic affairs. Low-cost, high-efficiency manufacturing was the key to Canadian prosperity, and that was particularly true of iron and steel manufacturing. Low costs could only be preserved if labour kept its demands moderate; if it did not, Canadian products would be priced not only out of the foreign market, but out of the domestic one too. Howe explained his attitude in a letter to his British Columbia friend Stanley Burke, Sr. Burke and his associates should hold the line on wages in negotiations with the unions. "It will be costly to teach this lesson," Howe wrote, "but [it will be] hopeless if further substantial increases are granted." Standards of living rose because of general prosperity, not because of high wage settlements. The only result of such settlements would be to produce costly and inefficient industries at the expense of the efficient sectors of the economy.[22]

Howe was a free trader in principle even if, as part of Canada's political heritage, he accepted high protection in practice. Howe, *Fortune* reported, estimated that 60 per cent of

Canadian industry would be "better off without tariffs." It went without saying that Canadian exports would be much better off if lower tariffs were broadly applied among the world's trading nations. As Howe liked to remind the House of Commons, Canada was the world's sixth largest industrial producer and fourth largest trader. The country's standard of living was second only to the United States' and far ahead of European rivals.[23]

But exports were not rising. In current dollar value, of course, they were, and there was a considerable jump during the Korean War. Nevertheless, in constant dollars, Canada was exporting less in 1952 (or 1957 for that matter) than in 1945. That was coupled with a steady rise in imports. Those, again in constant dollars, were up 50 per cent in 1952 over 1945; by 1955 they would be double. As a result, Canada rang up a massive deficit in its foreign trade. The difference in the balance of payments was made up by foreign investment.

Despite the relatively disappointing performance of Canadian exports, Howe continued to be optimistic. Canada was a developing country, and the new investments would set matters to rights. Canada still had a great deal that other countries wanted. In fact, they wanted it more than ever. In the same issue of *Fortune* that carried such a glowing portrait of Howe's accomplishments and Canada's future, there was another article, summarizing for its readers the contents of the Paley Report. This study, commissioned by the United States government, told Americans by how much they had already depleted their reserves of natural resources, and how much they would have to depend on outside sources of supply in the future.[24]

The American government was already aware that the United States would need Canadian resources in any future war. Aluminum, iron ore, nickel and platinum had already been the subject of discussions within the American government, and possibly with the Canadian government. But what was for some Americans a cause for fright was for Howe a sign of great good fortune. Canada's economy was sound as well as prosperous, he told an American audience in April 1953. Canada's resources in iron ore, copper, lead, zinc, timber and oil guaranteed its foreign trade and future prosperity. Canada was a "great storehouse" of "vast and increasing resources . . . of which other countries are short."[25]

The main beggar at the Canadian feast was the United States. That country's resources had been seriously depleted by the Second World War. The end of high-grade American iron ores was in sight; other shortages would follow. As early as 1947 Howe was trying to draw attention to Canada's ore reserves and especially to vast untapped deposits in Labrador, along the Quebec-Newfoundland border. Howe's information came from Jules Timmins, who held an interest in the Labrador ore along with George Humphrey's M.A. Hanna Company, of Cleveland, Ohio.

Howe had never met Humphrey; their first meeting took place in 1950. The subject was the development of Labrador's iron. The concession itself had nothing to do with the federal government. Natural resources were a provincial matter, and it was up to Humphrey's new company, the Iron Ore Company of Canada, to make what arrangements it could with Maurice Duplessis' and Joey Smallwood's provincial regimes. But Howe did control other things. He could dispense accelerated depreciation, and he controlled the allocation of steel. Steel for rails was essential if the Iron Ore Company were to link up its ore body with the port of Sept-Iles on the St. Lawrence, and accelerated depreciation would ease the company's financial burden considerably. Howe accommodated the company on both matters. He and Humphrey both wanted to see the iron ore developed as soon as possible, and this was a convenient way to make it so. Humphrey was impressed, and passed the word that Canada was a splendid place in which to invest. "The stability of the Canadian government" and the Canadian economy made Canada one of the best places in the world to place American capital.[26]

Relations with another iron ore company were not so happy. During the 1930's iron ore was discovered in Port Arthur's backyard, at Steep Rock Lake. A company was formed to exploit the mine, and General Donald Hogarth, a prominent Lakehead Conservative, became its president. But Hogarth and his company were overtaken by events. The war made financing difficult and priorities impossible. Thanks to help provided by the American Reconstruction Finance Corporation through the influence of the ex-Canadian Cleveland financier, Cyrus Eaton, Steep Rock managed to procure enough funds to develop its properties, and with some help from Howe a loading dock was built at Port Arthur.[27]

Steep Rock was in several senses a marginal development. Its ore body was much smaller than the Iron Ore Company's, and it had no guaranteed market for its product. It was no particular surprise that Steep Rock soon faced further financial difficulties. Hogarth had by this point become a friend and ardent admirer of Howe's – even to the point of publicly repudiating his Conservative allegiance in order to support Howe. Relations between Hogarth and Eaton were not good and Howe, who disliked Eaton, was only too happy to suggest an alternative source of funds to his friend. Had Hogarth not thought of trying his own Liberal brother-in-law from the Lakehead, Senator Norman Paterson? Hogarth had not; the two men were barely on speaking terms. Nevertheless, with his mine's future at stake, the general did as Howe advised. To his surprise, the money was available. Work could go on.[28]

If Steep Rock's prospects were improving, Hogarth's were not. The general had been battling an intestinal cancer for twelve years, and time was running out. The best he could hope to do was to provide for his successor as president. Howe himself would have been Hogarth's choice; failing that he asked C. D. if he had any suggestions. When Hogarth died, Howe took Steep Rock's presidency in hand. The best candidate, he decided, would be Frank Ross. Ross was an able man, forceful and ingenious. He was also a close friend, and at Howe's suggestion Ross allowed his name to stand for the presidency. Cyrus Eaton had another candidate, the mine's chief engineer, "Pop" Fotheringham. Howe had nothing against Fotheringham, but preferred a man with at least some outside connections. But within the Steep Rock board, Eaton had the votes, not Howe. Fotheringham, the minister was curtly informed, would be Steep Rock's new president.[29]

Howe quickly forgot the incident, but Eaton did not. The two men had contrasting styles and different interests – so different that Eaton cherished a lasting grudge against his Canadian "enemy," and began to accumulate a dossier on Howe. Eaton would not, as far as Howe was concerned, be admitted to the charmed inner circle of Canadian business.[30]

To Howe, the most intriguing of Canada's large corporate entities was the Aluminum Company of Canada, Alcan. Alcan provided the paradoxical spectacle of an American company that had, over time and through peculiar circumstances, become separated from its parent. Although Alcan's ownership was still

American, it was in every respect an independent Canadian company. Its president, R. E. Powell, like Howe, was born in the United States. He shared Howe's interest in fishing, golf and bridge – and in making Alcan a more Canadian company. Under Powell's regime Alcan's owners decided to move to Canada – an important symbolic recognition of Alcan's Canadian status.

Over the years Alcan received what Howe described as "enormous help" from the Canadian government in the form of accelerated depreciation, political support for its sales efforts, and the refusal to cooperate with American plans to erect a rival aluminum complex in the Alaska Panhandle. There was, however, an implied condition to Howe's ready assistance. It would not have been forthcoming, he wrote to Powell, "had Alcan been a subsidiary of an American company."[31]

Howe was aware that the expansion of American branch plants into Canada sometimes produced undesirable consequences. American companies usually refused to list their subsidiaries' shares on Canadian exchanges, and head offices had a tendency to dispatch a succession of American executives through Canada on their way to the top. Sometimes, too, American companies were more responsive to American needs, even those of the American government, than they were to the interests of their Canadian hosts. Howe believed that American corporate misbehaviour in Canada was the exception rather than the rule, and a comparatively rare exception at that. Yet he resented American restrictions on Canadian firms, and exerted whatever pressure he could to try to force U.S. subsidiaries to mend their ways.

The gloomiest news about Canadian problems with American priorities came in the summer of 1952. An American court rendered judgment on an international chemical cartel between Imperial Chemicals and DuPont of Delaware. The two companies were declared to be in violation of American anti-trust laws, and were ordered to stop their illegal activities. One such activity, the judge decided, was their joint subsidiary, Canadian Industries Limited, CIL.

CIL was a flourishing industry. It had played a major role in Howe's war production program, and in Canada's ongoing atomic energy program. When Howe heard the news that CIL's future was in jeopardy, he promised that he would advocate "every possible step to prevent this important Canadian corporation from being butchered." But as the implications of the

American judgment sank in, Howe modified his position. CIL's president, Greville Smith, and DuPont's top executives reassured the minister that although CIL would have to be divided, it would continue its Canadian operations. There would be simply two companies instead of one. And there would be a dividend. Because the two new companies would no longer be ruled by the original cartel agreement, they would be free to export their products wherever they chose, instead of being limited to the Canadian market as before. On balance, Howe decided the Canadian interest was better served by accepting the inevitable, and making the best of the opportunities it offered.[32]

Canada's unprecedented boom showed no signs of levelling off. Howe's defence production program was hitting its stride by the fall of 1952. Writing early the next year, Howe could spy no cloud on the economic horizon. But, he admitted, all good things come to an end: so would Canada's boom unless something more turned up. The economy, Howe liked to say, always needed one great project to keep it functioning properly. That did not mean the thousand and one small projects that postwar planners once envisaged, but something mammoth, something national in scope.[33]

Something like the St. Lawrence Seaway. Canals to bring deep-sea ships from the Gulf of St. Lawrence into the heart of North America were a gleam in an engineer's eye as early as the American Revolution. Mitch Hepburn and Maurice Duplessis stalled action on the grand design in the 1930s, but in 1941 Howe helped to negotiate an abortive Seaway treaty with the United States. Then American entry into the war and opposition from American railways and seaports kept the treaty mouldering in the U.S. Senate.

Lionel Chevrier, the Minister of Transport, liked the idea of a Seaway, and Howe shared his enthusiasm. Chevrier represented Stormont County, on the St. Lawrence. From there he could see wheat move down the St. Lawrence; soon iron ore would move up river, but only in small ships. It was time, both men agreed, to put the last link in Canada's transport network into place. It was up to Chevrier to carry the project. When he introduced the appropriate bills in the House of Commons on December 4, 1951, Howe sat beside him. Then, in a public statement, Howe put the Americans on notice that unless they joined up soon, Canada would build the Seaway by itself. Finally, after three years of constant badgering from Ottawa, the United States was ready. In 1954, a Seaway treaty was signed. Late in 1955 Howe attended the opening of construction. It would last four years, and would cost $900 million, for navigational improvements and hydro power works.[34] Once the Seaway was built, ocean-going ships could sail all the way to Port Arthur, to pick up Canada's export gold, its wheat. The transshipment of wheat at a St. Lawrence port would be a thing of the past.

Wheat produced other anxieties. In 1950 frost damaged the crop; the result was a smaller harvest than expected, and of inferior quality. Better times were expected in 1951. That year the weather produced a different disaster; before the wheat crop could be harvested the rains came. Much of what was left was buried under snow. The Wheat Board became the unhappy recipient of over 250 million bushels of tough and damp wheat. For thousands of farmers, the *Western Producer* wrote, the outlook was dismal: "For the life of them they couldn't see how the oceans of low grade, tough and damp grain could be moved out at any price." Howe's parliamentary critics professed to feel sorry for the minister. For once, Howe was indeed depressed. But Wheat Board chairman McIvor was not. The Wheat Board promptly rented all the available space for storing grain in Canada, and in Duluth and Buffalo too. Carloads of grain were rushed to the grain terminals, where it was dried and stored. It was, Howe smilingly told the House of Commons in March 1953, a simply "magnificent" job by the Wheat Board, and it had saved the 1951 crop from utter ruin.[35]

As the sun shone on the prairies in the summer of 1952, it was obvious that feast would follow famine. The wheat crop was the largest ever, 664 million bushels. Prices were good, and prosperity was rampant. But for the longer term, there was uncertainty. Cooperation among the world's wheat producers was shaky at the best of times, heavily dependent on and responsive to domestic political currents. Those currents were flowing strongly in the United States, where in November 1952 hundreds of thousands of farmers trooped to the polls to vote for a plain, unvarnished Republican administration, the first in twenty years.

The new Eisenhower administration took office in January 1953. President Eisenhower believed in leaving politics to the professionals. The professionals, in turn, devoutly followed the desires of their constituents, especially in the crucial midwestern farm states. And the constituents wanted to grow wheat, all the wheat they could, and to be paid for it by the government. The

American government proceeded to buy all the wheat its farmers could grow and then channel it into aid programs abroad.

Transportation jammed, markets were in chaos, and wheat prices plummeted. In the United States farm incomes remained stable, but in Canada they collapsed. In Saskatchewan farm incomes dropped by 40 per cent within a year. And when the wheat farmers were unhappy, prairie politics reacted quickly. It was with more than a tinge of apprehension, therefore, that Canadian politicians turned their eyes southward.

Nevertheless, Howe took comfort from the make-up of Eisenhower's cabinet. It was the most businesslike in twenty years. Two of its members, Treasury Secretary George Humphrey and Defense Secretary Charles ("Engine Charlie") Wilson, were personal friends of his and, as Howe put it in a letter to Humphrey, "friends of Canada who have a wide knowledge of public affairs in this country."[36] With the return of a Conservative government in Britain in 1951 and a business-oriented American government in 1953 Howe felt more comfortable about the destiny of Canada's two great partners.

In 1952 Clarence and Alice Howe bought a summer place at St. Andrews, New Brunswick, to replace their Rockport house on Cape Ann, Massachusetts. St. Andrews brought Howe even closer to a number of his business friends. Frank Ross was there, a major consideration; so was Sir James Dunn, the increasingly eccentric master of Algoma Steel. Howe now flew to St. Andrews with a pack of friends and acquaintances, who distributed themselves among the cottages of the rich near the seashore. Howe's cottage was in the St. Andrews' style; initially, Howe thought it had space enough for the children to gather with the growing crop of grandchildren. Later, the children and their parents were exiled to another cottage: they were too noisy for Howe.

The especially favoured at St. Andrews used to congregate in a back room at the country store to read the papers and exchange gossip before heading off for the golf course. There were parties and entertainments, and the grandest of all were at Dunn's summer mansion, "Dayspring." Dunn was getting fond of Howe; after all, they had a common Nova Scotian background, and even if Howe had crossed the multi-millionaire once or twice, he could now afford to forgive and forget. Dunn may have had his path eased in this direction by the fact that he wanted something from Howe. Howe was astonished at Dunn's proposition: he wanted Howe to become president of Algoma. The offer was first made in 1953; refused, it was repeated in 1955. Howe returned the compliment by investing heavily in Algoma shares.[37]

In St. Andrews the Howes were counted, in terms of actual wealth, among the minor rich. Dunn's fortune was fabulous, and so was that of the Killams. By comparison, Howe had a modest competency, estimated at roughly one million in 1952. The fortune was increased that year through one notable capital gain.

Back in the 1920s, Howe had helped out Ernie Buckerfield of Vancouver by taking part payment of his fee in one thousand shares in the Buckerfield Company, a private grain firm. It was a favour to a friend, which remained unrealized throughout the dismal thirties. It became an embarrassment, however, in 1948 when Howe became the minister in charge of wheat. Buckerfield was getting on in years and Howe's personal liking for him was not reflected in any great confidence in his business judgment. If Buckerfield died, his company would end in chaos. Accordingly, Howe began to urge Buckerfield to wind up his business in such a way as to allow Howe to get out of his affairs. Buckerfield was reluctant to go; his business was his life. Finally, in 1952, he went: the money realized from the sale gave Howe a large capital gain. He was relieved, partly at the size of his profit, but mostly because he had terminated an involvement that he felt compromised his position.[38]

In the summer of 1953 the Howes did not go directly to St. Andrews. Instead they travelled to London for the coronation, in company with the Dunns. It was enjoyable enough, the more so because they knew that when they got back Canada would be plunged into a federal election.

The government spent the spring of 1953 tidying up its affairs so that it could head off for the polls as soon as the coronation was over. Abbott produced a sunshine budget, his specialty. The only lingering embarrassment came from the Department of National Defence. There were charges of maladministration, waste and corruption. At Petawawa army camp, the opposition charged, there were even horses on the payroll. An investigation by George Currie, a Montreal accountant and former deputy minister of National Defence, agreed with some of the charges. Howe, when he read them, was scandalized. Not that the charges were serious in themselves, but that Brooke Claxton had

278

failed to prevent them arising. The direct cause, Howe decided, was a deplorable lack of business management in the Department of National Defence. That lack could be remedied, he and St. Laurent agreed, by inserting another minister into the department structure, an "Associate Minister of National Defence." Howe's choice was Ralph Campney, the diligent but uninspired member for Vancouver Centre. He was Mackenzie King's former secretary and J. V. Clyne's former law partner, as well as Howe's appointee as chairman of the National Harbours Board. Campney was currently accumulating virtue in the non-cabinet post of solicitor general.[39]

Campney was the latest in a series of additions that reconstructed the cabinet's junior ranks. Shortly after the 1949 election St. Laurent brought Hugues Lapointe, Ernest's son, into the government. Lapointe was followed by Walter Harris, who became Minister of Citizenship and Immigration in 1950, George Prudham of Alberta later that year, and James Sinclair of Vancouver in 1952, on the same day as Campney. There was still room for one more.

J. W. Pickersgill, St. Laurent's omnipresent adviser and one of the country's most powerful civil servants, had been thinking about a political career. Pickersgill's first choice was the Senate, where preferment was available and re-election no problem. But fate, in the form of Joey Smallwood of Newfoundland, intervened. Smallwood convinced Pickersgill that a Manitoba farm boy could find electoral happiness in Newfoundland; in return, Pickersgill could do more for Newfoundland with his knowledge of how Ottawa worked than any neophyte member from the island. For the oncoming campaign, Pickersgill would divide his time between local electioneering and travelling with the Prime Minister.[40]

The appointment of greatest concern to Howe, apart from Campney's, was Walter Harris. Harris was a teetotalling small-town Baptist lawyer from southwestern Ontario. He had arrived in Parliament by defeating the legendary Agnes Macphail in 1940. Though stern and rather aloof, Harris was bright and quick, a good speaker and organizer, as well as ambitious. In 1948, when the Ontario Liberals were switching leaders in their futile quest for office, Howe tried to persuade Harris to take the hopeless job. Harris, with his rural background as well as his political talents, might turn the trick. Harris refused, deciding there was more of a future in Ottawa. So there was: he became St. Laurent's parliamentary assistant in 1947 and kept the job until 1950. Harris' appointment to cabinet was intended to fill the dangerous gap in the Liberals' Ontario representation. Although that province rewarded the government party with 56 seats out of 83 in 1949, there was no outstanding minister from the province except Howe himself. And Howe, apart from his influence in the business community (which in Toronto obstinately continued to vote Conservative), was chiefly a regional minister. So were Lionel Chevrier, confined to eastern Ontario, and Paul Martin, in his independent duchy of Windsor. Decidedly there was need for new blood.[41]

Across Canada Howe interested himself, federally and provincially, first in Liberal survival, and secondly in Liberal success. He did not trespass far into others' preserves. If they could get Liberals elected, using his funds, he would be content. Much of his time was spent searching for political lieutenants, men on whose talents he could rely; when found, they would simply be handed larger and larger responsibilities in the conception and direction of political campaigns in their own areas. Despite Howe's continual activity, Liberal fortunes in provincial politics remained low, and in the five largest provinces the struggle for survival was well nigh desperate.[42]

But Howe refused to believe in the possibility of a federal Tory victory. There was always a good side to any situation, and if their programs were properly presented, Liberals would usually prevail. Party members liked Howe's infectious enthusiasm; many preferred it to Claxton's cautious, step-by-step tactical planning in which nothing was left to chance, and every disaster anticipated in his gloomy imagination. With Claxton, if the worst happened, the party would have a plan to meet it; but with Howe, it often seemed that tomorrow would be another day, and the future would, with a little financial help, take care of itself.

After eighteen years in office, the opposition hoped that the Liberals were riding to a fall on election day. As the campaign unfolded, however, it became apparent that another government triumph was in the making. St. Laurent toured the country emphasizing his government's responsible record and deriding the promises of the opposition. George Drew, still in command of the Conservatives, gave him a lot of promises to shoot at. Drew flailed away at the Defence Department's "horses on the payroll" and vowed to remove them; he boomed promises of reducing taxes and spending together, after reversing the Liberals' wasteful spending policies. After all, this ploy had worked in Eisenhower's campaign in the United States. (Implemented by the Republicans, it would in fact contribute to a North American recession that fall.) Why, the Conservative strategists asked, could Colonel Drew not follow where General Eisenhower had led? Looking at their leader, Conservatives failed to come up with the appropriate answer. But others did. And so Drew and his crew sailed away to defeat without even the consolation of running a glorious campaign. "Dear God," George Nowlan, the Conservative MP for Digby-Annapolis-Kings, moaned after the election, "where did we get that platform?" Dalton Camp, a party organizer, "professed surprise that Nowlan did not know. He was, after all, the party's national president."[43]

On election day, August 10, Howe chalked up another triumph in Port Arthur. There the local organization under Harry Black beat back another CCF attempt to defeat the sitting member: Wilmot, the CCF candidate, lost his deposit and Howe won with 49 per cent of the total vote. It was an enjoyable outing, nothing more. When the cabinet reassembled in Ottawa after the election they had every reason to congratulate themselves on a job well done: 171 Liberals elected, with five independents from Quebec who would doubtless support the government. Howe's own position was truly enviable. There was the usual rash of congratulatory letters, including one from Lord Beaverbrook who praised him as "the only first rank figure in public life escaping without a scratch." On top of that he had "never known," as Beaverbrook put it, "the misery of personal defeat."

As for Howe himself, he was at the peak of his form. He was, he wrote a friend, "enjoying the work. This job is so interesting that I doubt if I would be happy away from it until I slow down a bit more."

The St. Laurent government in the fall of 1953 was entering its Indian summer. It was apparently flourishing. No minister had been a casualty in the election. Just after the election the government machine stopped long enough to take on a new passenger, Jean Lesage, who became Minister of Resources and Development. Lesage succeeded Robert Winters, who was moved at Howe's suggestion to the portfolio of Public Works. These were minor changes. The top level of the cabinet – Howe, Gardiner, Abbott, Claxton, Martin and Chevrier – remained as it had been, unflappable and unstoppable.

When the autumn session of Parliament convened in

November, the government handled it with unusual aplomb. George Drew, de-clawed by the results of the election, was docile and cooperative – "statesmanlike," according to his followers. There wasn't much for Parliament to do. Some housekeeping acts were passed, the ministers uttered optimistic speeches, and the members were sent home to celebrate Christmas.

Howe rested up in Nassau over the holidays with a few rounds of his duffer's golf and evenings of keen but far from championship bridge; his main talent as ever was the luck that dealt him better than average hands, and the vigour rather than the skill with which he played them.

When he returned to the office early in the new year he was still overweight, he still had to contend with his angina, but for a man of sixty-eight who had worked at his driving pace for twenty years, he was surprisingly alert and fit. The immediate challenge he faced was the building of a pipeline to tap the vast resources of Alberta's natural gas for the energy-starved markets of central Canada.

Most of the interested parties, Albertans and Americans particularly, wanted to pipe their gas south and sell it in the rich markets of the American midwest. But Howe had decided that before he would let them do this a line must be built across Canada to supply the needs of Manitoba, Ontario and Quebec. It would be the longest pipeline in the world, over some of the world's most rugged terrain, an engineering feat the likes of which had never before been attempted. And if this were not a challenge enough to excite him, its construction would provide a great boost to Canada's economy, bringing in the foreign capital and creating the local jobs necessary to keep the boom going, so that Canada's great good times would roll on through the 1950s and beyond.

The way was blocked by staggering problems which only made the project more exciting as far as Howe was concerned. Certainly he was in no mood to retire until the job was launched. To do that he must first force the hand of the two rival groups of North American businessmen who were suitors for permits and support. He decided to make them forget their quarrelling, pool their resources, and form a single team to build the pipeline. And they would build it by the route and by the rules he had chosen.

CHAPTER SEVENTEEN

Pipeline

Early on a January morning in 1954 two groups of men crunched over the snow and up the wooden winter steps of Number One Temporary Building. Longstanding rivals for C. D. Howe's favour, they had come to hear his final judgment.

Howe's visitors represented a remarkable assortment of wealth and power, Canadian and American. Heading one group were two of his oldest friends: tall, bespectacled Alan Williamson of Vancouver, alumnus of Munitions and Supply, a Liberal fund-raiser; and Ray Milner of Edmonton, a small, alert bejowled individual, like Howe a Dalhousie veteran who went west during the wheat boom. Despite his Conservative allegiance, Milner flourished in Alberta's exotic political climate. He had been a friend of every Alberta premier (Liberal, United Farmer or Social Credit) and became the province's leading man of affairs.

The second group had a more continental sheen. It included no less than three partners of Lehman Brothers, the New York merchant bankers, a prominent Ottawa lawyer, Ross Tolmie, and a multi-millionaire Texan geologist; but its moving force was a mild little man with a casual old-fashioned manner and a Texas drawl: Clint Murchison. Appearances deceived; Murchison was one of the most dynamic of an active breed, the Texas oilman. On the side, he had recently helped a new-found friend, General Eisenhower, into the White House.[1]

What each group wanted was to build a pipeline to bring the natural gas reserves of Alberta to the energy-starved markets of central Canada and the United States. It offered the prospect of enormous risks and difficulties, and the potential of great wealth for the group that could build it.

For Clarence Howe no great work could have been better shaped to his heart's desire. He had always believed in having one big project ahead, to which he could bend his mind and his energies. This one was a labour of Hercules, certain to call forth again the classic cunning and Yankee ingenuity with which he had so many times confronted the intractable. It took him back to his university days: the tough, unarguable facts of physics were there to be discovered, reckoned with, and reduced to patterns of elegance. It reminded him of his first job at the Lakehead, forty years back, when he found a way for the farmers to build a terminal of their own; or when Lake Superior reduced that plan to ruins and he determined to soldier on; or of the day in 1929 when the white columns of Saskatchewan Pool No. 7 stood complete by the shore – the largest, the most modern, the most magnificent thing of its kind in the world.

As he approached the term of his three score years and ten, C. D. Howe could see in the pipeline a last great battle. As far as he was concerned, it entirely justified his decision the previous year to stay on in a government from which younger colleagues were now planning to depart; it confirmed him in his suspicion that he was now too old to retire. As he told the Toronto chartered accountant Walter Gordon, who was considering an invitation to join the Liberal cabinet that same year, "Where else could I get so big a job?"[2]

Once, when the head of the Canadian Broadcasting Corporation, Alphonse Ouimet, was asked what the corporation's greatest achievement was, without hesitation he replied: "the building of the network from coast to coast."[3] Alphonse Ouimet was an engineer. Canada was indeed an engineer's challenge – a wide gulf to be spanned, a sweeping curve of the world's geography to be bridged over. Howe had played his role in spanning the dominion from sea to sea – with the broadcasting network, with the national airline, and in reconstituting the national railway system. And now he would bind east and west together with a single link of steel. Howe saw the role of the trans-Canada pipeline in Canadian history as a second CPR.

The two groups of visitors were ushered separately into the minister's office. He saw each of them for about twenty-five minutes. Howe was friendly, but firm. Though he was seeing his visitors separately, he had just one thing to say to them both.

There would be one transcontinental pipeline, and it would run through Canada, and only in Canada. One company would build it, with any help in the government's power. But Howe would only issue a licence if the two parties would quit lobbying the various governments and interests concerned, if they would settle their differences and agree on a single plan. Each group, he remarked, had fine men in it. Each had a variety of skills and assets to contribute. They must return to the Château Laurier and meet. "The all-Canada line is national policy. I will make it feasible. Come back and see me at nine tomorrow morning. Together."[4]

It was a long night at the hotel. During the day the two groups had managed to eliminate all major obstacles but one: their respective shares in financing the proposed single new company. The group dominated by the New York investment bankers, which also included Clint Murchison, insisted that since the American investment market was at least ten times larger than the Canadian, their share should be a ten-to-one ratio. They also felt that Howe's new-found personal friendship with Murchison, and the fact that their group had committed itself to an all-Canadian pipeline route from the beginning, gave them two trump cards. The Canadian investment group, on the other hand, until Howe's firm decision in favour of an all-Canadian line, had long argued that building across the Laurentian Shield of Northern Ontario would make the line impossible to finance. They originally planned to build it as far east as Winnipeg and then south into the markets of the American mid-west. This group too had a good friend of Howe among them in the person of his wartime comrade Alan Williamson. They also had the advantage of Canadian direction and control. They held out all night for a fifty-fifty split.

Finally, the Canadian group's spokesman, Deane Nesbitt, convinced the Lehman partners that he and his colleagues had for many years successfully placed great quantities of Canadian securities on the New York market, and that Howe was deadly serious about a compromise that would be fair to both sides. At five A.M. Murchison's bankers went down to his room to advise him that they would agree to an even split in the financing of the new company. Already up and stirring by that hour, as always, Murchison immediately and cheerfully concurred. At seven A.M. they informed the Canadians that they were ready to go back to Howe's office with an agreement.[5]

The meeting went swiftly. Shortly afterwards, a plan for the new Trans-Canada Pipe Lines Limited was drafted and a fourteen-member board sketched out. Rather like a Canadian cabinet, it included influential people from every major interest and region, each of whom had their roles to play in the placing of sales contracts or securities or keeping in touch with one or more of the many governments and agencies concerned.

Howe had managed to leave each side feeling that he had done them a favour, and that despite all their bitter rivalry he could hold them together and see their project through. Williamson thanked him profusely on behalf of the Canadians. Murchison told him privately that until Howe intervened he had felt like a two-year-old about to have the "apple snatched from our hands"; if it had not been for "your aggressive attempt to get these people to work with us," the whole scheme would have collapsed.[6]

Howe soon found himself eagerly inquiring about deadlines, gas contracts and steel pipe supplies, prodding friends, politicians and regulatory bodies wherever they could help – in Edmonton, Washington, Ottawa, Toronto, New York, Montreal. He somehow seemed to be playing the roles of referee, linesman and coach all at once – never mind that there were usually several teams to be advised and more than one game going on at the same time. Howe loved helping his friends, and his friends were, almost by definition, the dynamic men – engineers, businessmen, academics, or indeed anyone with the right cast of mind and sense of urgency – who he believed would develop Canada.

Howe's role in the petroleum boom that hit Canada when Imperial Oil found oil at Leduc outside Edmonton in 1947 was relatively limited. The problems of finding the capital and technology to move Alberta oil east were well known and manageable compared to those of natural gas. Besides, Imperial Oil was a large company, long in the field, ready and able to procure financing for the pipeline from their wells in Alberta to their refineries along the route through the United States and finally into central Canada. Howe's chief role as Minister of Trade and Commerce had been to see that Imperial got their export permit for what they deemed the most efficient route available. It was typical of him that he made no attempt to change the company's chosen Great Lakes port of Superior, Wisconsin, to a Canadian terminus in his own home district of the Lakehead nearby. He readily accepted the argument that it would be more efficient to build into the United States so that the line would be aimed towards Chicago and ready to be extended when the time was ripe.

The natural gas business was different. There were far greater risks, variables and unknowns, and hence more need for intuitive decisions and for the helping or prohibiting hand of government at every turn.

In 1949 Howe advised Frank Ross, who was investing in the prospect of bringing gas south from northern British Columbia, that his chances looked good. Howe added that as minister he was ready and willing to expedite the export of gas across the United States border north of Seattle to help pay for the line to Vancouver and make the product cheaper there. He also advised Ross to discourage, if he could, the filibustering by western opposition members of Parliament against bills for rival pipelines out of Alberta. Besides, he added, "the government cannot let a group of Tories take charge of the Commons."[7]

By 1950 several groups were seeking permission to build natural gas pipelines out of Alberta in both directions – to Vancouver and to Winnipeg. It was assumed that they could only be financed if a large proportion of their ultimate market were found in adjacent American cities. It was also assumed that eastern Canada would only get its own supply by hooking up to Texas gas by means of a line across the Niagara River to Buffalo.

But then Clint Murchison appeared and introduced a new element into the game. He proposed that a line could be built across Canada without dependence on the American market. In August 1950 the Canadian subsidiary of his Delhi Oil Company was incorporated and it became the first major corporation in Alberta whose prime objective was to search for gas rather than oil. At the same time, he arranged to visit Howe. Like everyone else Howe was skeptical about his plans. He asked Murchison: "Have you ever travelled the Canadian Shield? I come from there and it is a little more rugged and a lot colder than Texas." But Murchison persisted. He knew that climate did not affect dry gas seriously and that the line, if necessary, could be laid on the surface rather than buried. As he told his company's Ottawa lawyer, Ross Tolmie, "You Canadians don't know the value of gas. When you do, you won't want to be on the far end of a line from Texas."[8]

Murchison also knew that the prospect of bringing foreign

gas into the United States would be anathema to his powerful competitors there. He did not think much of his chances of getting his Canadian product past their lobbies in Washington. An all-Canadian line would eliminate this major stumbling block. Murchison took Howe south with him on a winter holiday in January 1951 ("the best I've had in years," Howe commented in his thank-you note afterwards). And from that time on the two men were continuously in touch. The following year Howe was advising Murchison on which Canadians would be useful members of his company's board: Jules Timmins, the Northern Ontario mining magnate, for example. In due course Murchison invited Timmins to join and he accepted. Howe told Murchison that he would discuss the proposed all-Canadian line with Ontario Premier Leslie Frost, and later wrote that he and Frost agreed that "your willingness to construct the pipeline to Ontario is all the evidence we need that the line is feasible."[9]

Frost recalled Ontario's energy shortages during the Second World War and the fact that American sources were unreliable when there were power shortages across the border. Furthermore, both he and Howe had seen the St. Lawrence Seaway blocked by powerful sectional interests in Washington for many years. Frost was then in his prime, slipping easily from one to another of his old shoe roles – Lindsay lawyer, Old Man Ontario, Silver Fox of the back rooms and the board rooms, minor statesman of Confederation. Howe admired and liked this provincial Conservative politician as much as he had disliked Liberal Premier Mitchell Hepburn.

Frost was convinced that the energy needs of Ontario would soon be critical. He wanted the federal government's support in keeping sufficient Alberta gas reserves for Ontario before licences were granted for export to the United States. In October 1952 Howe told that other provincial eminence, Alberta Premier Ernest Manning, in Frost's presence, that he would not allow any gas exports to the American mid-west unless the needs of central and eastern Canada were provided for first. On March 13, 1953, Howe confirmed this decision and announced in the House of Commons that henceforth the building of an all-Canadian pipeline was to be government policy.[10]

At this point the most powerful of all American gas companies appeared on the scene. Tennessee Gas Transmission allied itself to a group of Torontonians led by Mayor Allan Lamport and the local utility, Consumers' Gas. They advanced a scheme to bring American gas across the border at Niagara. If they were successful they would establish a pattern that could kill any chance of the east-west all-Canadian pipeline. Howe immediately sprang into action. On March 28, 1953, he asked the Canadian ambassador in Washington, Hume Wrong, on behalf of both Premier Frost and himself, "to find out the facts as to the Tennessee Project and discourage it." And he asked Wrong to talk to Murchison's man in Washington, who would explain their position in detail. Murchison kept Howe posted on his rival's moves. He also advised on how the U.S. Federal Power Commission (FPC) might respond to the Canadian request for a licence to export Canadian gas south of Vancouver into the state of Washington. In a panic he asked Howe to "get your federal and B.C. Parliaments to enact Laws" guaranteeing export supplies on the west coast. Howe explained to his friend that his fears were unfounded: "In British law a statement by the Minister in the House" was quite sufficient. But since the FPC did not see it that way he said he would plan to amend both government regulations and the act. He did not bother to explain just what power he had to get "his B.C. Parliament" and Premier W. A. C. Bennett to do anything at all.[11]

In the meantime, he told Murchison that George Humphrey, the Cleveland iron ore baron who was President Eisenhower's new Secretary of the Treasury, had confided to him that he was soon going to make a couple of new appointments to the FPC. Howe advised Murchison that anything he could do to delay the FPC's ruling until these men were in place would be helpful. Murchison said that he knew who the new FPC chairman was going to be. After checking on him and his past operations, he told Howe "I have come to the conclusion that he is our sort of folks, and I know the President is." He wanted Howe to arrange to meet the man, along with President Eisenhower. "I know you can use your sagacity and turn on your personal charm and get any darn thing you want out of either of them."[12]

Murchison believed that if only his two good friends Ike and C. D. would get together they could also remove other obstacles to good neighbourly relations between their two countries and to the building of such projects as the St. Lawrence Seaway. "This Seaway situation is too complicated for me to try to work out politically just exactly what you want," he told Howe, "but I feel sure that if you take it out of diplomatic channels and go see the President yourself, you can get precisely what you want." Murchison tried to coax Howe away from a Commonwealth conference in London that April in favour of another trip to Mexico with him. "I know darn well we could show you a better time in Mexico, but I guess duty is duty."[13]

Howe was pleased by the attention of such a rich and powerful man, and indeed he was always a relatively easy mark for much less important and charming flatterers than Murchison. He was also genuinely fond of Murchison and enjoyed the naïve and direct personal approach to public affairs, though it was almost a caricature of his own. But he was too experienced to put much faith in Murchison's estimate of their common ability to orchestrate things to their own mutual advantage in Washington.

By August 1953 Tennessee Gas had acquired FPC approval to export American gas across the Niagara River. Howe and his department were left to search desperately for a Canadian legal device to stop them. The lawyers of Trade and Commerce found what they needed by using the Navigable Waters Protection Act, even though the only ship that sailed anywhere near the proposed pipeline was the *Maid of the Mist*. To their amazement and fury, Consumers' Gas and Tennessee were informed that the boiling waters below Niagara Falls were to be protected for navigation. This device held the fort until Howe could get legislation through the next session of Parliament requiring that Canadian imports, as well as exports, of gas would require a licence in the future.[14]

Howe next returned to the western front, where the Alberta gas producers, with the exception of Murchison, were clamouring for permission to ship their gas south to the United States without regard to the needs of central Canada. This was the other side of the pattern of the north-south continental energy grid which conventional wisdom, on both sides of the border, assumed to be inevitable. But under pressure from Howe, a way was found to keep the possibility of an east-west pipeline open.

At a meeting with Prime Minister St. Laurent on November 27, 1953, Premier Manning agreed to release enough gas from Alberta to supply the eastern Canadian market, provided there was a single Canadian applicant to transmit it and provided there was a spur line into the United States south of Winnipeg to make that applicant's company financeable. Howe was then in a position to force the shotgun wedding in Ottawa between the two leading contenders.

With the pipeline company launched at last, and Parliament still on vacation, the next few weeks looked unusually tranquil – so tranquil that the Prime Minister felt himself justified in taking a month to cross the world and consolidate Canada's new and prominent international standing.

Before he left, he and Howe talked over the situation. What would be the best strategy for the government's and the party's future? St. Laurent had several times considered retiring. Each time he held back, convinced that his duty bound him to stick by his party, whose most conspicuous asset he was. But he was now seventy-two. After two great victories surely he had done enough for the party. Howe agreed. It would soon be time to go. There were plenty of prospective successors; with four years before the next election there was time for an orderly transition. But there was no hurry: there would be time to decide what to do, and when to do it, when the Prime Minister returned. Meanwhile, as acting Prime Minister, Howe would steer the government through St. Laurent's absence.

St. Laurent left on February 4. For the cabinet it was almost a vacation. Howe addressed his colleagues by their first names and ran meetings in a swift but casual fashion. There was little urgent business and nothing to disrupt the smooth running of the next parliamentary session. In mid-February Howe took some time to help out an old colleague. Premier Angus Macdonald of Nova Scotia had a problem. The federal government was partly funding a causeway across the Strait of Canso, connecting Cape Breton with the province's mainland. But there was one embarrassment: the low bidder on the project was a Hamilton steel firm. It would be embarrassing not to give the project to the low bidder, but more embarrassing still to deny it to the local steel company in Sydney, Nova Scotia. Howe arranged matters. The president of the Hamilton firm was an old friend, he told Macdonald, and he was happy to do Howe a favour. "I approached him," Howe related, "on the basis of helping me out in solving a difficult problem."[15] Macdonald was delighted and expressed his thanks in a warm letter to his former colleague. It was Howe's last contact with Macdonald. In April he flew to Halifax to attend the Premier's funeral.

By then Howe had other concerns. They were caused by the condition of the Prime Minister. St. Laurent returned from his round-the-world trip on March 9, to a triumphal reception. Howe and the cabinet were there, and so was George Drew. St.

Laurent's appearance in the House of Commons was equally moving. In an age when world tours were great and unusual events, Canadians were proud and happy that their leader had so well represented their country in so many different lands. The results could be nothing but good.

No doubt they were for Canadian foreign relations. They were quite the opposite for St. Laurent. First his staff, and then his colleagues, were disturbed by what the photographs did not show – fatigue and exhaustion. At St. Laurent's age these were serious problems; they tended to express themselves in outward indifference and inner depression. For the first time his performance in Parliament suffered. When a tax dispute with Quebec was debated early in April, St. Laurent sat mute; finally he intervened, but it took an obvious effort to bring himself to do so.

Howe was by now seriously worried. On April 8 he wrote to St. Laurent's son-in-law, Hugh O'Donnell, to beg him to take St. Laurent along on an Easter vacation in Bermuda. Nothing of importance was coming up, he told O'Donnell, and he felt sure that he could hold the situation together in Ottawa for the next month. During that time it was imperative that St. Laurent recuperate.

What now worried St. Laurent was a prospect known only to him and a few of his innermost circle. Within months the government would face the loss of three of its most able ministers. Chevrier's departure was expected; he would become president of the new St. Lawrence Seaway Authority. But the two others were a shock. Brooke Claxton, as his friends knew, was worn out at the Department of National Defence. He learned, bitterly, that his work and ability had done him little personal good as far as his party was concerned. His chances of becoming leader after St. Laurent were, he finally realized, negligible. After toying with the idea of moving to another portfolio, Claxton decided to make a clean break: he would resign from politics and seek his fortune in business. The second was Douglas Abbott. Abbott had led a charmed existence as a politician; with his administrative record and his personal strengths – not least his affable manner – he was, unlike Claxton, a logical and likely choice for the party leadership. But Abbott did not want the job. He did not like the exercise of power enough to want to be prime minister.

St. Laurent was deeply grieved at his colleagues' decision to depart, but he was too proud to ask them to change their minds.

He would make the best of the situation. Howe and St. Laurent discussed what they could do. In the case of Transport, Howe suggested Jack Pickersgill, the Secretary of State. Pickersgill demurred; there was, in any case, another vacancy. When Howe and St. Laurent talked over the succession at Finance, they agreed that the logical successor, Stuart Garson, would be inappropriate. As Pickersgill later said, "Garson's lengthy presentations might cause strains in the Ministry and in Parliament"; the Minister of Finance was more in his colleagues' way and in the public eye than the Minister of Justice. Howe recommended Walter Harris instead. He was young and he was obviously a man of considerable abilities; he had made a good job out of Citizenship and Immigration. Harris was appointed. Transport was filled by a new man from Quebec, George Marler, whom the provincial Liberals could ill afford to lose; National Defence went, to Howe's satisfaction, to his old friend and early appointee to the National Harbours Board, Ralph Campney, who moved up from associate minister to minister. Roch Pinard, another new appointment, became Secretary of State, and Pickersgill replaced Harris at Immigration.[16]

The ministerial changes in the middle of 1954 had a far more serious effect than any election on the character and prospects of the St. Laurent cabinet. At a blow, half the cabinet's middle generation, men with ten years' service in the ministry, were wiped out, including the most acceptable choice for the next leader. Attention now focused on the survivors. Which of the younger men would run for the leadership, and how would they stand the wait? For the remaining three years of the government's life, the question of the next leader was never far from the political surface.

The most obvious candidates were Mike Pearson, whose personal popularity rivalled Abbott's and after that Walter Harris and Paul Martin. Most ministers had their preferences, usually for Harris or Pearson. Howe, despite his support of Harris for Minister of Finance, did not extend that support to the leadership; his own candidate, it was rumoured, was Robert Winters, the Minister of Public Works and his fellow MIT graduate. In Howe's eyes, Winters' principal strength was that he thought like a businessman – and, of course, like an engineer. Martin's chances he did not rate highly; in any case he did not like Martin's perennial sponsorship of welfare measures.

Howe made no overt sign of his preferences, but he must have been aware that with the new balance of forces in the cabinet his own position had become more important, and more vulnerable. St. Laurent needed him more than ever; some of his colleagues needed him not at all. As far as they were concerned, he was an embarrassment in the government, and especially in Parliament. Howe, Pearson moaned, was "the Tories' biggest asset in Parliament, as Drew was ours."[17] He had hoped that Howe would leave by taking over the St. Lawrence Seaway – or just leave.

The "Junior League" – Howe's scornful term for the younger members of the cabinet – was by no means wrong in its criticism of Howe. He was rough where a smoother man would prevail more easily. With his patience easily exhausted, and his estimate of his own ways and wisdom enhanced, he often treated Parliament with a contempt he made no effort to hide. He looked, some people thought, like a wounded bear, destined to be baited by the opposition, and doomed to rise to the bait every time. Old friends noticed that Howe's temper was perceptibly shorter and if he happened to lose it in public, where withdrawal would be difficult without loss of face for the whole government, the results could be disastrous.

It was bad enough in private, out of the public view. During the spring of 1954 the CBC decided to run a special on unemployment. Unfortunately, the special coincided with a debate on unemployment in the House of Commons. Davidson Dunton, the CBC's president, phoned Howe to ask him to say a few words on the subject. Howe blew up. Had Dunton nothing better to do than curry favour with the Tories? There would be no CBC special; if there was, he would fire everyone in the corporation from Dunton down. Dunton pointed out that he was responsible not to the cabinet but to the CBC Board of Governors. He could not and would not resign at a minister's request. Howe hung up, furious.

Dunton's phone call also coincided with a cabinet meeting. Howe steamed into the cabinet and told the other ministers about the proposed CBC special. St. Laurent was absent, and since Howe was presiding, he could shove the matter to the top of the agenda. Milton Gregg, the Minister of Labour, agreed: something would have to be done. Howe had a solution ready: stop the broadcast or fire everybody. A silence followed. "Most of the ministers," Pickersgill later said, "knew this was dangerous nonsense." Eventually Abbott spoke. Perhaps, he suggested, it would not be a good idea publicly to muzzle the CBC; but possibly the CBC would postpone its broadcast until a less embarrassing time. Abbott's intervention defused the situation, and Howe turned his attention to other matters; finally the cabinet adjourned for lunch. Howe sat next to Pickersgill, moody and silent. Finally he turned to his junior colleague. "Perhaps," he admitted, "I am wrong about this. The right thing for me to do is to call Dunton and tell him the cabinet is thoroughly annoyed but will not interfere. But if he cares to postpone the broadcast we will appreciate it." Howe duly called Dunton, apologized for his outburst, and said his piece.[18]

Unemployment reflected on the government's whole performance, and was beginning to cause concern. In June 1954 there were 221,000 people officially counted as jobless – 4.6 per cent of the work force. This figure was nearly double the 115,000 unemployed of a year earlier. When Howe dismissed this recession as a purely temporary slowdown in the booming economy, to many his optimism sounded hollow; but in the end he was proved to be right. But he could not take such a casual view of another slowdown. By the fall of 1954 the new centrepiece of his economic program, Trans-Canada Pipe Lines, was in serious trouble.

The new company was investing heavily in personnel and engineering plans in order to bring gas to Winnipeg by 1955 and begin building across northern Ontario the following spring. But in spite of its formidable membership and Howe's prodding on their behalf, the company's board could not persuade Alberta gas producers, and in particular Gulf Oil, the largest of the American-controlled companies, to sign supply contracts. Nor could they persuade such eastern utilities as Consumers' Gas of Toronto to sign purchase contracts. Without these contracts there was no hope of marketing Trans-Canada securities in New York at a tolerable interest rate. And without the prospect of financing, both gas producers and consumers were the more reluctant to tie themselves to contracts, and skeptical about the east-west pipeline.

Most people in the gas business were simply waiting for the Trans-Canada scheme to collapse; the logic of north-south patterns would then reassert itself. On top of this difficulty, Trans-Canada's request before the U.S. Federal Power Commission to allow export of some Canadian gas south of Winnipeg was stalled for lack of any concrete evidence that the company could guarantee any supply whatsoever, let alone finance the building of a pipeline across the prairies to the Minnesota border.

Throughout 1954 Howe and the Trans-Canada board members struggled to get their enterprise afloat. But the problems seemed to multiply. What Alberta gave with one hand, it withheld with the other. After Trans-Canada received permission to move gas out of the province in May, it was immediately faced with a new consortium of Alberta gas producers, Alberta Gas Trunk Lines, formed with the blessing of Premier Manning. This company would not even quote transportation rates for gas to the Saskatchewan border.

Premier Duplessis of Quebec met his Trans-Canada visitors personally, with teasing charm and smiling intransigence. The Trans-Canada representatives had come prepared. When Trans-Canada's spokesman, Frank Schultz of Dallas, asked, "Would it be presumptuous of us, Mr. Prime Minister, to ask who should be our lawyer in Quebec?" Duplessis roared with laughter. "No, Monsieur Schultz, it would not. It would be goddamn wise. You should have my personal attorney, Edouard Asselin." When the Trans-Canada directors went round to Asselin's office they discovered that Duplessis had already called and told him to accept. For good measure, Asselin was also put on the Trans-Canada board. The good it did, however, was not immediately apparent. After protracted negotiations, Quebec Hydro refused to get into the gas distribution business in any way.

Duplessis recalled for the edification of his Trans-Canada friends how the local gas company in his home town of Trois Rivières had failed, and lost people a lot of money, back at the turn of the century. In desperation the Trans-Canada directors tried to buy the old Montreal Manufactured Gas System so that they would have a customer. "Le Chef" expressed keen interest in selling it, then looked at the ceiling and told them that of course they would have to pay the full depreciated cost. This meant buying a vast quantity of antiquated equipment, such as several ancient coke ovens and $6 million worth of old coaling ships. That was the end of negotiations with Quebec for some years to come.[19]

With such examples of provincial cooperation before him, the socialist premier of Saskatchewan, Tommy Douglas, saw little reason to bail a private corporation out of trouble. So the Saskatchewan Power Commission also became sticky about terms and refused to sign a contract until it saw what others were planning to do.

The best prospects for sales were in southern Ontario, but even these remained difficult. Howe summoned the executives of Union Gas and told them they had better sign up with Trans-Canada – fast. He prodded the head of Consumers' Gas, Oakah Jones, whose cheerful pieties about the dynamic future role of gas in the Canadian economy infuriated him. "Why don't you sign a contract?" he demanded. Union Gas eventually did sign, but Consumers' held out another two years until there was no other possible recourse.[20]

By October 1954 the Trans-Canada people were desperate. Howe's oldest friend on the board, Alan Williamson, appealed to him on behalf of the staff they had hired, as well as the investors who were putting money into the company for surveys and right-of-way options.

> I have quite a responsibility to all these fine people who have come with Trans-Canada and given up fine positions elsewhere. Also to the many who are pouring in money on a no-profit basis, purely on my say-so that this is a national project. . . . If I weren't dealing with you I might be really worried.

Howe replied to Williamson that his government was "counting heavily on this programme and prepared to do what it can." Williamson was instructed by his board to tell Howe that in the light of their inability to get suppliers, customers or investors to take their scheme seriously, their only hope was a government bond guarantee. On January 6, 1955, true to his word, Howe told Williamson he would put such a proposal before cabinet. He said he expected their prompt concurrence. He was in for a rude surprise.[21]

Finance Minister Walter Harris, backed by his senior officials, and the Governor of the Bank of Canada, James Coyne, flatly rejected the Trans-Canada proposal as financially unsound. Howe pleaded with Harris. "This is no ordinary project, but the largest capacity and longest pipeline ever undertaken." He pointed out that with the resulting investment in gas-fired household and industrial equipment it would bring over one billion dollars into the Canadian economy. Above all, their government was "committed to the hilt" to an all-Canadian line, as opposed to a north-south supply pattern. "The project is comparable in importance to our transcontinental railroads. In my opinion, if the project is allowed to collapse the use of western gas in eastern Canada will be a dead issue for all time."[22]

But like Harris and his officials, the cabinet remained unconvinced, and the Prime Minister lacked both the will and the energy to assert himself and hammer out a compromise solution. Besides the financial objections, there was a strong political argument against guaranteeing a private corporation's bonds.

Howe was shaken. When Alan Williamson next visited his office he was appalled at the appearance of his old friend. Howe looked as if he had suffered a severe illness or shock. He had almost certainly experienced another bad bout of angina – although even his closest friends did not know he had a heart condition. Howe listlessly advised Williamson and Deane Nesbitt, who was with him, that he had suffered a defeat in cabinet and that they should try negotiating directly with James Coyne in his capacity as head of the Industrial Development Bank.[23] It was a course of action for which he obviously had little enthusiasm and even less hope. When a member of his staff approached him to try out an idea that the mandarins of Finance might accept, Howe growled: "You and all the other damn Rhodes scholars!" As for his colleagues in cabinet, Howe told an old friend that he was now part of "a government which has fallen into the hands of children."[24]

CHAPTER EIGHTEEN

Dictator Howe and Black Friday

Howe's defeat in the privacy of cabinet over his pipeline project was followed by a humiliating public retreat in the House of Commons on the question of his ministerial powers.

The debate began on March 10, 1955, when the Prime Minister presented a bill to extend the temporary emergency powers granted to the Minister of Defence Production during the Korean War. The Cabinet, anticipating a raucous and damaging confrontation between Howe and members of the opposition, agreed to Jack Pickersgill's suggestion that St. Laurent take charge of the matter himself. This he did in his best statesmanlike manner, full of lofty generalizations. But he could not conceal the weakness of the government's case. The powers had been granted during a period of wartime shortages and with an assurance from Howe himself that they would only be temporary. Now, though they had never actually been used and the emergency was over, the minister's emergency powers were to be made permanent.

The Tories' terrier of debate, Donald Fleming, leapt up scrapping the moment the Prime Minister finished: the bill was an outrageous attempt to mask "Dictator" Howe's lust for absolute power over the Canadian economy. The next day, St. Laurent was absent from the House, depressed and ill. Howe was given charge of his own bill and his younger colleagues' worst fears began to be realized. He utterly failed to perceive that the bill and his manner of defending it were a godsend to the opposition, They were able to convert what was a strong point in the public eye – his reputation for getting things done quickly and decisively – into a political liability. Why, they asked him, if he was promising not to use the powers arbitrarily, did he need them at all? He told them that if they were going to be so unreasonable he would not even listen to their proposals for compromise; he would put through the bill exactly as it stood.

Respite came while Parliament turned to other matters and Howe made an extended trip to Australia and New Zealand in his other capacity as Minister of Trade and Commerce. But when debate on the bill resumed on June 7, the Conservatives were readier than ever for battle. Encouraged by editorial praise for their resistance to the Liberal juggernaut, they decided on a bold new tactic. Instead of merely speaking critically of the government's arbitrary measure, they would dig in and obstruct its passage in the House of Commons.

To Howe's disgust, George Drew was back in fighting trim, his gorgeous golden self again, now that the humiliation of electoral defeat was wearing off. Ottawa temperatures soared to 90 degrees Fahrenheit and stayed there; but while members fretted restlessly about leaving for the summer, Howe told them that the government would "sit here until the snow flies," rather than accept any change in his bill. And he reminded them that over the years he had acquired "more experience in defence purchasing than any other man now living."

Day after day in the House the Prime Minister sat silent and drawn as the battle raged. Howe's only wholehearted support came from the other veteran of 1935, Jimmy Gardiner, who had been spoiling for a fight with the Tories and was determined to put them in their place. The CCF party supported the government on the grounds that the purpose of the emergency powers was to enable the minister to curb the greed of private entrepreneurs and protect the public interest if shortages of vital commodities appeared again. But it was the Conservative message – the picture of an arrogant old tyrant seeking to entrench himself permanently – that got through to the press and public. Donald Fleming conjured up the vision of a divided cabinet, with Howe at the helm instead of St. Laurent, steering the economy to the brink of socialism.

Howe was eventually driven to admit that he might not need to use the emergency powers, that he had "never missed yet" in getting the voluntary cooperation of Canadian manufacturers of defence products. But now he pleaded with the opposition. He told them he was launching a supersonic aircraft industry (an early reference to the ill-fated Avro Arrow) so big and complex it gave him "the shudders. . . . Some of you do not know how it feels to be out on a limb for $30 million or more of other people's money." The thought disturbed his sleep, he said. But the Tories simply taunted him with mock sympathy and cries of "What's a million?" They whooped and crowed the louder over his seeming signs of weakness.

Howe's belated appeal for sympathy and reason thus did him no more good than his earlier arrogant defiance. His pride was deeply wounded and his patience frazzled.

As the debate wore on into July, the Prime Minister was roused from his lethargy by accusations that he was deserting his own ship and his first mate and showing contempt for Parliament. He replied firmly that he and his colleagues fully expected to be around in three years' time to defend their stewardship of the powers they sought. This unexpected response was his first definite commitment to lead his party, unreformed and unrepentant, into the next election. His fighting Irish up, he repeated the pledge more explicitly on national television. So much for the thought that he and Howe would retire.

Walter Harris, as government House leader, next made a futile attempt to end debate on second reading by moving that "the question be now put." But the opposition shouted: "Closure!" "Gag!" and "Guillotine!" even as he was finishing. And since Harris' motion was itself subject to limitless debate, the filibuster continued.[1]

Howe had planned a long-weekend fishing trip into the wilds of Quebec with his friend Charlie Wilson, the American Secretary of Defense. Before leaving on Thursday evening, July 7, he casually told Harris and St. Laurent, perhaps without suspecting that they would take him literally, to deal with the matter as they saw fit in his absence. The next morning St. Laurent telephoned Drew and asked him to spend the weekend drafting whatever compromise amendment to the bill he thought reasonable. To Drew's delight and astonishment on Monday morning, St. Laurent accepted his proposal for a time limit to the minister's powers, and the compromise bill quickly passed that same day. One observer called it Drew's "greatest hour of triumph in the House." Back in Ottawa, Howe was furious, and imperiously summoned Walter Harris to his office in the House of Commons. The government of "children" had surely played false with him. Before Howe could start dressing down his "young" fifty-year-old colleague, St. Laurent slipped into the room unannounced and nodded at Harris to leave. He explained that the decision to compromise was entirely his own. Howe cooled down immediately and never raised the matter again.[2]

It was not the first time Howe felt that Harris was taking advantage of his absence. During Howe's Australian trip in the spring, the Finance Minister announced in his budget speech the formation of the Royal Commission on Canada's Economic Prospects. The idea came from Walter Gordon, who later recalled that he was increasingly worried about "the complacency with which Canadians were witnessing the sellout of our resources and business enterprise to Americans."[3] When the proposal was well received, Harris came to Gordon with a request from the Prime Minister that the commission chairman be, not a senior economic statesman such as Howe's wartime associate, Principal W. A. Mackintosh of Queen's, but rather Walter Gordon himself. It was less than a year since Gordon had refused St. Laurent's invitation to enter his cabinet, partly on the grounds that any policies he might propose would be vetoed by C. D. Howe. It was bad enough that the government should agree to the idea of a commission which Howe had opposed; after all, "an investigation of the Canadian economy was, in Mr. Howe's view, an investigation of C. D. Howe," as one commentator put it. But to choose a commissioner whose recommendations might well be unsympathetic to present policies was adding insult to injury. A western journalist said that Howe's cabinet defeat on the pipeline guarantee, by now common knowledge, was evidence of "the rise in power of Walter Harris and the decline in influence of C. D. Howe." Walter Gordon's appointment seemed to accelerate the trend.[4]

But Howe was never one to brood. With his stamina restored by a few days' summer recreation, he was ready to re-tackle his big project, the pipeline. On the fishing trip with Wilson he had broached the possibility of the United States administration forcing through permission for Canadian imports "on a national defence basis." But Wilson gloomily speculated that while that sort of businesslike efficiency was possible for Howe in Canada, he had to deal with hearings before the Federal Power Commission and the Supreme Court which might take years to complete.[5]

In August, at the suggestion of his deputy, Mitchell Sharp, Howe proposed to eliminate a major difficulty in financing the pipeline by putting responsibility for the costliest portion, the long bridge across the Precambrian Shield of northern Ontario, into the hands of yet another crown corporation, a device by which Howe had accomplished so many business miracles during his long career.[6]

At a meeting in the Prime Minister's office on September 1, followed by staff discussions later in the month, Howe got agreement from all parties concerned – Manning of Alberta, Frost of Ontario, his own colleague Walter Harris, the various regulatory board officials, Trans-Canada's directors, and even Canadian Gulf, the largest Alberta gas supplier – that the Northern Ontario bridge was acceptable. Its purpose was neither a subsidy to, nor an interference with, private enterprise; it was a means of putting Alberta gas into central Canada as soon as possible while avoiding the delays of running it through the United States. Once Trans-Canada was piping enough gas through, it would take over the northern Ontario section at cost, plus a reasonable return to the government for its investment.[7]

"I have never started anything that I could not finish," Howe wrote to Clint Murchison on September 30, 1955, "and one thing I intend is the building of the Trans-Canada pipeline. It seems to me that we have it licked for the moment." Murchison was getting nervous at the unfavourable publicity the pipeline was attracting, but Howe was unperturbed. He agreed that the Toronto group and their American consultants were still stirring up trouble in order to delay the project; that they hoped eventually to take it over and bring in American gas at Niagara. But action – the construction of Trans-Canada – not a battle of words, was the answer. Howe added that the pipeline was the last great project of their lives: "We are both young men yet, but I am reaching the point where I look forward to being able to come and go as I please . . . after which I will be camping on your doorstep." In the meantime Howe said he had "never been so busy or had so many difficult problems at hand."[8]

By the fall of 1955 press and public right across the country were becoming more critical of the Liberal government. The economy as a whole was buoyant, thanks in large part to increasing American investment in Canadian resource industries and a favourable balance of payments. But the fact that Howe and his colleagues appeared so uncritical of the Americanization of Canadian industry was becoming, for the first time, a matter of some public concern. Much more significant was the anti-American feeling generated by the rigid cold-war diplomacy of John Foster Dulles, and the fear the American Secretary of State's confrontation with Communist China over the defence of Quemoy and Matsu, small islands off the Chinese coast, could plunge the world into war.

Nineteen fifty-six would clearly not be an easy year for projects and policies whose success depended upon harmony between American interests and Canadian public opinion, and upon the cooperation of Parliament. But just as clearly, 1956 would be the year of make or break for C. D. Howe's pipeline. Trans-Canada was pouring money into staff, survey and right-of-way costs. It could not continue to do so indefinitely. It had few purchase or sales contracts, and clearly could not hope to get them until construction was under way. And that would not happen until Parliament approved the crown corporation for the costly northern Ontario bridge. Politically, the problem seemed equally urgent. Even if there had been business reasons for delay, Howe had no wish to enter an election year, as 1957 was expected to be, with his great work still in limbo.

To reach Winnipeg, the first big market for gas, from the Alberta border before freeze-up, construction crews would have to be in the field by June. That too was the expiry deadline for exercising Trans-Canada's option on the vast amount of scarce steel needed for the pipe-laying dash across the prairies. In order to acquire that option the company's directors found the bank unwilling to back them and reluctantly agreed to give 51 per cent ownership, and hence control, for a limited time to an American consortium of gas and pipeline companies big enough to pay for and absorb the steel pipe if anything went wrong. Thus to Clint Murchison's share in Trans-Canada was added a far greater American giant.[9]

Howe agreed completely with the company's move. Even the Canadian government could not have reasonably taken up this option because it had no alternative use for the pipe. The only way to make it work would have been immediate and complete nationalization, for which Canadian public opinion was unready, and to which the Alberta government and the American-controlled petroleum companies there were vehemently opposed. Howe was quite ready to take the route of public ownership, but only as a last resort.[10]

Since he was certain that American control would be the chief criticism of his pipeline bill in Parliament, he took steps to blunt it. He told Trans-Canada's president, the former Alberta politician and civil servant Nathan Tanner, that he, along with his leading Canadian financial adviser and his chief construction man, must be the company officers to appear in Ottawa for the duration of the battle. The less seen of the new American directors the better.[11]

Howe next conspired with his friend Premier Leslie Frost, the most powerful Conservative in the country, to have a quick vote of support for the pipeline in the Ontario legislature. Even the CCF joined the provincial Liberals, and on February 22 Frost's motion passed 88 to 0. Alberta was virtually run by a one-party government, and Social Credit Premier Manning made it clear, with the vociferous support of federal Conservative MPs from Alberta, that the province was now solidly in support of Trans-Canada.[12]

Nothing daunted, both federal Conservative leader George Drew and CCF leader M. J. Coldwell attacked Trans-Canada and its American owners, though Drew refused to recognize or commit himself to the only viable alternative of nationalization. The loudest alarm was sounded by John Diefenbaker, who went on the air on March 9 with a blast at the government's bungling of the whole pipeline issue and a warning of warfare to come. He recalled the opposition's successful filibuster against the proposed emergency powers for C. D. Howe during the previous summer. "That battle we won. But let me tell you that the fight we put on then will appear a mere skirmish beside the battle we will wage when the bill regarding the Trans-Canada Pipe Lines comes before Parliament." Diefenbaker invited his listeners to contemplate the government's "touching solicitude" for American big business and for a company which "would take for itself the profitable end of the project and pile the unprofitable on the backs of the Canadian taxpayers." Worse, such surrender of our natural resources to the Americans would make Canada "a virtual economic forty-ninth state."[13]

When he introduced the bill in the House six days later, Howe attempted to meet such arguments head on. He welcomed American experience and technical knowledge in fields new to Canada; he welcomed the loan capital that these would bring with them, which simply could not be raised here. But "if there is some uneasiness in this country about the extent and nature of United States investment in Canada," he continued, "this is the wrong place to focus it." Trans-Canada, compared to other foreign-controlled industries, "which for some reason have not been subjected to the same criticism, [is] a model which they might well study." He pointed out that the majority of the company's common stock was going to be offered to the Canadian public, that the majority of its directors were Canadian, and that the government had made it abundantly clear that it had the means and the will to make the company serve the interests of Canada and the Canadian energy market. Besides all that, the real point was that this would be a billion dollar enterprise, abounding in beneficial effects for the nation's economy.[14]

Howe had a strong case and he knew it. Furthermore, the kind of solid people in the business community whose judgment he most respected also knew it. Even Canada's leading business weekly, the *Financial Post*, which Howe had once called "the number one saboteur" of Canada's war effort, came out on March 30 with a strong editorial in support, headlined "The Main Thing Is to Get the Gas Line Built." Public ownership worked sometimes, but not here, the *Post* told its readers. Making the pipeline a crown corporation would expose it to a thousand and one political influences "for spur lines to Pint Pot Corner and Osmosis Centre." Canadians wanted a pipeline; it was clearly going to be an expensive "low interest rate affair"; only Trans-Canada was in a position to get it built; the facts of financial life remained the same whether "Trans-Canada management were changed overnight into 100 per cent fifth generation Canadians."[15]

Members of the government were so convinced their course was right that they did not really notice how little impact Howe's case was having on the popular press and the Canadian public. Or how hard Diefenbaker's kind of criticism was hitting home.

Two alert and powerful entrepreneurs were well aware of it and submitted to Howe quickly concocted schemes of their own for a Canadian-owned pipeline. The trouble was that one scheme, from a Toronto investment dealer, would require a far greater government commitment to his company's pipeline bonds than the proposed guarantee to Trans-Canada which the government had rejected more than a year earlier; and the other, from Frank McMahon, the Alberta oil man who was planning to build a gas pipeline through the Rockies to Vancouver, depended on selling most of its gas in the United States, a policy which the government had also rejected, in the interests of the Canadian consumer.[16]

But Howe, with what seemed to some observers ill-tempered and undue haste, denounced the first scheme as "a scavenger operation": its creator had invested nothing, and was trading on Trans-Canada's investment of time and money. And the other scheme Howe unwisely chose to conceal from Parliament and the public, on the grounds that Frank McMahon had marked his correspondence "private and confidential." The opposition and the press got wind of the McMahon scheme at an early date. Howe's position – that since it was private it did not exist – only helped them. Meanwhile their clamour for a Canadian-owned line was left unanswered.

April brought a different problem. At meetings between Trans-Canada people and Howe's deputy, Mitchell Sharp, the head of the American gas consortium controlling Trans-Canada told Sharp they were "distressed and embarrassed by the 'Gringo, Go Home' tone of the parliamentary debates and press comments." He offered to sell out their 51-per-cent share at cost to the government or anyone it might designate. He also said that the opposition* in the United States to their plan for importing Alberta gas via a spur line south of Winnipeg was so vociferous and effective that his group believed it would be too risky to go into the market just yet to raise the $80 million needed for construction of the pipeline from Alberta to Manitoba in 1956.

---

* The American group were opposed in Washington before the Federal Power Commission not only by their U.S. rivals in the gas pipeline business but also by a number of other lobbies. A spokesman for the American coal producers called the Trans-Canada scheme, with its spur into the United States, "a brazen attempt to force the American people to subsidize a costly and unnecessary pipeline across Canada." And that ancient volcano of the American labour movement, John L. Lewis, vowed with all the force of his mastiff jaw and black bushy eyebrows that he would stop the Trans-Canada scheme at any cost. Besides displacing with Canadian gas some 25 million tons of American coal being exported annually to eastern Canada, Lewis warned, the eventual import of "natural gas from a foreign country poses a dagger at the heart of [our] coal industry . . . and threatens to disrupt a broad segment of the American national economy."[18]

Unless Sharp advised them to sell out and leave, they proposed to wait until 1957.[17]

Informed of this, Howe was shaken, but determined to proceed anyway. As his friend Murchison remarked during an earlier crisis, quoting Maréchal Foch, "My centre is giving way, my right wing is in retreat. Excellent! I shall attack." Howe told Trans-Canada that he must go ahead in 1956. He believed their offer to get out at cost would be helpful in spiking the Canadian nationalists' guns. He would do his damnedest to get the government to furnish the necessary $80 million which neither the bankers nor the market would risk, in the form of a short-term loan. As security they must put up their total investment, which the government would take over at 90 per cent of cost if they failed to bring gas into Winnipeg by November 1. Reluctantly, Trans-Canada agreed; they had confidence in their construction crews, but they feared the worst when Howe's proposal reached Parliament.[19]

News of this plan leaked out on May 1, and until cabinet met to decide its fate on May 7, the government had an embarrassing week in Parliament. On top of this, the opposition peppered Howe with questions about Frank McMahon's "all-Canadian" scheme. Finally he was forced to admit he had had it in his hands, marked private, for five weeks. It hardly mattered that the scheme itself was little better than a fraud; Howe's concealment of it was denounced as flagrant contempt of Parliament. "The letter was marked private," he told his tormentors. "I get letters from my sister. I suppose I should announce in Parliament when I receive a letter from my sister."

"About the pipeline?" asked Diefenbaker.

Howe tried to undo the damage by obtaining McMahon's permission to table his correspondence. He stated at the same time that McMahon had withdrawn his offer. McMahon announced that since his pipeline to Vancouver had been successfully financed at the end of April, he was now too preoccupied to undertake another one. The opposition accused Howe of blackmailing him with the threat of future trouble. It was not true. McMahon did not need to be told that he had everything to lose by crossing Howe. But at this point anyone was free to believe whatever he wanted.[20]

On May 7 Howe got cabinet to agree to add his Trans-Canada loan proposal to the pipeline bill. House Leader Walter Harris warned his colleagues that the only way to have it passed before the June construction deadline would be by applying the rarely used practice of closure, at one or more of the four stages of unlimited debate permitted under the Commons' rules. Closure was the only procedure under which debate could be limited. It required a formal motion that the resolution or bill before the House (or its Committee of the Whole) "shall be the first business of the committee and shall not further be postponed." Harris and Jack Pickersgill worked out a timetable to allow the maximum number of debating days for each stage of the bill. They and their colleagues were now totally committed to pushing Howe's bill through. They were also aware that the government had for the present lost the battle for public support.

The opposition pressed their advantage brilliantly. By using points of order and other rules of debate, they managed to prevent Howe from even introducing his revised resolution into the House until May 14. They knew the government's deadline. It would only be a matter of a few more days' wrangling over procedure and Howe would either be forced to abandon his plans or cut off debate. The picture of an ageing, inflexible and tyrannical government was an even easier one to present to the Canadian people than that of a pro-American Liberal cabal selling out to a foreign-controlled corporation. And it was a picture which the Canadian public was ready to accept. They were tired of being told for twenty years that the Liberals were always right and knew what was good for people.

Howe's May 14 speech in defence of the pipeline bill was probably the best of his career. But at this stage, with the June deadline looming and closure the only hope of meeting it, his arguments hardly dented the opposition or got through to the public. As he rose to speak, Howe indulged in one contemptuous riposte to the wisecracks and derisive laughter from several members opposite. It showed, he said, "the vacancy of mind or easy irresponsibility of those who need not produce a workable course of action." But then he began pounding home his one simple theme: face the facts.

"Nothing that can be said in this House can change those facts. Nothing that can be said here is going to end the world shortage of steel pipe. No words spoken here can convince the owners of capped gas wells in Alberta or the would-be gas consumers in Manitoba and Ontario that there is no hurry about building an all-Canadian pipeline."

The Ontario legislature, Howe pointed out, had unanimously supported the bill for the northern Ontario section of the line, "the unproductive section," as the opposition dubbed it. "I suppose that when such Honourable Members water their gardens they turn on the tap and walk down the garden path with the unattached nozzle in their hands. They would regard a connecting hose as unproductive."

"Another fact with which we must deal," he continued, "was the unexpectedly long delay in the approval of the export of gas to the United States by the FPC. Perhaps the government should have foreseen this, but whether it could have or not," the point was that it had to deal with the situation as it existed now. Trans-Canada could not be financed in the ordinary capital markets; until it could secure such financing the government was tiding it over with a short-term loan – under stringent conditions.

Trans-Canada was not happy with the government's conditions:

> The company knows that unless it goes on to complete the line . . . it stands to lose its investment. If it does succeed in paying off the loan and building beyond Winnipeg, it has still a long way to go before it begins to reap any profit in it. If this were a sure thing I know plenty of people who would be only too willing to finance Trans-Canada today. But the picture of this proposal as a scheme to provide vast profits for Texas buccaneers is a fantasy, insulting to the ordinary intelligence and grossly insulting to the men who have sponsored this project with hard cash and hard work where most Canadians have been unwilling to venture.

Then, in a summary of his own experience with foreign investment, Howe told the House:

> The line will be built wholly within Canadian territory . . . the entire project is subject to Canadian law . . . not a cubic foot of gas can be exported to the United States without a permit from the Canadian government. In other words, whoever may own it, it is completely under Canadian control.
>
> If the public ownership is what the Official Opposition wants, let them stand up and be counted with the party to their left, who at least advocate public ownership out of intellectual conviction, not out of intellectual confusion.

George Drew had treated the government's pledge of majority Canadian ownership as a sham. Howe indignantly denied it: "I am more or less accustomed to the Leader of the Opposition accusing me of misleading the House, that being his idea of statesmanship, but his inability to understand a straightforward proposition continues to amaze me." Finally, Howe invoked the vision of a great project "of truly national scope, which we must either launch now or see languish for years to come. The means proposed are flexible, adaptable either to development by private enterprise, or if necessary by public ownership which, though less attractive, can still be moulded to our national needs."[21]

But Howe was not quite finished. Turning to the House leader, Walter Harris, he whispered, "Do I do it now?" Harris nodded. Howe turned back to the House. Bending forward, his fists on his desk, he said, "Mr. Chairman, it is obvious that some Honourable Members prefer to obstruct this motion rather than debate it." He picked up the paper from his desk and read out the fateful words which changed the course of the debate. "I beg to give notice that at the next sitting of Committee I shall move that further consideration of this resolution shall be the first business of the Committee and shall not further be postponed."[22]

Closure. The opposition drew in its breath, and then exploded: contempt for Parliament! "The guillotine!" "Dictatorship!" And from the Dictator himself.

In the opposition's mythology, Howe had finally torn the veil from twenty years of Liberal rule – twenty years of accumulating power, of growing contempt for the opposition, of overriding Parliament. Now a roused opposition would show what Parliament could do. They had an issue, and they had a leader.

The opposition general was not George Drew or M. J. Coldwell, but the CCF member for Winnipeg North Centre, the Reverend Stanley Knowles. A gaunt, angular, seemingly passionless being, Knowles had devoted his fourteen years in Parliament to a mastery of its secular theology – its rules and customs and privileges. No member of the House, not even the Speaker, could match Knowles' grasp of parliamentary lore, and few shared his superb sense of timing and tactics. The Liberals drew comfort from their majority; Knowles drew inner strength from parliamentary rectitude. In the impending struggle, Knowles deployed all his considerable skills to delay and obstruct the pipeline bill, and in the battle he had a singular and unwitting ally, the Speaker, René Beaudoin.

Beaudoin was a meticulous, handsome man with a trim black

moustache, who had cultivated and acquired a reputation for his knowledge of House rules. He showed elaborate courtesy and fairness in applying them. He was preparing a book on Commons procedure and was spoken of as a possible candidate for the office of permanent Speaker if it were to be created. But as Jack Pickersgill recalled, "he was inordinately vain. . . . Knowles played on this weakness . . . and encouraged Beaudoin to permit lengthy debates on points of order and, what was far worse . . . seduced him into allowing his decisions to be questioned and discussed after they had been made . . . [which was] contrary to the rules and wholly subversive of order in the House."[23]

After Howe had got the resolution to introduce his bill passed under closure, the Harris-Pickersgill timetable allowed for up to twelve more days of debate on the substance of the pipeline bill. But further application of closure, at the various stages – second reading, examination in committee and third reading – would obviously be necessary. All but a few hours of that time was spent debating not the substance of the bill but the rulings of the Speaker and the conduct of members of the government or the opposition.

Stanley Knowles recalled the last time closure had been applied (by Premier Bennett's government in 1932) and he quoted Opposition Leader Mackenzie King, who denounced its use as "autocratic power to the nth degree." Then, looking across at the government front bench, Knowles said: "If there is anything in spirits walking this earth after a man like Mackenzie King has passed on, I am sure his ghost must be haunting every cabinet minister every night . . . of this debate." By exercising closure for the sake of their pledge to Trans-Canada, they had allowed the demands of a private company to override the rights of "this free and independent Parliament of a sovereign nation."[24]

Since Louis St. Laurent had not participated in the debate, George Drew told the House he hoped that Howe had not imposed closure on the Prime Minister too. Drew called Howe the real head of the government now, and Fleming conjured up the spectacle of a weak prime minister hiding behind a reckless minister "unrepentant over his own lust for power, the same man who said 'if we wanted to get away with it who would stop us?' " St. Laurent was nicknamed "Louis the Silent," Canada was called "the Dominion of Howe," and Trans-Canada Pipe Lines the government's "Colombo Plan for Texas tycoons."

George Hees conjured up a scene in which its greedy directors plotted to "get good old C. D." to hand over Canada's resources. "You can just see the boys sitting around the room cutting up the melon in advance."[25]

"Through all this hubbub," Grant Dexter of the *Winnipeg Free Press* reported to his readers, "the most arresting figure on the government side of the House was Prime Minister St. Laurent. He sat impassive, expressionless, chin in hand, an open book on his desk, silent. His aloofness is almost unbelievable." St. Laurent had hoped he would not have to speak in the debate, but as each day passed it became clearer that he must.[26]

When he finally did, the signs of depression and weary old age vanished. He reviewed with great dignity, clarity and firmness the whole history of the pipeline project and its crucial importance to the nation, without a single reference to the insults heaped upon him. He only referred to closure briefly and euphemistically as "the distasteful responsibility of having to resort to the standing rules of the House," adding that the majority had its rights and duties as well as the minority.

His intervention put new life into the dispirited army of Liberal MP's, but it did nothing to abate the onslaught from the other side. In protest against rulings of the chair, both Fulton and Fleming refused to resume their seats when asked, and eventually Fleming got himself expelled for a day. As "St. Donald the Martyr" marched out, John Diefenbaker cried "Farewell, John Hampden!" invoking the name of a bygone parliamentary hero, and Ellen Fairclough unfurled a red ensign conveniently to hand, and draped it over Fleming's empty desk in eloquent mourning. Fleming got a hero's reception at home in Toronto, and in the press.

Language in the House became wilder as the debate lurched on. The Alberta Social Credit MP, Reverend E. G. Hansell, stated that anyone opposing the pipeline was following the communist line. Its Liberal and Social Credit supporters were in turn accused of turning the Commons into a pre-Nazi Reichstag; the bill was "the evil spawn of a fascist mentality." Two Quebec MP's became so heated in their exchange that they broke into French, a rare event in Parliament in those days, and the poor anglophone committee chairman had to plead with them as politely as he could to speak English so he could understand what was going on. Animal imagery was popular: the tread of C. D. Howe was compared to that of an elephant; MP's popping up and down from their desks were likened to gophers. Jackals, magpies, jackasses and the racehorse Citation all appeared for benefit of Hansard. Trans-Canada itself was called a pampered pet and a Liberal dog. Its coat of arms should be an octopus on a maple leaf shield with stars and stripes in the background. The Leader of Her Majesty's Loyal Opposition got into a heated debate with the chairman of the Committee of the Whole as to whether he should withdraw the words "trained seals" he had applied to Liberal MP's. Drew solemnly insisted that he had heard seal-like barking sounds emitted from the government backbenches and refused to retreat from his assertion.

As the June deadline approached, Knowles and his colleagues debated House rules with the Speaker on into the night, and the clamorous division bells rang through the corridors hour after hour to call members into the House for recorded votes on challenges to his rulings.

Caught in the glare of television lights one morning as he left the Parliament building at the crack of dawn, Howe mustered a jaunty manner and a cheery remark about how the pipeline was doing just fine, thank you, while opposition MP's solemnly warned the people of Canada that this man and his government were depriving them of their liberties.

Howe spoke but briefly as the debate raged on, and then only in obedience to Harris' instructions as to when he must move the various stages of closure on his bill. But he was far from unmoved at the cheap shots about his being an American immigrant and a betrayer of Canada to his friends from Texas. He told the House that he had lived in Canada for forty-eight years, had worked to build his country, and did not appreciate being called "a second-class citizen" because he had come from the United States.

The climax of the debate came late in the afternoon of Thursday, May 31, with just two more sitting days left to meet the deadline. Beaudoin was again allowing the opposition to argue at length a point of order. When the dinner break arrived at six P.M. the bill was still mired in procedural tangles. But the Prime Minister had moved closure, and a vote must come after the House reconvened for its evening sitting.[27]

The opposition had only one ploy left. On a question of privilege Colin Cameron of the CCF drew the Speaker's attention to two letters in the Ottawa *Journal* harshly critical of his conduct. Stung, Beaudoin leapt at Cameron's bait. If Cameron wished to make the two letters the subject of a parliamentary motion, the Speaker would show him how. And Beaudoin proceeded to do just that. Cameron hastily scribbled a motion according to Beaudoin's prescription. By the time the House adjourned at ten P.M. the opposition was merrily engaged in a new debate that promised to last for days.[28]

Howe left the House in despair. "Our bill is dead," he remarked to Pickersgill, as they adjourned to St. Laurent's office to decide what to do next. Pickersgill, fertile in stratagems, worked out a plan that he thought might succeed, and with his colleagues' consent, went to see Beaudoin to explain it to him. But Beaudoin refused to listen. He knew he had been wrong, he told Pickersgill, and he knew how to put things right. With misgivings, the minister left.[29]

Beaudoin put his thought into action when the House met on the morning of June 1. After a careful reading of the letters Cameron complained of, he had decided they were not in fact breaches of privilege, and he would now rule Cameron's motion out of order. The opposition challenged his ruling, and as the vote was being recorded, shouts came from both sides of the House. Someone passed the word that a cabinet minister's car had been spotted earlier at Beaudoin's house. One MP then charged that there was another pipeline – the one "running between the government front bench and the Speaker's chair." Others called out: "What took place in the dark?" and "Why did you change overnight? Are you afraid?" Beaudoin paled, hesitated and seemed to totter on his feet. As more shouts came from the opposition benches, Dr. James McCann, the Liberal cabinet minister, rushed forward to ask the Speaker if he was all right and would he take a glass of water; Liberal MP John MacDougall, who had a heart condition, offered his glycerine pills.* With an effort, the Speaker recollected himself and proceeded to recount his further error of the previous afternoon. The House should not suffer for the Speaker's error, and therefore business should return to where it had stood the previous afternoon at 5.15 P.M. Cameron's point of order and motion would be treated as if they had never occurred. As opposition and government members gaped in astonishment, Beaudoin then put what was effectively a motion from the chair – itself a breach of parliamentary procedure.

* Macdougall collapsed and died on June 6.

The venerable M. J. Coldwell, pince-nez dangling, moved towards the Speaker's chair shaking his fist. Liberal members began banging their desks, and in spite of Walter Harris' attempts to stop them, a small group began singing "Onward Christian Soldiers." Met with cries of "Shame! Shame!" the Liberal chorus struck up their improvised song, "We've been working on the pipeline." Tory MP's shouted "Hitlerism!" and "This is Black Friday, boy." The Canadian Press reported that Beaudoin "sat white-faced in the Speaker's chair looking straight ahead, at one point he tapped his left foot, at another he fiddled with his robe. He did not try to restore order."

Reverend Dan McIvor, at eighty-three the oldest member of the Commons, deaf to the shouts but excited by the threat to the Speaker, had to be pulled back by the coat tails by a fellow Liberal. Jack Pickersgill later wrote of the scene: "I shall never forget the tension . . . as I sat there watching an orderly assembly turning almost into a mob. . . . I was frightened to see how fragile the line was between deliberation and disorder and how easy it might be for disorder to turn into violence."

Beaudoin's motion was finally passed, 142 to 0. The House gratefully adjourned for lunch.

When it resumed sitting at 2.30 P.M., the business proceeded as if there had been no yesterday. A leftover motion was put, the House went into committee under the unflappable Deputy Chairman of Committees, E. T. Applewhaite. Applewhaite ignored or rejected opposition efforts at further delay. Closure was put and voted, and at 1.47 A.M. on Saturday, June 2, passage was completed. This obstacle overcome, the pipeline bill moved inexorably to its final passage in the small hours of Wednesday, June 6. [30]

The bill now went to the Senate, which unspectacularly but thoroughly debated its substance – a consideration largely omitted in the uproar in the Commons. Only hours before Trans-Canada's steel pipe option expired, the bill received royal assent, on June 7. While the Liberal cabinet, the opposition and the press gazed at the parliamentary wreckage, Trans-Canada got ready to lay pipe across the prairies.

CHAPTER NINETEEN

Defeat

I would not like to face an election at the moment," wrote Howe to an old friend on the Saturday morning after the pipeline debate finished. Fortunately we do not have to."[1]

Howe had no idea how close he was to being wrong. At that very moment Stanley Knowles and his chief liaison officer with the Conservatives, Davie Fulton, were working out a scheme which would force the Prime Minister to ask the Governor General to prorogue or dissolve Parliament. The government was running out of money. Within a few days it required a parliamentary vote of interim supply, something that was usually passed as a matter of course. Knowles believed that in the present mood of the country a brief filibuster to prevent the voting of funds and so force a general election would be widely supported. When Parliament was not sitting, the government was empowered to pay its bills by governor general's warrants, but such a situation could not in practice last long.[2]

George Drew went to Toronto that weekend, however, and on Monday he told Fulton that the plan to force an election must be cancelled. He had been talking to some Tory fund-raisers and other people close to Premier Frost. There was no doubt about their views on the pipeline, and the dim prospects of uniting the party on that issue in an election. Several Conservative MP's from the West also disagreed with the federal leadership's stand on the pipeline. Carl Nickle of Calgary denounced it in the House; Howard Green of Vancouver was silent throughout the debate. And as Howe rightly pointed out, "our business friends are supporting . . . the government, though we have lost some ground with labour and the man on the street."

"I think that this ground can be regained in time," he added cheerfully. "It looks to me as if we will be net gainers by next June."[3]

Howe frequently made two other points in his many letters to people who wrote in support or criticism of his actions. Sensitive to the anti-American talk directed at him, he defended the use of closure as "the British answer"* to "the American type of filibuster . . . imported into the House of Commons" by the opposition.

He also said he doubted "if the sudden application of closure made much difference in the long run. Both the Tories and the CCF had announced that they intended to block passage of the Bill, and we were working against the deadline. The main thing is the pipeline is now under construction. I must say I enjoyed the battle, and the newspaper criticism does not bother me. I feel that the end will justify the means."[4]

What pleased Howe most was that the amount of gas being signed for by Canadian customers after the bill passed was far beyond anyone's expectation. It might even make Trans-Canada independent of extra sales to the United States: "I would like nothing better than to tell our U.S. friends that we have nothing to offer them." His major concern now and for the next several months was to help the company ensure a successful financing of its securities. "The future of our government depends to a considerable extent on the ability of Trans-Canada to finance the pipeline and pay off the government loan."[5]

For several months it was touch and go. An American steel strike that summer stopped the flow of pipe delivered into Canada, and the company failed to finish the first section of the line by fall. Howe's critics made the most of it; but since stoppage due to strikes meant no forfeiture, the company was not seriously damaged by the delay. That year's difficult New York bond market was a much greater problem. Exacerbated late in the fall by the Suez crisis, it nearly spelled disaster for Trans-Canada. In the end the Canadian market, with much cajoling

---

* Though rarely used in the Canadian Parliament, closure was a much commoner and more accepted practice at Westminster.

and encouragement from Howe, took a higher proportion of the bonds than the financiers had expected.[6]

The final crisis came near the end of the year as Tennessee, the leader of the American gas consortium in control of Trans-Canada, tried to use the company's delicate condition to settle a ferocious battle with rival pipeline companies in the United States. Through its lawyer, the former Secretary of State Dean Acheson, Tennessee proposed that three of its American rivals buy into Trans-Canada and be given representation on the board. In a fury, Howe instructed the Canadian ambassador that "Acheson must be told Canada has lost all patience." He took the risky course of threatening to cancel Tennessee's permit to export Canadian gas to the United States. "Parliament . . . has always been hostile to export. 1957 being an election year, the pressure will be that much more intense. . . . We cannot concern ourselves about empire-building by Tennessee in the middle west."[7]

Howe followed up with instructions to another intermediary, Senator Peter Campbell, once the Liberal party's chief bag man, who had resigned his position on the Trans-Canada board when the pipeline bill came before Parliament. "Now you warn [the American companies] there may be no Canadian gas unless there is a quick settlement . . . it is now or never." And he added that the company heads should "meet without lawyers until agreement is reached. Lawyers can then put the agreement into proper form but I think that in the meantime they can only muddy the waters."[8]

Howe's gamble paid off, and in the meantime Trans-Canada's financiers in Canada and New York managed to close in on the final necessary total of bond commitments. As rumour of impending success leaked out, there was a wild rush of demand for company stock. Howe next had to caution Trans-Canada to see that all small orders were filled in full, because he was besieged with letters "from small people across Canada . . . some of them quite bitter when they find that brokers give them little hope." Deane Nesbitt replied that he agreed and was already taking steps in anticipation of Howe's wishes. In the end some thirty-five thousand individuals and corporations succeeded in buying shares; by far the largest number of shareholders to whom a new issue had been allotted in the history of Canadian financing. With cash on hand and signed contracts pouring in, the company could now build flat out to meet Howe's target: gas into Toronto and Montreal by 1958.[9]

One thing the Trans-Canada affair made clear to Howe was that he must be more explicit about the role of American investment in Canada. Clearly the level of public apprehension about it was rising, even within the Liberal party. Walter Gordon was due to issue the preliminary report of his royal commission on the economy soon, and Howe fully expected it would be critical, perhaps intemperately so, of the behaviour of American companies in Canada. Perhaps he should seize the initiative in the debate.

Howe took the opportunity of an October visit to the Canadian Club of Chicago to lecture businessmen on both sides of the border. He knew better than anyone how much American investment had contributed to Canada's rate of growth. "We are not allergic to outside capital," he said. But American parent companies should remember that they were in Canada, a foreign country, not Ohio. They should give Canadian investors a chance to buy shares in their Canadian subsidiaries, and Canadian employees proper opportunity for promotion. They should make public more information and they should treat their Canadian branches as autonomous enterprises with the right to seek their own export opportunities without parental interference or greed.[10]

At bottom, however, Howe's opinions did not change. He hoped, as always, that American branch plants in Canada would be good corporate citizens. And he believed they brought advantages which Canada needed in order to develop and prosper. If they did not behave well, he was confident of his ability to bring them to heel. He never really thought about a time when he would not be around to do so. Privately, he considered criticism of the Canadian-American relationship to be "synthetic complaints." Every sensible Canadian, he later wrote, "realizes that we cannot prosper except through our friendship with the United States." The opinions of those who did not know this were of no account. When Walter Gordon's preliminary report appeared, Howe dismissed it with one word: "Bullshit!"[11]

After repeating his Chicago sermon in Milwaukee, Howe took off on a trip to promote trade between Canada and Japan. It was during his pleasant and apparently fruitful stay in Tokyo that a grave international crisis erupted. At the end of October and the beginning of November 1956, the world was pushed to the brink of total war. The people of Hungary rose in revolt against their native communist masters and the Soviet army.

Britain, France and Israel invaded the Suez Canal zone to punish Egypt for its presumption in nationalizing the canal. And the Russians took advantage of the confusion to put down the Hungarian revolution in blood. Under these competing pressures the western alliance almost fell apart. John Foster Dulles was very blunt about American disapproval of the Anglo-French action in Egypt; for Canada, Prime Minister St. Laurent indignantly denounced the ageing "supermen of Europe." Thanks largely to the efforts of Lester Pearson, the worst was avoided, and the invading armies around the Canal were replaced by a United Nations peace force, including some Canadian troops. Pearson won the Nobel Prize for his efforts, as well as the respect of world opinion, but the St. Laurent government collected brickbats at home.

Howe's principal contact with the Suez crisis was the telegrams St. Laurent sent him, asking his chief English-Canadian colleague for advice and support. The support Howe readily gave; as for advice, he thought that his colleagues in Ottawa were far better equipped than he was to make the necessary decisions. But when he came back, he found anti-American feeling at a new high, this time combined with the conviction in parts of English Canada that the St. Laurent government was recklessly anti-British.[12]

The best news the Liberals thought they had that fall was the selection of a new leader of the Progressive Conservative party. John Diefenbaker, Howe's long-time adversary in the House of Commons, was selected at a December convention in Ottawa to replace the ailing George Drew. Diefenbaker was not overwhelmingly popular in his own party; many of his colleagues in the House secretly shuddered at what might lie ahead. Diefenbaker, they knew, had a difficult disposition at the best of times, self-centred and wilful. The Liberals believed they would have little trouble disposing of Diefenbaker's sonorous, old-fashioned rhetoric on the hustings. Surely people were not so backward as to take Dief seriously.

These happy thoughts were confirmed by the public opinion polls. In January 1957 the Gallup organization reported that the Liberals had the support of 48.2 per cent of the electorate compared to 31.4 per cent for the Conservatives – almost exactly the same figures as in the 1953 election. The 1957 election ought, therefore, to be a walkover. Had the Liberals given the matter a closer look, they might not have been so confident.

The weakness of the opposition was no guarantee that

Diefenbaker would fail, nor that the Liberals would succeed. The veteran Conservative MP George Nowlan compared the opposition's function to placing baskets under apple trees. "Then they must shake the trees. If the apples are ready to fall, they will get them. If they are not ready to fall, their efforts will have been wasted." An investigation of the government tree early in 1957 would have disclosed several wobbly apples.[13]

The first made its appearance in the autumn surveys of the Department of Trade and Commerce. There were, Howe was informed, some disquieting signs. Investment intentions for 1957 indicated that investment would not grow as fast as in previous years; unemployment was up, sharply, in October; shortages of commodities like steel and newsprint had been overcome. Howe brought these facts to the attention of Walter Harris when the Minister of Finance was preparing his spring budget. Harris, Howe knew, was concerned about inflation; his officials warned him of the danger of over-stimulating the economy by an expansionist budget. Harris was therefore inclined to prescribe a very modest dose of election favours for 1957, and to keep the lid on expenditures and prices. That, Howe wrote on February 21, was short-sighted. If his own figures were correct (and he was certain they were), "a continuation of present [fiscal] restraints is likely to result in the curtailment of desirable expansion."[14]

Harris was unconvinced. Inflation, not recession, was the problem, and his budget would concentrate on restraining the boom. When Harris presented it to Parliament on March 15, it was a very modest package: taxes were cut slightly, and family allowances were increased slightly. Old age pensions were up by $6 a month to $46. There would be a budgetary surplus. Predictably, it was not Harris' sound finance that attracted either praise or attention: it was the $6 increase to pensioners, rather than the $10 more generally predicted. "Six-buck Harris," as the Finance Minister was quickly dubbed, became an electoral liability.

Harris had not definitively rejected Howe's advice. He consoled himself with the thought that if the Trade and Commerce predictions proved correct there would be plenty of time later in the year, after the election, to bring in a supplementary budget and rectify matters.[15]

A second source of weakness for the government lay in the dubious performance of the wheat economy. World prices were falling in the face of a vast, subsidized American giveaway program. In 1955 prairie farmers' net income in Canada was less than half of what it had been in 1953, and the granaries of the west were bulging with unsold wheat. Howe's Wheat Board officials were already negotiating for sales in the one potential market that the United States could not touch; but the effects of the first Canadian sales to China were still in the future. Howe and his government in the meantime got blamed for the farmer's plight in the midst of general prosperity. Howe's palliative gesture to the farmers, an increase in government-guaranteed loan limits, was likened by the Saskatchewan provincial Liberal leader to using "a stirrup pump in a brush fire" and denounced as "mere tinkering" by that traditional bastion of Liberalism, the *Winnipeg Free Press*. When he went west to preach patience for the present and optimism about the future, Howe's message of cheer, coupled with his firm refusal to consider special subsidies, only roused further hostility.[16]

The third problem was a paradox. The most popular Liberal in Canada was the Prime Minister. When St. Laurent turned seventy-five in February, Liberals from across Canada journeyed to Quebec City to pay homage to the party's own "Mr. Canada." Howe introduced the Prime Minister at the birthday banquet in a rare burst of eloquence. "I sometimes hear it said," he told his audience, "that Prime Minister St. Laurent carried on where Mackenzie King left off. I have heard him referred to as a second Laurier. These are meant as tributes to our Prime Minister. But to me, he stands in the shade of no man, living or dead." The crowd roared its approval; St. Laurent was moved to tears.[17]

But the Prime Minister was, after all, seventy-five, four years older than Mackenzie King had been in his last campaign. His stamina was not what it had been, and those close to him knew that he was often abstracted and indifferent to the day-to-day business of politics. Nevertheless, as one Liberal strategist proclaimed, "St. Laurent will be seventy per cent of the campaign. What do we need a program for if we have him?" Or, as the press put it, less politely: "They'll run him stuffed if they have to." President Eisenhower, after all, had just been brought back from death's door to an overwhelming victory at the polls.

The Liberals *had* a program, expounded at length in a four-hundred-page handbook for Liberal candidates. Quoting Howe, it informed its readers that St. Laurent stood in the shade of no man. As for what the party itself had to offer, the handbook had no doubts: "strong leadership" came first; "a constructive program" came later. One constructive program not mentioned in the handbook was the hastily organized admission of thirty-five thousand Hungarian refugees, who had fled their country after the 1956 revolution was suppressed. Howe approved. As he and Jack Pickersgill, the responsible minister, left a cabinet meeting shortly before the election was called, Howe burst out: "That's the only constructive thing we've done this year."[18]

The Liberals' reliance on St. Laurent to see them through was matched by a dependence on their regional ministers' ability to keep their own areas under control. Some, like Robert Winters in Nova Scotia, thought there would be no great difficulty. Others, like Walter Harris in Southern Ontario, took a gloomier view of their prospects. George Prudham was so gloomy about Alberta that he decided not to run at all. But with the party still riding high in the polls, it was hard to imagine that it could lose. Only minor adjustments were made before the election.

One obviously weak area was Toronto. There had been no minister from Toronto since 1935, and it was time, the Liberal chieftains reasoned, to appoint one. The obvious candidate was Paul Hellyer, the 33-year-old MP for Trinity. Howe and Harris discussed the matter, and Harris then checked out what Toronto Liberals' reaction would be. Hellyer was appointed on April 26.[19] By then the election campaign was already two weeks old. Parliament had been dissolved on April 12, and the election set for Monday, June 10.

Howe's first duty to the party was to find funds for the campaign, and there is no doubt that he was generally successful. Later estimates placed Liberal spending during the 1957 campaign at between $6 and $10 million, and in any case the Liberals disposed of much more money than their Conservative rivals. Howe's appeal to prominent Liberals for funds was apparently issued late in April, and it evidently produced the desired effect by mid-May. As a result, Liberal candidates could count on the usual ration from party headquarters, and more besides. As the dispenser of funds in Northern Ontario, Howe encouraged his candidates to spend. There would be more available at the end of the campaign.

As before, Howe took to the campaign trail himself. His role was especially important in western Canada where he functioned as an auxiliary regional minister. He found that the

Manitoba Farmers' Union had made the anti-Liberal cause its own. In some wheat-growing areas it was difficult for him to get a hearing at all. On May 19 at one spectacular meeting in Morris, Manitoba, he was subjected from the outset to a cacophony of boos and catcalls. When one member of the audience shoved his way to the front and demanded to speak, Howe was in no mood to accommodate him. "When your party organizes a meeting," he growled, "you'll have the platform . . . and we'll ask the questions." The man turned out to be president of the local Liberal association. With the meeting out of control, Howe tried to escape, but he was made to stay and endure a question-and-answer session with all the questions loaded against him. At last the crowd parted, but just as Howe was getting into his car one heckler came back for more. Why had Howe not answered his question, put earlier in the meeting? "Look here, my good man," the minister replied, "when the election comes why don't you go away and vote for the party you support? In fact, why don't you just go away?"[20]

Matters failed to improve a few days later when Howe met another heckler in a group of farmers. Once again Howe was asked why he was indifferent to the farmers' economic plight. Howe was not, but it would have been pointless to expect his audience to believe that. "It looks like you've been eating pretty well under a Liberal government," Howe replied, poking his finger into his questioner's ample midriff.[21]

Close by on the prairie the construction crews of the Trans-Canada pipeline were working full blast. The first Alberta gas would reach Winnipeg by summer's end, and the Lakehead by early winter. But it was the pipeline debate, not the pipeline, which had caught the public's imagination. The Conservatives published a pamphlet called *Black Friday* and placed newspaper ads across the country under the same title, in mourning for the death of parliamentary liberties. When Prime Minister St. Laurent spoke at a rally in Winnipeg he was greeted by hecklers crying "Closure!" and "Guillotine!" and "Supermen!"* *Spring Thaw* in Toronto that year restaged the pipeline debate with savage satire, and the "Governor General" in the smash hit musical *My Fur Lady* brought down the house with lines to his prime minister like "Hello Louis! How(e)'s everything!"[22]

---

* This last jeer was a *double entendre*, referring both to St. Laurent's outburst against the ageing "Supermen" of Britain and France who had invaded Suez, and to the Supermen of Ottawa like himself and Howe.

The Liberals' campaign strategy was to pinpoint problem areas while identifying those regions which could well be left alone. One such region was Northern Ontario where, a memorandum composed in early April indicated, "no . . . seats are thought to be at stake." But in mid-May Howe got a frantic call from his campaign committee in Port Arthur. Things were going badly. He must come home immediately.[23]

It was decided to cancel the remaining engagements of an already disastrous tour, and return the minister to the Lakehead. When he arrived, he found that his executive had not exaggerated. The main challenge came from the CCF, who had nominated Douglas Fisher, a 37-year-old history teacher from a local high school. Fisher had been born in Sioux Lookout, the son of a Liberal railwayman. He had an attractive and cheerful personality, was popular with his students, and had discovered an interest in politics. The previous year Fisher had made the acquaintance of Donald MacDonald, the CCF leader at Queen's Park. MacDonald was impressed by Fisher and urged him to run for his party. Fisher found the idea attractive, and in October was duly nominated CCF candidate for the federal riding of Port Arthur.

Fisher's candidacy attracted a certain attention. The first to notice was the Cleveland tycoon Cyrus Eaton, who had never forgiven C. D. Howe for his part in the Steep Rock mine affair. Eaton decided it was time to take his revenge. Unbidden, information about Howe began to arrive at Fisher's headquarters. In several envelopes, Fisher found details about Howe's relations with Sir James Dunn and government subsidies to Algoma, and about Howe's close acquaintance with various business leaders. Eaton firmly believed that Howe's rich friends would be a vulnerable point. Fisher was at first puzzled and then excited. He decided that the election could well be fought on Howe's close connections with the beneficiaries of his department's policies as well as on the government's abuse of Parliament. But Fisher's wife thought differently. The election could be won fairly, without resorting to Eaton's scandalmongering. Ironically, Judith Robinson, the Toronto *Telegram's* bitterly anti-Howe columnist, passed on extra money from Eaton; it was not needed – but it was accepted, to swell Fisher's campaign surplus.[24]

For once, the CCF was ready. When the election was announced in April, the local party in Port Arthur had more than enough money to fight the campaign, raised from individual contributions and from union sources. Fisher was able to march down the street with his campaign manager and pre-empt the best spots on the local TV station. It was owned by a friend and supporter of C. D. Howe's, but the Liberals were not bidding on television time, and the owner saw no reason not to sell where he could. Every night from April until June, the viewers of Port Arthur were treated to the comfortable sight of Douglas Fisher, the friendly local high school teacher, looking like a rumpled bear, explaining simply and patiently what was wrong with the Liberal record, and what was right about his own proposals to remedy it. Even people who disliked the CCF were favourably impressed.[25]

The decision not to buy television time was the first mistake of Howe's campaign. It was understandable; there had been no television in any previous campaign, and it was not part of the political experience of any of Howe's managers. They simply didn't think of it.

If Howe's first mistake was unconscious, the second was induced by the enemy. Every night after school Fisher and his supporters would head out of Port Arthur for the bush, to tour the logging camps. Spring was the season for logging, and the camps were heavily populated with itinerant workers. Though many of them were ineligible to vote, it was still good publicity to make a strong impact there. Fisher had the support of the union, and every night when he showed up at the mess halls, the local shop steward would introduce him. Fisher would deliver a short rousing address and then move on, leaving behind several cases of beer as a token of his affection. Fisher was understandably popular. Reports soon reached Howe's organizers that the CCF candidate was taking advantage of the woodworkers. Their concern was increased when Fisher explained on television that since Howe had won by 6,000 votes in the previous election, that meant the CCF had to turn around 3,001 votes to win this one. There were, he considerately explained, 3,500 votes in the camps. Fisher knew this to be an exaggeration, but he hoped that it would panic Howe's organizers into making a strategic mistake.

Fisher's guess was right. Though Howe's return to the Lakehead bolstered the sagging morale of his campaigners, it also demonstrated to anyone who cared to look that the "great C. D. Howe" was now afraid of losing his own seat. Howe was belatedly sent dashing from camp to camp in the backwoods. He soon discovered that without the support of the union shop stewards, he could not find enough men together in one place to make much difference. In any case, by the time the election came in June, most of the camps had been wound up and the men dispersed to their original homes. It was an aggravating and futile exercise.

Howe found little comfort among his old supporters. Many of the old familiar faces were gone: moved away, dead, or preoccupied. Fisher exploited to the full a $175 donation sent to him from a former Liberal supporter in one of the railway towns. This man, Fisher told his TV audience, had actually got the money from Howe's campaign committee, which had told him to spend it as best he could. But since 1953 he had changed his mind, and no one thought to ask him what his opinion now was. He happily put the money to the best use he could think of – electing Douglas Fisher. Everywhere Howe went within range of Port Arthur television, he found that Fisher's personable television appeals had made startling inroads among his own supporters. He was now goaded into another mistake.

Under Canadian election law, the last day for broadcast political appeals is two days before the election day. Howe's supporters forced the local station to remain open longer than usual, in order for Howe to broadcast a last-minute message to the voters of Port Arthur. But when Howe arrived at the station, he found Fisher just leaving after another broadcast of his own. The minister glared at his challenger, then muttered that he thought that Fisher might well win. Howe stalked into the TV studio and treated his viewers to the spectacle of a tired, harsh old man, telling them that the nice young fellow that they had been seeing on television for the last couple of months was, if not a communist himself, then associated with the communists. No one believed him.[26]

Election day in Port Arthur was cloudy and by the evening a light rain was falling. At 7:30, half an hour after the polls closed, it was obvious that Fisher had carried the city. Only an overwhelming surge for Howe in the outlying townships would save the day. Howe waited with a few faithful workers until the results came in from Terrace Bay and Nipigon. Howe had carried both polls, but by a slim margin. The other polls could not make up the difference and Fisher stood to win the seat by at least a thousand votes. Howe swore for five minutes, in a style that would have commended him to his lumberjack constituents. He then turned around and kicked a pile of beer cases, which had been set aside for the victory celebration. Then he turned around to his appalled supporters. "Okay, where do we go to concede?" No one seemed to know. It was decided to drive to the local television station.

There once again Howe found his young nemesis waiting for him, this time in the company of his wife and his mother. The elder Mrs. Fisher was distressed. She herself had always voted for C. D. Howe, up until this election, and she was crushed to see her hero defeated, even though she was happy about her son's victory. "Oh, Mr. Howe," she mourned, "what will you do now?"

"Why, Mrs. Fisher," said Howe, comforting her, "there are so many things to do! The only thing that worries me is that I might not be around long enough to do them." He shook Fisher by the hand, and walked onto the set to make his concession.[27]*

The news of Howe's defeat was broken on national television a few moments later by an excited CBC announcer. Until that point, since western returns were not yet in, it had seemed as if the Liberals might squeak by with a reduced majority or a plurality in the House of Commons. But with the fall of their titan, they suddenly seemed less like a government. By the time all the votes were counted, the Liberals had won 105 seats with 40.9 per cent of the popular vote, while the Conservatives won 112 seats with 38.9 per cent; nine cabinet ministers had been beaten in their own ridings. The CCF and Social Credit parties held the balance in the new Parliament.

After twenty-two years, the unthinkable, the impossible, had happened. In spite of obvious omens of change in scattered localities, next to no one had expected such a national result. *Maclean's*, to its embarrassment, was already in print with prognostications and advice for the next Liberal government. Editors of the dailies, when they recovered from the shock, generally expressed their pleasure in the surprises that a democratic electorate could spring on its masters and on the pundits. Some openly rejoiced in the government's defeat and in particular that of its most senior member. Only "in the constant enlargement of his own power," wrote the *Globe and*

* The final result in Port Arthur was: Fisher, 12,228; Howe, 10,813; and Vigars (Conservative) 5,261.

Mail, "did Mr. Howe show authentic genius. . . . Never before have so many Canadians feared, so many Canadians bowed the knee before, one man. Perhaps that was his greatness. But it is not the type of greatness we would wish to see enshrined in this country's history."[28]

Howe flew back to Ottawa after performing one last industrial ceremony at Sault Ste. Marie. He found Prime Minister St. Laurent depressed and shaken, and in no mood to compound his humiliation by waiting for defeat in the House. The government had clearly been repudiated by the country and must resign, he told his colleagues. Howe agreed with his old friend. On June 21 they formally left office, and John Diefenbaker became Prime Minister of Canada.

More than any man, Howe had played a major role in his party's defeat. The way in which the power of his presence and the sheer force of his personality had come to symbolize government during the last years of the old regime is well illustrated by the comments of two fellow Liberals. Walter Gordon in 1954, weighing an invitation to join the cabinet, was urged by the Prime Minister to talk to Howe about it. Howe "could not seem to understand why I was hesitating," Gordon recalled. But when asked what his reaction would be to Gordon as a new member criticizing a proposal Howe might bring to cabinet, "his reply was one of astonishment: 'You'd do *what*, young man?' " That was all the answer Gordon needed: "Mr. Howe was not going to change and neither was the government."[29]

Walter Tucker, a veteran Saskatchewan Liberal MP first elected to Parliament in 1935 and narrowly re-elected in 1957, wrote feelingly of Howe during his last year in power: "I understand now, and for the first time, the meaning of Lord Acton's phrase 'all power corrupts, absolute power corrupts absolutely.' [It is] not a moral corruption but a corruption in one's attitude toward other human beings over whom one feels one has great power."[30]

Howe blamed himself for not getting out when the getting was good. And on reflection, he acknowledged that, like himself, the party and the Prime Minister were suffering from old age. Back in 1953, he later explained, "I had an understanding with our leader that we would both retire after a year or two in office and give the new leader time to get organized. Unfortunately, our leader changed his mind about retiring, which was a mistake both for him and for the party. The plain fact is that the Liberal dynasty had run out of ideas."[31] As George Nowlan observed, oppositions do not win elections. They pick up the pieces when the government party loses. Over twenty-two years in office the Liberals eventually managed to offend more people than they gratified. Proud of their "responsible" record in government, their statesmanlike view of the broad national picture, they were constitutionally unable to respond to demands that they alter their policies to gratify special interest groups, what they chose to dismiss as regional grievances or mere popular desire. After creating a massive public service (up from 41,000 in 1935 to 179,000 in 1957) in order to match the expansion in governmental powers, they found themselves taking political responsibility for the growing number of administrative decisions made by the bureaucrats. The Liberals were the prisoners of their own success; and when their machine could no longer expand, they became vulnerable.

Howe was the visible symbol of the government's ossification. The least bureaucratic of men, ironically he came to embody the Ottawa mandarin attitude that the electorate so decisively rejected. His age, his ill health, his worsening temper, all made him appear more autocratic and unfeeling than he was and, indeed, than the government collectively was. Like all of them, Howe was convinced that nothing more remained than to fine-tune the administrative apparatus. Leave visions – and charades – to the opposition. If sober common sense was what the country needed, that was what the country would get. The government knew best, they would act for the best: as Howe had once asked his critics, who would stop them?

CHAPTER TWENTY

"Sitting on the Beach"

C D. Howe did not leave public life a poor man. His investments, organized in two personal corporations, Penryn (for Alice) and Cloud (for Clarence) were worth well over a million dollars in book value alone and their market value was considerably higher. From his investments Howe took a steady and respectable income: over $20,000 a year in the mid-fifties which, added to his $25,000 a year salary as an MP and minister, placed him high in the statistical lists of privileged Canadians. At seventy-two, he could afford to sit back, clip coupons, speechify at banquets, and follow most of his colleagues into an honourable obscurity. Which he most decidedly did not do. As it turned out, Howe was soon immersed in several new projects – new careers, as some might have called them.[1]

Appropriately, however, his first decision on retiring from office was financial. He ordered his broker to sell some of his stocks, and within days Howe's comment was drifting around Ottawa: "I don't trust this new bunch." For those who thought that the earth had trembled on June 10, 1957, this was scarcely reassuring. When Howe got around to explaining matters, it was too late. "I did cash in some securities," he admitted, "but not to any great extent." He suspected that "business is in for a bad time in 1958," and like any good businessman he was following the proper strategy for bad times and liquidating some of his assets.[2]

Ottawa was suddenly a very lonely town for C. D. Howe. His

office staff was gone, though Ruth Thomson followed her boss into retirement as his personal secretary. And the civil servants found it wise to keep a discreet distance. The Conservatives had not been in power for twenty-two years, and the new government was known to believe that the upper reaches of the civil service were incurably tainted with infectious Liberalism. Of Howe's deputy ministers, Fred Bull was far away across the Pacific enjoying his post as ambassador to Japan. Mitchell Sharp was left to cope with new political masters who were already convinced that he would best be employed elsewhere, anywhere, out of government.

As for the rest of official Ottawa, the political part, many of the faces were new: Tory ministers learning the ropes and basking in the unexpected glory of their offices and the fulsome praise of the press. The Liberals were scattered across the country, picking up the pieces, and wondering how to adjust to indefinite unemployment and to paying their campaign debts. One defeated candidate from Northern Ontario had taken Howe seriously about spending extra money in the stretch drive. He called the minister in a panic shortly after the election, and asked for party funds to reimburse him. "Haven't you heard?" Howe replied. "We lost." And hung up.

The defeated Liberals were the lucky ones in Howe's view. Those who had the misfortune to be re-elected were condemned to under-employment and public impotence. "I am not unhappy about my personal defeat," he wrote to his young friend John Turner,* who had written him a long eulogy "in an election that swept our party from office." But Howe had a lingering grievance against the electorate that had done the deed. "I never want to go inside the Parliament Buildings again," he told a friend in the summer of 1957.[3]

That was too drastic. In September Howe received a pained letter from St. Laurent, asking if he really meant to desert his friends of decades and leave them to face a grim future alone. Contrite, Howe quickly made amends. He told his leader he would help the party "in any way I can, and I do intend to be active in the Liberal cause wherever and whenever opportunity

---

* He also urged Turner to consider taking up a political career – a deeply satisfying one for a young man of his ability. While Howe often told people he was gratified that he himself had turned to politics, this is the only letter in his papers urging such a course on someone else.

offers.'' St. Laurent was retiring from politics himself, and a convention to choose the new leader was to be held in January 1958. Howe decided to stay around and watch the show, and do what he could.[4]

The summer months passed slowly in Ottawa and then in St. Andrews. There was nothing to do but go down to the corner store and chew the fat in the back room with other members of the elderly rich. In August two messages arrived which touched Howe deeply. He was asked to join the board of governors of Dalhousie University. Then, shortly after, Dalhousie upgraded its offer. Would Howe become the university's chancellor, Dalhousie's first? Howe would. It was an office that would bring him back to Halifax, a city that he always liked. He even considered retiring there, and inspected properties in the older part of town. The move would take him closer to the place that gave him his first start in Canada, and close to Bill, who was stationed at Halifax with the Royal Canadian Navy. Howe never did move back, but he changed his personal routine in order to be present at the board of governors' meetings.[5]

Howe decided later that summer to pull up stakes and move from Ottawa to Montreal. There was nothing for him to do in Ottawa anyway, except play golf and bridge and haunt the Rideau Club to watch the new ministers at play. Ottawa was a one-industry town, and Howe no longer belonged to that industry. He decided to move closer to the action in the business world, and that, he decided, would be Montreal. ''I know,'' a friend wrote, ''you have always liked [Montreal] much better than either Ottawa or Toronto.'' When the Howes returned from New Brunswick in September, Alice stopped off in Montreal to look for an apartment.[6]

It took months to organize the move. Meanwhile, Howe coped as best he could in Ottawa. Writing to Beaverbrook late in September, he lamented the life of a ''gentleman of leisure, which I find boring.'' Howe was waiting for an intervention, and it came from two of his old associates: Beaverbrook himself and E. P. Taylor.[7]

One day at the Rideau Club Taylor stopped at Howe's table. Perhaps Howe could do him a favour. There was a vacancy on the board of Domtar, a paper firm controlled by Taylor's Argus Corporation. He would be honoured if Howe would take the position. Howe was touched. Incredibly, nobody else had yet asked him to join any corporate board. The fear of Diefenbaker's vengeance on any major corporation that presumed to take him aboard was likely one reason for leaving Howe discreetly in limbo for a time. The order had gone out immediately that the Howe engineering firm, with which he had not been involved since 1935, was to be cut off government contracts. So Howe accepted the offer with alacrity. It was "a compliment to me," he wrote Taylor, "and I know I would enjoy the association."[8]

If E. P. Taylor was happy to do a friend a favour, Beaverbrook was anxious to put the friend to work – in their mutual interest, of course. Beaverbrook held a large interest in Price Brothers, an old Quebec City pulp and paper firm with extensive holdings along the lower St. Lawrence. Price Brothers was one of Howe's preferred investments. Over the years, he had bought steadily into paper company stocks, earning on the way a considerable unrealized capital gain. Beaverbrook wanted to put Howe on the Price Brothers board, and Howe was happy to accept. There were only two snags: Price was a competitor of a subsidiary of Taylor's Domtar; and Beaverbrook hated E. P. Taylor, who had tried to take over Price Brothers in a spectacular raid a few years earlier. Howe, who liked both men, would be caught between them.[9]

He sensed trouble coming, and in November suggested to Taylor that it might be as well to leave his appointment to Domtar unannounced and ineffective because of the conflict of interest between Price and its rival. Taylor dismissed the suggestion. Between Domtar and its subsidiary which competed with Price, there was a gulf fixed; Howe would never be asked to compromise himself in the board meetings of Domtar. He then wrote Beaverbrook in January that Taylor had no further designs on Price Brothers, and that to irritate him by throwing up his directorship would be needlessly offensive. "Eddie is sentimental," he added, "and to quarrel with him might be expensive."[10]

Beaverbrook was certainly sentimental about Taylor, but not in Howe's sense. He redoubled his efforts to bind Howe to Price Brothers' cause. The chairman of its board and Howe's old friend, Herbert Symington, was ailing, and Beaverbrook wanted to replace him. His candidate was C. D. Howe.

While Beaverbrook's plans for Price Brothers were maturing, Howe was enjoying a brief return to backroom politics. At the Liberal leadership convention of January 1958 it was becoming obvious that there would be only two serious candidates, Paul Martin and Mike Pearson. Robert Winters would have had little chance even if he had not lost his Nova Scotia seat in 1957. Walter Harris, also defeated in the general election, reluctantly decided not to run, thereby leaving the field open to Pearson. Howe knew whom he would support: "our man" for these purposes was Pearson. Like Howe, Pearson did not look the part of the professional politician and in his sunny way shared Howe's impatience with the merely political approach to a problem in favour of getting on with whatever larger task was at hand. In fact both Howe and Pearson were, though unaware of it, much subtler and more ruthless politicians than Paul Martin. While Howe remained publicly uncommitted, privately he raised a bit of money for Pearson's campaign. A passionate and tearful last-minute appeal from Paul Martin at Howe's home in Rockcliffe astounded him but left him unmoved.* Pearson it must be, and Pearson it was, "hands down," as Howe jubilantly wrote to his old friend R. E. Powell.[11]

Howe's own part in the convention was confined to a speech and a tribute. The delegates applauded warmly, and yesterday's men stepped out of the limelight. It was not quite a year since St. Laurent's triumphant banquet in Quebec City.

The inheritors set to work immediately. Parliament had been recessed for Christmas, and would meet again on January 20. When the House assembled, Pearson was ready with a motion demanding that Diefenbaker and his ministers submit their resignations forthwith and allow the Liberals, the people who knew how to run Canada, to return to their proper position as the governing party. Diefenbaker was incredulous, and then delighted. Pearson, as he sat down, realized that something had gone wrong: his speech was "a failure, indeed a fiasco."[12]

Pearson's speech centred on the economic deterioration that

---

* Howe recounted the next day at the Rideau Club that Martin had pleaded with him to support a francophone candidate like himself in order to help preserve good relations between the two founding peoples of Canada. Such an outburst of feeling only confirmed Howe in his opinion that Martin was the wrong man for the job. Besides, Howe partially shared Jimmy Gardiner's perception that the Liberals had lost a lot of ground in 1957 because English-speaking voters believed that French-Canadian influence was too great in Ottawa. While he rejected this criticism where St. Laurent was concerned, Howe believed it was not the time to break the Liberal party's tradition of alternating between French and English leaders. On top of all that, Martin's commitment to heavy spending on social security had never appealed to Howe, while Pearson's involvement in External Affairs had placed him in a field in which Howe felt no compelling interest or expertise, and no occasion to quarrel.

had occurred since the new government had taken office. Diefenbaker's reply concentrated on a document that he waved in Pearson's face: "The Canadian Economic Outlook for 1957," prepared for C. D. Howe by his officials in March 1957. What the report said was hardly news to Howe, because it predicted what he had warned Walter Harris against a year before. What Diefenbaker did not stress, however, was that the "hidden report" (as it was quickly dubbed) was one opinion among many furnished by the government's advisers. That consideration was lost to sight under the hubbub created by Diefenbaker. He utterly demolished Pearson's naïve claim that Liberal times were better times. How could they be, when the Liberals had known, and deliberately concealed from the people, that there would be a recession?[13]

Pearson had handed Diefenbaker a ticket for re-election. On February 1 Diefenbaker cashed it in. Parliament was dissolved and an election set for March 31. The news came as an unpleasant surprise to C. D. Howe. His plans for spring were well advanced. He and Alice were to sail for Europe with Sir James' widow, Lady Dunn. When they came back, later in the spring, they would move to Montreal. In the meantime they would be free of the dreary slush of an Ottawa winter. Howe was doubly annoyed: at having his vacation cancelled (there was no alternative but to stay and help the party), and at seeing his advice ignored in the campaign. At first he swore that he would have "nothing to do with this one, financial or otherwise." But he soon softened. As he later wrote, after the slaughter was completed, he was "so shocked by the direction of the campaign, that I decided to take no part in it, other than help with the financing. Pearson's advisers were about as inept as could have been gathered together." Howe had advised Pearson not to do anything to provoke an election. When Pearson realized his mistake Howe believed that he was foolishly blaming everyone but himself. This was "quite unfair," he wrote. "Mike's excuse for everything is that he accepted the advice of those he gathered around him. I hope he will soon appreciate that a leader must decide what advice is appropriate to the occasion, and that his own judgement and responsibility are required."[14]

Election day brought the predictable disaster. The banner of "Peace, Prosperity, Pearson," had been no match for Diefenbaker's northern vision and his supporters' cry of "Follow John!" The Liberals garnered a pathetic 49 seats, 25 of them in

Quebec. It was by far their worst showing since Confederation. Pearson saved his own seat, but across Canada the party was decimated, with nothing at all west of the Ontario-Manitoba border. The last returns were in from the wheat farmers – a final judgment on Howe from the group he had begun working for forty years before.

There was no point looking back. What was done could not be undone and Howe turned his energies to the reconstruction of the Liberal party. He was even prepared to bury the hatchet with Walter Gordon, whom he had pointedly snubbed for many months. One day, finding himself near Gordon at the Rideau Club, Howe got up from his chair and walked over to Gordon's table. "Walter," he began, "there are so few of us left." After that, Howe made a point of calling on Gordon whenever he came to Toronto; personal peace was made between the two men. He had long ago ended his feud with Walter Harris. In the spring of 1958 he and Harris were discussing Harris' political future and Howe urged him to run for the leadership of the Ontario Liberal party. Writing to a friend in Vancouver, Howe advised that "as I see it, our best opportunities lie in restoring our Provincial organizations." He remained a substantial contributor to the funds of the Liberal party both nationally and in Port Arthur.[15]

As for the new government in Ottawa, Howe did not find Diefenbaker's presence on the ministerial benches as much of an affront as did some of his former colleagues (or some of Diefenbaker's own followers). Diefenbaker, he wrote to Powell in September 1957, "has been a friend of mine since he entered the House of Commons and, although I still like him personally, I am wondering what kind of Government his will prove to be." Though it was too soon to tell, there were a couple of disquieting portents. "Every one of his listeners" during the election campaign "was assured that taxes would be lowered and rewards were to be all that could be desired." What would Diefenbaker do when he faced up to the demands of office?[16]

With 207 followers behind him in the House of Commons, Diefenbaker would soon provide the answer. But Howe was not in Ottawa to see it. In May, after clearing out his files, he finally faced the "miserable job" of moving. The records Howe did not take with him, he burned, or left sealed in the Public Archives. Then, in June, he left.[17]

The Howes took an apartment at 3468 Drummond, on the

top floor of a new building perched on the side of the mountain. From here they enjoyed a view down the street to the Ritz Carlton, a few blocks from the Mount Royal Club, which Howe proposed to make his new luncheon headquarters. It was, Howe wrote, "a great view" whose only drawback was the steep climb up the hill – "which becomes steeper as the evening wears on."[18]

The days were busy. After several months of idleness, Howe was finding new opportunities thrust upon him. A number of corporations began to court him. By the end of 1958 he had joined no less than fourteen boards (all Canadian companies, he noted with satisfaction), including those of the National Trust Company, the Canadian Investment Fund Limited and the Bank of Montreal. Disappointed by the failure of the Bank of Nova Scotia to appoint him to its board of directors (he had banked there for fifty years), Howe transferred the bulk of his business to his new bank. Becoming a new boy on the board of such an august and formidable body as the Bank of Montreal was an experience, even for the Right Honourable C. D. Howe, P.C. At his first meeting, he assumed that it was like the cabinet, and when an interesting item came up, Howe asked a question. He received a glacial stare from the chairman of the board, and his question was ignored. Howe after all had never been a member of the old corporate establishment, and while a number of his wartime recruits were already on their way to becoming Canada's new business elite, few of them had yet reached the bank board, let alone changed the aura of nineteenth-century conservatism which lingered there.[19]

Howe was entrusted with larger responsibility when he assumed the chairmanship of the board of Ogilvie Brothers, the flour millers. Ogilvie's had a reputation as a staid and unimaginative business. His old friend George McIvor, president of Ogilvie's rival, Robin Hood Flour, told his staff that things were going to change with Howe at the helm. No longer should they assume that Robin Hood would automatically have little competition from their rival. Howe travelled across the country with Ogilvie's representatives, exploiting to the full his connections in the grain trade, and trying to re-establish the firm as first-class competition. Howe was back in his element, working hard on many enterprises at once and enjoying it all thoroughly. He regularly ran across many of his old friends and subordinates from Munitions and Supply, Reconstruction or Trade and Commerce, who were now increasingly the shakers and movers of the Canadian business world. V. W. Scully, for example, who ran Victory Aircraft for Howe during the war, had gone to the Steel Company of Canada on his boss' recommendation and had just been made chief executive officer; Douglas Ambridge, who had built Polymer for Howe and then worked on wartime merchant shipping, was now head of the giant Abitibi Pulp and Paper Company; Max Mackenzie, Howe's former deputy at Trade and Commerce, was with Chemcell in Montreal; Mitchell Sharp worked for Henry Borden, chairman of Brazilian Traction; T. N. Beaupré was soon to be president of Domtar, and Bill Bennett of Iron Ore of Canada; there was Eric Phillips and Eddie Taylor of Argus Corporation; and the list was still expanding.

Howe even saw some of his business friends on Sundays. Alice had managed to get him out to church regularly for the first time in their married life. An Episcopalian by conviction, she had joined the Church of England in Canada, and belonged to a high church parish in Ottawa; she was now a pillar of the cathedral parish of the Anglican Diocese of Montreal. Clarence, hitherto unconfirmed, late in 1957 had knelt to receive the Holy Ghost at the hands of the Lord Bishop of Ottawa – pleasing Alice was now well worth a mass – but he was reluctant to venture further. When he saw some of his old friends in the cathedral, however, he changed his Sunday habits. "This is my kind of church," he remarked enthusiastically.[20]

Howe lunched regularly at the Mount Royal Club, when not dashing off by TCA to a board meeting in Toronto or Vancouver. He enjoyed listening to the mounting chorus of muttering and grumbling against the follies and outrages of Prime Minister Diefenbaker, particularly from those who had raised money for the Conservative party in the 1958 elections. "Well," Howe commented loudly and cheerfully, "*I* didn't vote for him."[21]

But when the Prime Minister got himself into political trouble in February 1959 by cancelling the expensive Avro Arrow program and throwing thousands of highly skilled Canadians out of work, Howe refused to join the critical chorus. He said Diefenbaker had done the right thing: there were limits to government spending and there would be no international market for the plane, however magnificent it was. A couple of months earlier, Howe had the satisfaction of hearing that his greatest single project was complete. In a blinding sleet storm outside Kapuskasing, the last weld was made in the Trans-Canada pipeline, and on October 27, 1958, the first Alberta gas flowed in to Montreal. *Trade and Commerce* magazine hailed Howe as its man of the year for an achievement which "rivalled in his time the significance of the driving of the last spike" in the CPR.[22]

In due course, Howe became, as Lord Beaverbrook had intended, the new chairman of the board of Price Brothers. For Howe, it was the most important of his companies, both in terms of his personal investment (9,450 common shares valued at $266,000 in 1959) and in terms of the attractiveness of its prospects. The company was doing well; it was expanding its plant and its sales, and its markets looked rosy. There was only one nagging annoyance: Beaverbrook's notion of the proper functions of a chairman of one of "his" companies. If the chairman were not himself, he was presumed to be a minor member of the Beaver's lodge, one whose actions were determined by the shrill cries of command issuing from headquarters in London, Nassau, Fredericton, or wherever he happened to be at the time.[23]

What worried Beaverbrook most about Price Brothers was that he did not by any means have complete control. He had beaten back Taylor's earlier raid only with the help of other interests on the board, and the thought made him nervous. Howe's selection as chairman was intended to provide the services of a generalissimo in his war with E. P. Taylor. But Howe's chairmanship was shaded by his doubtful associations with the enemy camp itself. Requests, demands, pleas that Howe resign from Domtar flooded Howe's new Montreal office in the Sun Life building. Howe patiently replied to each. "I will certainly resign," he wrote in July, "the minute that it is reported to me that the Taylor interests are enlarging their shareholding in the Price Company." He would not, however, resign without reason, and for the moment there was none.[24]

Beaverbrook next tried to have his friend K. C. Irving, the multi-purpose magnate of New Brunswick, added to Price's board. Irving's appointment would have helped strengthen Beaverbrook's position there and also served to warn off the Taylor interests in case they thought of trying another takeover raid. But Irving was, in the eyes of the other Price directors, a rival and competitor in the pulp and paper business. Equally important, he came from outside Quebec, a point of some interest to the provincial government of Maurice Duplessis. Premier Duplessis knew how to make his opinion count, because Price's hopes of expansion were tied to further concessions of Quebec timber limits. An interview between Howe and the Premier in mid-November was a great success. "I am satisfied," Howe reported to Beaverbrook, "that he will be helpful whenever Price Brothers needs help. [And] we need his help." The last thing a Quebec company needed was an infusion of Anglo-New Brunswick imperialism.[25]

Beaverbrook refused to give up, however. He issued more orders and demanded to know why his wishes were being ignored. Irving has "no competing interests whatsoever with Price Brothers," he told Howe. "Whoever makes such a suggestion is foolish." As a sop, Howe and the Price board agreed to invite Beaverbrook's son Max Aitken to join them.[26]

Unsatisfied, Beaverbrook fired off a declaration of war on July 12, 1960. Citing a bill of grievances, including a recent presumed slight to Max, he informed Howe that he was completely disappointed at the company's dismal record. He told Howe that in future Price could not expect to reach an agreement with Beaverbrook's newspaper companies for the purchase of Price Brothers' newsprint.[27]

Howe refused to budge. "[I will not] join in your personal vendetta against Eddie Taylor, and force Mr. Irving on the board regardless of the feelings of other members." He hoped, however, that Beaverbrook's attitude would not mean "our personal friendship is ended." But it was.[28] When the two men met next, in October, it was as rivals. This time they were contending in a different sphere, and for a different goal: academic honour and academic money. The money was Lady Dunn's; the question was whether it should go to Dalhousie or to Beaverbrook's pet project, the University of New Brunswick.

Howe took his job as chancellor of Dalhousie seriously. Although it was one of the oldest universities in Canada and had a distinguished list of alumni, it had never entered the university big leagues. By the fifties, Dalhousie was very much a small-time local college, operated on a shoe-string budget under the anxious eye of its president, Dr. A. E. Kerr. Kerr believed in expanding student enrolment and putting up new buildings, if necessary at the expense of academic standards. He had always managed the university's budget so as to avoid the need for fund-raising appeals. In his first conversations with Kerr after

342

being appointed chancellor, Howe said it was no good for him to try raising money when the university was so obviously in the black. Without a deficit, any demand for funds from the alumni would be met with skepticism. Howe told Kerr that he wanted money spent on making Dalhousie a first-rate institution. "Dalhousie has become obsessed by buildings," he complained, "and is allowing its staff to deteriorate." The salary program "gives much evidence of penny-pinching." He was right of course: a full professor's salary had far less, in fact, buying power than the $2,000 a year which Howe earned as a neophyte back in 1908.[29]

Howe examined Dalhousie's endowment and investments. He suggested that the university was investing too cautiously; the money it had salted away was simply not producing a sufficient return. At Howe's urging, the board decided to invest more of the university's money in growth stocks rather than in sober-sided bonds. Howe was also anxious that the money that he helped to raise should be turned into the establishment of a larger, permanent endowment.

Finances were only one aspect of Howe's work for Dalhousie. He wanted the university to recover the kind of national and international reputation it had possessed in the days when he was there. That could be most immediately achieved, he decided, by inviting prominent people to appear for the awarding of honorary degrees. In 1960, for example, at his own expense, he brought Sir John Cockcroft, the illustrious Cambridge nuclear physicist, to Dalhousie for an honorary degree.

Howe's most spectacular intervention in Dalhousie affairs did, however, involve a building. Dalhousie had kept an anxious eye on the estate of one of its richest graduates, Sir James Dunn, an estate now organized in part as the Dunn Foundation.* When Howe accepted the chancellorship, he was pleased to note that "our relations with the Dunn Foundation are on a very solid basis." Dalhousie persuaded Lady Dunn to pay for the erection of a splendid new Science Building.[30]

Lady Dunn, however, was a friend of Lord Beaverbrook,

* When Sir James died, Howe had been named an executor. It was an awkward position for a minister of the crown, but he sold his stock in Algoma Steel which Dunn had controlled, took no fee for his work, and carried out his task in order to place the steel company, Canada's second largest, in competent hands and protect its future and that of the Canadian steel industry generally.[31]

whom she later married. When it came time to open the building, she indicated that Lord Beaverbrook "as Sir James' oldest friend" would do the honours. Howe professed himself "very much annoyed." "Beaverbrook's interest," he pointed out to Kerr, "is in the University of New Brunswick, and certainly he is no friend of Dalhousie. As far as that goes, he was no particular friend of Sir James, when both were active in London business circles." Nevertheless, it was Lady Dunn's right to dispose. "I suppose," Howe concluded resignedly, "that we must live with it." Lady Dunn, Beaverbrook, and an entourage of friends from New Brunswick duly arrived for the opening.[32]

There would, of course, be a banquet. But Howe learned to his dismay that Kerr, a Presbyterian teetotaller, refused to taint the university premises with alcohol. Howe reacted swiftly. If Dalhousie's guests could not be properly entertained by the university, he would do it himself elsewhere. Accordingly, he held the celebratory banquet off campus at the Nova Scotian Hotel, and it was a grand affair indeed. For the moment, Howe had potlatched the Beaver: "My purpose was to show New Brunswick that we in Nova Scotia could also arrange a dinner. I think that Beaverbrook got the point." The next day, when President Kerr complained that a university function had been polluted with alcohol, Howe glared at him: "When my wife and I give a party we entertain our friends in a way we think is appropriate."[33]

Howe's relations with Kerr were by this point strained in every sphere. Howe found the president a man of little vision, lacking the necessary graces and abilities of a modern university president. He began planning for Dalhousie's future as soon as Kerr could be decently disposed of. He wrote to President N. A. M. Mackenzie of the University of British Columbia, "I can tell you in confidence that Dalhousie badly needs a different type of president." One candidate Howe had in mind was Mackenzie's associate, Geoffrey Andrew, but another was closer to hand. Largely at his insistence, Henry Hicks, the former Liberal premier of Nova Scotia, who had been defeated by Robert Stanfield, was recruited as dean of arts and science. It was obvious that Hicks would be Kerr's successor.[34]

Howe had won a minor skirmish against Beaverbrook with his grand opening of the Dunn Science Building. The main engagement lay ahead. Beaverbrook's threat to boycott Price Brothers paper products was obviously intended to bring the Price board to heel. But Beaverbrook did not control all the markets; even in England he had rivals, and powerful ones. One of these rivals, Rothermere's Associated Newspapers, owned the Anglo-Newfoundland Development Company, which in turn owned large pulp and paper interests in the island province. It might be possible to stymie Beaverbrook by merging with his rival. With the backing of Royal Securities, Howe flew to England in October 1960, and got an agreement in principle. Price Brothers would merge with Anglo-Newfoundland. Beaverbrook was out, Rothermere was in. Howe returned, triumphant but exhausted, to Montreal.

But he scarcely paused to unpack. His many other interests had been neglected during his twelve days in Britain. He had paid visits to Halifax and Port Arthur before leaving; on his return, business meetings took him on separate trips to Ottawa, Welland, Winnipeg, Toronto, and then back to Winnipeg, where his fellow directors of Federal Grain were having their problems. Now that he had become such an important member of Canada's corporate world, he was all the more conscientious about helping old friends who needed his counsel. Nor would his pride and enthusiasm let him miss a meeting, if he could help it, of the Massachusetts Institute of Technology board's executive committee, the blue ribbon group of distinguished Americans who governed his old alma mater.[35]

Howe was still in great demand as a recipient of honorary degrees. In recent years he had been awarded several of North America's highest honours in applied science and public service. For his fostering of TCA, he became the first Canadian to win the prestigious Guggenheim Aviation Medal; previous recipients included Orville Wright. When asked to speak on such occasions Howe worked hard at giving his listeners the benefit of his experience and advice. As the first Canadian to give the Society of Chemical Industry's Messel Lecture, for example, he presented a thoughtful defence of the crown corporation's function in the making of industrial Canada.[36]

In 1960 Howe also played a significant role in Quebec politics. His former cabinet colleague Jean Lesage was the new leader of the little band of Liberals in the Quebec Assembly who for so long had failed to dent the armour of Premier Duplessis' Union Nationale. The Montreal business establishment always contributed heavily to Duplessis' election funds, and saw little advantage and some risk in helping the opposition. Howe's support of Jean Lesage made his party credible in the board rooms. For the first time in decades, the provincial Liberals were decently funded when the 1960 elections were called. Howe thus helped prepare the way for the Quiet Revolution which opened Quebec to the winds of change and brought Lesage and with him a new Liberal recruit named René Lévesque to power.[37]

Howe kept in touch with Lesage after he became premier. For how long the new government's directions would have pleased him we shall never know. But he was becoming distinctly uneasy about the federal Liberals. In September 1960, he and a number of business friends supported the holding of Pearson's Kingston conference – billed as an exchange of ideas among "liberally-minded Canadians." Howe was distressed over what happened at the conference. His old deputy Mitchell Sharp may have been chairman, but there were far too many left-wing intellectuals featured for his taste, one of them being Pearson's own staff man, Tom Kent, whom Howe heartily disliked. His friends at the Mount Royal Club told him exactly what they thought of the "socialists" sounding off at Kingston. Howe gloomily agreed.[38]

In November there was a testimonial dinner for him in Ottawa, attended by such admirers as his old cabinet colleagues, former U.S. Treasury Secretary George Humphrey, CCF party leader M. J. Coldwell, *Ottawa Journal* publisher I. Norman Smith, and the Tory sage Grattan O'Leary, who praised Howe as "one of the most distinguished and rabid conservatives in the country." He enjoyed himself greatly, but he did not miss a step in the busy round of his new business and university careers. During one three-day period in mid-December he attended successive meetings in New York City, Welland and Quebec City. A number of acquaintances recall seeing him sitting alone in airports during his retirement years, waiting for his plane to be called, looking exhausted – the sepia patches under the eyes heavier than before, the broad face somehow both haggard and a bit puffy. It was a gruelling schedule for a man in his seventies; it was also the kind of routine he had not really experienced since he was a young man in private practice. In Ottawa people had come to him, to be fitted into the ordered routine of a well-run office.[39]

One December afternoon in 1960, Bill Bennett was told his old boss had been kept in with a heavy cold and would like to see him. "He was sitting in a corner of the den in his dressing gown, looking absolutely terrible," Bennett recalled. They had a drink and Howe mentioned his latest invitation to help out an old friend: Jules Timmins wanted him on the Hollinger Mines board. Bennett advised against it. Instead, Howe would be better to drop all his boards except the ones that met in Montreal. "What do you want me to do?" Howe grumbled. "Go sit on a beach somewhere and think about dying?" Then he relented: "Maybe you're right. But I've got one more big job to finish off," and he mentioned the Price Brothers-Rothermere deal. "I could ease up after that."[40]

Howe had coped with his severe colds and his angina pains before by taking a winter holiday or a nap. A few days out of Ottawa or a few hours of sleep, and his stamina was restored. This time the doctors insisted he spend Christmas at home in bed. He managed to obey until Thursday the 29th when he felt well enough to go into the office and catch up on his correspondence. The next day, he felt a little weaker, and decided to stay home. On December 31, he watched the Saturday night hockey game on television as usual. Part way through, he complained of feeling unwell and retired to his bedroom. There, a few minutes later, Alice Howe found him, dead of a heart attack.

C D. Howe was buried from Christ Church Cathedral on St. Catherine Street on January 4, 1961. The Anglican Archbishop of Montreal, the Most Reverend John Dixon, officiated, and Alice Howe chose two appropriately vigorous hymns: "Lead on, O King Eternal" and "Ten Thousand Times Ten Thousand." She also asked for a reading of the 91st Psalm: "Whoso dwelleth under the defence of the Most High, shall abide under the shadow of the Almighty." Arrangements were kept as simple as possible. There were only four pallbearers, Howe's sons Bill and John, and his sons-in-law, Jim Dodge and Bob Stedman. But some things were not simple. Crowds of politicians, executives, friends and admirers were present; to handle them Bill Bennett and John Turner worked for three days on plans and protocol out of an office in the Sun Life Building on Dominion Square. C. D. himself had already made his definitive if flippant pronouncement about such matters. When told by a member of his family of a dream that he had died and they found it impossible to pick and choose among honorary pallbearers, Howe replied, "Don't worry. Just ring up the Mount Royal Club and get the first ten members with plug hats." There were no honorary pallbearers.

Everyone came. St. Laurent travelled down from Quebec City and was seated in the front pew beside Prime Minister Diefenbaker. Opposition Leader Pearson attended, as did Howe's old cabinet colleagues Abbott, Pickersgill, Chevrier, and Martin along with Norman Lambert and a dozen of his fellow senators. From Quebec City came Premier Jean Lesage, with a collection of Liberal legislative councillors. From all over the province, Howe's French-Canadian comrades – past and present members of the Commons – poured into the cathedral. The most unexpected member of the congregation was Howe's oldest political colleague, Jimmy Gardiner, who had jumped in his car and driven all the way from Saskatchewan to pay his respects. Whatever their differences, Howe was, in Gardiner's mind, a great Liberal. Having travelled two thousand miles non-stop, Gardiner simply turned round and drove back. Most of the other members of the congregation adjourned after the burial at Mount Royal Cemetery for a reception.

Editorialists were almost unanimous in their homage. The *Gazette* informed its readers that Howe was a man who "would think and act in large terms. He had hardiness and a scorn of delay." The *Montreal Star* gave Howe's death over a column of editorial comment as well as three full pages of biography, pictures and reminiscence. Howe was a "big man" who had set his mark on Canada. "His vast charm and personal magnetism, his easy unruffled humour, his loyalty to the men he worked with, set Howe apart." For *La Presse*, Howe's passing meant that "un géant entre dans sa légende." Papers from Ontario and the West which had celebrated his defeat in 1957 now voiced their praise. Even the Toronto *Telegram* momentarily dipped its sails in salute to the "indomitable optimist." More predictably, the *Toronto Star* told its readers that "Howe's Monument is Everywhere": he was "the chief builder of modern industrial Canada" and "one of the greatest Canadians of all time."

On the corner of Bank and Sparks streets in Ottawa there stands a splendid new palace of chrome and reflecting glass, built to house the Department of Industry, Trade and Commerce: it is called, naturally enough, the C. D. Howe Building, after the department's greatest minister. It may have seemed fitting to house so many trade bureaucrats under one shiny roof, to administer the legacy of C. D. Howe. Bureaucrats, however, were the least of Howe's legacies, and it is difficult to imagine the glittering prizes of Ottawa in the late 1970s reflecting C. D.'s soul. "Does it work?" he might have asked.

Howe's essence was power; his spirit was action; his style was rough and ready, but effective. No other man in Canadian history has combined political and economic power in the manner of C. D. Howe. Some, certainly, have wielded political power more wisely – as Howe himself readily admitted. Others have been more powerful economic leaders. But no one has been so successful in bringing together politics and business, using political power first to dominate and then to guide. His relation to Canada's big businessmen was indeed the most remarkable aspect of Howe's career. He was their leader, even though he did not come from their ranks.

The origins of Howe's power were strictly political; his leadership in 1940 was imposed, not sought; at that time Howe would never have ranked on any list of business candidates for the post of "industrial statesman" that the crisis demanded. But it is the political power that dominates, not the unshaped desires of a disorganized business elite. Having accidentally found their leader and discovered his effectiveness, Canadian business clung to him: through the war, the 1945 election, through the postwar reconstruction, the Korean crisis and the boom of the 1950s.

The secret of Howe's leadership lies in his performance in that confused, glorious year, 1940. In the midst of crisis, he took a calculated risk: he shaped Canada's war program, renewed Canada's industrial plant, and reconstructed the Canadian economy with the aid of his chosen advisers and a blank cheque from the Canadian government. It was the only blank cheque he would ever get, but it was enough. By the end of 1941 Canada was endowed with a modern industrial plant, a trained industrial work force, and a reformed group of executives who were gradually being shaped into a single managerial class. Using the men who came to work for his department, and those who worked for the government on contracts, Howe created a common group of managers, with allegiance to himself, the one man to whom the whole economy made sense, its chairman of the board and chief executive officer.

In looking beyond the exigencies of wartime, Howe knew that the real reconstruction had already taken place. It was, in the first place, economic. But it was also psychological, a matter of confidence: confidence in oneself and confidence in Canada. The Great Depression would not resume, he believed; the postwar world would present problems of shortage, not overabundance. From that insight Howe moved into action, dismantling Canada's siege economy, muffling the would-be state planners, removing the most complex and absolute of wartime regulations while keeping the key controls, over steel and fuels, in his own hands. Whether by encouraging them or driving them, or if necessary threatening to put a public company of his own into the field, Howe led Canada's reluctant businessmen, who feared the return of hard times, into a program of dynamic expansion.

Howe, M. J. Coldwell shrewdly observed, would have done well under any system, provided he was allowed to manage what he wanted. What counted was the political power he could use, and that it was strong enough to influence the economic power. The theory under which he wielded his power – socialism, free enterprise, corporate liberalism or whatever – was of little concern, although his deepest instinct was that the freeing of reasoned self-interest would be the best way to stimulate the economy.

Howe's attitude to equity capital was much the same. It mattered little where the money came from, provided it was invested in Canada and produced Canadian jobs. American money, American industrial organization and American technology could help to transform Canada. Without them, Canada would quickly become a stagnant backwater. An American investor, coming to Canada, must play by the rules of the game as Howe understood them. They must employ Canadians, shape their decisions to conform to Canadian needs, and become, as the trite phrase had it, "good corporate citizens." Those were the rules that should apply to all significant firms, foreign-owned or not, and it was up to the Canadian government to see that they were enforced.

The great debate over the pipeline only served to reinforce Howe's views. It was Howe, not some American corporation, who decided that western gas must be brought across Canada rather than simply sent south into the United States. It was he in the end who was responsible for enforcing a faster timetable, severe penalties for non-performance and ultimate Canadian ownership and control upon the American owners of the company. Even before he died, it was evident that the pipeline was a success, and probably his greatest single achievement. Within a decade of its first full year of operation the flow of cheap western gas into central Canada had increased sevenfold and the company was 94 per cent Canadian-owned. Without Howe, the line would not likely have been built at all and by the 1970s

Canada would have been more thoroughly locked into a north-south continental energy grid.

Even in the 1950s, however, and with increasing shrillness since, Howe's critics have argued that under his evil genius Canada traded a contented, if modest, independence for a fur-lined foreign domination. "It must be a great satisfaction to Mr. Howe," Judith Robinson wrote in 1956. "When he came to power Canada was poor like all the world but it had a free Parliament. . . . Now Canada is rich and it no longer has a free Parliament." Howe had scant sympathy for such concerns. He believed he knew how economic relations between Canada and the United States worked, and he believed that the government of Canada did not march to the beat of the American drum. In any case, much of the American investment in Canada was pouring into the hungry fields of provincial jurisdiction and even had he wanted to stop it, which he did not, neither provincial politicians nor public opinion would have agreed with him.*

The problem of American investment was more a political and cultural one than it was economic. For Howe, American investment was *investment*; for his critics it was *American* investment. It was associated with Canada's historic continental rival. American money arrived already tainted by its origins. So had Howe. Donald Fleming had found it useful during the pipeline debate to slip in a reference to Howe's immigrant origins, and Fleming's point has been often repeated since. Howe was "an

---

* Six years after Howe's death, one economist summarized the performance of firms in the Canadian economy in terms Howe would have approved. "The evidence . . . suggests that in significant part the direct investment firm has contributed to the development objectives favoured by governmental authorities in recent years. Where it has not done so there are often good economic reasons why it cannot perform as expected, reasons often related to the framework of public policy within which it operates."

The real question of foreign ownership, in Howe's mind, was whether it brought more benefits to Canada than it cost. Economically, it was obvious that it did. Direct foreign investment in Canadian industry meant foreign risk-taking. The cost of servicing foreign investment, the sum of interest and dividends flowing out of the country, was significantly lower in percentage terms when Howe left office than it had been in the booming twenties. To use another indicator, the total foreign long-term capital invested in Canada in 1957 ($17.5 billion) was *lower* as a percentage of gross national product (55 per cent) than it had been in 1926 (117 per cent) or 1945 (60 per cent). The growth in Canada's gross national product ($11.8 billion in 1945 and $31.9 billion in 1957) – a growth largely attributable to the inflow of foreign capital – was proof positive of the desirability of capital inflow.

American import," Donald Creighton has written, "a very good North American, quickly responsive to the militant moods of Washington and New York." Echoing Creighton, sociologist Wallace Clement described Howe as "the American import to the Liberal St. Laurent cabinet." Presumably Howe imported national subservience along with his flat New England accent.

Howe was "an American by birth, a Canadian by choice." To understand him fully it must be remembered that he lived the first years of his maturity in Nova Scotia, nearly a quarter-century in the Canadian West, the twenty-two years of his public life in Ottawa and his last days in Montreal. He travelled as widely in Canada as any politician in our history, and he developed an unparalleled network of connections and friendships throughout the country. His attitudes and character were profoundly shaped by his adopted land.

He brought with him, unquestionably, certain American qualities which he never lost. There was a largeness and a generosity, a decisiveness and a simplicity in his temperament which was reminiscent of certain other great Americans – the railway builder Van Horne, the neurosurgeon Wilder Penfield, the urbanist Jane Jacobs – who have committed themselves to Canada. However lamentable Howe's faults and ignorances, they are not, any more than his virtues, those of pettiness, caution or inhibition. Howe could never be confused with that archetypical Canadian Man who, as Frank Scott put it, "never did things by halves which he could do by quarters."

Faults and limitations Howe certainly had and they were serious ones. He was in the first place an utter philistine with respect to an appreciation of the arts and architecture, of religion and of the natural world – even though he could be readily convinced of the value of their appreciation by people he respected. The nature of his commitment to the practical uses of higher education, like his sunny liberal philosophy of life, was something he scarcely questioned or examined. His understanding of British political institutions, whose superiority to American ones he often proclaimed, was crude to say the least. It was understandable enough: quite apart from the enthusiasm and commitment of a convert, he knew full well that the checks and balances of the American system would never have allowed any politician, even in wartime, to wield the awesome collection of economic powers which he held in Canada. Howe has been often accused of lacking sympathy for labour, and for the poor and the disadvantaged in society; but he contended that a healthy economy best protected their human rights and economic needs. Certainly he loved the company of the rich and powerful, and tended to accept uncritically many of their social views. In his final years, Howe's age and ill health brought out the bully in him and made it harder for him to rein in his explosive temper. His frequent repentances and apologies did not always undo the damage. And it is fortunate, too, that there were always a few colleagues or opponents or subordinates with the courage to stand up to him and stop him when the worst of his anger and prejudices, or the more misguided of his objectives and methods, carried him and the country onto perilous ground.

Howe was a man of complete integrity, keen intellect, humour, charm, warmth and decency. He was a great leader of men. To his friends, his employees, his students and his colleagues he was utterly loyal, and to even the most humble and ungifted of them he gave his trust and respect as human beings. And they in turn gave him their complete commitment; even a number of his political opponents, from M. J. Coldwell to Grattan O'Leary, were devoted to Howe, no matter how much they disagreed with his views and his party. And of the thousands of men and women who were personally acquainted with the man, however briefly or superficially, there were few who were not moved by the experience. Howe's acts of personal kindness to people in need were legion and must far outnumber the personal encounters that led to harsh words or frustration. Henry Borden spoke for many Canadians when, after Howe's death, he recalled "the deepest admiration, affection and love" in which they held him.

Notes

NOTES

Preface

1. Early in 1958 I needed Mr. Howe's help with a business history I was writing. His friend and fellow engineer, Hugh Hilton of the Steel Company of Canada, spoke to him for me and I was promptly instructed to be at the Rideau Club in Ottawa at noon the next day. Besides my research on the Canadian steel industry, I was collecting for the same book the reminiscences of several formidable ancients – among them Lord Beaverbrook, Sir Edward Peacock, Col. R. S. McLaughlin and Joseph Chamberlain's friend, Sir Ian Hamilton-Benn (a sprightly 97 at the time) about the financial worlds of Britain and Canada in the early 1900s. It sometimes seemed as if I were encountering characters who had strayed out of an unwritten novel by Henry James. To my surprise the one with the most powerful presence of all was C. D. Howe.

   Standing alone waiting, he looked unspeakably old and haggard. In repose, the bronzed wrinkled reptilian skin, the heavy sepia patches under the eyes, gave him the mask of a sort of living monument. Animated suddenly, with a flash of the dark glittering eyes and a broad smile, his face shed fifty years. The flat Boston accent rang out: "How *ah* yuh!"

   After the cordial little procession of old comrades to his table had subsided, Mr. Howe wrote out our "dinner" order in a sort of phonetic shorthand and proceeded to make short work of my prepared questions. He then turned to the topic of the day which was the Liberal leadership contest between Lester Pearson and Paul Martin. After various blunt personal remarks on that subject, he began gossiping about other things he probably shouldn't have, not at least to an inquisitive young stranger. To my astonishment we were quickly into 1957 cabinet debates or anything else I had the wit to ask about. His Privy Councillor's oath of secrecy, as I was to discover much later from others, never did extend to the premises of the Rideau Club. As we were about to leave, he told me there were several mountains of his papers out in Tunney's Pasture which I might like to look through some time, in fact some of his friends were after him to have them used for a book and would I be interested in doing that sort of thing? As I was already otherwise occupied, I did not pursue the matter.

The last time I saw him was several months later, in Beaverbrook's flat at the Waldorf in New York City, where his lordship was apparently getting him involved in a big pulp and paper company he owned. Howe looked absolutely exhausted. (W.K.)

Prologue

The account of the ocean trip is based on entries in C. D. Howe's "Diary of Events from Wednesday December 4th, 1940, to Sunday January 26th, 1941 inclusive" (Public Archives of Canada, Howe Papers [hereafter HP]). Other details are from E. P. Taylor, Alice Howe, Ruth Thomson interviews; letter of Howe to Elisabeth Howe, 6 Dec. 1940; J. W. Pickersgill, *The Mackenzie King Record*, I, *1939-1944* (Toronto: University of Toronto Press, 1961), 153-54; House of Commons, *Debates*, 1945, 22 Nov., 2442; Beaverbrook interviews.

Chapter 1

1. Howe and Worcester family genealogies, courtesy Alice Howe; Alice Howe, Agnes Howe Bettinger and Barbara Worcester Porter interviews; Stanley Howe, "C. D. Howe and the Americans," Ph.D. thesis (Orono: University of Maine, 1977), chapter 1.
2. Ibid., and Stanley Howe, unpublished notes on family recollections of C. D. Howe; memorabilia in Waltham Public Library Archives.
3. Carl Lawson, quoted in Boston *Globe*, July 28, 1940, and Stanley Howe, unpublished notes and "C. D. Howe."
4. "Waltham High School Graduation Exercises," courtesy of Alice Howe.
5. David F. Noble, *America by Design* (New York: Alfred A. Knopf, 1977), 50-51, 64, 263-67, 320; MIT Calendar, 1907, MIT Archives; see also Daniel Calhoun, *The American Civil Engineer* (Cambridge, Mass.: 1960).
6. S. C. Prescott, *When MIT was 'Boston Tech'* (Cambridge, Mass.: 1954).
7. Ibid. and MIT student records courtesy the Registrar; Class of 1907 Year-book (*Technique*) and other MIT student publications, MIT Archives; B. W. Porter and A. H. Bettinger interviews.
8. B. W. Porter and A. H. Bettinger interviews.
9. James Barker interview.

Chapter Two

1. Postcards, Sept. and Oct. 1908, C. D. Howe and Mary Hastings Howe to various members of Howe family, courtesy of Stanley Howe.
2. J. H. L. Johnstone, Denis Stairs, C. J. Mackenzie, R. McCullough, and H. W. L. Doane interviews.
3. HP, speech files.
4. See note 2 above; Horace Read interview; catalogues of Dalhousie University and Minutes of Senate and of Arts and Science Faculty meetings, 1908-13, Dalhousie University Archives.
5. Ibid.
6. Ibid.
7. J. H. L. Johnstone, H. W. L. Doane, and R. McCullough interviews.
8. PAC, Magill Papers, contain information about Magill's character and career including a biographical sketch by his wife; when Robert Magill

died Alice Howe wrote to her that "Clarence has always felt, and often said, that he owed his whole career to him. . . ." Alice Howe to Susan Magill, 28 Jan. 1930.

Chapter Three

1. *Fort William City Directory, 1913,* Thunder Bay Public Library; H. J. Symington interview.
2. The classic work on the western wheat economy is V. C. Fowke's *The National Policy and the Wheat Economy* (Toronto: University of Toronto Press, 1957); on points of detail, however, it has been superseded by C. F. Wilson, *A Century of Canadian Grain* (Saskatoon: Western Producer Prairie Books, 1978).
3. PAC, Magill Papers, Cora Hind to Robert Magill, 28 Sept. 1915, quoting Magill back to himself; ibid., memo by Magill to the Dominions Royal Commission, undated but c.1914; ibid., Magill to George Perley, 22 July and 16 August 1913.
4. Norman Lambert, "C. D. Howe: a Memoir," (privately held); Howe long afterward referred to "a sharp disagreement" between himself and Bennett in Calgary in 1915: HP, vol. 187, file 90(69), Howe to Beaverbrook, 1 Dec. 1959.
5. George McIvor interview. Howe was helped by the relative simplicity of grain elevator construction. Building an elevator comprised three basic phases. In the first, the engineer bored a hole in the earth to test the ground on which the elevator would rest. Then he returned to the drawing board to prepare plans for an elevator of appropriate size. During the third phase, construction, the engineer supervised the laying of the foundation (usually millions of board feet of Canadian pine), and then the pouring of the concrete. Concrete was poured into slip forms which rose up round the towers of the elevator. Howe was fortunate that the technology for slip forms had been perfected just before he became an elevator engineer; the book he used, Milo S. Ketchum's *The Design of Walls, Bins and Grain Elevators* (New York: McGraw-Hill, 1907), remained standard for many years. We are greatly indebted to Joseph Carr of Carr & Donald, Toronto, for this information.
6. A. W. Rasporich, "A Boston Yankee in Prince Arthur's Landing," in *Canada*, Winter 1973, 22-23; George McIvor interview.
7. George McIvor and Murray Fleming interviews.
8. Alice Howe interview.
9. Port Arthur *News Chronicle*, 9 Dec. 1916; Rasporich, "Boston Yankee," 23-24; George McIvor, Alice Howe interviews.
10. Port Arthur *News Chronicle*, 28 April 1920.
11. Ibid., 8 Dec. 1922.
12. John Stirling, Murray Fleming interviews; information supplied by Murray Fleming.
13. Ibid. and George McIvor interview; Noble, *America by Design*.
14. John Stirling interview.
15. Rasporich, "Boston Yankee," 27; Lakehead University Archives, C. D. Howe scrapbooks and clipping file.
16. Alice, William and John Howe, Elisabeth Howe Stedman, Barbara Howe Marshall, Mary Howe Dodge, Nellie Fisher Wright interviews.

17. The house is still in good condition and has been used during the 1970s by the Children's Aid Society of Thunder Bay. The quotation about the view is from J. W. Pickersgill interview.
18. Alice Howe, Elisabeth Howe Stedman, Nellie Fisher Wright interviews.
19. C. J. Mackenzie interview.
20. George McIvor interview.
21. W. J. Bennett, George McIvor, H. J. Symington interviews; MIT Archives, C. D. Howe to MIT Alumni Association for their 1926 newsletter.
22. W. J. Bennett, George McIvor, David Mansur interviews.
23. Murray Fleming, William Peach interviews; Rasporich, "Boston Yankee," 27-28.
24. Murray Fleming and William Peach interviews; C. D. Howe to William Peach, 17 Jan. 1933, courtesy Alice Howe.

Chapter Four

1. Lambert, "Memoir," 2.
2. Ibid., 2-3.
3. Salter Hayden interview.
4. John Stirling interview. Charles Dunning also claimed later that he strongly encouraged Howe to go into politics. A story appeared occasionally in the press during the 1940s that Mackenzie King persuaded Alice Howe that she would see more of her husband at home if he were a politician rather than an engineer. A number of people who knew the Howes during the 1930s and 1940s believed she encouraged him to go into politics, though she herself does not recall anything more than leaving the decision to him.
5. Lambert, "Memoir," 5; Lambert Diary, 1934.
6. B. A. Culpeper, Murray Fleming interviews; Lambert, "Memoir," 3-4.
7. Ibid.
8. Port Arthur *News Chronicle*, 30 Nov. 1934; Rasporich, "Boston Yankee," 28. Howe's reputation as a friend of labour was based on his attitude to the old craft unions and railway brotherhoods of his home town. When the industrial unions came across his path in the 1940s, his reputation took a decided turn to the right.
9. Lambert, "Memoir," 5-7.
10. PAC, King Diary, 12 June 1935.
11. Port Arthur *News Chronicle*, 25-27 Sept. 1935.
12. A. W. Rasporich, "Boston Yankee," 29; *Atlas of Canada* (Ottawa: Department of Mines and Resources, 1967), Plate 108.
13. Port Arthur *News Chronicle*, 7 and 9 Oct. 1935; Rasporich, "Boston Yankee," 29-30.
14. Rasporich, "Boston Yankee," 29.
15. Ibid., 30.

Chapter Five

1. King Diary, 19 Oct. and 5 Nov. 1935.
2. Toronto *Globe* 16-19 and 22-23 Oct. 1935.
3. King Diary, 17-19 and 21-23 Oct. 1935. On King's 1935 cabinet-making, see also H. B. Neatby, *William Lyon Mackenzie King,* III: *The Prism of Unity* (Toronto: University of Toronto Press, 1976), 126-33; F. W. Gibson, "The Cabinet of 1935," in Gibson, ed., *Cabinet Formation and Bicultural Relations* (Ottawa: Queen's Printer, 1970), 105-41; Neil

McKenty, *Mitch Hepburn* (Toronto: McClelland and Stewart, 1967), 73-74.

4. W. J. Bennett, J. W. Pickersgill, Ruth Thomson, Annette Saint-Denis interviews. Senator Salter Hayden also recalled later that Howe was in one respect "very hard on his staff because he would readily promise things to someone he liked," and the staff then had to cope with the generous promises as best they could.

5. King Diary, 28 Oct. 1935.

6. Ibid., 29 Oct. 1935.

Chapter Six

1. Murray Fleming and William Peach interviews; HP, private financial files.

2. Alice Howe, Elisabeth Howe Stedman and Mary Howe Dodge interviews.

3. W. J. Bennett, J. W. Pickersgill interviews.

4. See note 2 above.

5. Thérèse Casgrain, *A Woman in a Man's World* (Toronto: McClelland and Stewart, 1972) 96-97.

6. Hugues Lapointe, W. J. Bennett, Alice Howe, Elisabeth Howe Stedman interviews. Years later, in 1949, Howe was presiding at cabinet two weeks after young Lapointe's appointment as solicitor-general; Lapointe's first recommendation to cabinet was for commutation of the death sentence for a young Sudbury man convicted of murder. A number of ministers, he knew, were strongly for hanging, in this as in almost every case, and they gave their new colleague a rough time. The pro-clemency members contested the matter hotly but it appeared they were losing, and Howe could be counted on to vote against them. After forty-five minutes of argument, Howe got restless and to everyone's surprise abruptly declared "As Mr. King would say 'the consensus of the meeting' is for clemency." Afterwards Howe took Lapointe aside and told him: "I wasn't going to see you lose your first case in cabinet," and then added "but you had better get up a better case next time."

7. Queen's University Archives, Lambert Diary, 1936-39. With his responsibilities for ordering marine, railway and radio equipment, among other things, C. D. Howe was from the beginning the greatest single source of industrial contracts from government and crown corporations. He discussed these contracts with Lambert frequently. He also discussed advertising contracts (e.g., Lambert Diary, 31 Dec. 1936). On Liberal party funding and patronage, see J. L. Granatstein, "Financing the Liberal Party," in M. S. Cross and R. Bothwell, eds., *Policy by Other Means* (Toronto: Clarke, Irwin, 1972), and Reginald Whitaker, *The Government Party* (Toronto: University of Toronto Press, 1978).

8. On the National Harbours Board, see C. A. Ashley and R. G. H. Smails, *Canadian Crown Corporations* (Toronto: Macmillan, 1965), chapter 14.

9. House of Commons, *Debates*, 1936, 21 Feb., 425-31; 19 Mar. 1262-65; 24-27 Mar., 1412-32, 1508-16, 1556-65; 21-23 Apr., 2049-2120; 20 May, 2997-3008; 26 May, 3105-3119.

Chapter Seven

1. T. C. Keefer, *Philosophy of Railroads*, edited with an introduction by H. V. Nelles (Toronto: University of Toronto Press, 1972), lx, xxviii, xxxix, xl.

2. G. R. Stevens interview.
3. House of Commons, *Debates*, 1936, 27-28 Apr., 2178-2228 and 3-5 June, 3367-3459. At the first working session of the 1935 cabinet, Howe had recommended getting rid of the Board of Trustees; he said they had helped the Conservative government to do "everything possible to sabotage the National Railways" and were even yet plotting to sign an agreement with the CPR that would do more damage still. King basically agreed and, dismissing counsels of caution from other ministers, carried cabinet with him in favour of drastic action. King Diary, 28 Oct. 1935.
4. King Diary, 7 July, 1936; G. R. Stevens interview. The CNR board was appointed 10 Sept. 1936 and took office on 1 Oct.
5. G. R. Stevens interview; Dexter Papers, Dafoe to Dexter, 30 Oct. and 2 Dec. 1936.
6. Frank Peers, *The Politics of Canadian Broadcasting* (Toronto: University of Toronto Press, 1969) 22-26, 69-71, 178, 186; E. Bushnell and G. Spry interviews.
7. House of Commons, *Debates*, 15 June 1936, 3710.
8. Frank Peers, *Politics*, 193, 209-10, 205; Austin Weir, *The Struggle for National Broadcasting in Canada* (Toronto: McClelland and Stewart, 1965), 207, 212-18; E. A. Pickering, E. Bushnell and G. Spry interviews. In his diary for 21 Jan. 1937, King recorded that he had seen Howe personally to straighten out the "differences he had been having with his Board." He complained afterwards that "Howe is a good business executive but lacks political experience."

Chapter Eight

1. J. R. K. Main, *Voyageurs of the Air; a History of Civil Aviation in Canada* (Ottawa: Queen's Printer, 1967); K. M. Molson, *Pioneering in Canadian Air Transport* (Altona, Manitoba: 1974); John Swettenham, *McNaughton*, I, *1887-1939* (Toronto: Ryerson Press, 1968), 286-99. The J. A. Richardson Papers and the unpublished work on civil aviation of Margaret Mattson of the PAC were also consulted. There is very little in the Howe Papers on TCA or its background before 1939. There is a useful unpublished manuscript on the Richardsons by Donald Creighton in the Richardson Archives, Winnipeg.
2. Richardson Archives, Canadian Airways – TCA – Howe correspondence, 1936-37.
3. Ibid.
4. Lambert Diary, 29 Sept. 1936 and 24, 25 Oct. 1936.
5. King Diary, 19 Nov. 1936.
6. Ibid., 26 Nov. 1936.
7. Howe to Beattie, 15 Mar. 1937 quoted in K. Molson, *Pioneering*, 196-97.
8. Richardson Archives, Richardson to Howe, 26 Apr. 1937 and Howe to Richardson, 25 May 1937.
9. Extract from Minutes of CNR board meeting, courtesy Norman MacMillan, CNR Chairman, 1970.
10. Extract from minutes of TCA board meetings, ibid.; Gordon McGregor, H. J. Symington interviews; C. A. Ashley, *The First Twenty-Five Years: A Study of TCA* (Toronto: Macmillan, 1962).
11. Ibid. and *Air Canada: the First Forty* (Air Canada pamphlet, Montreal,

1977) and *Horizons* (Air Canada house magazine), 10 Apr. 1977 (Anniversary number).

12. Richardson Archives, Richardson to Beatty, 14 Aug. 1937.
13. Ibid., Beatty to Richardson, 24 Aug. 1937.
14. Air Canada publications, see note 11.
15. Floyd Chalmers interview.
16. The passages on Howe's administrative style in the 1930s are based chiefly on interviews with W. J. Bennett, J. W. Pickersgill, C. J. Mackenzie, George McIvor, Ruth Thomson, and Annette Saint-Denis, but are also derived from interviews with some of those who worked with him later, particularly David Mansur, Frederick Bull and Deane Nesbitt.
17. McKenty, *Hepburn*, 165 and elsewhere; Lambert Diary 1938; Rasporich, "Boston Yankee," 30 and 33.
18. W. J. Bennett interview; Lambert Diary, 2, 3, 5 and 7 Dec., 1938.
19. W. J. Bennett interview; Lambert Diary, 12 Dec. 1938; Neatby, *King*, III, 268-73; McKenty, *Hepburn*, 165-70. Howe argued for organizing a frontal attack against Hepburn before King was persuaded it was wise. At this time Hepburn and Duplessis were supporting a campaign in Montreal and Toronto business circles for amalgamation of the CNR and the CPR. Hepburn denounced Norman Rogers as "a pink socialite" for his left-wing views.
20. McKenty, *Hepburn*, 174.

Chapter Nine

1. C. P. Stacey, *Arms, Men and Governments, The War Policies of Canada, 1939-1945* (Ottawa: Queen's Printer, 1970), 1-6, 67-108; Swettenham, *McNaughton*, I, *1887-1939*, chapter 10; J. G. Eayrs, *In Defence of Canada*, II (Toronto: University of Toronto Press, 1965), 134-54.
2. House of Commons, *Debates*, 1939, 9 Feb., 771-75; George Drew, "Canada's Armaments Mystery," *Maclean's*, 1 Sept. 1938; Leslie Roberts, *C. D.: The Life and Times of Clarence Decatur Howe* (Toronto: Clarke, Irwin, 1957), 52-68.
3. King Diary, 24 Aug. 1939.
4. House of Commons, *Debates*, 12 Sept. 1939; Roberts, *C. D.*, 67-68.
5. Pickersgill, *King Record*, I, 27.
6. Ibid.
7. Ibid., 23; J. L. Granatstein, *The Politics of Survival* (Toronto: University of Toronto Press, 1967), 43-47.
8. Pickersgill, *King Record*, I, 62-65.
9. Ibid., 66.
10. Ibid., 72; J. L. Granatstein, *Canada's War: The Politics of the Mackenzie King Government, 1939-1945* (Toronto: Oxford University Press, 1975), 89.
11. Rasporich, "Boston Yankee," 33; Pickersgill, *King Record*, I, 62-63.

Chapter Ten

1. King Diary, 5, 9 April, 1940.
2. Ibid.
3. Henry Borden interview.

4. Interviews with Mrs. Frank Gibson, H. Carl Goldenberg and Henry Borden.
5. Henry Borden interview.
6. Ibid.
7. Ibid.
8. E. P. Taylor interview; Richard Rohmer, *E. P. Taylor* (Toronto: McClelland and Stewart, 1978), 86-87.
9. W. J. Bennett interview.
10. HP, vol. 5, Report by W. A. Harrison and E. A. Bromley, no date but early 1940; Henry Borden interview.
11. Ibid.
12. Public Record Office, London, (PRO), AVIA/22/3/66, memorandum by Sir Henry Self, 23 Aug. 1940.
13. PAC, Privy Council Papers, series 18, vol. 47, Gordon Wismer to Mackenzie King, 11 June 1940, and Arnold Heeney to King, 13 June 1940; on controls generally see J. de N. Kennedy, *History of the Department of Munitions and Supply*, II (Ottawa: King's Printer, 1950).
14. Bruce Hutchison interview.
15. Duncan McDowall, "Steel at the Sault: Sir James Dunn and the Algoma Steel Corporation, 1906-56," Ph.D. thesis, Carleton University, 1978, 312-14.
16. Stacey, *Arms, Men and Governments*, 500-501; E. P. Taylor interview.
17. United States National Archives, Washington, State Department Papers, 842.002/105, J. P. Moffat to Secretary of State, 9 Sept. 1940.
18. Ralph Bell interview.
19. Ibid.; Henry Borden interview.
20. PAC, J. W. Dafoe Papers, vol. 12, Grant Dexter to Dafoe, 25 Jan. 1941; Ray Lawson interview.
21. Stacey, *Arms, Men and Governments*, 496.
22. AVIA 22/3/70/2058/331, James Crone, "Canadian Reminiscences," written in 1944.
23. J. P. Moffat had just been appointed American minister to Ottawa. His dispatches, always well informed, were the first reliable information the U.S. government received on Canada's war effort.
24. Ibid., 842.002/107, Moffat to Secretary of State, 26 Feb. 1941.
25. Austin Cross, *The People's Mouths* (Toronto: Macmillan, 1943), 68.
26. Order-in-Council PC 6601; House of Commons, *Debates*, 20 Nov. 1940.
27. On Beaverbrook's impact on British supply, see State Dept. Papers, Hickerson files, Box 6, R. F. Simmons memorandum, 24 Feb. 1941.
28. Ray Lawson Papers (privately held), Howe to Lawson, 6 Dec. 1940.
29. Elisabeth Howe Stedman Papers (privately held), Howe to Elisabeth Howe, 6 Dec. 1940.
30. Woodward's observation is quoted in Douglas E. Harker, *The Woodwards* (Vancouver: Mitchell Press, 1976), 144; Privy Council Papers, series 18, vol. 47, Howe to J. K. Sheils, 1 and 6 Jan. 1941.
31. *Ottawa Journal*, 27 Jan. 1941; King Diary, 25 and 26 Jan. 1941.
32. PAC, Dafoe Papers, vol. 12, H. J. Symington to J. W. Dafoe, 19 Feb. 1941.
33. Lambert Diary, 23 Nov. 1940, 26 Dec. 1940.
34. Ibid., 2 Nov. 1940; "Need War Chief," *Financial Post*, 23 Nov. 1940, 26

Dec. 1940, *Ottawa Journal*, 10 Jan. 1941, mentioning Carmichael's appointment.

35. The minutes of the Wartime Requirements Board reveal Henry's uncharacteristic inactivity; the secretary of the board, Carl Goldenberg, recalls that Henry was undoubtedly looking out for Howe's interests; the suggestions of Pickersgill and Turnbull, dated 1 Dec. 1940 and 21 Jan. 1941, are in King Papers J4, file 2067.

36. On Carmichael, see Lambert Diary, 11 Jan. and 6 Feb. 1941 and C. J. Mackenzie Diary (privately held), 27 March 1941; Dafoe Papers, vol. 12, Dexter to Dafoe, 5 Feb. 1941. A biographical sketch of Carmichael (and of many of Howe's other officials) may be found in Carolyn Cox, *Canadian Strength* (Toronto: Ryerson, 1946), 20-23.

37. King carried into the War Committee meeting a memorandum by Harry Ferns, dated 20 Jan. 1941, highly critical of Federal Aircraft; King Diary, 29 Jan. 1941; Gardiner's comment is in Lambert Diary, 3 Jan. 1941.

38. The MacMillan report appeared in *Votes and Procedures* of the House Commons, 27 Feb. 1941; House of Commons, *Debates*, 26 Feb. 1941, 1055-57.

39. Dafoe Papers, vol. 12, Dexter to Dafoe, 30 Mar. 1941.

40. HP, vol. 170, file 90(2), Howe to Henry, 22 Nov. 1941.

41. Taylor was first appointed "executive assistant" to Howe: Rohmer, *Taylor* 98-99.

42. AVIA 22/3/62, Taylor to Sir H. Brown, 15 May 1941.

43. King Diary, 3 Feb 1941; Cabinet War Committee Minutes, 18 Feb. 1941.

44. State Dept. Papers, 842.20 Defense/62, A. A. Berle to Sumner Welles, 28 Feb. 1941.

45. Clark, Memorandum, 21 Mar. 1941, Clark to King with enclosures, 9 April 1941, and Howe to King, 8 Apr. 1941, Documents on Canadian External Relations, VIII, 295-321. On these negotiations and the Hyde Park Agreement in general, see J. L. Granatstein and R. D. Cuff, "The Hyde Park Declaration, 1941: Origins and Significance," *Canadian Historical Review*, LV (1974).

46. J. W. Pickersgill, *The Mackenzie King Record*, I (Toronto: University of Toronto Press, 1961), 192-93.

47. Ibid.

48. Quoted in the *Toronto Star*, 3 Jan. 1961.

49. King Diary, 3 Feb. 1941; Stacey, *Arms*, 491-92.

50. HP, vol. 170, file 90(12), Henry to Howe, 3 Dec. 1941.

51. Borden interview; Carmichael interview.

52. HP, vol. 170 90(2), Howe to Henry, 22 Nov. 1941; Mackenzie King Diary, 27 Mar. 1941.

53. HP, vol. 170, file 90(2), Howe to Henry, 22 Nov. 1941.

54. House of Commons, *Debates*, Nov. 1941.

Chapter Eleven

1. Emmett Murphy ("Murph") became a favourite of the entire Howe family. He was not as highly regarded by other civil servants, especially when, under Howe's patronage, he became deputy minister of public works: John Stirling interview, John Connolly interview.

2. "Backstage at Ottawa," *Maclean's*, 15 Dec. 1942, 45; Elisabeth Howe Stedman interview.
3. Alice Howe interview.
4. Elisabeth Howe Stedman interview.
5. Ibid.
6. Frank Brown interview.
7. Grant Dexter Papers, Dexter memorandum, 6 Jan. 1942; Mackenzie Diary, 5 Feb. 1942.
8. PAC, Eric Hehner Papers, vol. 1, Minutes of the War Industries Control Board, 12 Dec. 1941; McGill University Archives, H. R. Donald Papers, "A Chemist's Yesterdays," 127: "More meetings in Ottawa before the end of the year with Mr. Howe urging us on to greater efforts."
9. J. R. Nicholson interview.
10. Howe's statement is in House of Commons, *Debates*, 16 June 1943, 3714.
11. Dexter Papers, B. T. Richardson memorandum, 28 Feb. 1942; Brown interview; for an example of Cottrelle in action, see PAC, Henry Borden Papers, vol. 2, Cottrelle to Borden, 18 Jan. 1943. On one famous occasion, Cottrelle revoked the special gas ration of an executive who offered him a lift to work.
12. During the war $514 million of private investment received tax concessions: Department of Reconstruction and Supply, *Encouragement to Industrial Expansion* (Ottawa: King's Printer, 1948), 21.
13. McDowall, "Dunn," 325-27; T. F. Rahilly interview.
14. Borden interview; K. R. Wilson, "Welter of Confusion Fogs Malton Seizure," *Financial Post*, 14 Nov. 1942; Lambert Diary, 26 Jan. 1943.
15. Roosevelt Library, Hyde Park, NY, Harry Hopkins Papers, vol. 312, "Canadian Labor and the War," unsigned memorandum, 9 Sept. 1942.
16. The CMA's warning is quoted in A. F. W. Plumptre, *Mobilizing Canada's Resources for War* (Toronto: Ryerson Press, 1941), 271; Howe's reaction to the CMA is in minutes of a meeting with the CMA, 8 May 1941, King Papers, J4, file 2395; King Diary, 30 May 1941; Minutes of the War Industries Control Board, 8 July 1941; PAC, J. L. Ralston Papers, vol. 38, Harry Crerar to Ralston, 26 July 1941; King Diary, 27 July 1941; Pickersgill, *King Record*, I, 229-33; Lambert Diary, 28 July 1941; King Papers, J1, vol. 306, Lapointe to King, no date but probably 31 July 1941.
17. Lapointe's letter to King was based on RCMP information; PAC, Lapointe Papers, vol. 11, C. Vaillancourt to Howe, 31 July 1941; Ralston Papers, vol. 38, contain two relevant memoranda: "Re: Arvida: Summary of Intelligence Reports, Aug. 11th" and an unsigned memorandum dated 3 Sept. 1941.
18. Goldenberg interview.
19. Cited in Whitaker, *The Government Party*, 138.
20. King once described Humphrey Mitchell as "a great talking machine": Bennett interview; for Carmichael's intervention on Mitchell's behalf, see Goldenberg interview.
21. Lambert Diary, 27 April 1942.
22. Ibid., 31 May 1942; House of Commons, *Debates*, 16 June 1942, 3369, 3371; "Backstage at Ottawa," *Maclean's*, 15 July, 1 Aug., 15 Aug. 1942.
23. HP, vol. 170, file 90, Howe to Beaverbrook, 10 Aug. 1943; Cabinet War Committee Minutes, 23 Sept. 1942; Ralston Papers, vol. 115, WICB memorandum, 30 Sept. 1942.

24. Bennett interview.
25. Ibid.
26. The best brief accounts of Canada's early involvement in atomic energy are to be found in C. P. Stacey, *Arms, Men and Governments*, 515-28, and James Eayrs, *In Defence of Canada*, III (Toronto: University of Toronto Press, 1972), chapter 5.
27. Ralston Papers, vol. 41, Carswell to Howe, 16 Feb. 1942.
28. Ibid. Ralston to Howe, 16 Feb. 1942; Cabinet War Committee Minutes, 12 Feb. 1942.
29. Cabinet War Committee Papers, Document No. 112, Howe, "Re: Joint U.S.-U.K. Boards for Allocation of Finished Munitions, Distribution of Shipping and Distribution of Raw Materials," 5 March 1942; Cabinet War Committee minutes, March to September 1942, passim; Mackenzie Diary, 28 July 1942; FO 371/31543/4284, Sinclair to Lyttelton, 4 Sept. 1942 for the British reaction.
30. Cabinet War Committee minutes, 28 Oct. 1942. For a differing view, see Stacey, *Arms, Men and Governments*, 167-78.
31. Bennett interview.
32. Lambert diary, 1 and 2 Nov. 1940; Howe's reaction to demands for political criteria to be applied to contracts is in King Papers, J4, vol 254, file 2607, Turnbull to King, 23 Oct. 1940; Rasporich, "A Boston Yankee," 34. Some traces of Howe's wartime political activities in Port Arthur may be gleaned from his travel files in the Howe Papers.
33. Lionel Chevrier interview; King Papers, J1, vol. 342, Howe to King, 14 Jan. 1943.
34. Pouliot is quoted in Norman Ward, *The Public Purse* (Toronto: University of Toronto Press, 1964), 189; for an example of opposition cooperation with Munitions and Supply see the exchange between Howe and Gordon Graydon, the Conservative MP for Peel, in PAC, Graydon Papers, vol. 7, in May 1943. Howard Green, in an interview, confirmed Howe's generally good relations with the opposition.
35. See Blair Fraser, "Victory in Aluminum," *Maclean's*, 1 Feb. 1944; a press release containing Brown's testimony may be found in the PAC, M. J. Coldwell Papers, vol. 62; Brown interview.
36. Bennett interview; Ross Tolmie interview; J. H. Perry interview.
37. HP, vol. 39, file 9-13(1), Powell to Howe, 25 Feb. 1949 and Howe's reply, 1 March, 1949.
38. For a summary of contract review, see the Department of Munitions and Supply's *Quarterly Report* for the fourth quarter of 1945 (Ottawa, mimeo, 1946), 65-69.
39. Brown interview; Department of Munitions and Supply, *Quarterly Report*, second quarter of 1944, 14; K. R. Wilson, "DMS to Renegotiate Many War Contracts," *Financial Post*, 17 June 1944; ibid., 24 June 1944; House of Commons, *Debates*, 19 June 1948, 5522-3.
40. HP, vol. 170, file 90, Howe to Beaverbrook, 10 Aug. 1943.
41. Quoted in McDowall, "Dunn," 355.

Chapter Twelve

1. Cabinet War Committee Document No. 653, Wartime Information Board to Cabinet, 9 Nov. 1943.

2. Stirling interview.
3. See Granatstein, *Canada's War*, 269-71.
4. HP, Howe Speech to Maritime Chambers of Commerce, November 1943. Howe followed up this speech with another to the Montreal Reform Club, predicting an orderly reconversion to peacetime industries: *Montreal Gazette*, 29 Nov. 1943.
5. King Papers, J1, vol. 342, Howe to King, 17 Nov. 1943; Pickersgill, *King Record*, I, 632.
6. House of Commons, *Debates*, 27 Jan. 1944, 1-3.
7. According to "Backstage at Ottawa," *Maclean's*, 1 Dec. 1943, 15, Howe already had "pretty definite ideas of the part which his department should be playing in postwar planning." According to Grant Dexter, Howe wanted reconstruction "very much": Dexter Papers, vol. 3, memorandum, 23 Dec. 1943.
8. PAC, Ian Mackenzie Papers, vol. 66, file 527-168, for a memorandum of discussion among ministers, 10 Jan. 1944; see also King Diary, 24, 27, 30 March, 1944.
9. Bennett interview.
10. J. W. Pickersgill and D. F. Forster, eds., *The Mackenzie King Record*, II (Toronto: University of Toronto Press, 1968), 96-98.
11. King Diary, 6 Oct. 1944.
12. Ibid., 12 Oct. 1944; King Papers, J1, vol. 361, Howe to King, 24 Oct. 1944.
13. C. J. Mackenzie interview; John Baldwin interview; Privy Council Papers, series 18, vol. 30, file D-29, Baldwin to Howe, 10 Oct. 1944.
14. HP, vol. 170, file 90(4), Howe to Cyrus MacMillan, 22 July 1945.
15. Ibid., vol. 69, Howe to George Bateman, 4 Oct. 1944.
16. King Papers, J1, vol. 361, Howe to King, 31 Aug. 1944.
17. Department of Reconstruction and Supply, *Encouragement to Industrial Expansion in Canada* (Ottawa: King's Printer, 1948), 15, 47; HP, vol. 170, file 90(4), Gordon Farrell to Howe, 6 April 1945 and Howe to Farrell, 9 April 1945.
18. J. B. Carswell was brought home from Washington to head Howe's surplus disposal program: "Expect War Assets Head to be J. B. Carswell." *Financial Post*, 11 Dec. 1943; "75% of Surplus Material Unsalvageable – Carswell," ibid., 24 Feb. 1945.
19. Department of Munitions and Supply, *Quarterly Report*, fourth quarter 1944 and first quarter 1945.
20. See Department of Reconstruction and Supply, *Quarterly Reports*, 1944-46.
21. The Canadair sale was authorized by PC 242 of 1947. The Electric Boat Company took over Canadair with a promise to invest $2,000,000, and to pay $175,000 annual rent for the plant.
22. See Robert Bothwell and J. L. Granatstein, forthcoming article, in the *International History Review*, 1980.
23. Ibid.
24. HP, vol. 186, file 90(65), Howe to Mitchell Sharp, 14 Dec. 1959.
25. See PAC, Finance Department Papers, vol. 3580, file M-04, W. A. Mackintosh, "Another Note on the Department of Reconstruction," 18 Oct. 1944; Dexter Papers, Dexter memorandum, 17 March, 1945.

26. Privy Council Papers, series 18, vol. 35, file D-29, Baldwin to Henry, 2 Jan. 1945; Mackenzie Papers, vol. 66, file 527-168, Senior to Mackenzie, 6 March 1945; Mackintosh, "The White Paper on Employment and Income in its 1945 Setting," in S. J. Kaliski, ed., *Canadian Economic Policy Since the War* (Ottawa: 1966), 15.
27. Ibid.
28. Bennett interview; David Mansur interview; O. J. Firestone interview.
29. Ibid.
30. House of Commons, *Debates*, 12 April 1945.
31. Mackintosh, "White Paper."
32. *White Paper on Employment and Income with Specific Reference to the Initial Period of Reconstruction* (Ottawa: King's Printer, 1945).

Chapter Thirteen

1. HP, vol. 170, file 90, Howe to Beaverbrook, 10 Aug. 1943.
2. George McIlraith interview.
3. Liberal arrangements are well described in Whitaker, *The Government Party*, especially 156-57.
4. Ibid., 153-58.
5. J. W. Pickersgill and John Baldwin were especially enlightening on LaFlèche and McLarty.
6. Each of the new ministers was surprised to find the others in King's anteroom: Martin, Chevrier and Abbott interviews.
7. Baldwin interview.
8. Ibid.; PAC, Claxton Papers, memoir notes, vol. 225.
9. See Whitaker, *Government Party* and Granatstein, "Financing the Liberal Party," for alternative interpretations of the same material. The Lambert Diaries, the principal source for Liberal fund-raising for this period, give no indication that the Liberals used secret lists of contributors, or that undue pressure was exerted on businessmen to contribute. According to Henry Borden, the chief Conservative fund-raiser, there was no evidence that the Liberals misused government contracts to procure funds during the war: Borden interview.
10. Lambert Diary, 16 May 1945. Frank Sherman, an innovative industrialist, was an active Liberal and a particular favourite of Howe's: Bennett interview.
11. Granatstein, "Financing the Liberal Party," 194-95; Lambert Diary, 25 May 1945.
12. Granatstein, "Financing the Liberal Party," 195: "In all likelihood the Conservatives spent more than the Liberals in the election of 1945."
13. Virtually every Canadian periodical ran this ad: this version is taken from *Saturday Night*, 19 May 1945.
14. *Ottawa Journal*, 25 May 1945; *Ottawa Citizen*, 30 May 1945.
15. Rasporich, "Boston Yankee," deals briefly with the federal election; see also Rasporich, "Faction and Class in Modern Lakehead Politics," *Lakehead University Review*, VII (1974), 53-55; Lambert Diary, 6 April, 1945; Port Arthur *News Chronicle*, 3, 11, 17, 22, 31 May, and 2, 4, 7, 8, 9 June 1945.
16. Ibid., 12 June 1945.
17. Goldenberg Papers (privately held), Minutes of a meeting of the Directors-

General and Co-ordinators of the Department of Reconstruction held in the Minister's Office, 22 June 1945.

18. King Diary, 6 Aug. 1945.
19. See Wilfrid Eggleston, *The Road to Nationhood* (Toronto: Oxford University Press, 1946), chapters 5 and 6; a British diplomat's impression of Drew's performance may be found in DO 35/1121/G629/3, Stephen Holmes to Secretary of State, 11 May 1946.
20. Ibid.; John English, "Dominion-Provincial Relations and Reconstruction Planning," in *Proceedings* of the first conference of the Canadian Committee for the History of the Second World War (Ottawa: Department of National Defence, mimeo, 1977).
21. Goldenberg interview; *Ottawa Citizen*, 22 Aug. 1945; King Papers, J4, vol. 299, file 3068 for the REL incident: United Steelworkers of America to all MP's, 10 Sept. 1945.
22. Stirling interview; on the housing shortage, see Blair Fraser, "Hovels for Heroes," *Maclean's*, 15 Oct. 1945.
23. King Papers, J4, vol. 280, file 2894, Heeney to King, 24 Nov. 1945; Mansur interview; cabinet conclusions, 6 March, 1 April 1946.
24. HP, vol. 171, file 90(5), Howe to H. B. Hosmer, Concord Mass., 7 May 1946; housing figures are taken from the *Canada Year Book 1948-1949*, 607; during 1946-47 the federal government made over $100 million worth of loans under its housing legislation.
25. See J. J. Brown and Ralph Allen, "Assets to Ashes," and "Assets into Junk," *Maclean's*, 15 July and 1 Aug. 1946.
26. Tom Bryson interview. Bryson, as assistant private secretary, frequently travelled with Howe.
27. Pickersgill and Forster, *The Mackenzie King Record*, III (Toronto: University of Toronto Press, 1970), 93. When British Prime Minister Attlee raised the subject, King responded: "I said undoubtedly Ilsley . . . and St. Laurent . . ."
28. King Diary, 15 Jan. 1946.
29. Pickersgill interview.
30. Ibid.; Pickersgill and Forster, *King Record*, III; Bennett and Bryson interviews; see also the sour note about "dollar-a-year men" in King Diary, 1 May 1947: praise for such men, wrote King, showed "a curious lack of proportion."
31. Ibid.
32. Gerald Hawkins, "Here's Howe," *Liberty*, 15 Mar. 1947.
33. Elisabeth Howe Stedman interview; King Diary, 23 Dec. 1946.
34. The most heartfelt congratulations came from Howe's Tory friend, Grattan O'Leary editor of the *Ottawa Journal*: "Right Honorable 'C. D.' ", *Ottawa Journal*, 13 June 1946.
35. Bennett, C. J. Mackenzie and V. W. Scully interviews.
36. King Papers, J4, vol. 315, file 3328, Heeney to cabinet, 6 Nov. 1946; Howe to Heeney, 8 Nov. 1946, ibid: ibid., file 2392, Heeney to King, 3 Dec. 1946; ibid., file 2648, Heeney to King, 17 Jan. 1947.
37. C. J. Mackenzie, J. R. Nicholson interviews.
38. Bennett interview.
39. Ibid.
40. Ibid.; see also W. Eggleston, *Canada's Nuclear Story* (Toronto: Clarke Ir-

win, 1965); Margaret Gowing, *Independence and Deterrence*, I (London: Macmillan, 1974), 131-46.

41. King Diary, 11 Feb. 1947.
42. Ibid.; the sale was ratified by P. C. 242, 21 Jan. 1947; Walter Gordon and Arthur Irwin interviews.
43. *Ottawa Citizen*, 25 July 1947; HP, vol. 172, file 90(8), Howe to T. A. Crerar, 15 Sept. 1947.
44. King Diary, 21 Aug. 1947.
45. We are greatly indebted to John Holmes for permitting us to see his memorandum on Howe's European trip.
46. J. L. Granatstein and R. D. Cuff, *American Dollars, Canadian Prosperity* (Toronto: Stevens, 1978); see also Robert Bothwell and John English, "Canadian Trade Policy in the Age of American Dominance and British Decline," *Canadian Review of American Studies*, VIII (1977), 52-65.
47. House of Commons, Debates, 16 Dec. 1947, 345. Howe's speech was read to the House by J. M. Macdonnell.
48. Ibid.
49. This information was volunteered by a bystander who wishes to remain anonymous; Baldwin interview.
50. External Affairs Papers, file 288(S), Hume Wrong (Canadian ambassador in Washington) to Lester Pearson, 28 April, 1948.
51. Ibid., Pearson to King, 3 May 1948 and King to Pearson, 6 May 1948; Pickersgill and Forster, *The Mackenzie King Record*, IV (Toronto: University of Toronto Press, 1970), 272. There was some support, inside and outside the cabinet, for some kind of Anglo-American-Canadian economic and/or political union: HP, vol. 172, file 90(10), E. P. Taylor to Howe, 21 June 1948 and Howe to Taylor, 24 June 1948. In his letter Howe referred to "the views which you and I share," presumably on the subject of free trade with the United States. The next year, after the 1949 general election, Taylor expressed the hope that, if "Britain does not come to her senses and collapses . . . we will lose no time in merging our economy with that of the United States, even if it means political union at some later date." Howe replied that "there is no doubt in my mind about the desirability of tying up with the United States," but advised against any hasty action. (HP, vol. 174, file 90(15) Taylor to Howe, 8 July 1949 and Howe to Taylor, 11 July 1949).
52. McDowall, "Dunn," 425; N. Ward, ed., *A Party Politician: The Memoirs of Chubby Power* (Toronto: Macmillan, 1966), 394-97; the diaries of Ralph Maybank, the MP for Winnipeg South Centre, are replete with pre-convention gossip during the spring and summer of 1948: Public Archives of Manitoba, Maybank Papers, "Diary," 15, 19, 20 April, 1948.
53. Glenbow Institute, Calgary, Gardiner Tapes, interview with Una McLean, 3 Jan. 1962.
54. State Dept. Papers, 842.00/8-948, Elizabeth Armstrong, "Visit to Ottawa," 9 Aug. 1948.
55. *Ottawa Journal*, 8, 9 Aug. 1948.

Chapter Fourteen

1. *Toronto Star*, 3 Jan. 1961.
2. There is a compelling description of St. Laurent's impression on a reporter

in Bruce Hutchison, *The Other Side of the Street* (Toronto: Macmillan, 1976), 220.

3. Quoted in Dalton Camp, *Gentlemen, Players and Politicians* (Toronto: McClelland and Stewart, 1970), 4-5.

4. Claxton's voluminous unpublished memoirs in the Claxton Papers furnish a vivid picture of the Montreal minister; Paul Martin interview.

5. Quoted in W. A. Matheson, *The Prime Minister and the Cabinet* (Toronto: Methuen, 1976), 159.

6. Paul Martin interview.

7. Abbott, Gregg, Martin and Pickersgill interviews. Pickersgill noted that by 1953 new junior ministers, including himself, called Howe Mister.

8. See A. F. W. Plumptre, *Three Decades of Decision* (Toronto: McClelland and Stewart, 1977), 108-109; Abbott interview.

9. HP, vol. 179, file 90(35), Howe to Gordon Farrell, president of BC Telephone, 13 March 1952; ibid., vol. 175, file 90(18), Howe to B. E. Hutchinson, 1 Oct. 1949, and Hutchinson to Howe, 22 Dec. 1949; ibid., vol. 181, file 90(44), E. P. Taylor to Howe, 26 March 1953 and Howe to Taylor, 4 April, 1953.

10. King Papers, J4, file 2648, Hume Wrong to King, 4 Oct. 1943, Norman Robertson to Prime Minister, 27 Dec. 1943, Robertson to Prime Minister, 20 Jan. 1945. Robertson commented on the "rather defensive state of mind and something approaching an inferiority complex within the Department." Max Mackenzie was Robertson's suggestion for deputy minister.

11. On MacKinnon, see Norman Ward, "Hon. James Gardiner and the Liberal Party of Alberta," *Canadian Historical Review*, LVI (1975); Max Mackenzie, J. W. Pickersgill and C. F. Wilson interviews.

12. Max Mackenzie interview.

13. George McIvor and Charles Wilson interviews.

14. McIvor interview.

15. Ibid.; see Wilson, *Grain*, chapter 44.

16. Quoted in J. G. Diefenbaker, *One Canada* I (Toronto: Macmillan, 1975), 213.

17. Wilson, *Grain*, 858-64; see also Bothwell and English, "Canadian Trade Policy," 60; Howe himself thought the policy of governmental grain contracts was a very bad business, likely to produce more friction than satisfaction: HP, vol. 171, file 90(6), Howe to James Rank, 18 July 1946.

18. Wilson, *Grain*, chapter 42.

19. J. W. Pickersgill, *My Years with Louis St. Laurent* (Toronto: University of Toronto Press, 1975), 149-52.

20. Ibid.; House of Commons, Debates, 12 March 1951, 1172; Merrill Menzies interview. Menzies, then Stuart Garson's executive assistant, was astonished at Gardiner's unconvincing performance.

21. Granatstein and Cuff, *American Dollars*, 84; Plumptre, *Three Decades*, 82-85 and 97-101.

22. See Statistics Canada, *Canadian Statistical Review: Historical Summary* (Ottawa: Information Canada, 1972), 123, 125.

23. The success of controls on imports from dollar countries was startling: imports under Howe's Schedule One (Luxury Goods) sank from $200,402,000 in 1947 to $83,457,000 in 1948. Howe mourned the inability of the British to replace American imports (HP, vol. 174, file 90(15): Howe

to Sir Clive Baillieu, 9 Aug. 1949): "We are doing all we can to import from Britain, but, unfortunately, lines that can be sold here readily are not available in great supply." See also "Backstage at Ottawa," *Maclean's*, 15 July 1949.

24. HP, vol. 4, file S4-12 Pearson memorandum, 19 April 1950, and Howe memorandum, 21 April 1950.

25. Ibid.

26. House of Commons, Debates, 1 March 1949, 1010-14.

27. Dexter Papers, Max Freedman to Dexter, 16 Jan. 1948.

28. David Wolfe, "Economic Growth and Foreign Investment; A Perspective on Canadian Economic Policy, 1945-1957," *Journal of Canadian Studies*, XIII (1978), 10.

29. Ibid., 11; Max Mackenzie interview.

30. House of Commons, *Debates*, 24 Feb. 1948, 1562.

31. Green interview.

32. Ibid.

33. House of Commons, *Debates*, 16 Feb. 1948, 1261-62.

34. Ibid., 19 Nov. 1945, 2251; 20 Nov. 1945, 2297-98; see also Roberts, *C. D.*, 151-59, for a good description of Howe's postwar troubles with Parliament.

35. Pickersgill, *St. Laurent*, 73; see also Dale Thomson, *Louis St. Laurent, Canadian* (Toronto: Macmillan, 1967), 255-59.

36. HP, vol. 173, file 90(12), Howe to Ross, 22 Feb. 1949; ibid., file 90(13), Howe to Harry Hodges, editor of the *Victoria Times*, 18 March, 1949.

37. Maybank Papers, Maybank memorandum, 6 April 1949.

38. HP, vol. 174, file 90(14), Howe to Ross, 9 April 1949; Whitaker, *Government Party*, 199-203.

39. State Dept. Papers, 842.96/8-1349, US Embassy to State Department, 15 June, 1949; by June 7, Norman Lambert could write to T. A. Crerar that the Tories were going to get "a first-class licking" in Ontario: Queen's University Archives, T. A. Crerar Papers, vol. 88.

40. HP, vol. 174, file 90(15), Borden to Howe, 28 July 1949 and Howe to Borden, 2 Aug. 1949.

Chapter Fifteen

1. House of Commons, *Debates*, 2 Nov. 1949, 1369.

2. Ibid., 3 Nov. 1949, 1396; as Gideon Rosenbluth and Hugh Thorburn note in their study, *Canadian Anti-Combines Administration, 1952-1960* (Toronto: University of Toronto Press, 1963), 7, the anti-combines administration had been unusually active in the postwar period.

3. House of Commons, *Debates*, 7 Nov. 1949, 1500.

4. Ibid.

5. Pickersgill, *St. Laurent*, 107-108. Howe himself had no regrets about his role in the flour milling affair; as for McGregor, he wrote to a friend, the ex-commissioner would not be missed: HP, vol. 175, file 90(17), Howe to Frank Ahern, 23 Nov. 1949. As for the Combines Act, there is no direct evidence as to Howe's attitude, but it seems safe to conclude, as Rosenbluth and Thorburn do (*Canadian Anti-Combines Administration*, 15), that Howe had no love for the principle of anti-combines where it interfered with larger economic objectives.

6. House of Commons, *Debates*, 1 Dec. 1949, 2551-53.

7. HP, vol. 175, file 90(18), Neal to Howe, 18 Dec. 1949; Howe to Carswell, 27 Dec. 1949; PAC, St. Laurent Papers, vol. 86, file C-30, Howe to St. Laurent, 10 Jan. 1950.
8. House of Commons, *Debates*, 31 March 1950, 1434.
9. "Backstage at Ottawa," *Maclean's*, 1 July 1950; State Dept. Papers, 842.00/11-2448, US Ambassador L. Steinhardt to Secretary of State, 24 Nov. 1948; Denis Stairs, *The Diplomacy of Constraint* (Toronto: University of Toronto Press, 1974), 104.
10. House of Commons *Debates*.
11. Stairs, *Diplomacy*, 104.
12. Dexter Papers, Bruce Hutchison memorandum, 25 Oct. 1950.
13. HP, vol. 176, file 90(23), Howe to Billy Woodward, 3 Aug. 1950.
14. House of Commons, *Debates*, 8, 9, 11 Sept. 1950. The bill passed, 136 to 33.
15. HP, vol. 176, file 90(24), Howe to Sir James Dunn, 15 Sept. 1950.
16. Howe's speech (6 Oct. 1950) is in the St. Laurent Papers.
17. Dexter Papers, Bruce Hutchison to Dexter, 27 Oct. 1950.
18. HP, vol. 177, file 90(25), Frank Sherman to Howe, 23 Nov. 1950; Howe to Sydney Pierce, 2 Dec. 1950; Howe to Sir Cecil Carr, 16 Dec. 1950.
19. "The Great Aluminum Farce," *Fortune*, June 1951, 93ff.
20. Ibid.; Howe's efforts to secure American purchases of Canadian aluminum are chronicled in an extensive correspondence with R. E. Powell, especially Powell to Howe, 25 Oct. 1950 and Howe to Powell, 28 Oct. 1950 (HP, vol. 177, file 90(25)), and in HP, vol. 39, file 9-13(1). A file at the Truman Library, Independence, Mo., Truman Papers file OF 541 (1948-50), details the political pressure brought to bear by American aluminum firms on their government to avoid purchasing Canadian uranium.
21. HP, vol. 177, file 90(26), Howe to Sir Cecil Carr, 16 Dec. 1950; Max Mackenzie interview; J. W. Pickersgill interview.
22. Pickersgill, *St. Laurent*, 133-34; Thomson, *St. Laurent*, 309; House of Commons, *Debates*, 2 March, 1951, 836-39.
23. Ibid.
24. Ibid.
25. Department of Defence Production, *Report, April 1-December 31, 1951* (Ottawa: King's Printer: 1952), 16.
26. House of Commons, *Debates*, 30 May 1952, 27-81.
27. Department of National Defence, Directorate of History, Frank McGill Papers, Frank McGill speech (undated), "Thoughts and Experiences in Connection with the Department of Defence Production."
28. HP, vol. 177, file 90(29), Howe to Sir Cecil Carr, 14 April 1951.
29. Interviews with Alice Howe, Elisabeth Howe Stedman, and William Howe.
30. Dexter Papers, Hutchison to Dexter, 28 Jan. 1952; Pickersgill interview.

Chapter Sixteen

1. "C. D. Howe of Canada," *Fortune*, Aug. 1952, 118.
2. These quotations are taken from random *Financial Post* issues during 1952.
3. The best description of Howe's unique relations with Canadian business is

in Mitchell Sharp, "Reflections of a Former Civil Servant," in W. D. K. Kernaghan, ed., *Bureaucracy in Canadian Government* (Toronto: Methuen, 1969), 82-87.

4. D. C. Abbott interview.

5. HP, vol. 179, file 90(35), Howe to Sir David Robertson, 10 April 1952. Howe added that he felt "the pressure of Government work a little more than formerly." See also HP, vol. 182, file 90(47), Howe to W. O. Bovard, 14 Sept. 1953.

6. Sharp, "Reflections," 83.

7. McDowall, "Dunn."

8. Ross and Powell were especially frequent and favourite correspondents. Williamson and Godsoe kept Howe in touch with local Liberal politics.

9. HP, vol. 195, file S.D.7-1, Sherman to Howe, 24 Sept. 1955, Howe to Sherman, 30 Sept. 1955, Sherman to Howe, 4 Oct. 1955, and Howe to Sherman, 6 Oct. 1955.

10. Ashley and Smails, *Crown Corporations*, 237, 246. In 1952 Howe also reported to Parliament on behalf of Atomic Energy of Canada Ltd., Canadian Patents and Development Ltd., Crown Assets Corporation, Defence Construction Ltd., the National Research Council, Eldorado Mining and Refining Ltd., Eldorado Aviation Ltd., Northern Transportation Co. Ltd., the Export Credits Insurance Corporation, the Canadian Wheat Board and the Canadian Commercial Corporation.

11. Bennett interview. Howe also resisted American efforts to refine some of Eldorado's uranium in the United States.

12. In his Wallberg lecture at the University of Toronto on 22 Jan. 1952, Howe predicted "large atomic plants" across Canada, producing electricity, in the foreseeable future. Bennett interview; W. Eggleston, *Canada's Nuclear Story* (Toronto: Clarke, Irwin, 1965), chapter 14.

13. HP, vol. 179, file 90(34), Howe to Jack Berry, 21 Dec. 1951. Berry had recently resigned from Avro, and Howe extended his sympathy, noting "how bad the top management was" before Gordon arrived. In an exchange of letters with Brooke Claxton in Nov. 1951, Howe commented that British aircraft firms concentrated too much on development, too little on production: HP, vol. 48, file 9-85-30(5).

14. Ibid., file 9-85-30(4), Howe to Claxton, 19 Dec. 1952.

15. House of Commons, *Debates*, 28 June 1955, 5380.

16. Firestone and Sharp interviews; Blair Fraser, "Backstage at Ottawa," *Maclean's*, 15 Jan. 1953 and 15 Feb. 1954.

17. Sharp interview.

18. Ibid.; Bull interview.

19. Max Mackenzie interview.

20. HP, vol. 176, file 90(24), Howe to Sam Bronfman, 21 Sept. 1950; ibid., vol. 178, file 90(29), Howe to Clyne, 24 Jan. 1951, Clyne to Howe, 26 Feb. 1951, Howe to Clyne, 1 March 1951; Bennett interview.

21. Ibid., vol. 180, file 90(37), H. Blancke to Howe, 11 Feb. 1952 and Howe to Blancke, 27 Feb. 1952. Of top management in U.S. subsidiaries in Canada in 1955, 57 per cent were Canadians: see Benjamin Barg, "A Study of United States Economic Control in Canadian Secondary Industry," Ph.D. thesis, (Columbia University, 1960), 53.

22. HP, vol. 180, file 90(40), Howe to Stanley Burke, 9 June 1952; ibid., vol.

179, file 90(35), Howe to Hugh Hilton, president, Stelco, 8 April 1952 and Howe to T. R. McLagan, Canada Steamships, 25 April 1952.

23. "C. D. Howe of Canada," *Fortune*, Aug. 1952.

24. Ibid.; see also Hugh Aitken, *American Capital and Canadian Resources* (Cambridge, Mass.: Harvard University Press, 1961), chapter 3.

25. C. D. Howe, "Canada's Economic Future," in *Canada: Nation on the March* (Toronto: Clarke, Irwin, 1953), 203.

26. "The Great Labrador Venture," *Fortune*, Dec. 1948; HP, vol. 176, file 90(21), Jules Timmins to Howe, 4 April 1950, J. B. Carswell to Howe, 13 April 1950, Howe to Carswell, 15 April 1950, R. A. C. Henry to Howe, 15 April 1950 and Howe to Henry, 18 April 1950; David Golden interview.

27. As early as 1945, Howe learned that there were problems inside Steep Rock's board: in February of that year Eric Phillips resigned from the board in protest at the transfer of Steep Rock's bank account to Cleveland: HP, vol. 21, file R-8-2(51), Phillips to Howe, 23 Feb. 1945.

28. Bennett interview.

29. HP, vol. 21, file R-8-2(49). Howe stated his basic complaints about Steep Rock in a letter to Donald Gordon, president of the CNR, on 7 Aug. 1950: "I may tell you in strict confidence that I am not at all pleased with the present management of Steep Rock. Cyrus Eaton seems determined to retain control of the management, which might be all right if it were not for the fact that Eaton holds a personal contract for selling the product [through his company Premium Ores], which would seem to disqualify him for control of the management. I am trying to arrange that a Canadian president be appointed who will give aggressive representation to the interests of the shareholders." Howe reiterated these objections in a letter to Eaton on 8 Aug. 1950.

30. Bennett interview; John Connolly interview; Harry Crowe interview. Eaton stored away information about Howe's activities for his own future use.

31. HP, vol. 188, file 90-6, Howe to Powell, 13 Feb. 1959.

32. Ibid., vol. 180, file 90(38), Greville Smith, president of CIL, to Howe, 1 Aug. 1952, Howe to Smith, 2 Aug. 1952, Howe to M. N. Campbell, Hamilton, 6 and 27 Oct. 1952; ibid., vol. 186, file 90(64), Howe to Smith, 20 Nov. 1958; Herbert Lank interview.

33. Ibid., vol. 180, file 90(38), Howe to Essington Lewis, Melbourne, 16 Feb. 1953.

34. Secretary of State Dean Acheson took up the Seaway with the Canadian cabinet during a visit to Ottawa on 22 November 1952, expressing President Truman's sympathy with the Canadian position and agreeing that Canada was entitled to proceed by itself with the development of the waterway: Truman Library, Independence, Mo., Acheson Papers, memorandum 22 Nov. 1952. Truman's successor, Dwight Eisenhower, had by April 1953 concluded that he was "almost sorry I ever heard the project mentioned." Eisenhower Library, Abilene, Kansas, Eisenhower Papers, Whitman files, box 12: D. D. Eisenhower to Milton Eisenhower, 29 April 1953.

35. McIvor interview; House of Commons, *Debates*, 30 March 1953, 3417.

36. HP, vol. 180, file 90(39), Howe to Humphrey, 22 Nov. 1952.

37. McDowall, "Dunn."

38. Howe's efforts to persuade Buckerfield to sell are recorded in HP, vol. 275-76; ibid., vol. 178, file 90(32), Howe to Buckerfield, 6 Sept. 1951: "We will both be much safer when our business interests are dissociated, particularly while Mr. Drew was on the warpath."
39. Campney, Howe wrote to St. Laurent on 12 Dec. 1952, was "a good business man and could clear up that situation." HP, vol. 181, file 90(43).
40. Pickersgill, *St. Laurent*, 181-85.
41. Ibid., 105; Harris interview.
42. Ibid.
43. Dalton Camp, *Gentlemen, Players and Politicians* (Toronto: McClelland and Stewart, 1970), 139.

Chapter Seventeen

For a fuller account of the Trans-Canada affair see W. Kilbourn, *Pipeline* (Toronto: Clarke Irwin, 1970), including its bibliography, and J. W. Pickersgill, *My Years with St. Laurent* (Toronto: University of Toronto Press, 1975). The pipeline correspondence in HP is in files 8-2-1 and 75 unless otherwise marked.
1. D. Nesbitt, N. E. Tanner, E. L. Kennedy, H. R. Milner, M. Gutman, M. Natelson, F. Schultz and J. R. Tolmie interviews.
2. Walter Gordon interview.
3. J. R. Haggan interview.
4. See 1 above.
5. Ibid.
6. HP, Murchison to Howe, 15 Jan. 1954.
7. HP, Howe to Frank Ross, 17 Nov. 1949, and 21 Sept. 1950.
8. Tolmie and Schultz interviews.
9. Schultz and Nesbitt interviews; HP, Howe to Murchison, 22 Jan. 1951 and 5 Dec. 1952.
10. Leslie Frost and Ernest Manning interviews.
11. HP, Howe to Hume Wrong, 28 Mar. and 5 May 1953; Murchison to Howe 9 Apr. 1953; Howe to Murchison, 14 Apr. 1953.
12. HP, Howe to Murchison, 14 Apr. 1953; Murchison to Howe, 15 Apr. 1953.
13. HP, Murchison to Howe, 16 Apr. 1953.
14. Tolmie interview. Tolmie suggested use of the Navigable Waters Protection Act to Trade and Commerce.
15. HP, Macdonald to Howe, 12 Feb. 1954 and Howe to Macdonald, 16 Feb. 1954.
16. J. W. Pickersgill interview and Pickersgill, *St. Laurent*, 214-19.
17. L. B. Pearson interview. One of the things that disturbed Pearson most was Howe's penchant for tearing down old buildings. With Howe's support, Public Works Minister Robert Winters proposed to tear down the magnificent but inefficient old West Block on Parliament Hill; it was all Pearson and his allies in cabinet could do to get the Prime Minister to overrule them. Similarly, when the Parliamentary Library was badly gutted by fire, Howe thought it should not be restored but rather replaced by a sleek new building on cheaper vacant land; books requested by members could be moved into the Parliament Buildings via tunnel and a conveyer belt. With respect to architecture and the arts Howe was a complete

philistine, but he could be readily persuaded to support specific cultural policies by the right person and a well-put case. During a Rideau Hall state dinner, the voluble and charming Père Georges-Henri Lévesque of Laval was seated next to Howe by Governor General Massey, after Massey learned that Howe and St. Laurent were hesitant about backing the proposed $100 million endowment for a national arts council. Before the evening was over Howe was favourably impressed, and not long afterwards the Canada Council Act was put before Parliament. As for setting high standards in design, Donald Buchanan of the National Gallery got to Howe through his father the Liberal senator, and thereafter Howe was a firm supporter of the Gallery committee which eventually became the National Design Council. (Alan Jarvis and John C. Parkin interviews.)

18. Pickersgill and A. D. Dunton interviews. The broadcast went on the air as scheduled.
19. Schultz interview.
20. HP, Howe to Oakah Jones, 7 Oct. 1955.
21. Trans-Canada Pipelines Archives, Alan Williamson to Howe, 1 Oct. 1954; Howe to Williamson, 12 Oct. 1954 and 6 Jan. 1955.
22. HP, Howe to Harris, 15 Jan. 1955.
23. Nesbitt interview.
24. Jack Davis, Nesbitt and Tolmie interviews.

Chapter Eighteen

1. House of Commons, *Debates*, 1955; 10 Mar. 1904-7; 7 June, 4513; 28 June, 5376-77; Liberal *Newsletter*, July 1955, quoted in Thomson, *Louis St. Laurent*, 401.
2. Walter Harris, Louis St. Laurent interviews; Thomson, *St. Laurent*, 402-403.
3. Walter Gordon, *A Political Memoir* (Toronto: McClelland and Stewart, 1977), 59-60.
4. Gordon interview; Thomson, *St. Laurent*, 395, quoting a Calgary *Albertan* correspondent.
5. Nesbitt interview.
6. Sharp interview; Trans-Canada Pipelines Archives, N. E. Tanner to Trans-Canada directors, 15 Aug. 1955.
7. Sharp interview; HP, Minutes of Sept., 1955, meetings of Sharp et al. See also Kilbourn, *Pipeline*, 91-92.
8. HP, Howe to Murchison, 30 Sept. 1955.
9. Tanner and Nesbitt interviews. See also Kilbourn, *Pipeline*, 95 ff.
10. Ibid.
11. TCPL Archives, Howe to Tanner, 27 Feb. 1956.
12. Ibid. and Frost interview.
13. CBC radio broadcast, 9 Mar. 1956.
14. House of Commons, *Debates*, 1956, 15 Mar. 2165-66.
15. *Financial Post*, 30 Mar. 1956.
16. *Pipeline*, 105-10; and HP, Gairdner to Howe, 26 Mar. 1956, and McMahon to Howe, 16 and 24 Apr. 1956. The latter are still in the personal files of HP!

17. HP, Minutes of meetings Apr. 6-11, 1956, between Trade and Commerce officials and Trans-Canada directors, also occasionally attended by Howe.
18. T. J. McGrath and J. L. Lewis quoted in *Financial Post*, 24 Dec. 1955.
19. See 17 above; HP, Murchison to Howe, 23 Mar. 1955; Nesbitt interview and D. Nesbitt, *Memoir* (privately held).
20. House of Commons, *Debates*, 1956, 2 May, 3482, and 4 May, 3562.
21. Ibid., 14 May, 3860-65.
22. Ibid., 3865; Pickersgill, Harris and Tanner interviews.
23. Pickersgill, *St. Laurent*, 282-83.
24. House of Commons, *Debates*, 1956, 15 May, 3927-28.
25. Ibid., 18 May, 4089.
26. *Winnipeg Free Press*, May 23, 1956.
27. House of Commons, *Debates*, 1956, 17-31 May, 4025-523; the general comments are derived from all the interviews referred to in notes 1 to 23 above; see also Kilbourn, *Pipeline* chs. 8 and 9.
28. Eugene Forsey interview; House of Commons, *Debates*, 1956, 31 May, 4524-34.
29. Pickersgill, *St. Laurent*, 292-93; Pickersgill interview.
30. Pickersgill, *St. Laurent*, 293-99; Thomson, *St. Laurent*, 434-43; House of Commons, *Debates*, 1956, 1, 4 and 5 June, 4537-775; Kilbourn, *Pipeline*, ch. 9.

Chapter Nineteen

1. TCPL Archives, Howe to Williamson, 9 June 1956, quoted in Kilbourn, *Pipeline*, 138.
2. Stanley Knowles and E. D. Fulton interviews.
3. See 1 above.
4. HP, Howe to E. L. Blair, 6 June 1956; Howe to D. R. Harrison, 18 July 1956.
5. See 1 above; HP, Howe to Douglas Stuart, 24 June 1956.
6. Nesbitt interview.
7. HP, Howe to Arnold Heeney, 15 Dec. 1956.
8. HP, Howe to Peter Campbell, 17 Dec. 1956.
9. TCPL Archives, Howe to Nesbitt, 22 June 1956; Nesbitt interview and *Memoir*.
10. Text in HP, speech files.
11. Mitchell Sharp interview.
12. *Cf.* James Eayrs, *Canada in World Affairs, October 1955 to June 1957* (Toronto: Oxford University Press, 1959), 182-91.
13. Quoted in Margaret Conrad "George Nowlan," Ph.D. Thesis, University of Toronto, 1979.
14. Harris Papers (privately held), Howe to Harris, 21 Feb. 1957.
15. Harris interview.
16. Returning from a trip to southern Alberta in August 1955, Howe wrote that "the country is enjoying a wave of unparalleled prosperity." (HP, vol. 184, file 90(54): Howe to James Muir, chairman of the Royal Bank of Canada, 4 Aug. 1955.)
17. Thomson, *St. Laurent*, 498; the text of Howe's speech was reprinted in

Liberal Action (Ottawa: National Liberal Federation, 1957), the Liberal speaker's handbook for the 1957 campaign.

18. Ibid.; Pickersgill interview.
19. St. Laurent Papers, vol. 172, file C-20-H, Howe to St. Laurent, 20 April 1957, and Harris to St. Laurent, 22 April 1957.
20. When Howe returned to Ottawa, however, he described his run-in with the farmers as greatly exaggerated and as of no consequence: Claude Bissell diary, 27 May 1957.
21. Thomson, *St. Laurent*, 513.
22. Ibid., 512. The most famous line in *My Fur Lady*, sung by a chorus of Liberal MP's, was: "Uncle Lou, Uncle Lou, tell us what to do – and Howe!" After the election it was changed to "Uncle Lou, Uncle Lou, what's become of you – and Howe?"
23. Douglas Fisher interview.
24. Ibid.
25. Ibid.
26. Peter C. Newman, *Renegade in Power* (Toronto: McClelland and Stewart, 1963), 55.
27. Fisher interview.
28. *Globe and Mail*, 12 June 1957.
29. Gordon, *Political Memoir*, 57.
30. Maybank Papers, Walter Tucker to Ralph Maybank, 15 July 1957.
31. HP, vol. 107, file 75(2), Howe to Irvin Studer, 23 May 1958.

Chapter Twenty

1. Howe's personal corporations were designed with an eye to the future. Penryn ensured Alice Howe's personal financial security after Clarence's death; more generally, both companies were meant to avoid double provincial succession duties on Howe's eventual estate. As W. J. Bennett commented, when questions were raised about Howe's personal finances, "had Mr. or Mrs. Howe been attempting to hide the fact that they held certain securities they would not have incorporated holding companies, since these corporations are required to make an Annual Return" (W. J. Bennett to John Wintermeyer, 5 Dec. 1957). It was also alleged that Howe owned stock in pipeline companies. An examination of Howe's financial records discloses no holdings in any pipeline company, either directly or indirectly; moreover, according to Howe, "no member of my family owns stock in any pipeline company" (Howe to Wintermeyer, 5 Dec. 1957).
2. Newman, *Renegade in Power*, 59; HP, vol. 188, file 90-6, Howe to R. E. Powell, 21 Oct. 1957.
3. Gordon Dryden interview; HP, Howe to Turner, July 1957; HP, vol. 107, file 75(5), Howe to St. Laurent, 17 Oct. 1957.
4. Ibid.
5. Dalhousie University Archives, Board of Governors file: A. E. Kerr to Howe, 8 Aug. 1957, Howe to Kerr, 16 Aug. 1957. Howe's appointment as chancellor was approved at a Board of Governors meeting on 29 Aug. 1957, and the news telephoned to Howe. Howe accepted in a letter to Kerr on 4 Sept. 1957.

6. HP, vol. 187, file 90(69), Howe to Beaverbrook, 27 Sept. 1957; ibid., vol. 186, file 90(64), Douglas Stuart to Howe, 9 July 1958.
7. Ibid., vol. 187, file 90(69), Howe to Beaverbrook, 27 Sept. 1957.
8. Ibid., vol. 125, file 82-8, Howe to Taylor, 8 Oct. 1957.
9. Howe's joining the Price board was first raised in a letter from Beaverbrook to Howe, 1 Oct. 1957 (HP, vol. 187, file 90(69)). The dispute between Beaverbrook and Taylor, apart from its personal aspects, was an episode in the Toronto-Montreal financial rivalry: it also included struggles in brewing and farm machinery.
10. Ibid., vol. 125, file 82-8, Howe to Taylor, 16 Nov. 1957, and Taylor to Howe, 18 Nov. 1957; vol. 187, file 90(69), Howe to Beaverbrook, 25 Jan. 1958.
11. Ibid., vol. 188, file 90-6, Howe to Powell, 17 Jan. 1958. Howe added: "You will get a letter from him thanking you for your help towards organizing his campaign."
12. L. B. Pearson, *Mike*, III (Toronto: University of Toronto press, 1975), 32.
13. See Peter Stursberg, *Diefenbaker: Leadership Gained* (Toronto: University of Toronto Press, 1975), 88, and Patrick Nicholson, *Vision and Indecision* (Toronto: Longmans, 1968), 68-71 and 80-81.
14. HP, vol. 186, file 90(63), Howe to John Hammel, 12 Feb. 1958; ibid., vol. 107, file 75-8, Howe to Walter Harris, 5 May 1958.
15. Gordon interview; Harris interview; HP, vol. 186, file 90(64), Howe to John L. Haar, 22 Aug. 1958; Howe to R. M. Campbell, 7 Oct. 1958.
16. Ibid., vol. 188, file 90-6, Howe to Powell, 21 Sept. 1957.
17. Ibid., Howe to Powell, 27 May 1958: the worst part of the move, Howe added, was "the weeding out of office records that go back over forty-five years."
18. Ibid., vol. 186, file 90(63), Howe to W. M. Neal, 24 June 1958; as for Ottawa, Howe wrote to G. W. Cavey on 25 Aug. 1959, "I have been there only once since I moved to Montreal and have no plans for another visit."
19. Ibid., vol. 188, file 90-6, Howe to Fred Bull, 24 March 1958; Pickersgill interview.
20. Alice Howe interview.
21. Bennett interview.
22. *Trade and Commerce*, Jan. 1959.
23. HP, vol. 186, file 90(64), Beaverbrook to Howe, 18 July 1958 and Howe to Beaverbrook, 7 Oct. 1958.
24. Ibid., Howe to Beaverbrook, 24 July 1958.
25. Ibid., vol. 187, file 90(69), Howe to Beaverbrook, 17 Nov. 1958.
26. Ibid., vol. 186, file 90(65), Howe to Symington, 15 Jan. 1959; Beaverbrook to Howe, 7 Dec. 1958.
27. Ibid., vol. 187, file 90(69), Beaverbrook to Howe, 12 July 1960.
28. Ibid., Howe to Beaverbrook, 25 July 1960.
29. MacKay, McNeill, Aitchison and Read interviews; Dalhousie University Archives, file "Howe, the Rt. Hon. C. D. (Chancellor)," Howe to Kerr, 12 Mar. 1960; Howe also suggested that Claude Isbister, J. E. Parkinson and O. J. Firestone be invited to leave Ottawa and join the Dalhousie economics department: Howe to Kerr, 16 April 1958.
30. Ibid., Howe to Kerr, 4 Sept. 1957.
31. Ibid., Howe to Kerr, 7 Sept. 1960.

32. Ibid., Howe to Kerr, 11 Nov. 1960.
33. HP, vol. 187, file 90(67), Howe to Mackenzie, 29 Sept. 1960; ibid.; as early as March 1959, Howe commented to a friend that on one particular issue he had no doubt "Dr. Kerr will do all he can to prevent a reasonable agreement" (Howe to Ray Milner, 11 March 1959, HP, vol. 137, file 86-3-1).
34. Ibid., vol. 187, file 90(67), Howe to W. A. Arbuckle, 12 Dec. 1960.
35. Bennett and Beaverbrook interviews; HP, Howe's personal engagements schedule, Sept.-Dec. 1960.
36. C. D. Howe, Messel Lecture, "Industry and Government in Canada," at the Society of Chemical Industry, Montreal 15 Sept. 1958.
37. Lesage interview. "This," Howe wrote to Frank Ross, "will mean the end of the Union Nationale and a sweep of Quebec in the next Federal election by the Liberals." And that in turn would be the end of Diefenbaker (HP, vol. 186, file 90(66), Howe to Ross, 23 June 1960).
38. HP, vol. 187, file 90(67), Mitchell Sharp to Howe, 2 Aug. 1960, Howe to Fraser Bruce, 15 Aug. 1960, Sharp to Howe, 14 Sept. 1960, Howe to Sharp, 20 Sept. 1960.
39. Bennett interview; I. Norman Smith, " 'C. D.' Among His Friends," *Ottawa Journal*, 3 Jan. 1961.
40. Bennett interview; HP, vol. 187, file 90-1, Howe to Elisabeth Howe Stedman, 29 Dec. 1960.

Index

INDEX

Bennett R. B.: clashes with CDH, 33, 87-88, 89-90, 97; and wheat, 51, 57n; and "New Deal," 57-58; as leader of Opposition (1936), 83-84; and harbours commissions, 85; and air policy, 106; mentioned, 53, 59, 69, 73, 74, 312

Bennett, W. A. C., 289

Bennett, William, assistant to CDH, 72, 73, 80, 114, 117, 118, 131-132, 137, 160, 174, 184, 198, 202, 203; at Eldorado Gold Mines, 213, 265; at AECL, 265; at Iron Ore of Canada, 340; visits CDH, 346-347; at CDH's funeral, 348

Berle, Adolf, 151

Bertrand, Ernest, 86-87

Bethel, Maine, 16n, 17, 18

Black, Harry, 54, 55, 117, 118, 281

"Black Friday" (June 1, 1956), 315-316

Board of Grain Commissioners, 30, 32, 33, 34

Board of Railway Commissioners, 99

Board of Transport Commissioners, 99-100

Borden, Henry: at Dept. of Munitions and Supply, 129, 130, 131, 138, 154; as a Conservative, 129, 173, 201, 202; on 1949 election, 242, 243; at Brazilian Traction, 264, 340; last word on CDH, 354

Borden, Sir Robert, 30, 93, 129

Bracken, John, 238

Brazilian Traction Company, 264, 340

Bren gun debate, 121-122

British Commonwealth Air Training Plan, 125, 138

British Supply Council in North America, 141, 150

British Supply Mission, 134

Broadcasting, see Radio broadcasting

Brockington, Leonard, 103

Bronfman, Samuel, 269

Brophy, Reg, 102, 103

Brown, Frank, 175, 177, 269

Bruce, Fraser (Scotty), 175, 264

Bryson, Tommy, 114, 117, 210

Buck, Tim, 60

Buckerfield, Ernie, 278

Bull, Fred, 268, 333

Burke, Stanley, Sr., 270

Cabinet (federal): formation of (1935), 65-71; changes in (1940) 134, (1942) 166, (1945) 199-200, (1946) 211, (1949-1953) 279, (1954) 292-293; members of (Nov. 1948), 224-227

Cahan, C. H., 83, 86, 88, 90

Cameron, Colin, 314, 315

Camp, Dalton, 281

Campbell, Senator Peter, 201, 319

Campbell, Wallace, 123, 124, 129

Campney, Ralph, 279, 293

Canadair Limited, 190, 214-215, 242

Canadian Airways Limited, 106, 107, 109, 110, 111, 113

Canadian Arsenals Limited, 249-250, 265

Canadian Association of Broadcasters, 101

Canadian Bank of Commerce, 94

Canadian Broadcasting Corporation: bill founding, 82, 100, 102; building of stations, 103, 284, 294-295

Canadian Commercial Corporation, 249, 255

Canadian Industries Limited (CIL), 274-275

Canadian Manufacturers' Association, 162

Canadian National Railways: reform of, 82, 91, 96-98, 99; creation of (1923), 93, 94; problems of, 93, 95, 99; Royal Commission on, 95, 97; and broadcasting, 100; and TCA, 108, 109, 112

Canadian Northern Railway, 35, 93, 94

Canadian Pacific Airlines, 113, 190

Canadian Pacific Railway, 35, 93, 94, 95, 99, 108, 109

Canadian Radio Broadcasting Commission, 82, 101

Canadian Radio League, 101, 102
Canadian Wheat Board, 51, 57n, 230, 231, 232, 276, 323
Cardin, P. J. A., 67, 69, 70, 163, 167
Carmichael, Harry, 145, 146, 154, 166, 168, 186-187, 212, 264
Carswell, J. B., 171, 248
Carter, W. H., 76
C. D. Howe Company: formed, 35-36; initial disaster recouped, 39-40; business expands, 40-45, 50; effects of Depression on, 51; CDH sells, 76, 77; John Howe joins, 241
Celanese Corporation, 269-270
Central Mortgage and Housing Corporation (CMHC), 208
Chamberlain, Neville, 122
Chandler, Ralph, 35, 36, 51
Charlesworth, Hector, 82
Chase, Howard, 164, 165
Chevrier, Lionel: parliamentary assistant to CDH, 174; joins cabinet, 199-200; Minister of Transport, 222, 224, 280, 281; and Seaway, 275, 292; at CDH's funeral, 348
Chicago conference on aviation, 191
Chrysler of Canada, 139
Church, Tommy, 83
Churchill, Winston, 12, 141, 169, 259
Citadel Merchandising Ltd., 133
Clark, Clifford, 140, 144, 145, 147, 151, 152, 193, 268
Claxton, Brooke, 102, 188; Minister of National Health and Welfare, 199; and CDH, 200; and election campaigns, 200, 202, 242, 280; Minister of National Defence, 211, 224, 225, 226, 227, 252, 257, 266, 267, 278, 281; resigns from politics, 292
Clement, Wallace, 353
Closure, 309, 311, 312, 313, 318
Clyne, J. V., 269, 279
Coal supply, 207, 215
Cockcroft, Sir John, 343
Cockfield, Brown (advertising agency), 202

Coldwell, M. J., 84, 175, 244, 247, 305, 316, 346, 351, 354
Collins, Frank, 72
Combined boards for war production, 170-172
Combined Production and Resources Board (CPRB), 171, 172
Combined Raw Materials Board (CRMB), 171
Combines Investigation Act, 245, 246, 247
Communist Party of Canada, 60
Conscription, 165, 166; crisis of 1942, 166-167; crisis of 1944, 191n, 199, 221
Conservative Party: members in House (1936), 83-84; criticism of CDH, 87, 88, 89-90, 97, 147, 175, 238-241, 242, 256, 299, 300, 301, 305, 307-309 *passim*, 311-314 *passim*
Construction, postwar, 207
Consumers' Gas Company, 288, 289, 290, 295, 297
Contracts, war, 176, 177, 178
Co-operative Commonwealth Federation (CCF) Party, 60; members in House of Commons (1936), 83; criticism of CDH, 89, 98, 175, 311-312
Corning Glass Company, 189, 190
Cottrelle, George, 135, 160
Covert, Frank, 211
Cox, Charles, 62, 116, 117, 173, 203
Coyne, James, 297, 298
Creighton, Donald, 353
Crerar, General Harry, 163
Crerar, T. A., 69, 70, 108, 134, 148, 199
Croll, David, 61
Crown corporations: CDH and, 89; use in wartime, 133, 153, 161, 178
Currie, George, 278

Dafoe, John Wesley, 31, 65, 99, 147
Daigle, Senator Armand, 222
Dalhousie University, Halifax, 22, 23, 27-28, 334, 342, 343, 344
Dandurand, Raoul, 66, 69, 134
Defence planning, 120

Hitler, Adolf, 84, 100, 119, 123, 178, 180
Hogarth, General Donald, 272, 273
Hopkins, Harry, 152
Housing, postwar shortage of, 207-208
Howe, Agnes (sister of CDH), 17
Howe, Alice Worcester (wife of CDH), 12, 22, 117, 210, 277, 340, 347; CDH proposes to, 36-37; character, 37, 40; marries CDH, 38; as homemaker, 46-47; 79, 81; arranges move to Ottawa, 76, 77; life in wartime, 157, 158; accompanies CDH to Europe, 248; funeral of CDH, 348
Howe, Barbara (daughter of CDH), 46, 211
Howe, Clarence Decatur: birth, 15; ancestors, 15n; parents, 15, 16, 17; boyhood, 17-19; appearance, 17, 21-22, 34, 131; education, 18, 19, 20-22: professor at Dalhousie (1908-1913), 23-30; with Board of Grain Commissioners (1913-1916), 31-35; forms C. D. Howe and Company (1916), 35-36; marriage (1916), 36-38; business successes and growing reputation, 39-45, 49, 50; participates in civic life, 41, 45-46; develops new unloader for grain, 43; effects of Depression on business, 51; enters politics, 52-57; first election campaign (1935), 60-62; selected for cabinet post, 65, 66, 68-70 *passim*; appointed Minister of Marine and Railways (1935), 71; chooses staff, 71-74; recommendations on harbour commissions, 74-75; moves to Ottawa, 76, 77; and Liberal Party fund-raising, 81, 200-201, 324; becomes Minister of Transport (1936), 81; defends Harbours bill, 85-91; and CNR reforms, 91, 93, 96-98, 99: sets up Board of Transport Commissioners, 99-100; creates CBC, 100-103; and TCA, 103, 104-113; enjoyment of political life, 113-114; administra-

tive style, 114-115, 158, 160; and feud between federal and Ontario Liberals, 116-118; and Bren gun debate, 121-122; on approaching war, 122-123; accepts responsibility for defence production (Nov. 1939), 124, 125; election campaign (1940), 127; named Minister of Munitions and Supply (April 1940), 128; forms executive team, 129-131; office routine, 131-132; growing political importance, 132; joins War Committee of cabinet, 134; emergency powers: (wartime) 134-135, (import controls) 217, 218, 235, 238-239, (Korean War) 253, (Defence Production Act) 256, 258, 299-301, 305; and steel supply, 135-136; and aircraft production, 137, 138, 266-267; and Americans, 139, 152, 153, 214-215; and business, 139-140, 175, 245-246, 263-265, 270, 272-275, 326, 350-351; trip to Britain (1940), 9-12, 142-143, torpedoed and rescued, 9-11, 142; internal conflicts in department, 143-149; and lend-lease, 150, 151; changes in department, 153-155; war production expands, 158, 159; and labour, 161-165, 206, 270; conscription, 166, 167; and manpower, 167-168; and atomic bomb, 168-169, 205; and combined boards, 171, 172, 173; financial policies, 176, 177, 178; restructuring of Canadian economy, 178-179; appointed Minister of Reconstruction (Oct. 1944), 185-186; industrial conversion, 187-188; war surplus disposal, 188-189; aviation policy, 190-191; and economists, 191-192, 193-194, 195, 196, 267-268; election (1945), 197, 199, 202, 203; and dominion-provincial relations, 204, 205; housing shortage, 207-208; Minister of Reconstruction and Supply (Jan. 1946), 208, 212: privy councillorship, 209-210, 211; and atomic

MacDonald, Donald, 326
MacDonald, Malcolm, 151, 168, 209
Macdonnell, James M., 218, 238-239, 253, 258
MacDougall, John, 315
McGill, Air Vice-Marshal Frank, 257
McGregor, F. A., 245, 246, 247
McIlraith, George, 240
MacInnis, Angus, 88
McIvor, Reverend Dan, 58, 59, 63, 127, 316
McIvor, George, 230, 231, 276, 339
McKay, Lois, 27
McKeen, Senator S., 222
Mackenzie, Alexander, 78
Mackenzie, C. J., 26, 154, 168, 169, 186, 212, 214, 265
Mackenzie, Ian, 71, 121, 127, 199, 200, 211, 219, 231
Mackenzie, Maxwell W. (Max), 229, 230, 245, 255, 268, 269, 270, 340
Mackenzie, N. A. M., 344
MacKinnon, James, 218, 219, 229, 230
Mackintosh, W. A., 185, 186, 192-194, 195, 204, 267, 268, 302
McLagan, Rodgie, 269
MacLaren, D. L., 203
Maclaren, D. R., 110
McLarty, Norman, 159, 162, 199
Maclean's magazine, 121, 208, 329
McMahon, Frank, 307, 308
MacMechan, Archibald, 28
MacMillan, H. R., 135, 141, 142, 144-149 *passim,* 154, 168
MacNab, Sir Allan, 92
McNaughton, General A. G. L., 105, 120, 200
Magill, Robert, 29-30, 32
M. A. Hanna Company, 272
Management, Canadian, 160, 161, 269
Manhattan project, 169, 213
Manion, Robert, 53-54, 58, 63, 71, 73, 95; Opposition leader, 118, 121, 123; election of 1940, 126, 127
Manitoba Free Press, 31
Manning, Ernest, 288, 290, 296, 303, 305
Manpower, 165, 166, 167-168

Mansur, David, 208
Marine, Dept. of, 71, 72, 73, 78
Marler, George, 293
Marshall Plan, 234, 235, 249
Martin, Paul: Secretary of State, 200; Minister of National Health and Welfare, 211, 224, 227, 280, 281, 293; at Liberal Party convention (1948), 221, (1958), 335, 336; at CDH's funeral, 349
Massachusetts Institute of Technology, 20-21, 22, 345
Massey, Vincent: Canadian High Commissioner in London, 12, 81; and National Liberal Federation, 52, 53, 54, 70; Governor General, 259, 260; mentioned, 101
Maybank, Ralph, 221, 222, 242
Meighen, Arthur, 45, 59, 93, 166
Michaud, Joseph, 71, 107
Milner, Ray, 283
Mitchell, Humphrey, 166, 222
Morgenthau, Henry, 139, 151, 152
Mount Royal Club, 339, 340
Mulock, Sir William, 64
Munitions and Supply: CDH appointed Minister of, 128; executive committee of, 130-133 *passim,* 136, 137: deputy minister of, 130, 132; crown corporations set up, 133-134; accounting methods of, 140-141; internal struggles, 143-149; Hyde Park Agreement, 152; personnel changes in, 154; production, 154, 155, 158, 168, 170; expansion of quarters, 156; and manpower, 167-168; sales to U.S., 169-170; and the military, 170, 172; and combined boards, 170-172: opposition criticism of, 175-176; financial practices, 176, 177-178; fluctuations in munitions requirements, 178; and Canadian economy, 178-179; and reconstruction, 186; winding down of war production, 187; and war surplus disposal, 188-189; and White Paper on Unemploymnt and Income, 195
Munitions and Supply Act, 133, 134

Price Brothers Ltd., 264, 335, 341, 342, 344
Provisional International Civil Aviation Organization, 191
Prudham, George, 279, 324
Purvis, Arthur, 141, 143, 150, 153

Quebec provincial election campaign, 125

Radio broadcasting, 100-103
Rahilly, T. F., 161
Railway Committee of the House of Commons, 95
Railways, 57, 92-93; and air service, 106, 108. *See also* Canadian National Railways
Railways and Canals, Dept. of, 71, 73, 78, 92
Ralston, J. L., 59; Minister of Finance, 124, 125, 129; Minister of Defence, 134, 136, 143, 163, 221; clashes with CDH, 167, 168, 171, 172, 173
Reciprocity negotiations, 219, 220
Reconstruction, Dept. of: proposed, 183, 184; CDH appointed Minister, 185-186; and industrial conversion, 188, 191; and economists, 192; and White Paper on Employment and Income, 195; and dominion-provincial relations, 204-206; and end of war, 206; and housing shortage, 207-208; CDH's work at, 211-212
Reconstruction Party, 59
Reed, Captain John, 10, 11
Research Enterprises Limited, 155, 168, 189, 206
Richardson, James, 105-106, 107, 108, 109, 110, 111, 112
Rideau Club, 79, 334
Rideau Hall, 77
Rinfret, Fernand, 70, 71
Robertson, Norman, 229
Robinson, Judith, 326, 352
Rockcliffe Park, 77
Rogers, Norman, 67, 102, 118, 127, 132, 134

Roosevelt, Franklin, 57, 100, 151, 152; impressions of CDH, 153
Ross, Frank, 145, 241, 242, 264, 273, 277, 287
Rothermere, Lord, 345
Royal Commission on Broadcasting (1929), 101
Royal Commission on Canada's Economic Prospects, 302, 320
Royal Commission on Transportation (1932), 95, 97
Royal Commission on the Grain Trade (Saskatchewan), 29
Rubber, 133, 159

St. Andrews, N.B., 277, 278, 334
Saint-Denis, Annette, 73
St. Laurent, Louis: joins cabinet, 166; Minister of Justice, 185, 194; privy councillorship, 209; Minister of External Affairs, 211, 219; and CDH, 217, 294, 333; at leadership convention, 221, 222, 223: elected leader of Liberal Party, 223; as Prime Minister, 224, 225; first cabinet, 224-227; and wheat policy, 233, 234; first parliamentary session, 241; election (1949), 242; and Korean War, 251, 252; and Defence Production Act, 255-256; considers CDH for governor-generalship, 258, 259; and cabinet changes, 279; and election of 1953, 280, 281; and pipeline, 290, 298; world tour, 291, 292; and cabinet changes (1954), 292-293; and Defence Production Act (1955), 299, 300, 301, 302: pipeline debate, 312, 313, 315; Suez crisis, 321; in election of 1957, 323, 325, 330; retires from politics, 334; attends CDH's funeral, 348
St. Lawrence Seaway, 275-276, 288, 289, 294
St. Lawrence Seaway Authority, 292
Saskatchewan Cooperative Elevator Company, 34, 35, 39, 41-42